MEMORIES and THOUGHTS

MEN—BOOKS—CITIES—ART

BY

FREDERIC HARRISON

AUTHOR OF "THE CHOICE OF BOOKS," ETC.

New York
THE MACMILLAN COMPANY
LONDON: MACMILLAN & CO., LTD.
1906

PR 4759
H 31 m

Norwood Press
J. S. Cushing & Co. — Berwick & Smith Co.
Norwood, Mass., U.S.A.

NOTE

THIS volume is the reply to frequent appeals to the
writer to collect pieces which within the last ten or twenty
years have appeared in America and in Reviews and Journals at home. The first was called out by friends in the
United States who desired a slight biographical sketch, as
it is their custom to expect. It is indeed a chapter from
certain *Memoirs* that the writer intends to retain in manuscript *penes se*. Various as are the other pieces in subject,
and occasional as they were in origin, the author in his old
age submits them to his readers as permanent impressions
left on his mind by a somewhat wide experience. He now
arranges in order some reminiscences of the famous men
and women he has known, the great books he has studied,
the splendid memories of Nature and of Art which he will
cherish to the last. He has to thank the courtesy of pub-
lishers for permission to use pieces which appeared many
years ago in America — in *The Forum, The North American
Review, Harper's Magazine;* and at home, in *The Fortnightly, Nineteenth Century*, and *Contemporary Reviews;*
in *The Times, The Daily Chronicle, The Tribune, The
Speaker*, and some other periodicals.

HAWKHURST, October 1906.

CONTENTS

vii

CONTENTS

MY MEMORIES

1837–1890

[*The Forum of New York, October 1890, Vol. X., in reply to a request to write some reminiscences.*]

THOSE of us who are approaching sixty years of age have the good luck, I often think, to bear the memory of a most extraordinary time. We are still young enough, as we fondly flatter ourselves, to hope that we may yet see great changes in the world. And we are old enough to remember what the world was without some of its most familiar institutions, and without what now seem indispensable appliances of life. As a child, I can remember things which are now thought barbarous relics of the past; and I often wonder how we managed to live without lucifer matches, railways, telegraphs, penny post, or even household suffrage.

My memory reaches back from 1837 over the whole reign of the Queen, whose fifty-three years of rule have witnessed wonderful things — things which have transformed our external life and have deeply modified our inner life. Among my earliest recollections is the return home one day of my father with the words, "The King is dead!" My first definite impression of public life was the coronation of the Queen, of which I witnessed the procession in Palace Yard at Westminster. There for the first time I began to conceive what living history means; to think about statesmen, nations, and government. I saw the great Duke and the heroes of Waterloo — it was then only three years further off than is Sedan from us now — I remember Marshal Soult, and Esterhazy, and the ambassadors of many kings. There too I first heard the roar of a vast crowd; and I was told how the Abbey and the Hall at Westminster before me had been the scene of the coronation of a score of kings and queens, and had been built by men who fought in the Crusades and at Crecy and Agincourt. I can recall now, like a series of historical pictures, every separate scene in that long, and to me, a small country child, most wonder-stirring day.

The American people, spread over an almost boundless continent, where everything around them is the work of one or two generations, wonder not a little at our slow and old-world English ways. In this small, centralised, densely-packed island, we grow up from childhood with the roots of the old order always around us. I was born in the days of rotten boroughs, bribery, and pocket seats; when noble-men's butlers returned members to Parliament in his lord-ship's hall. The widow of an M.P. used to frank our letters, and that saved us sometimes eightpence apiece. Omni-buses, cabs, and policemen had just been invented; but they were still thought new-fangled fads. Post boys, hackney coaches, and watchmen were still familiar figures of the streets. It was the era of Pickwick. We did without railways. From London to Brighton or to Bath we had to drive; and if with the same horses, no faster than thirty miles in a day. Ocean steam navigation was an experiment; our only telegraph was the wooden semaphore; there was no fire brigade, and our only fire engines were hand pumps; the water supply came in part from wells; there were no main sewers, and cesspools existed in great cities. Slavery existed in our colonies and possessions beyond sea, and nearly a million of Negroes were bought and sold in the King's dominions. India was gov-erned by a company of private merchants, who had a monop-oly of the trade to China. Men were hanged by the score, and sometimes in chains. Forgery and other felonies were still punishable by death. Southey was our poet laureate, though Scott and Coleridge, Campbell and Lamb, still lived. Landseer and Maclise formed our ideals in art, Bulwer-Lytton was our model in literature, and Count D'Orsay in manners. Tennyson, Macaulay, Carlyle, Mill, Dickens, Thackeray, Darwin, and Gladstone were unknown youths. The memory of the old system was still quite fresh. Many living men could remember Washington, Jefferson, and Madison, and the last war between England and the United States. My own grandfather was born under George II., and my father could remember the victories of Nelson. My mother told anecdotes of Napoleon, which she had from the family of Sir Hudson Lowe, while the Emperor was a prisoner at St. Helena. The brother of Louis XVI. had just ceased to be king of France, and was living at Holyrood, as the ex-King Charles X. Metternich was supreme in Germany, the Czar Nicholas in Russia, and Louis Philippe in France.

My childhood was thus passed in the great epoch of progress which followed on the break-up of the old absolutism in Europe after 1830. It was also the epoch of the vast material changes which have arisen out of the railway system, ocean steam navigation, the telegraph system and the manifold uses of electricity, the cheap postal system, popular literature, the development of journalism, the enormous expansion of great cities, and the settlement of Australia, South Africa, and of the western continent of America. More especially in England, the period covers the immense succession of reforms which come between the Reform Act of 1832 and the free-trade legislation of 1846. As may be supposed, this series of changes was but dimly understood by a boy. But it gave me a general sense that everything around me was an open question; that there was no habit of life which we might not expect to see changed. My father, a cautious city man, conservative by instinct and by conviction, shook his head, even while his good sense admitted the improvement. For my part, I liked the new thing; waited to see what would come next; and, except that I admired Alcibiades, the Crusaders, and Charles I., had no particular prejudices. Though I lived in a quiet country village, all my real interests were in London, which could be seen across miles of rich open meadows, from the lovely northern hill on which our house stood. A walk from town then would take one into an exquisite rural solitude, unbroken by the roar of the engine, unpolluted by the pall of smoke. My tranquil days were passed in many a leafy copse and sloping glade, beyond which the dome of St. Paul's seemed to hang in the atmosphere of the dim distance, as does that of St. Peter's from the Campagna. In those days it was quite possible to belong to the capital by interest, society, and habits, and yet to dwell in a beautiful country and in a peaceful rural solitude. I have lived to see London increase 150 per cent in population, and 500 per cent in area; and now I must go forty miles away from it to find the same rustic peace. And, with all our railways, telegraphs, post offices, and newspapers, it is no longer possible to dwell in a pure country and yet to belong to a great city. In my boyhood it was.

SCHOOL LIFE

At the age of nine I went to reside in London, and for two years was taught in a day school by Joseph King of Maida Hill, the most admirable schoolmaster I have ever known. I began Greek with Homer and Latin with Virgil, the grammars being taught verbally, without books. At the age of eleven I went to King's College School, which I left as second in the school in 1849. My schoolfellows were sons of Charles

Dickens, T. Landseer, Richard Lane, Macready, the actor,
Lord Westbury, the Chancellor; afterwards the only son of
Edward Irving, and in the sixth form for two years I sat next
to Henry Parry Liddon, late Canon of St. Paul's. I was a
boy at school when the great movement of 1848 swept over
Europe, shook down so many thrones, and opened the era of
so many wars of race and of frontier. Cram full of Livy
and Tacitus, Thucydides and Xenophon, Corneille and
Schiller, Milton, Byron, and Shelley, at the precise age when
youths debate whether despotisms or republics are to be
preferred, when they write essays on the character of Julius
Cæsar or Cromwell, compose odes to Liberty and Latin
verses on Brutus and Tarquin, we were just ready to be impressed with the tumultuous succession of events which
surged across Europe in 1848–49. I delighted to note that
Louis Philippe lost his throne on the 24th of February —
the *Regifugium*, or day when Rome celebrated the expulsion
of her kings. It was a stirring time, when kings, emperors,
and popes fled in disguise, when new republics were being
proclaimed, when socialism, communism, and imperialism
fought it out in a dozen great cities, when Chartism was
thought to be revolutionary, and when Bright and Cobden
were dangerous demagogues. It was difficult for a youth
entering manhood between the years 1848 and 1852 not to be
an ardent politician. And, passing my time, as I did, between
the whirl of the great city and the studies of the university, I
took a lively interest in all the political and social events of
that era. I do not remember that I fell into precise party
lines or that I formed dogmatic opinions. We were all too
full of political theories and classical examples to be mere
Tories, Whigs, and Radicals. And we were too much
impressed by the burning questions which arose day by day
to be satisfied with any abstract politics. London and Oxford

corrected each other. Plato and Lord Palmerston taught very different codes of politics. We were interested by both, and by a thousand new events which neither of these masters seemed able to explain. Like most of my companions, I came to the conclusion that society in the middle of the nineteenth century was an extraordinarily complex thing — a thing of intense interest and of profound meaning. Gradually I settled into a deep, lasting, and passionate sympathy with the popular cause everywhere and in all forms. Having no hereditary or acquired prejudices in favour of any class or of any special type of society, I slowly parted with my boyish liking for conquerors, cavaliers, and princesses in distress, and took my side with the cause of oppressed nations and the struggling people. I had seen the Chartist movement in London and had heard great debates in Parliament, and I became a convinced free trader and an ardent nationalist. Aurelio Saffi, the friend of Mazzini and one of his colleagues in the Triumvirate at Rome in 1849, settled at Oxford, and he became my teacher in Italian and my close friend. He introduced me to other Italian exiles; and from them and from Francis Newman, whom I knew later, I received a deep interest in the cause of nations struggling to be free. At the same time I read much French, and knew France and Frenchmen. As a schoolboy, three times I passed my autumn in France; once, in a French family in Normandy, connected with my own. While living among them, I saw every phase of French provincial life as described by Balzac in the forties. This commenced my close familiarity with France, which for forty years I have visited almost without the interruption of a single year. I was three times in France during the reign of Louis Philippe, and again during the second republic, just before the *coup d'état* of 1851. The atrocities of that time and the infamies of the empire of 1852 stirred me to the soul. By the time I was twenty-five, I had seen most of the principal cities of France, Germany, and Northern Italy; I had some knowledge of the language, circumstances, and recent history of all of these countries; I was a republican by conviction, had a deep enthusiasm for the popular cause throughout Europe, and was inclined to the socialist solution of the great class question.

OXFORD

I went up to Oxford from school in 1849; at a time when the great controversy in theology, which shook the Church and led to the conversion of Cardinal Newman, Cardinal Manning, and many others, was passing into a new phase. Liberalism was in the ascendant, and the dominant type of thought presented to me was Positive rather than Catholic. J. Stuart Mill, George Grote, Arnold and his historical school, Carlyle and his political school, Comte and his Positive school, were the influences under which my mind was formed. I was still a student when Kingsley published *Alton Locke* and *Yeast*, Ruskin his *Modern Painters* and *Seven Lamps of Architecture*, and F. Denison Maurice his *Theological Essays*. The minds of raw youths are influenced first, not by the great masters of thought, but by the masters of expression and of pathos. I spent six years at Oxford as student, fellow, and tutor. And besides the regular curriculum of the ancient and modern historians and philosophers, I became saturated with Mill's *Logic* and *Political Economy*, Grote's *History of Greece*, the works of Carlyle, the earlier pieces of Lewes, Herbert Spencer, and Miss Martineau, the English classical historians, and Guizot, Michelet, Mazzini, and Quinet. Comte I knew only through G. Lewes, Littré, and Harriet Martineau.

At the same time I read not a little theology, both orthodox and unorthodox. Cardinal Newman's *Parish Sermons*, Keble's *Christian Year*, Jeremy Taylor, Bishop Butler, Dante, *Paradise Lost*, and the Bible, were my constant reading, along with Robertson of Brighton, F. D. Maurice, Francis Newman, Theodore Parker, Strauss, Lewes, and the two Martineaus. John Henry Newman, the cardinal, and Francis Newman, the theist, interested me almost equally; Lewes's *History of Philosophy* and the *Lives of the Saints* occupied me alternately; I hardly ever missed a university sermon or a number of the *Westminster Review*. Whilst at Oxford, with science and metaphysics I took no serious pains, though I tried to make out what they came to in the end. But almost every phase of theology, every age in history, and every scheme of social and political philosophy, supplied me with matter for thought, and in turn commanded my sympathy. I imagine that is a very common form of the Oxford mind, at least it was so in the fifties. And if I took the complaint in any unusual mode, it was simply in this — that I saw a good deal to respect in all of these different views of the "great problem."

I was brought up as a High Churchman, my Godfather being an intimate ally of Henry Phillpotts, Bishop of Exeter, and he took care to give me a thorough training in orthodox divinity. At school I had been something of a Neo-Catholic, and took the sacrament with a leaning toward transubstantiation. As a student at college, I slowly came to regard the entire scheme of theology as an open question; and I ultimately left the university, about the age of twenty-four, without assured belief in any form of supernatural doctrine. But as the supernatural died out of my view, the natural took its place, and amply covered the same ground. The change was so gradual, and the growth of one phase of thought out of another was with me so perfectly regular, that I have never been able to fix any definite period of change, nor indeed have I ever been conscious of any real change of mind at all. I have never known any abrupt break in mental attitude; nor have I ever felt change of belief to involve moral deterioration, loss of peace, or storms of the soul. I never parted with any belief till I had found its complement; nor did I ever look back with antipathy or contempt on the beliefs which I had outgrown. That which was objective law to me as a youth, has become subjective duty to me as a man. I have found theology to be a fine moral training, when it ceased to be an external dogma. I have at no time of my life lost faith in a supreme Providence, in an immortal soul, and in spiritual life; but I came to find these much nearer to me on earth than I had imagined, much more real, more vivid, and more practical. Superhuman hopes and ecstasies have slowly taken form in my mind as practical duties and indomitable convictions of a good that is to be. Theology, with its religious machinery and its spiritual consolations, has gained a fresh meaning to me, now that I look on it as a mode of moral evolution and not as historical reality. I read the Bible, my Christian mystics and poets still, and with greater pleasure and deeper insight than I did when I was told to believe in thirty-nine articles and to repeat the three creeds and the catechism.

Happily, both at school and at college, we were left pretty free to learn what we pleased (so that we did really learn), and to cultivate our minds as thinking beings and not as machines. Our teachers succeeded in instilling into our minds a zeal for work and a passion for self-improvement. But neither at school nor at college were we ever put through the mill. I read the classics with delight, so as to enjoy them for themselves, without ever grinding them up into verbal exercises. In history, I believe I had from Richard Congreve the very best of teaching; for which I am ever grateful. And in philosophy, we were taught to use our own common sense, and not to repeat tags of windy systems. I managed to satisfy my tutors; but they taught me to read for my mind's sake, and not for the sake of "the schools." I always felt complete indifference to prize-winning in all its forms, and I was happy enough not to be pressed into that silly waste of time by parents, tutors, or friends. I read what I enjoyed, and I enjoyed what I read. Poetry, art, history, politics, and religion gave us unfailing matter for thought and interminable topics of debate. Both at school and at college we passed much of our time like the Athenians in the days of Paul, but I do not think it was time ill spent. In my experience, these discussions turned most often on questions of religion, though those of politics, especially of the international order, were nearly as constant. Over social problems we ranged freely, without forming systematic doctrines and without crystallising into any prejudice.

EDUCATION

I have now an experience of some forty years as student, teacher, and examiner; and it forces on me a profound conviction that our modern education is hardening into a narrow and debasing mill. Education is over-driven, over-systematised, monotonous, mechanical. At school and at college, lads and girls are being drilled like German recruits — forced into a regulation style of learning, of thinking, and even of writing. They all think the same thing, and it is artificial in all. The round of endless examination reduces education to a professional "cram," where the repetition of given formulas passes for knowledge, and where the accurate memory of some teacher's "tips" takes the place of thought. Education ought to be the art of using the mind and of arranging knowledge; it is becoming the art of swallowing pellets of special information. The professor mashes up a kind of mental "pemmican," which he rams into the learner's gullet. When the pupil vomits up these pellets, it is called "passing his examination with honours." Teachers and pupils cease to think, to learn, to enjoy, to feel. They become cogs in a huge revolving mill-wheel, which never ceases to grind, and yet never grinds out anything but the dust of chaff. The academic mill, which runs now at high pressure, like a Cunard liner racing home, seldom forms a fresh mind. From this curse of modern pedantry, my companions and I were happily saved by the influence of Richard Congreve.

For the first thirty years of my life I was essentially a learner, but only in part a student of books. Never having been a great reader, and not having acquired the passion of pure study, I cared mainly for men, things, places, and people. As a student, and then a barrister of Lincoln's Inn, I read quite as much history and philosophy as law; and I tried to correct my defective training in science by following the lectures of Owen, Huxley, Tyndall, Liveing, and others, with the proper text-books and studies in the Museums. In these days we must give ourselves up either to literature or to practical life, if we wish to succeed, and perhaps if we wish to be useful. But I have never been able to give up problems of religion and philosophy for politics, nor yet to drop interest in politics for the sake of books. My interests have always led me to study movements on the spot, and from the lips of those who originate them. In this spirit I have sought to understand the various social and labour questions by personal intercourse with practical men. For some years I worked as a teacher in the Working Men's College, under F. Denison Maurice, along with Tom Hughes and his colleagues. For three years I served on the Trades Union Commission, and then was Secretary to the Digest Commission. I have thus been in close relations with all the leading workmen and with the leading economists of recent times. I have known intimately the principal leaders of the trades unions, of all the labour leagues, and of all the social and co-operative movements of the last thirty years. I have followed up the history of the trade questions and of the labour societies in London and in many provincial and foreign towns. I have attended trades-union, co-operative, industrial, international, and socialist congresses, both in England and abroad; and have visited conferences, committees, and meetings in all parts of the country. A thousand blue-books and treatises on economics would not have taught me what I learned from the Rochdale Pioneers, from trades-union congresses, from strike or union committees, from international congresses, and from men like George Odgers, Allen, Burnett, Applegarth, Howell, Holyoake, Arch, and Burns. Economists who lay down the law on industrial problems, without personal knowledge of a single workman or of a single fact in a workman's life, are like the philosophers in Laputa extracting sunbeams from cucumbers. No political economy is worth a cent if it is not based on personal knowledge; it is not merely the "dismal science," but it is the pedants' science.

In the same way, I have always tried to make out political problems by personal intercourse with those who led them. The franchise question, the industrial question, the American civil war, and Home Rule, are not to be understood from newspapers and reports. I went to Italy after the campaign of 1859, at the crisis of the foundation of the Italian kingdom, and had conversations with Mazzini, Garibaldi, Minghetti, Saffi, Poerio, Farini, Pepoli, and many of the men who governed Italy in 1859 and who made the northern kingdom. In the same way, I followed up the history of the third republic in France and the communal insurrection of 1871. I have had conversations with Gambetta, with his lieutenants, and with the leaders of many socialist and republican parties. During the great struggle which established the republic in 1877–78, I journeyed through all parts of France, and saw the political leaders of each district. The movements of Germany and of the United States I have never had the opportunity to study on the spot; and I am conscious of the enormous difference between reading newspapers and seeing men. To hunt up and to "interview" men of note is a silly and odious habit of our day. But no study and no books can supply the place of personal intercourse with those who know and those who lead. I am sure whole libraries would not give me what I have gained in converse with Gambetta, Mazzini, Renan, Michelet, Louis Blanc, Tourguénieff, F. Newman, G. H. Lewes, John Bright, J. Stuart Mill, Carlyle, G. Eliot, Ruskin, Cardinal Manning, John Dillon, John Burns, Spencer, Comte, John Morley, and Gladstone.

On questions political, industrial, and international, I have often addressed the public; but I have always declined to enter politics as a profession. My business always seemed to me to endeavour to teach. Compromise is the soul of politics, and personally I loathe compromise. The statesman's duty is to reckon with the opinions of the majority; and personally I feel scanty respect for the majority, and I cannot bring myself to profess it. For five-and-twenty years my essential business has been to teach the principles of Positivism. Every other aim or occupation has been subsidiary and instrumental to this. The field is large enough for a lifetime; and it is one which makes impossible any career whatever, either literary, political, practical, or social. I have enlarged to the public on Positivism *usque ad nauseam*, and I will not return to it now. To one point only would I refer — the prolonged study and the gradual stages by which I came to adopt it.

A VISIT TO A. COMTE

I was quite thirty-five before I fully absorbed the Positive system. I had been a systematic student of it for ten or twelve years before. Comte's system was known to me as an undergraduate, but it was not completely published until I was twenty-five. Before that, I had paid him a visit in Paris, and had had a long and memorable conversation with him. My college tutor, Richard Congreve, a pupil of Dr. Arnold of Rugby, afterward became the first preacher of Positivism in England; and several of my intimate college friends are now my colleagues at Newton Hall. But none of us adopted Positivism until after we had left Oxford. For my part, the acceptance of the general principles of Auguste Comte has been the result of very long and unremitting study, and it proceeded by a series of marked stages. First his view of history commanded my assent; then his scheme of education; next his social Utopia; then the politics; after that his general view of philosophy; and finally the religious scheme in its main features. During the whole of the process, up to the last point, I reserved large portions of the system, to which I felt actual repugnance, or at least confirmed doubt. And during the various stages I kept up lively interest, and no little sympathy, with many kindred, rival, and even antagonistic systems, philosophical and religious. Even now I am regarded by some Comtists *pur sang* as a pro-

fane amateur, a schismatic, and a Gallio. And while cynics
outside accuse me of fanaticism, some of my fellow-believers
suspect me of heresy.

LITERARY LIFE

I hope that I am not expected to say anything about
literary methods, habits, or theories. I no more pretend to be
a man of letters than I pretend to be a politician. I have
even less of the man of letters about me than of the politician.
In matters literary, I have but one advice to give. Keep out
of literature, at least till you feel ready to burst. Never write
a line except out of a sense of duty, or with any other object
save that of getting it off your mind. About literature I
have nothing to say. I have always felt myself more or less
of an amateur. Nor do I remember to have wasted an hour
in thinking about style, or about conditions of literary success.
As I have sought to teach many things, and have fought hard
for many opinions, I have tried to put what I had to say as
well as I could. But as I have always some practical object
in view, my eagerness keeps me from spending thought over
the mode of saying it. Mark Pattison, of Oxford, used to
say to a pupil who happens to be now both a brilliant writer
and a leading statesman: "My good friend, you are not the
stuff of which men of letters are made. You want to make
people do something, or you want to teach something; that
is fatal to pure literature." I am afraid that I have a dash of
the same vice, and something of the Jacobin within me
murmurs that "the Republic has no need of men of letters."
Once or twice in my life I have taken up the pen in a vein
of literary exercise — I began this very paper in that mood —
as a man turns to a game of billiards or to gardening after
his day's work. But the demon soon rises, and I find myself

in earnest trying to bring men over to our side. It is hopeless to make a man of letters out of a temper like that. Literature is art, and the artist should never preach.

It was lucky for me that I recognised this defect at once; for the critics have made a dead set at Positivism, and to be known as its advocate is to be turned into the literary world like a dog suspected of rabies. All my formal Positivist teaching is necessarily gratuitous; and as I have had to print and to circulate most of my pieces at my own cost, I have long found literature not so much a profession as an expensive taste. I was nearly thirty before I published anything at all. My first article happened to be on "Essays and Reviews," and I was not so foolish as to attribute the interest it aroused to anything beyond the accident of the subject and the circumstances of the time. I did not pursue literature as a calling. For ten years I occasionally entered into discussions on political, industrial, or philosophical questions, but I did not use my pen professionally. My profession was the law, the practice of which I followed for some fifteen years without great zest and without any ambition. I afterward taught jurisprudence as professor; and, having inherited a modest fortune, which I have had no desire to increase, I eventually withdrew to my present occupation of urging on my neighbours opinions which meet, I must admit, with but moderate acceptance.

MELIORIST AT LAST

Here ends my confession, which I am told my American readers wish me to make. As they know nothing about me but my name, they have a right to ask me how I came by the bundle of opinions with which I am credited. I have no objections to tell them, though one cannot do so without an abominable dose of talking about one's self.   As I look back over my life, which, though not yet a long one, has been passed in a very critical time, I am struck with this — the essential persistence of the social organism in the midst of universal change.   Every aspect and appliance of practical life has been transformed within my own memory; and yet, in all its essential conditions, human life remains the same.   Railways, telegraphs, the post, journalism, steamships, electricity, the doubling of the population, and the shrinking of the planet, do not really change society.   My children live much as I did fifty years ago.   And all these revolutions in the material world but slightly affect the moral and the mental world. On the other hand, the greatest empires, the most rooted institutions, the oldest prejudices, the most sacred beliefs, crumble almost without warning; and what was a wild paradox yesterday is a harmless truism to-morrow.   I have seen the downfall of so many habits, ideas, laws, and systems of thought, that I can imagine no reform and no new dispensation as beyond our reasonable hope.   And yet again, amidst endless, rapid, universal change, I find that the vital essence of things remains.   Creeds die; but not the spiritual life they nourished.   Societies suffer revolution; but the living elements do not greatly vary.   Our knowledge enlarges, our formulas change, our methods grow; but everywhere it is growth, not destruction.   What I have witnessed is not really revolution: it is normal evolution.   The cells and germs are forever in perpetual movement.   The organism — Humanity — remains, and lives the life of unbroken sequence.

POSTSCRIPT, 1906

The sixteen years that have passed since I set down my experiences for an American public have witnessed memo-

c

rable changes in our own land and in the world — a new reign, many obstinate wars, the recasting of international relations, the new East, the transformation of Russia, the filling up the vacant parts of our planet, the growth of Democracy, and Socialism, and an enormous expansion of Wealth, Trade, and Mechanical inventions. But I see no cause to vary the language with which I closed the foregoing paper. It is still evolution, not social revolution. Dogmas are continually melting away, but the essentials of religious feeling remain healthy and active. And in spite of the appalling bloodshed of some recent wars and the delirious multiplication of armaments, there may be heard deep down in the murmurs of the masses and in the aspirations of the wise, a heart-felt yearning for peace and international friendship.

As for myself, I am not conscious of having seriously altered my convictions or my habits. It is a curious accident that I can distinctly recall all the leading events and nearly all the famous persons of the sixty-four years of the reign of Queen Victoria, and have witnessed all the State ceremonies from her Coronation to her Burial, as well as the public funerals of the men illustrious in politics, literature, and art. Visits from time to time to Paris, Rome, Berlin, Holland, and the United States, and again to Athens, Constantinople, and Egypt, enabled me to enlarge my understanding of public affairs, and to see something of those who administer them. Four years spent at the London County Council gave me some inkling of the difficulties of municipal business. After a service of twenty-five years I resigned my tasks as President of the English Positivist Committee, and, being now in my seventy-fifth year, I have for some years past withdrawn from London and live in a quiet country, occupied with my books, my garden, and in stringing together the loose ends of a rather scattered activity.

I can hardly now claim that detachment from letters, which was true enough in 1890. Since then, having quitted the legal profession, I have published a variety of books, and have even committed myself to what my friends tell me is the senile weakness of a romance and then a tragedy. The habit of writing, like other indulgences, is apt to grow upon one; and, as I gradually withdrew from active affairs, I did not resist the temptation to give form to occasional thoughts, memories, and fancies. Some few of these I now offer for a leisure hour to the general reader.

HAWKHURST, 1906.

THE BURIAL OF TENNYSON

1892

As the throng which gathered to the funeral of our great poet slowly melted away from the Abbey, the same thought was borne in upon many of us — Have we then no poet left in England? The passing away of a great figure which for two generations has filled the mind and speech of men is always wont to leave this impression of a void. Forty years ago, when Wellington was laid beside Nelson in St. Paul's, Tennyson groaned out: "The last great Englishman is low." And as we left the Laureate alone with his peers in Poets' Corner, there rose to a hundred lips the murmur: "The last English poet is gone!" It was a natural feeling, an unthinking impulse; perhaps a blind mistake.

It is inevitable that we should seek at times like this to compare, to judge, to anticipate the verdict of our posterity. But the impulse should be resisted: it is futile and worse than useless. We are far too near to judge Tennyson truly or even to decide if he has left a successor. The permanent place of a poet depends on his one or two, three or four, grandest bursts, and his inferior work is forgotten. So too the poetry which startles and delights its immediate generation is almost always much weaker than the poetry which mellows like wine as generations succeed. It needed for Dante five entire centuries before his real greatness was admitted; it needed two centuries for Shakespeare.

It would be strange if English poetry were to close its glorious roll with the name of Tennyson. For three hundred years now our race has never failed to find a fine poet "to stand before the Lord." Shakespeare had done immortal things while Spenser still lived. Ben Jonson survived until the early lyrics of Milton. Dryden was in full career when *Paradise Lost* was published, and when Dryden died Pope was already "lisping in numbers." Pope survived till Gray was a poet and Cowper a youth; and with Burns, Coleridge, Wordsworth, Byron, and Shelley, the list comes down to the poet whom we have just buried. In these three centuries, from the *Faerie Queene* until to-day, the only gap is for the ten years which separate the *Rape of the Lock* from the death of Dryden. But at Spenser's death, who really knew what Shakespeare was, and at that of Byron and Shelley, who thought of Tennyson as their successor?

They who were present at the burial in the Abbey had opened to them, as in a vision, some glimpse down into the depths of the poetry, the persistence, and solemnity of English life — into that deep under-current which flows far below our gross and common everyday life. What a flood of memories from ancient history, what a halo of heroism, art, and devotion, consecrate that spot! A church built in the age of the Crusades, with foundations and memorials, tombs and crypts, that go back to the Saxon kings, in the history of which Agincourt, the Civil Wars, the Reformation, and the Commonwealth are mere episodes, and wherein even three centuries of a long succession of poets form but the later chapters — such a building seems to hold the very heart of the English people. Statesmen, artists, churchmen, poets, men of science and men of business, all schools, creeds, and interests, came that day together; sect, party, and rivalry ceased to divide men — all were Englishmen come to do honour to their poet.

There was no parade, no eloquence, nothing of unusual show; no trumpets, helmet, or plume, no "guard of honour" or officials in uniform or robes; there was no concourse of elaborate music or feats of epideictic oratory. It was the daily service of the Abbey choir, the ordinary burial, with no feature of it uncommon, except the great Union Jack spread out upon the coffin. Not a word was spoken outside the Prayer-Book; nothing was done which is not done every day when honoured men are buried. Merely this — that the vast cathedral and the square in which it stands were filled with silent and eager masses, that around the coffin were gathered men of every type of activity and thought which England holds, that the whole English-speaking race was represented and was deeply stirred.

In the whole world there is nothing left which in continuity and poetry of association can be put beside a burial in our Abbey. It is doubtful if anything recorded in history ever matched it altogether in the volume and beauty of its impressiveness, or ever before so mysteriously blended the sense of antiquity with the sense of life. For there is nothing artificial, nothing of mere antiquarianism, in the Englishman's love for the Abbey and its sacred dust. The common seaman in Nelson's fleets felt it; the American citizen feels it more intensely often than the Londoner; they feel it in their hearts at home in Africa and in Australasia; to the whole English-speaking people the associations of the Abbey are both profoundly historic and vividly modern. The Abbey suggests to us all three things in equal force: the Past, Poetry, Living Work. That is the true strength of England, which to the German is a metaphysical enigma and to the Frenchman seems an amazing paradox — that below our eternal money-grabbing and vulgar routine there is a sense among us that the Past and the Future are really one, and that we must be the link between the two. That makes the most material and most conventional of European nations at bottom the most capable of great poetry.

HIS SUCCESSORS

So let us not despair of one day finding a poet worthy to carry on the torch. It is plain that no one is yet acknowledged as the real equal of Tennyson. But we may have such a one among us even now. Although for three centuries the succession of English poets has never failed, there have been some brief periods when the most discerning eye must have failed to recognise the man. When Dryden died there must have been searchings of heart until the star of Pope rose above the horizon. And when Byron died young, like Keats and Shelley before him, and Coleridge, the poet, had long subsided into interminable monologues, neither Campbell, nor Scott, nor Southey, nor even Wordsworth, could be said to hold the poetic field. Wordsworth's, indeed, is a very striking case. His general reputation as a poet was hardly established till more than forty years after his first poems were published, and he was more than seventy before he received any public honour. And it may well be that we are all blind now, and that a new Tennyson, another Shelley or Milton, is in our midst, did we only know it. There is an element of hope perhaps in numbers. The English-speaking race is to-day quite three times as numerous as it was at the death of Byron, twelve times as numerous as it was at the death of Dryden, and those who can and who do write verses may be forty or fifty times as many. So the field is vastly larger.

But, alas! in poetry numbers count for much less than in elections and other practical affairs. Indeed, in poetry, numbers and genius seem almost to stand in inverse ratios. When Shakespeare produced his plays, there were certainly not half a million persons living who could write pure English; and when the *Iliad* was first chanted at a festival, there was no man living who could write his name. There are now at least sixty millions who can write our language, and of these some millions, we may be sure, in public or in secret, compose lines that they fondly believe to be verse. What! not one prime poet in some millions of versifiers? We do not see him yet! Neither Tennyson, Hugo, Heine, nor Longfellow has left any recognised equal and successor.

The strange part of it is that there never was an age when so great a quantity of very excellent verse was produced as in our own. There can be no doubt about it. We have to-day scores of elegant poets and hundreds of volumes of really graceful verse. Of educated men and women, at least one in three could turn out a passable lyric or so, far better than the stuff published as poetry in the age of Pope, or Johnson, or Southey. There are not so many true poets, perhaps, as there were in the lifetime of Spenser and of Shakespeare. But it may be truly said that at no period in the long history of English poetry has it been so free from affectation, mannerism, false taste, and conventional commonplace. Since verse began there has never been so high, so pure a level of third-rate verse. There are a dozen writers whose exquisite technique makes that of Dryden or Byron look quite careless and that of Pope monotonous, and there are at least a hundred writers who far surpass the imitators of Dryden, Pope, or Byron.

That perhaps is the ominous side of our high poetic standard. If out of such a mass of graceful verse we find no really great poetry, it would look as if there were something amiss. Can it be that we all think too much of this graceful form that so many can reach? Is it that we are all, writers and readers alike, under the glamour of a style which is not the less a "fashion" by being subtly harmonious and severely subdued? As the poet said, "All can raise the flower now, for all have got the seed." Poetry is raised too much now from another's seed, from a single seed, from what is indeed a highly specialised seed. And poetry mayhap has begun to suffer from the maladies which follow upon "breeding in-and-in": rickety bones, transparent and etiolated skins, exquisitely refined impotence. Neither readers nor writers intend it or even know it, but we are all looking for echoes of the *Idylls* or *In Memoriam*: it becomes our test and standard; the poet is afraid to let himself go, lest he be thought Byronic and impatient of the "slow mechanic exercise" which not only soothes pain but produces poetry. No age that ever fell under the spell of a style knew it at the time. Their contemporaries could not hear the eternal jingle in the papistic couplet when Pope's imitators produced volumes. People who listened to songs "in the manner of Tom Moore" were deaf to the doggerel of the words. Dryden in his day was the ruin of the poetasters who tried to catch his swing. So was Pope the ruin of his followers: they caught his measured cadence; they could not catch his wit, his sparkle, and his sense. Dr. Johnson latinised the English language for a whole generation. And perhaps the perfections of Tennyson's art are among the causes that we have no perfect poetry.

His Special Form

Perfection of form is often, nay, is usually, a snare to its own generation. Raffaelle ruined "the school of Raffaelle," and so did Guido ruin the school of Guido. Intense attention to form, especially to a form which is capable of a high

degree of imitation, too often leads to insipidity. How
common now in the scholastic world is the art of elegant Latin
verse! Our schools and colleges can show thousands of
"copies" of faultless elegiacs and sonorous hexameters, with
fewer flaws than you might pick in Statius and Claudian.
But how dull, how lifeless, how artificial are these prize compositions if we read them as poetry! Faultless, yes; but we
wish the author would now and then break loose into a sole-
cism, and but for ten lines forget Ovid and Virgil. Much of
our very graceful, very thoughtful, very virginal poetry is
little but "exercises" in English verse composition to the
tune, not of Ovid's *Tristia*, but of *In Memoriam*.

Now, the exquisite jewelry of Tennyson's method, subtle
as it is, is imitable up to a certain point, just as Virgil's
hexameter is imitable up to a certain point, and for the same
reason. Both are the poetry of intense culture, inspired by
the worship of form. I take a stanza typical of this art —
a stanza not surpassed in melody by any poetry of this century
— a stanza which is wonderfully prophetic of the poet himself and his enduring influence:

> His memory long will live alone
>   In all our hearts, as mournful light
> That broods above the fallen sun
>   And dwells in heaven half the night.

That is simply perfect: a noble thought, an exquisite simile,
a true and splendid analogy between Nature and Man, the
simplicity as of marble, and a music which Shelley only has
equalled. Yet it is imitable up to a measure: we can analyse
the music, we can mark the gliding labials, the pathetic cadence in the "mournful light" and "dwells in heaven,"
the *largo* in "broods above." It is beautiful, but it is imitable, as Milton and Shakespeare are not imitable. Take
Milton's —

> He must not float upon his watery bier
> Unwept, and welter to the parching wind,
> Without the meed of some melodious tear.

Or again, "that last infirmity of noble mind," or "Laughter holding both his sides," or "thy rapt soul sitting in thine eyes." When Shakespeare says "the multitudinous seas incarnadine," or

> We are such stuff
> As dreams are made on, and our little life
> Is rounded with a sleep : —

this is not imitable. Both thought and phrase are incalculable. No other brain could imagine them; once heard they are indelible, unalterable, unapproachable. It is not the music which rivets our attention first, but the thought. The form matches the idea, but the idea transcends the form. Poetic form, we are often told, must be "inevitable." True, most true. But poetic thought also must be incalculable. For this reason the greatest poets who clothed incalculable thought in inevitable perfection of form — Milton, Shakespeare, Dante, Æschylus, Homer — never misled their generation into imitation, never founded "a school." We shall have a poet worthy to succeed Tennyson when we no longer have Tennyson on the brain: when we are all less absorbed in the technical mastery of the instrument, and are intent on the great human message which the instrument merely transmutes into music.

THE BURIAL OF RENAN

It was passing strange that France should lose her greatest writer of prose within a few days of the blow by which England lost her greatest writer in verse. And some friends of both were present at the funeral in the *Panthéon* and in the Abbey. It was an eloquent contrast, suggestive of profound differences in our national idiosyncrasies and condition. The burial of Renan was a great ceremony of state, with military and official pomp, academic and bureaucratic dignity, pageantry, oratory, and public consecration in a civil monument now for the third time wrenched from the Church. The burial of the English poet was a simple and private act of mourning to which a multitude came in spontaneous sympathy. It had no dignity but that which was given it by the place — by the historic Past, by Poetry itself, and by at least the pathos of the old faith. France has broken with her Past, with the old religion, and she has no continuous poetic traditions. France is deliberately pushing forth on the ocean to find a New World. Nor has any one of this generation done more to stimulate this movement than Ernest Renan. The founders of New Worlds cannot look to robe themselves in all the poetry and solemnities of the Old Worlds, but they may bear within them the Life and the Future.

Ernest Renan was a consummate master of the French language; and masters of language exercise a power in France which is not known to other nations and which is hardly to be understood in some. He was a scholar, a man of learning, a subtle and ingenious critic. With his learning, his versatility, his romantic colouring, and his exquisite grace of form, it would have been singular if he had not acquired great influence. It was, of course, the influence of the critic: the solvent, dispersive, indefinite influence of the man of letters who hints his doubts and hesitates his creed. Renan assuredly had no creed, needed none, and was mentally incapable of conceiving himself as having a creed. I knew him personally, and have heard him expound his ideas in conversation and in lectures and also in private interviews. I do not believe that there was left in his mind an infinitesimal residuum of dogma, old or new. As the Cambridge scholar said, when he was asked to define his view as to the Third Person in the Trinity, Renan "would not deny that there might be a sort of a something" behind all that he knew and all that interested him so keenly. But for himself, his whole activity of brain was absorbed in the romantic side of history, in the lyrical aspect of religion, in the decorative types of philosophy.

Ideas of such mordant potency have seldom been clothed in a mantle of more spiritual religiosity of external hue. One can fancy the terror that he once struck into the tender Catholic spirit who for the first time heard these ghastly doubts issue forth, as it were, from a dreamy patristic hagiology. It was as when the Margaret of *Faust* kneels down in her agony before the image of the Madonna and hears her prayer answered by the strident mockery of Mephistopheles. But the tender Catholic spirit is grown stouter now and is inured to many things. We can see how Renan, so negative himself, so vague, and so allusive, is leading on to a knowledge more systematic than his own, more positive, more definite and real. He has been an influence in his generation, even though he hardly knew whither he was tending, and though such ignorance or mistiness appeared to him to be the true philosophic *nirvana* to which only the wise attain.

We are now in the age of mist. We are becoming very "children of the mist"; for the one dogma that seems destined to survive is the duty of being undogmatic. We have all learned to say with the poet, "Our little systems have their day"; with the critic we all believe in "the power, not ourselves, that makes for righteousness." That is comprehensive, large, suggestive. The definite, perhaps the intelligible, is limited: limitations mean narrowness, hardness, slavery, somewhere. "O friends," cries the popular preacher of to-day, be he layman or cleric, "let our spirits be free, let us seek to know, not to decide; to analyse, not to believe. Away with the system-mongers and the slaves of any 'doxy.' Let us sip truth from every flower and leave the drones to brood over the honey!" The cultivated mind is becoming incapable of giving final assent to anything definite. It sees something in everything and error only in attempts to give that something a form. Of this philosophy and religion of the Great May-be, Monsieur Ernest Renan is the chief of the apostles; he is Peter and Paul and Doubting Thomas all in one very charming writer of French prose.

SIR A. LYALL'S "TENNYSON"

1903

ALTHOUGH ten years have passed since Tennyson's death and half a century since the appearance of some of his best pieces, his latest biographer can claim with truth that he still holds the field in poetry, that none has yet come forth even to challenge his crown. We may take the wisely balanced estimate of his complete works by Sir Alfred Lyall as that which will prove the final and authoritative judgment of the Twentieth Century on the supreme poet of the Victorian Era

Sir Alfred is himself a poet of distinction, with more than a tincture of philosophy and scholarship, and, withal, a man whose life has been passed in the government of men. Here, then, we have a judgment of our great poet, at once subtle, sympathetic, and authoritative. Agreeing as it does in substance with the brief sketch that I ventured to put out two years ago, I propose to examine it in detail and to add further criticism of my own.

As do all judicious men, Lyall seizes at once on the dominant note of Tennyson's poetry — his supreme mastery of form, especially in all modes of lyric art. He rightly calls the Laureate "an essentially lyric poet." In speaking of *In Memoriam*, he says: "His sure and never-failing mastery of poetic diction carries him through this long monotone with a high and even flight." I hardly find Lyall's cooler phrases quite warm enough to express the enthusiasm I feel myself for what I have called his "unfaltering truth of form," "his infallible mastery of language"; "the rhythm, phrasing, and articulation are so entirely faultless, so exquisitely clear, melodious, and sure." No doubt, Lyall uses language much of the same kind. But nothing satisfies me unless we place Tennyson quite alone, unapproachable, in an order by himself, amongst the Victorian poets, if only by virtue of this unique perfection of style. No man honours more than I do the intellectual power of Browning, the serene meditations of Arnold. But perfect poetry must be perfect in form.

Almost the only estimate on which Lyall seems to be open to question is in placing Tennyson's zenith too soon in his career. To rank the early volumes as containing "some of the most exquisite poetry that he ever wrote," so that "The Lady of Shalott" is an "example of his genius at a period when he had brought the *form* and *conception* of his poetry up to a point which he never afterwards surpassed," — this is surely anticipating things. To tell us that "his genius had reached its zenith fifty years before death extinguished it," — that is to say, in 1842 — is too hasty a view. It means that neither in form nor in conception did *The Princess*, or *In Memoriam*, or *Maud*, or the *Idylls*, rise to a higher level of perfection than "Mariana," "The Lady of Shalott," and "The Palace of Art." Certainly, these lovely lyrics of 1832 and 1842 have abundance of Tennyson's peculiar charm; and it is to us to-day wonderful that critics and public failed at once to see all that they heralded to come. But to say that Tennyson therein had reached his zenith, that he never afterward surpassed them, is to do him scant justice.

"The Lady of Shalott" is indeed an exquisite poem, full of imagination and colour, but the riper and more pathetic "Lancelot and Elaine" is grander in art as well as more powerful in its human realism. And though the versification of the early poem is both subtle and musical, it has weak points such as Tennyson's more finished poem would avoid. The rhymes are not at all faultless. Even if we allow that license which Tennyson constantly asserts — as of "two" rhyming with "true," "barley" with "cheerly" — the license is a fault where it requires a mispronunciation of a word according to a cockneyism or a vulgarism. To make "girls" rhyme with "churls" suggests the speech of the streets. We almost expect "gals." I doubt if "holy" is a good rhyme to "wholly," for the two words are identical in sound. Somewhat higher up the rhyme is mere repetition, for "river" rhymes to "river," and also to "mirror," another cockney mispronunciation.

I am not a convert to the new theory of rhyme, which would make any general similarity of sound a good rhyme. No doubt, to lay down a rule about similar spelling, or "rhyme to the eye," is absurd. Rhyme ought to mean *harmony of sound*, where the words are correctly pronounced. What I object to, is a homophony obtained by a vulgar enunciation of either word, as "gurl" and "churl," or "lidy" and "tidy." As I noted formerly, Tennyson's "Six Hundred" makes a false rhyme with "blunder'd," "thunder'd," "wonder'd," "sunder'd," because it involves our pronouncing *hundred* as "hunderd," — which only vulgar persons say. Any one who knew how readily the poet could slip into rustic dialect can understand how he made the mistake.

But a close view of "The Lady of Shalott" will show us rhymes and phrases which are certainly short of the "Tennysonian perfection." One doubts if four such rhymes as "early," "barley," "cheerly," "clearly," should be immediately followed by three rhymes so close in sound as "weary," "airy," "fairy." No doubt, the good fellows who towed barges down to Camelot pronounced *barley* as

D

"bearly" and "weary" as "wairy," but we do not so speak to-day in polite society. Nor does it seem like Tennyson's best to write —

> She floated by,
> . . . between the houses high.

One cannot imagine an adjective more jejune and childish than "houses high." No! "The Lady of Shalott" is a sweet fantasy, but not to be mentioned in the same breath with "Come into the Garden, Maud," "Tears, Idle Tears," or "Come down, O Maid," "Old Year," "Ring out, Wild Bells."

Lyall very justly praises the lovely blank verse of the classical romances and the *Idylls*, and justly rebukes the deaf ears of the orthodox and conventional critics of the old *Quarterly* who could not hear it; but he does not note that, in power and majesty, Tennyson never quite reached the level of *Paradise Lost*, and some rare bursts of Wordsworth. "Ulysses" and the original "Morte d'Arthur" contain the grandest lines of heroic metre that the Laureate ever wrote. But even these do not reach the diapason of the "mighty-mouth'd inventor of harmonies," with his swelling organ-voice, as when the multitude of angels cast to the ground their crowns of amarant and gold; and then, taking their golden harps, begin their sacred song with the words:

> Thee, Father, first they sung, Omnipotent,
> Immutable, Immortal, Infinite,
> Eternal King; thee, Author of all being,
> Fountain of Light, thyself invisible.

This, indeed, is the only English heroic verse which can be set beside Homer.

It is amusing to read that the poet specially valued himself on his "shortness," and on his inexorable rule of throwing away hundreds of verses that he judged not to be perfect.

It is quite true that he suppressed thousands of such lines, and, as the *Memoir* shows us, with invariable judgment. But as to "shortness," the *Works* even now comprise some 60,000 lines, more or less — at least three times the output of Milton. And the Poems, with few exceptions, would be more effective if they were not so long. Even the "Two Voices" suffers by being in 150 stanzas, when one hundred would be ample for the argument, vague and indecisive as it is. Much the same may be said of *Maud*, of the *Idylls*, and, lastly, of the historical dramas. The scheme, the intellectual motive, the form of none of them is adequate to sustain such elaboration, so much monotonous detail. The *Idylls of the King* contain far more lines than *Paradise Lost*, which, indeed, would bear being shorter.

Tennyson would too often paint vignettes upon a canvas which was fit for a cartoon of life-size groups. As Lyall points out, his habit was to paint a picture by elaborating a succession of local features, not by broad strokes. And in conducting an argument, or developing a plot, he sought to obtain his effects by a multiplicity of kindred, but distinct points. The whole was always beautiful and often impressive. But it was at times tedious, and was never the highest form of art. The Homeric and sculptured figures of Œnone, Ulysses, Tithonus, became long-drawn subtle romances of love, disappointment, destiny, and ambition, more akin to the modern novel than to classical simplicity. Tennyson, no doubt, was never diffuse in words, and wrote with a cultured brevity and economy of phrase. But he was certainly most profuse in images, ideas, and colours; and, in arguing a thesis or in narrating a story, he relied on artful elaboration, rather than on the flash, the thunder, of the greatest poets.

How many stanzas, how many pages, would Tennyson have filled if he had conceived such an invocation as this:

> Thou, O Spirit, that dost prefer
> Before all Temples th' upright heart and pure,
> Instruct me, for Thou know'st: Thou from the first
> Wast present, and with mighty wings outspread
> Dove-like sat'st brooding on the vast Abyss
> And mad'st it pregnant: what in me is dark
> Illumine, what is low raise and support.

Hamlet's soliloquy, "To be, or not to be," goes in thirty-two lines, and it contains as much thought as the whole of *In Memoriam* in 3000 lines, and it is quite as impressive.

The truth is this. Tennyson phrased each thought with masterly concision. But he framed each picture with a laborious multiplication of touches; he told his tale with a continuous stream of subtle suggestions, just as Samuel Richardson does in *Clarissa*; and he works up a recondite philosophical thesis by piecing together a *sorites* of ingenious arguments, on no one of which is he willing to rely as conclusive. It is a mode of art singularly popular, but it is not the art of the greatest masters of song.

An excellent point made by Lyall is the attention he draws to the versatility of the Laureate, even from the first. How any men pretending to be critics could talk, as the *Quarterly* men did, about "fantastic shrines" and "baby idols" in speaking of volumes which passed from "Mariana" to "Œnone" and thence to "Morte d'Arthur," "St. Simeon Stylites," "Fatima," "Three Voices," "Locksley Hall," and "The Vision of Sin" — this seems strange indeed to us. But, after all these, we have seen the Poet of "Come into the Garden, Maud," produce the "Passing of Arthur," "The Revenge," "Rizpah," "Vastness," "The Foresters," and "Becket." Since Shakespeare, no one of our poets, unless it be Byron, has shown anything like the same range of invention and grasp of diverse themes and all modes of the lyre.

Lyall is again entirely just in treating *In Memoriam* as Tennyson's masterpiece, "of all the continuous poems the longest and the most elaborate." It is, as I said, "one of the triumphs of English poetry," and it would not be easy to name any other poem of such length so faultless in form, so consummate in music and in harmony of tone. Sir Alfred also shows how greatly the success of *In Memoriam* was due to its "sympathetic affinity with the spiritual aspirations and intellectual dilemmas of the time." Of course, Lyall rejects the curious notion of some Tennysonians, that *In Memoriam* founded a Theodicy, or religious philosophy of its own. The poet had a too "dubitating temperament," as Lyall phrases it, to found any scheme of philosophy or theology whatever, even if his "musical meditations" had been more definite. "Dogmatic theology had long been losing ground"; science, he says, had introduced the conception of *law* in lieu of *will* or caprice. Tennyson had lived from his Cambridge days in 1828, "in communion with the thought and knowledge of the day." It took a strong hold of his imagination, says Lyall. Down to his latest years, Tennyson was constantly shaken with the enigmas of the Universe, the Infinite, Death, the petty and transitory nature of our Earth. As he recognised no authoritative Revelation, Creed, or Church, all this hung over his subtle and brooding soul, and made him almost a pessimist, in spite of his resolute will to "believe where we cannot prove." Such was the tone of the cultured academic mind of the first half of the nineteenth century. Tennyson lived his whole life in this atmosphere, and transfigured its hopes, its doubts, its horror, and its yearnings in a series of exquisite, but depressing, descants.

Lyall's account of Tennyson's religious position is admirably worked out and quite convincing. He rightly fulfilled "the poet's mission, which is to embody the floating thought of the period." "The poet leads us to a cloudy height; and though it is not his business to satisfy the strict philosophical inquirer, he offers to all wandering souls a refuge in the faith." Nothing can be put more accurately. And, as Lyall shows, the clouds rather thickened than dispersed with the advancing age of the poet. "The sense of the brevity of human existence and the uncertainty of what may lie beyond, although Tennyson fought against it manfully, did undoubtedly haunt his meditations and depress the spirit of his later inspirations." Such pieces as "Despair" and "Vastness" indicate a morbid tone in man's view of life, duty, and religion; and, with all their sublimity and pathos, they tend to debilitate and unman us. As Lyall says, "they have a tendency to weigh down the mainsprings of human activity." "They are beautiful as poetry, but they are neither philosophy nor religion."

The second chapter of the *Memoir* shows where and how, at the age of twenty, the poet's intellectual interests grew. At Cambridge, from 1828 to 1830, he lived in the society of the "Apostles," described in Carlyle's *Sterling*, the brethren who, as Sterling said, "are waxing daily in religion and radicalism." Arthur Hallam, one of the most brilliant of them, wrote that the spirit of the young society had been created by Frederick Denison Maurice. Maurice had left Cambridge a year or two before; but he had already begun to exert on young inquiring minds the remarkable influence which he so long retained. With a really beautiful nature and high social aspirations, Maurice was, as Ruskin found him, "by nature puzzle-headed and indeed wrong-headed." In spite of this, the poet formed a close friendship with the theologian, made him godfather to his son, and thought that, had he been less obscure to the ordinary mind, he might have taken his place as the foremost thinker among the Churchmen of their time.

Churchmen of that stamp were certainly of a flabby, inconclusive order of mind.

In æsthetic parsonages they grumble at the impression Lyall seems to convey that the Laureate's mood was too often inconsequent and gloomy. But such was his frame of mind, and it grew on him with age. The problems of Infinity, Eternity, the brevity and littleness of human life, loomed ever darker, and never rested in any complete and final answer. He was ever "in many a subtle question versed," and "ever strove to make it true." But to the last he never quite beat his music out. He faced the spectres of the mind; but he never absolutely laid them. I remember as a young man when first admitted to his company, he turned to me, with that grand assumption which he affected to those with whom he disagreed, saying with a most cadaverous air: "If I thought as you do, I should go and drown myself." I smiled; for the absurdity as well as the ill manners of such an outburst amused me. I replied quietly, looking, I am sure, as cheerful as he looked disconsolate: "No! Mr. Tennyson, if you thought as I do about Life and Death — you would be a happy man!" Personally, the poet seemed to be even more unsatisfied with his own beliefs than the poems showed. But if it did not tend to peace of mind and energy of action, the pathos and the dreaminess of this habit of thought were the inspiration of much exquisite poetry. Like other people, he mistook his own gift of words for profound thought.

We shall all agree with Lyall as to the rare charm of the lyrics of *Maud,* especially of the songs, which are amongst the most exquisite in all modern poetry. But he points out with a sure hand the essential weakness of the "Monodrama," where violent storms of passion, ecstatic love and happiness, and actual madness have to be told of himself by a single speaker. *Maud* is a very singular, almost unique, example of a rare type — an elaborate and passionate lyric, wherein is rehearsed a romantic and indeed sensational story, such as we expect in a psychologic novel or a rousing melodrama. Lyall dwells enthusiastically on all the beauties of the poem; but he is forced to admit that the task which the poet had set to himself was beyond the reach of lyric art.

The Princess is one of the Laureate's delicious masterpieces for which even the least friendly critics have never had anything but praise. It was a theme that gave scope to every one of Tennyson's gifts — his fancy, his exquisite sense of beauty both material and moral, his glowing imagination and deep sense of purity, the reign of love, the perfection of Woman. For my part, I always count this poem as Tennyson's most typical triumph, for whilst it gives every opening to his peculiar genius, it has nothing whereof he was other than perfect master. *Maud* may have structural defects; the *Idylls of the King* are a cross between Idyll and Epic, and are not quite faultless in either sense; and even *In Memoriam* is somewhat long-winded, lugubrious, and unsettling to the general reader. But *The Princess* has perennial delight for the whole reading world, whilst it satisfies every canon of the most searching criticism.

No part of Lyall's estimate is more elaborate and more just than the very subtle study he has made of the *Idylls of the King*. He analyses the sources of their sustained popularity — the colour, the imagination, the fine symbolism and the marvellous versatility of the twelve cantos. But he cannot close his mind to the incongruity inevitable in such a scheme — the transmuting Malory's magical myths, told in frank mother-tongue, into ethical allegories, psychologic subtleties, and modern delicacy of thought and speech. The Arthurian romance in its original form never was a thing for young ladies to dream over, for ministers to preach about, or for

the hierophants of culture to expound in elaborate "keys"
and commentaries. As in *Maud*, as in *The Promise of May*,
in "Vastness" and in "Despair," the poet set himself a task
where the conditions of real success were unattainable by
any art. The author of these exquisite Pastorals, songs,
lyrics, fantasies, medleys, and meditations forced himself to
produce an Epic of 11,000 lines, a crowded stage of heroes,
battles, supernatural beings, of passionate love and tragic
death, all predetermined by a mysterious destiny; and yet
the poet will not put off his love of dulcet Pastoral, psychologic
analysis, and ethical homily. The result, as Lyall says, is
too much of a "splendid anachronism," something in places
almost tame and artificial. But it is strangely fascinating
and deserves its immense popularity with the general public.

Equally subtle is Lyall's analysis of the Romances, Ballads,
and Pastorals. He is enthusiastic over their grace, refinement, fancy, and imagination, whilst recognising that Tennyson's genius was "essentially cultivated and picturesque."
This does not accord with the unconscious simplicity of the
true ballad or the rustic power of plain speech now and then
reached by Burns, Lady Nairne, and by Wordsworth.
"The Twa Corbies" and "Edwin and Angelina" are both
said to be ballads: but how wide is the gulf between them!
Difficile est proprie communia dicere; and that camel will get
through the eye of the needle after all, before culture and
word-painting will ever produce the pathos that rings in the
genuine speech of rude men. Tennyson's two "Northern
Farmers" are a rare success. But they were enough. The
prolonged imitation of mere provincial vulgarisms becomes
dull and unpleasing, if carried too far, as does the music of
whistling in imitation of the voice or the violin. It is a
wonderful trick but soon grows tiresome. Lyall has put this
excellently. But it is a pity that he has not said quite enough

of "Rizpah." This poem was Tennyson's supreme triumph in the weird, tragic, and ghastly romance. It has true directness, horror, and realism. And, dreadful as it is, it is within the range of poetry, nor has modern poetry done anything grander in that vein.

It is pleasant to find that Lyall does full justice to the Dramas, especially to the gallant attempt to revive a genuine historical drama, which our new historical precision has made an almost impossible task. The best of Tennyson's Plays have not been properly valued. They inevitably want the grace, music, and glow of the lyrics and idylls and the subtlety of the meditative poems. And Tennyson's genius was lyrical, not dramatic. Accordingly, none of them, except *Becket*, succeeded on the stage with a London public eager for very different spectacles. Nor have they in full measure all the charm that the cultured reader finds in the Lyrics. But they have sound qualities of their own, and will doubtless be played to more worthy audiences when a real reform of the theatre has been achieved. In the meantime, they ought to be read by all who care for serious poetry and the idealisation of great historic catastrophes.

One regrets that the poet did not take King Alfred for one of his heroes. The scantiness of the historical record would have given ample scope to his imagination, whilst the nobility of the great King and his mission as saviour of the English name would have given fire to the poet's patriotism. After some reflection, he rejected William the Silent as subject for a drama, because he clung tenaciously to English history and legend. Lyall truly remarks on the singular tendency of Tennyson to restrict his subject to his own country. He confines his vision, except for the antique, to England and even particular parts of England. Chaucer, Shakespeare, Milton, Dryden, Pope, Byron, Shelley, Wordsworth, Coleridge, Keats, and Browning are full of interest in other lands. Foreign travel did not inspire Tennyson; foreign history, legend, and art left him cold; he rarely alludes even to Scotland or to Ireland. He is the most intensely English of all our poets, unless it be Cowper or Crabbe. That has been Tennyson's strength. It may hereafter prove to be a weakness.

Lyall does full justice to Tennyson's command of every type of metrical resource. But he does not seem to complain of that peculiarity of his later manner which at last became a mannerism and even an offence. To me the enormously long rhymed lines of his decline are quite intolerable. Lines of sixteen syllables as in "Despair," or of eighteen and even twenty in "Vastness," are abortions in English verse; and that for the sound reason that the English language has an inordinate number of consonants in proportion to vowels, and consequently piles up an agglomeration of letters in every long line. No other poetry has ever burdened itself with verses of sixty letters and twenty syllables. Such monstrosities in poetry are not verses but tumours. Hardly any modern language is so ill-fitted for them as is our own.

Another tendency which grew on the Laureate with years was the constant resort to trochaic metres (— ◡), and also to three-syllable feet, such as dactyls (— ◡◡) or anapæsts (◡◡ —). We all enjoyed the "May Queen," "Locksley Hall," the "Light Brigade," and felt the quick, eager, and tripping trochees well fitted for a short ballad. But when it came to dactyls in lines of sixteen and eighteen syllables, when long-winded metaphysical debates were spun out in verses consisting of seven feet and a half, with twenty syllables and sixty letters — Tennyson or not — the effect is wearisome. The rattle of the three-syllable foot is quite unsuited to philosophical homily. The poet, in his earlier mode, quite felt

the futility of English hexameters and pentameters when he
wrote in his "Experiments":

> When was a harsher sound ever heard, ye Muses, in England?
> When did a frog coarser croak upon Helicon?

Although after the "experiment" of "Boädicea," he did
not resort to pure hexameters, for which our language is so
utterly unfit, he constantly resorted to long lines of *octameters*
full of dactyls, the effect of which to our ears is even less
pleasing than that of "Boädicea." [1]

There seems to be very good reason for the more sparing
use in English poetry of trochees, dactyls, or anapæsts. The
excessive quantity of letters in English syllables, as compared
with the classical or Latin tongues, causes an English three-
syllable foot to bulk larger, both to the ear and to the eye,
than does a Greek, Latin, or Italian three-syllable foot.
The first line of the *Iliad* has only eleven consonants; the
first line of the *Æneid* has nineteen; the first line of *Paradise
Lost* has twenty-one; the first line of "Vastness" has thirty-
one consonants. And they tumble over each other, choke
the mouth and disturb the eye.

A peculiarity of English speech is the tendency to throw
back the accent to the antepenultimate syllable, to clip and
hurry the pronunciation, and this especially in the more
vulgar language. The trochaic and dactylic metres naturally accentuate this tendency; and, however suited for ballad
purposes and for impetuous bursts of emotion, these verses,

---

[1] The fourth line of " Vastness " scans thus:

```
 1        2          3          4          5          6
 _  ᴗ ᴗ   _  ᴗ ᴗ    _  ᴗ ᴗ    _  ᴗ ᴗ     _   ᴗ ᴗ    _ _
What is it | all but a | trouble of | ants in the | gleam of  a | million
      7        8
 _   ᴗ ᴗ    _
 million of | suns |,
```

a dactylic octameter catalectic (*i.e.* cut short).

with the accent on the penultimate and antepenultimate of the foot, are not suited for sustained narration, grave reasoning, and dignity of tone. English heroic verse has always chosen an iambic metre — *i.e.* feet of two syllables, one short and one long, with the stress on the last syllable, not on the first. We could not stand *Paradise Lost* in a dactylic or ballad metre.[1]

Tennyson has shown himself to have consummate mastery of the iambic metres in all their forms, and all his noblest pieces are so cast. The nature of our language and all the traditions of our poetry point to some of the iambic forms as best for all continuous, grave, and stately poems. And this makes it the more unlucky that he so often abandoned them in his later verses for trochaic and dactylic types, indelibly associated with ballads, burlesques, and even nursery rhymes.[2]

We may offer these criticisms without at all impugning Tennyson's undoubted claim to be looked on as the supreme poet of the Victorian Era, and one of the chief lyric poets of our English tongue. It is unworthy of him and of ourselves to exalt him to a superhuman pedestal, where it is counted profanity to hint at a weakness or a fault. Like almost all our poets, except Milton, Gray, Coleridge, and Arnold, he published a great deal more than he need have done. Tennyson no doubt published far less of careless, ill-digested, and

[1] Suppose it ran in dactyls :

```
   1        2           3          4          5          6
 _   ᴜ ᴜ  _ ᴜ ᴜ  _ ᴜ    ᴜ   _ ᴜ ᴜ   _   ᴜ   _ _
Man's want of | proper  ob | edience  and | tasting of | disallowed | apples.
```

[2] The trochaic metre suits :
"John Gilpin," "The Babes in the Wood," "Three Jolly Huntsmen," and "Lord Bateman."

Dactylic metre suits :

```
     1          2            3          4          5
 _   _     _   ᴜ ᴜ   _ ᴜ    ᴜ   _   ᴜ   ᴜ   _
'Tis the | voice of the | sluggard I | heard him com | plain.
```

poor work than almost any of our poets. All of them, except Milton and Gray, sank at times into bathos unworthy of them. This Tennyson never did. But he published much, in his later career, which is inferior to his best. The future will no doubt be content to remember little more than a half, or even a third, of his immense output. Most of his poems would be more effective if they were only half as long as they are. Again, his best work was all completed in the first thirty years of his very long course of active work. But having accepted these provisos, let us make the most of him who was the greatest poet of the last three generations; let us delight in his grace, soothe our spirit in his music, revel in his fantasies, and honour his noble ideals, his pure imagination, his profound seriousness.

THE MILLENARY OF KING ALFRED

[*An address given in 1897, proposing the celebration of the thousandth anniversary of Alfred's death. This took place in October 1901, when the Statue was unveiled by Lord Rosebery at Winchester.*]

ON the 26th of October 1901, exactly four years hence, a thousand years will have passed since the death of our greatest King. We are a little overdone with anniversaries, and those not always of the worthiest. But this is no ordinary occasion; for it will be the thousandth anniversary of him to whom England owes an incalculable debt of gratitude, one whom our best teachers describe as the noblest Englishman recorded in our history. Alfred's name is almost the only one in the long roll of our national worthies which awakens no bitter, no jealous thought, which combines the honour of all; Alfred represents at once the ancient Monarchy, the army, the navy, the law, the literature, the poetry, the art, the enterprise, the industry, the religion of our race. Neither Welshman, nor Scot, nor Irishman can feel that Alfred's memory has left the trace of a wound for his national pride. No difference of Church arises to separate any who would join to do Alfred honour. No Saint in the Calendar was a more loyal and cherished member of the ancient faith; and yet no Protestant can imagine a purer and more simple follower of the Gospel. Alfred was a victorious warrior whose victories have left no curses behind them: a King whom no man ever charged with a harsh act: a scholar who never became a pedant: a Saint who knew no superstition: a hero as bold as Launcelot — as spotless as Galahad.

47

The commemoration of this glorious Founder of our national unity — of a man so close to the very roots of the throne, so dear to the sympathies of the people, bound up with all our traditions and institutions, the inspiration of our early literature and language — such a commemoration should be a national, not a private, concern. The House of Commons might well vote the cost of a torpedo-boat for the Founder of our maritime power, for him to whom we largely owe it that there exists any England at all.

If it be done, it should be done royally; in a form at once magnificent and national. I do not presume to say what form it should take. I trust that, when the time comes, the Government itself will take counsel of the most competent advisers it can find. In my daydreams I have imagined a grand *Mausoleum*, dedicated to the memory of Alfred, and in manifold forms of art recording the great events of his life. I use the word — *Mausoleum* — not in the commercial, but in the true, the historic, sense — the monument erected to King Mausolus in the fourth century B.C. by the piety of his wife.

It was one of the triumphs and one of the wonders of the ancient world: and itself exerted a dominant influence over the development of Hellenic art. All visitors to the British Museum are familiar with the fragments of it which time has spared, and have seen the suggestions of its original form over which the learned dispute. It contained colossal statues of the King and his wife Artemisia — still noble even in their ruined state — a grand monumental edifice, adorned with a multitude of statues, reliefs, friezes, and finials, the least fragment of which is to-day a study and a joy. Now, I do not suggest that we should imitate that or any other monument of antiquity; but I can imagine the boundless opportunities for great commemorative art which a monument of this kind presents.

In my daydreams I have seen rising in some conspicuous spot in Wessex a shrine in that Byzantine manner which was the dominant architecture of Europe in the age of Alfred — the style of the Holy Wisdom of Constantinople, or possibly of that Pantheon at Rome which Alfred knew — but in any case, a building wherein could be worked out in marble, in mosaic, in bronze, and in enamel, scenes to recall to us the aspect and events of our Hero's life — his terrific combats with the Dane on land and sea, his council-hall, his midnight meditations, his studies, his prayers, his boyish experiences in Rome.

What a scope for the artist in every form of art is presented by the varied incidents of that crowded life and heroic age, when all costume was noble, all accessories picturesque, and manners Homeric in simple nature. It seems to me that any fine works of art should be under a roof, and not exposed to our climate, and that a covered building might contain not only the principal monument, but a Museum to which might be transferred Alfred's Jewel at Oxford and any other genuine relic of his time, with coins, carvings, enamels, arms, robes, and any contemporary manuscript and illumination which it was possible to obtain.

Or a simpler form would be a colossal statue to be seen afar off on the top of some historic down in a more massive and bolder type of art. And if such a monument were raised in the open air, there is little doubt where it should be placed. I was the other day again in the ancient and famous city of Winchester — the royal city of Alfred, where his bones still crumble in their thrice-desecrated tomb — I thought fresh efforts should be made to identify the exact spot — and I felt how deep a debt lies on Winchester and on England to replace that lost grave at least with a cenotaph and a monu- ment — "the tomb," says the Annals, "made of the most

E

precious porphyry marble." How fitly it might stand on the historic Hill which looks down on College, Cathedral, and wall!

A Mausoleum which should combine a grand statue of the King with various illustrations of his life and deeds would open great opportunities to several artists in different arts. And it would be a narrow patriotism indeed which limited these artists to our own land. It would dishonour the memory of Alfred to do this. No English ruler has ever been so large-minded in all his interests, so Catholic in his taste, so pre-eminently European in his type of mind. To him of all men, Art, Learning, Culture were too wide and human to know any local habitation. He sought out for his service, his biographer tells us, Welshmen, Irishmen, Bretons, Franks, Scots, Frisians, and Danes; "he was munificent towards foreigners of all races"; he sent abroad for teachers, artificers, discoverers, and seamen. It would be a pity if a monument to commemorate his name were not open to the genius of the civilised world.

Another thought, indeed, has occurred to me. Our Westminster Abbey is at last crowded to excess, and must very soon cease to be the resting-place of the great men whom the nation delights to honour. We need a new Abbey, a *Campo Santo*, where in ages to come the noblest sons of England may be laid (as the poet says) "to the noise of the mourning of a mighty nation." It is easy to say that future ages will take care of themselves. But there is one thing that the Future cannot do — it cannot create a Past. And what it will want for its *Campo Santo*, when the venerable Abbey can serve no longer, is a Past. A national Mausoleum of King Alfred may at least suggest a Past — a past more ancient than the Abbey of the Edwards and the Henrys — it might grow into the nucleus of a national *Heröum* — just as

Poets' Corner grew into a sanctuary of art round the tomb of Chaucer in the Abbey. And I can conceive that in ages to come Nelsons' famous phrase of, "Victory or Westminster Abbey," might be replaced by the hope of warrior, statesman, or poet to be thought worthy to lie in the Mausoleum of Alfred.

When the thousandth anniversary of Alfred comes round, we all trust that the royal Lady, the forty-ninth sovereign since Alfred, may be able and willing to give her personal sanction to a national Festival. Modern history has no such sequence of national continuity to present — no throne, no institution, no organic patriotism, no literature of such vast duration and such venerable traditions. And this is a healthy and fruitful form of patriotic feeling. It can offend no man, neither in these islands nor in the Empire, nor abroad in other nations. The little Englander and the greater Englander, the Englishman and the Imperialist, Old England and New England, can unite in honour of the great King who ruled an England far smaller than any little England of to-day, yet whose genius and heroism made it the nucleus — the *pou stô* — of all that his descendants ever held in their dominion, of all that his descendant, Her Majesty, holds in dominion at this hour [1897]. The memory of Alfred calls up no thought of Conquest, but the noblest form of Defence, it calls up international sympathies and co-operation, a great civilising and missionary task, it suggests schools, temples, libraries, industries, courts of justice, civic organisation: — all the boundless influence of a great brain and a majestic character, be the field of his energy as small as a single province and the materials to his hand of the simplest sort.

Many other modes of using for ourselves and our children this matchless occasion occur to me, on which to-night I can only touch. There is still needed a perfectly complete and critical edition of every line of the King's authentic writings. We should never forget that Alfred is the Father of English History, the Founder of English prose. He is in the true sense the Father of the History of the English people — in a sense more literally true than Herodotus ever was the "Father of History" — in that Alfred gave an impulse and form to the *English Chronicle*, the oldest national record in modern Europe; and himself wrote or inspired the writing of some of its typical parts. He is the Founder of English prose, in that he not only formed an organic prose, but his influence caused the maintenance of English prose until the Conquest for the time superseded it by Latin and French. No perfect collection of these noble pieces of our scholar King has yet been made: and it would form a worthy task for a company of Scholars to achieve it.

Nor, again, is there any adequate English biography of our great Hero. After all that has been done by eminent scholars who have given us every authentic fact ascertainable in Alfred's career, there is yet no full and adequate biography of the King by an English hand. The splendid pictures drawn by Green and by Freeman, in more than one work of each, remain after all but glowing sketches; and they are but episodes embedded in voluminous works. And, excellent as is the German work of Dr. Pauli, it is possible to imagine a new biography based on more recent research, and worthy to rank with the masterpieces of English prose.

Perhaps it is not too late for the Holy See to repair its neglect to place Alfred amongst its canonised Sovereigns. There are already twelve of these in the Calendar, we are told: not one of the twelve was the peer of the Saxon King — whom four centuries ago our Henry VI. vainly besought the Pope to canonise. Rome acts always with deliberation.

But, after a thousand years, it may yet recognise the holiness of a saint the halo of whose glory will last as long as the Church.

Some commemoration of the great King there is certain to be in the millenary year 1901. I would raise a voice in hope that it may be at once national and worthy of the nation: that it may not degenerate into a scramble or a farce. It would be an occasion to call for representation of every side of our national life — as the pulse from Alfred's mighty heart throbbed into every vein of the nation's organism. Soldiers, sailors, scholars, churchmen, missionaries, teachers, councillors, judges, prelates, artists, craftsmen, discoverers — chiefs and people — all alike might gather to do honour to the royal genius who loved them all, who breathed into them all his own inspiration. I can imagine an assemblage of chosen delegates from our regiments and our fleets, from cathedral, abbey, church, and chapel (without distinction of creed), from universities and schools, from art and science academies, from libraries and institutes, from Parliament and from Government, from courts of justice and from county halls and city councils, from the labourers in town and country — all joining around a national monument to our first great Hero. Such military display as was thought right would best be furnished forth by the volunteers and naval reserves in honour of the King who first organised a regular militia at home for the defence of our shores by sea and land — whose very name as a warrior spells "*Defence — not Defiance.*" Such a national commemoration would be a real festival of industry, art, order, union, peace, and religion.

No people, in ancient or modern times, ever had a Hero-Founder at once so truly historic, so venerable, and so supremely great. Alfred was more to us than the heroes in antique myths — more than Theseus and Solon were to Athens, or Lycurgus to Sparta, or Romulus and Numa were to Rome, more than St. Stephen was to Hungary, or Pelayo and the Cid to Spain, more than Hugh Capet and Jeanne d'Arc were to France, more than William the Silent was to Holland — nay, almost as much as the Great Charles was to the Franks.

The life-work of the Great Alfred has had a continuity, an organic development, a moral, intellectual, and spiritual majesty which has no parallel or rival amongst rulers in the annals of mankind. And I cannot doubt that four years hence the English-speaking people will remember him who gave them the precious germs of that which our forefathers have made a thousand years of national life and honour.

THE TERCENTENARY OF CROMWELL

THREE hundred years have come and gone since the mightiest spirit that ever held command over these three kingdoms came into the world. For two hundred and fifty years the English people who owed him so much (all but a remnant of stalwart men) reviled his memory and ridiculed his life. He was despised and rejected of men. We hid our faces from him. At last, in the latter half-century, a man of genius drove home to the bottom of our conscience as a people, our folly, ingratitude, and shame. Years and years of remorse will hardly suffice to expiate our offence.

Thomas Carlyle spoke, we may admit, with passion, with something of a prophet's rage and excess. In fifty years we have grown calmer, more judicial, more amply informed of the truth. And recognising as we do the substantial justice of Carlyle's story — nay, seeing in many things how even his high estimate may be amplified and coloured — we have no temptation to-day to exaggerate qualities or to palliate faults. We are willing to admit the sad and dark side of this vast national epic, as well as the immortal and heroic side we see to-day. We are all no longer under the spell of an advocate's passion. We are penetrated with the conviction of a weighty and unanswerable judgment, all errors weighed and measured out in the issue. And we, the most ardent Oliverians of us all, are no longer battling for Revision of an unjust sentence. We come, like pilgrims, to bow the head in silent meditation at the foot of an empty and desecrated tomb.

It has taken three hundred years for Englishmen to know

what they owe to one of the greatest men their race has produced.　It is a wise rule that we should in general observe
anniversaries of death rather than of birth, for all public and
historic purposes.　Birthdays belong to family occasions, and
are proper to theological and mystical festivals.　Except
from the point of view of some miraculous and superhuman
birth, the coming into the world of a statesman or poet is a
thing of which the public at the time took no note, and which
affected nobody and nothing outside the home itself.　The
effect of a great life upon fellow-men is only complete and
perceptible when the life is closed, and often not till long
afterwards.　No one outside a plain home in Huntingdon
noticed the fact that Elizabeth Cromwell was brought to bed
of her fifth child, and for forty years few people supposed
that a great event in English history had happened on the
25th of April 1599.　But when Oliver, Protector, died, all
Britain and Ireland held its breath in hushed expectation —
and all Europe breathed more freely.　It is the end of a great
career which concerns nations — not the unnoticed birth
of a baby who may live to have a great career half a century
later.　Real centenaries should run with the date of death,
not of birth, or we shall all get bored by anniversary commemorations, as some affected people even now profess to be
bored.

But, as many honest men refuse to postpone the commemoration of Oliver until 1958, and as the first statue to him
in London is to be raised this year, we need not adjourn our
remembrance of a great man to a date which only our children
will see.　Let us ask ourselves to-day the simple questions
— In what things was Cromwell a great Englishman?　What
is the teaching of his life?　What are the effects he left on
the history of England?

Oliver Cromwell is by general consent a typical Englishman, having that union of somewhat incongruous forces which is to be found in the English people, which has made England — English in his courage, in his patience, his self-control, his masterful stubbornness, his pitiless crushing down of opponents when he felt himself to be on the path of duty, his disdain of forms, theories, doctrines, and utopias, his passion for freedom with personal self-will, his Biblical religion, his sterling honesty of aim and yet great capacity for intrigue, his fierce hold on certain root ideals with a boundless spirit of compromise, opportunism, toleration of all things and all men that he judged to be instrumental to his ends. An eminent historian (himself a descendant of the Protector) tells us to regard him "with all his physical and moral audacity, with all his tenderness and spiritual yearnings, in the world of action what Shakespeare was in the world of thought, the greatest because the most typical Englishman of all time" — not a model but a mirror, wherein we may see alike our weakness and our strength.

The "most typical" of Englishmen is wholly true: as to "the greatest," it is a term rather too strong for those who admit great faults, and perhaps some crimes. It is true that both faults and crimes were essentially those of the age and of the moral standard of the party he led; and what we most condemn to-day met with nothing but praise from some of the best spirits of the time. Yet perhaps in "the greatest" of Englishmen we would ask for a career more entirely spotless, and a nature of more heroic beauty. King Alfred, whom Freeman called "the model Englishman," would be more fairly matched with Shakespeare, if we choose to imagine the greatest of our national types, for to King Alfred neither crimes nor faults are imputed. Cromwell is of us, is near to us; we are living still in the daily influence of his work; we know every incident of his life, almost every thought of his mind. We feel for him as we feel for our own country, when unconsciously, instinctively, often in spite of the pricking of conscience, we murmur — England ! with all thy faults I love thee still ! We honour Cromwell in spite of his faults; some of us, it may be feared, because of his faults.

It is as an Englishman that Cromwell must be judged, and it is unreasonable to ask Scots or Irish to join us to-day. Though Cromwell gave Scotland good government for the first time in its history, so that a Scotchman and an enemy writes : "We always reckon those eight years of the usurpation a time of great peace and prosperity;" though he certainly prepared the way for the ultimate Union — the source of Scotland's happiness and glory — yet it will not be forgotten that Cromwell conquered Scotland, and ruled it as a conqueror. As to Ireland, Cromwell remorselessly carried out the atrocious policy of his age, and of our country. For my part, I never will palliate or condone it. And the "curse of Cromwell" in the mouths of Irishmen will long rest on his memory and on our peace.

The teaching of Cromwell's life is plain. The silly legend about his ambition and demagogic intrigues has long died away. If ever any English ruler had power forced on him step by step, or ever lived a reserved, austere, domestic life till roused by tyranny to play the man as a citizen should, if ever English statesman having absolute power stood clear of personal interests or sordid desires, it was he. As our Hero-King wrote : "You need not be solicitous about power, nor strive after it. If you be wise and good, it will follow you though you should not wish it." The meditations of Alfred upon Power form a key to the career of his successor eight centuries later. Nor let it be forgotten that for the first time in our history, and almost for the last time, morality and religion were the titles for entrance to Oliver's Court, and notorious vice unfitted all men for Oliver's service. His tolerance of honest convictions, his patience under open hostility, his loathing of confirmed profligacy, his contempt for conventional formulas — were alike unalterable and boundless.

As a statesman, the unique merit of Cromwell's government was his genius for administration, for securing efficiency in every department, for selecting the right man for every duty, for recognising and using every kind of capacity in every department. His success in this crowning art of the statesman has perhaps never been equalled in our own history, hardly in that of Europe, unless it be by Richelieu and Frederick the Great. This plain yeoman, who had tilled his farmstead until past forty years, stepped forth into public life, made himself a thorough soldier, created a consummate army, decided a tremendous civil war, conquered two neighbouring kingdoms, guided a national revolution, stemmed it back by organising a solid conservative government, chose as his deputies the most capable soldiers, seamen, governors, diplomatists, financiers, lawyers, ministers, and publicists who could be found to serve the Commonwealth, and in five years he had formed the strongest Government in Europe, and had made his country the leading Power in the world.

In what we now call opportunism (that is, the instinct of the statesman to change his tactics under circumstances and to seize the occasion of the hour) Cromwell has rarely been equalled by any man in all recorded history. His note as a born statesman is the union of matchless audacity with inexhaustible wariness. No great man so brave and so daring was ever so untiringly prudent and watchful. In his whole career Cromwell never met with a single disaster, either in war or in government. He was never off his guard, was never once caught napping, never relaxed his intense hold on the smallest detail, or allowed a single point to be unguarded. In this he is like Elizabeth, Wellington, or Marlborough, but he surpassed them all in sleepless vigilance and unbroken success. His were not the triumphs of a Napoleon alternating with hideous catastrophes, nor the generous imprudences of a Cæsar or a Henry IV. In one of the most complex and arduous careers in history, Cromwell is almost the one great chief who in peace and in war never met with a rebuff which more perfect prudence would have sufficed to avert.

What permanent results did Cromwell stamp upon the history of England? In the broadest sense he gave us modern England. Not, of course, alone, but as chief leader in the English Revolution, much as Frederick made modern Prussia, as Nelson won Trafalgar, or as Wellington won Waterloo. Cromwell made modern England with the blood and sweat and heart of the flower of the English people. It is far from clear that without him the finer part of the English people would not have succumbed to the baser part, that the Stuarts would not have founded at last some such monarchy as that of the Louis in France. Those who understand the inner history of the Civil War know that, down to the battle of Marston, if not down to the New Model, the issue was far from clear — and Marston and Naseby were essentially Cromwell's triumphs. And those who understand English history know that the struggle was a long one, that it lasted for at least sixty years from the Long Parliament to the Act of Settlement, that what old Whigs call the "Revolution" was a mere episode and after-glow of the Commonwealth. Modern England begins with the Act of Settlement: this was the direct fruit of the Civil War: and the Civil War might have ended in a Malignant Monarchy — but for Oliver Cromwell and his genius as soldier and statesman.

An exalted Personage once asked a certain historian to tell

him what Cromwell had left of permanent to the nation?
"Well, sir," was the answer, "our most gracious Majesty,
and our present Dynasty." This may pass as an after-dinner
phrase, but it is not altogether a paradox. We have to look
at these problems in a large way and from an ample perspec-
tive. The Commonwealth and the Protectorate destroyed
the Old Monarchy and the Feudal Constitution, and they
opened the ground for all our Liberal Institutions. It is
true that Stuarts, Monarchy, and Church returned, but only
for a space, mere shadows of their ancient form. Look at
England as a whole, as it was at the accession of Charles I.
and as it was at the accession of Queen Anne, and note the
enormous change within those two generations. Monarchy,
peerage, parliament, law, justice, finance, toleration, equity,
commerce, religion — all were transformed, and stood on a
wholly new social system. Who, along with the people of
England, and their sense of freedom, justice, and truth, had
made this possible? Who — but Oliver Cromwell?

Of course, the Protectorate was followed by the Restoration,
and most of its direct acts of State were annulled. It is
true that Parliamentary Government, as understood by the
Whigs, was far from an idea of Cromwell, who contemplated
rather the Presidential system of the United States. But,
though Cromwell did not found Parliamentary Government,
nor religious liberty, nor the legal and administrative system
that he prematurely set up, he made all these things possible
in the end, little as he foresaw what he was doing. Our
subsequent history, no doubt, was a compromise, and much
of it was as anti-Cromwellian as it could be. But it was
Cromwell who, in the evolution of the English nation, made
our subsequent history possible.

The eminent historian quoted above now tells us that
Cromwell has left nothing permanent, that not only his

institutions, but his ideas failed of result, that his negative work lasted, but his positive work vanished. This is an over-statement which, if it were pressed, would be a paradox or a sophism. It is a matter of language. In great revolutions of nations and societies there is no arbitrary distinction between negative and positive results. To destroy for ever an effete political and social system is practically to found a new system. And if new institutions improvised on the cleared ground do not take permanent root, they prepare the way for modified institutions of a kindred sort. It would be easy to show that Alexander, Julius Cæsar, Charlemagne, Richelieu, or Napoleon left no permanent results on history, because their positive work vanished, and their institutions were swept away, or developed in new forms. That Cromwell's "ideas" have failed is manifestly untrue. What, then, mean our eulogies, centenaries, statues, and honours to his memory — our grateful sense of his hatred of oppression, of persecution, of his zeal for good government, justice, morality, religion in things public as well as private? Let us not make ourselves blind over the records of institutions and negotiations. The ideas of Cromwell live deep down in the hearts of Englishmen.

We hear too much of the objection that Cromwell was a soldier and ruled by the sword. He was a civilian — not a soldier — a citizen by nature, and always a statesman by the summons of the nation, a soldier for a brief spell by dire necessity. Cromwell was forty-three when he first drew a sword, and of the fifty-eight years of his life he spent but nine under arms. Great soldier as he was in the field, he was far less the professional soldier than George Washington, or William the Silent. If we study his whole career after Worcester we see him continually labouring to return to a civil government, and all his ways differ essentially from the ways of a Frederick or a Napoleon, though he held absolute power, and was beset by enemies within and without. The Protectorate, which lasted less than five years, was a constant effort to restore the ravages and calm the passions of civil war.

We are told again that Cromwell's rule rested wholly on the Army, that it was a military despotism, and that a military despotism was an impossibility in England, doomed to an abhorred collapse. In words, it is true that the Protectorate, like the Long Parliament, rested on armed men, who, perhaps, were at all times a minority of the nation. Neither Parliament nor Protector were any product of manhood suffrage. But the armies of Parliament and Protector were formed of men wholly different in origin and in character from the troops who followed Frederick or Napoleon, or even Wellington or Moltke. The "Ironsides" were ardent politicians, usually religious and political enthusiasts, who held their own Parliament in the camp, a Parliament more able and honest than the Rump at Westminster. The *Clarke Papers*, so admirably edited by Mr. C. H. Firth, have shown us what these men were like, and how they affected the State. With all their faults and follies they were the flower of England, and the most genuine politicians of their age. And far into the Restoration the old "Ironsides" were known, up and down the country, as the most trusty, virtuous, and industrious citizens in their villages or towns. Most revolutions are carried through by a minority of enthusiasts. It was so in the Commonwealth. And the larger part of what was brave, pure, and just in England gathered round the great man who, of all English chiefs since Alfred, was the most brave. the most sincere, the most just, the most devout.

THE STATUE OF OLIVER CROMWELL

1899

At last, after two centuries and a half, London has a statue of the greatest ruler who ever governed the three kingdoms. The hatred of his memory, which so long kept him in exile from the Palace of Westminster, has at length fizzled out in the whining of a handful of Ritualists, Jew financiers, and Jacobites. That Churchmen, the parasites of smart Society, Irishmen, mediæval æsthetes, and the like should feel sore at honours paid to the great Protector is not unnatural. But they were not expected to subscribe to the statue and were not invited to attend the commemoration. They have vented their ill-humour; and now at last a grand effigy of Oliver stands in the precincts of the ancient Hall, on the gateway of which his mangled head rotted for twenty years. It looks on the Abbey, where the nation entombed him with royal honours at the premature end of his short dictatorship.

To oppose the erection of a statue to Cromwell shows a curious misunderstanding of what such a memorial implies. It does not mean that we approve of all that the man commemorated did in life: much less that all parties and sections of the public approve his career. If so, there could be no statues of Wellington, Gordon, Jenner, or George III. If warm approval of all the acts of such an one and absolute unanimity were needed, before a statue could be raised, there would be no statues at all, or none but that of Alfred the

Great. And, even in his case, uniform admiration seems almost to dull the public interest; and we perhaps want a few grumblers, as Devil's advocates, even for Alfred.

But just consider those of whom we have statues in London already — Charles I., James II., Richard Cœur de Lion, George IV. — four of the worst Kings who ever occupied the throne — to say nothing of Francis, Duke of Bedford, Benjamin, Earl of Beaconsfield, the Duke of Cumberland, and the Duke of York of the last century. There would be plenty of black balls in the box, if these noble persons were submitted to a public ballot. Nobody asks to have the statue of any of these removed — not even that of the miscreant James II., whom Macaulay describes as "a libertine, narrow in understanding, obstinate, harsh, and unforgiving" — one whom the nation drove from the throne in favour of the present Dynasty. There must be a give-and-take in such things. And if the mass of the public can tolerate the sight in bronze of a sinister brute like James II., we have a right to claim a place for one who represents the good side of that great national struggle, whereof James II. was the incarnation of the evil side.

A memorial of Oliver rests on the fact that he was the leader of a movement which transformed the course of English history, and then, for nearly five years, was the paramount ruler of the three kingdoms at an epoch eminent for skilful administration and national power. The most ardent Oliverians do not to-day pretend to justify many things in the Protector's public action, nor do they dream of celebrating him as a perfect character. No one now repeats the extravagant hyperboles of Carlyle, whose sardonic idolatry tends rather to stimulate hostility to the memory of Cromwell, not to disarm it. But the reaction against Carlyle's old-Cameronian hero-worship seems to be going too far; and even some who

F

deeply approve the overthrow of the Stuart absolutism and all that it meant in Church and State, rather minimise the part that Oliver had in the work, and insist on his failure to bring the work to its full completeness. In these days of so much flabby theology and playing with mediævalism on one side, of so much conventional liberalism and pedantic special-ism on the other side, the occasion is one to insist on the su-preme importance of the entire life of Cromwell in the success-ful evolution of the English people.

It is now plain that the Stuart absolutism in Church and State could not have been broken down without civil war. Of that civil war, one marked by rapid and complete success not elsewhere recorded in modern history, Cromwell was the soul. All the great battles were victories of his, were won by his genius alone when all seemed lost. The conquest of the other two kingdoms was also his sole task. No one now, even of his most bitter opponents, doubts Cromwell's great place as a soldier. But his supreme part in the Civil War was much more than that of a soldier. The organising of a regular army, having consummate discipline and efficiency in all its arms and resources, out of the raw farmers and workmen hastily enlisted, was Cromwell's own achievement, and was perhaps even more decisive than brilliant tactics in the field. But this is to say that, but for Cromwell, the Monarchy and Feudalism might have beaten down the Parliament and people, might have established a retrograde absolutism and a persecuting Church.

But it is as the instrument of a great political and social evolution, much more than as a consummate soldier, that we celebrate Cromwell; it is as statesman, not as warrior, that he stands to-day at the gateway of Parliament, looking down on the minor politicians in Parliament Square. We are told by some eminent historians of the Protector that his negative or destructive work was invaluable and permanent; his positive and constructive work was mistaken and evanescent. Part of this statement is a mere matter of language; part of it is due to the viewing the broad course of English history from a standpoint somewhat too special and narrow.

What is *negative*, what is *positive* work, in things political and social? Destructive work, in statesmanship, provided it be *permanent*, is *ipso facto* constructive, if it enables the new system to form and to grow. As Luther, Wickliffe, Latimer were primarily destructives in theology, or as Voltaire, Hume, Kant were primarily destructives in metaphysics, though vast constructions have grown up on the ground which they cleared and laid bare, so some of the most mighty founders of political reconstruction left at their deaths nothing permanent except their decisive work of destruction. In societies, to destroy the effete, at *the right* time, in *the right* way, and *once for all*, is to reconstruct. Sulla, Attila, Philip II., Robespierre, and Marat were mere destructives and anarchists, because their destruction was evil, and what they destroyed was destined to revive. But those who sweep away what is destined to perish past any revival, and, after finally preparing the new ground, design a new type of society and show forth an ideal of a better world, these men are constructive statesmen, even though their direct foundations are entirely modified and rebuilt.

Alexander, Julius Cæsar, Charles the Great, Godfrey de Bouillon, Louis XI., William the Silent, effected memorable works of reconstruction. The first three transformed the world and the whole course of civilisation, and the latter three made possible great national reconstruction. And yet the State system, the institutions laboriously founded by each of these, quickly perished; and hardly one of them left anything absolutely permanent behind him, unless it were the city of Alexandria and the Calendar. If we use terms very strictly, and press things rigidly, the residuum of their entire work may be said to lie in destruction, or negative results. Especially would this be true of William the Silent, whose whole career was one of failure and disappointment; for, at his murder, almost everything he had toiled to found was crumbling away. And yet after three centuries the nation he created reveres him as its Father, and the British Empire is now fighting on the Orange River in Africa, with the mere offshoot and emigrants from that nation.

Almost every criticism now urged against the statesmanship of the Protector might be made with tenfold force against that of William the Silent. William's great scheme of uniting the seventeen provinces utterly failed and for ever, his attempt to harmonise Lutheran and Calvinist, Walloon and Hollander, noble and democrat, broke down before his own eyes. He turned from France to England, from England to Germany, from monarchs to people, from Princes to preachers, from magnates to tradesmen. His diplomacy was one long tangle of changes, conflicting principles, ever-varying combinations, as was that of Henry of Navarre, Mazarin, Cavour, or Bismarck. The failures, abortive schemes, vacillations, high-handed acts, and arbitrary blunders imputed to the Protector may all be matched in the history of these statesmen; and, in the case of William the Silent, they were tenfold as great. And yet the world has long been agreed that William created a nation, and that his negative success has really proved to be a positive success of the first order.

That destructive statesmanship should be constructive in result, requires many important conditions. The destruction must be necessary and timely; it must be final; it must prepare a permanent reconstruction. The Protectorate fulfilled all these conditions. Mr. John Morley, in his new

and fascinating *Life of Cromwell*, quotes a sentence of mine
wherein I speak of Oliver's success as a constructive statesman. If Mr. Morley will look again at chapter xi. of my
little book he will see that his quotation omits the most important phrase in my sentence. I wrote that Oliver was one
of the rare order "of constructive *and conservative* statesmen."
By that I meant that a statesman who, after a great revolutionary clearance, stems the current of destruction, conserves
and re-establishes order and good government, *ipso facto*
constructs a new and sounder system. After Worcester
Cromwell was in supreme authority for exactly seven years,
during which his policy was essentially Conservative. As he
truly said, the needs of the time were "Healing and Settling."
For seven years he did heal and settle in the only way possible,
often by arbitrary acts, now and then by unjustifiable acts,
constantly trying new methods, but always bent on honest
settlement. And this seven years of heroic, but often abortive, striving towards settlement in a conservative, but not a
reactionary sense, made possible the final Settlement, which
thirty years later was brought about in the time of the third
William of Orange.

Although many of the Protector's schemes and arrange-
ments disappeared with him and some of them before him,
they were ultimately succeeded by institutions of a similar
order and having like purpose, which never could have been
founded at all had not Cromwell's reforms and experiments
preceded them. Like William the Silent, Cromwell failed
at times because he was in advance of his age, especially in
the matter of religious equality, official competence, law
reform, and the proper spheres of Parliament and Executive.
Had Cromwell had his way he would have made the political
system of England akin to that of the United States; and in
my opinion it is a pity he did not have his way. But his

failure to fall in with the Parliamentary system, which was hardly established for more than a century after his time, was one of those failures for which he is deserving of honour and not of blame.

It is quite true that his rule as Protector was based on the Army, that much of it was oppressive to the defeated party, that it was unconstitutional, such as could not be permanently established in England. Quite true: but the effectual destruction of the old divine-right Monarchy could not have been made decisive in any other way. Feudalism could not have been crushed by a few defeats in the field. And the mediæval *régime* in law, local administration, religious persecution, and arbitrary taxation could not have been broken down without years and years of a military *régime* based on a different spirit. Marston Moor, Naseby, and Worcester were not enough to transform England from a Feudal Monarchy and semi-Catholic Church into a free Commonwealth and Protestant toleration. It needed the five years of the greatest ruler that England has ever known; and if the five years had been fifteen it would have been better for us now. The government of Scotland was oppressive; the conquest of Ireland was atrocious; the foreign policy of the Protectorate was selfish. But all of these were involved in the very nature of the Englishmen of that day. To ask of Cromwell that he should be of different mould was to ask him not to be an Englishman of the seventeenth century, not to be an Englishman at all. At any rate, in all this he did not go counter to the best hopes and aims of the worthiest men of his own time and nation. In his fine address, Lord Rosebery has summed up, in a curiously happy phrase, the essential force of Cromwell's nature. He was truly "a practical mystic, the most terrible and formidable of all combinations." He combined spiritual inspiration with the energy of a mighty man of action.

THE REMAINS OF OLIVER CROMWELL

1899

THE munificent gift to the nation of a statue of the great Protector has naturally awakened a new interest in the supposed fragment of his remains; and, as having given some attention to the matter when preparing my little book on Oliver's *Life*, I wish to support the very reasonable demand for a serious and official inquiry into the facts. I do not pretend to pronounce any decisive opinion; nor am I inclined to a hasty or sentimental view of the case. What we ask is a thorough examination with convincing authority, not crude action without adequate investigation. I certainly believe, as was remarked by others, that a strong *primâ facie* case for inquiry exists. Experts of much more weight than laymen can have in such a matter think the same. What I wish to urge is, that now is the time for inquiry, and that it very much concerns the good name of our nation to make it.

Let us consider what is at stake, *supposing* that the mummy head is truly that of Oliver himself. Many competent men, some on historical and some on physiological grounds, believe that it is. If so, a really dreadful responsibility lies upon us. Whatever view we take of the Civil War and the Usurpation, whatever we hold about Oliver's character and designs, no one doubts that he was *de facto* ruler of England in a time of glory and power, that his is one of the greatest names in the roll of English history, that he was laid with

71

magnificent ceremony in the Abbey by the *de facto* Government of these islands. There he lay with official sanction until the Restoration, when one of the most foul and barbarous outrages recorded in our history was perpetrated upon his remains. It was not the action of a mob, it was not done in the fury of revolution or civil war, nor was it the inconsiderate act of irresponsible subordinates. It was deliberately done by Parliament, the Government, and the Crown with every form of loathsome brutality. And in the judgment of many of us it still stands an unatoned stain on our monarchy and our national history. The sickening details of this outrage rise to our gorge when we think of the Restoration and the annals of Westminster.

The outrage is one almost without example in our history. In France, in the Netherlands, in Germany, the tombs of the great dead have been desecrated by furious mobs in civil and religious insurrections. But our history is happily almost wholly free from that peculiar type of brutality. The one stain on our history of this odious kind is the official and monarchic outrage on the Protector's bones. It would be difficult to find in European history another instance when a monarchy and a Parliament had inflicted in cold blood this vindictive desecration on the ruler who for years had maintained its honour amongst the nations, and had carried its flag to a foremost place in the earth. Suppose that a Spanish Viceroy had desecrated the tomb of William the Silent at Delft, or that a Bourbon Restoration were even yet to desecrate the tomb of Napoleon in the Invalides. What would be the feelings of a Dutch patriot, or of a French patriot, if he had good reason to believe that the severed head of William, or that of Napoleon, were this very day to be seen in a box in a country house? Every Frenchman or any Dutchman, of decent feeling, whatever his religion or his politics, would exclaim in wrath and disgust — "In God's name, let us know if this thing can be!" Now a great many of us think that it is quite possible such a thing really is, with regard to the outraged remains of Oliver, and we think it becomes this nation's honour to find out the truth.

I have never pretended to offer any conclusive opinion in a difficult problem of the kind; and I only took up the inquiry with great hesitation and repugnance. The subject is a gruesome and painful one in any case; and, to those of us who profoundly revere the memory of our great Protector, almost horrible and repulsive. No one with such a sense can witness the uncovering of a relic which, whatever it be, is an appalling sight, without a qualm of divided feeling that, maybe, he is looking at the features of one of the grandest spirits our English soil ever reared — or, it may be, on some nameless skull that curiosity or imposture may have invested with interest. In my own case, the very depth of veneration with which I should bow my head before the true remains of the hero made me very loth to admit that so extraordinary a survival of such a relic was possible. I believe that was the feeling of Carlyle, and that he could not bring himself to examine it with patience.

Gradually, and by a convergent set of testimonies, I have come to think that such a survival is not only possible, but probable. The documentary history of the relic is very far from adequate; but it is perfectly reasonable and consistent so far as it goes. Under the circumstances, a perfectly unbroken and complete history would be, in the highest degree, unlikely to exist. If the head which undoubtedly fell one night from Westminster Hall be still above ground, it would only be preserved in a secret and surreptitious way. The principal evidence I take to be, the obvious correspondence of the mummy head with the authentic portraits and

busts of Oliver, and especially with the cast taken after death
on which Carlyle relied. I have made a study of all these
portraits and busts, and I cannot detect one feature or one
circumstance wherein the relic fails. The extraordinary
combination of incidents is this — an embalmed mummy
head, corresponding minutely to the portraits and busts of
Oliver, *severed from the body long after death, and after embalming,* fixed upon an ancient halberd head, itself bearing
marks of long weathering, and the whole piece with its in-
teguments, hair, bony structure, flesh, and iron spike minutely
corresponding to the history of the relic — itself extremely
probable and consistent. What ingenuity could combine all
these elements — the head of a mummy resembling Oliver
so closely as to convince biologists and sculptors, which had
been severed from the body after embalming, and was en-
crusted on an antique lance head? And to what end was
such strange ingenuity directed? The relic is not for sale,
nor on show, nor has it been thrust upon the public notice.
For nearly the whole of the century it has been honourably
preserved by two families, who regard it as a sacred trust.

I am very far from asking any one to take my opinion on
the matter, which after all only amounts to a *primâ facie*
case of strong probability. What we ask for now is an inquiry
— an authoritative and conclusive inquiry — to place the
matter at rest before the statue is set up. It is really a cruel
thought that, for aught we know, the grandest head that ever
sat on English shoulders may be lying loose in the house of a
private owner; the head, be it remembered, which an English King and Parliament so foully disinterred, cut off, and
set up in mockery at the gateway of Parliament. To leave
this possibility floating about as a matter of periodical gossip
is really to continue and approve the original outrage.

Now, the inquiry can be made a very simple and easy one.

I suggest that a small Commission should be asked to investigate and report to the Home Secretary. It so happens that there are many descendants of the Protector amongst our public men, especially in the present Government and party in office. Foremost stand a late Cabinet Minister, and our most learned living historian. Lord Ripon, the highest in rank of the known descendants of Oliver, would make an admirable chairman; Mr. S. Rawson Gardiner, another descendant, would, of course, be at his side. Sir John Lubbock, also a descendant, would represent the scientific question; the Regius Professors of History at Oxford and Cambridge, and certainly Mr. C. H. Firth, as a Cromwellian expert, should be added. There might be a sculptor, say Mr. Thornycroft, who is preparing the statue, and possibly an expert in craniology and in taxidermy, or the like. All we want is an authoritative opinion from men of varied experience. A month or two of careful sifting of evidence, a few hours of actual inspection, and half a dozen sittings would dispose of the whole affair. And, whatever were the report of the Commission, the matter would be set at rest for ever.

But in case such a Commission were to report that in their opinion there is sufficient ground to believe the relic to be in truth the outraged head of our great Protector, then the Government should address the Dean of Westminster, having obtained the sanction of the Crown, and ask Parliament to efface the atrocious blot upon its annals by formally replacing the surviving fragment of our great Dictator in the very vault where the nation laid him in glory and honour nearly two centuries and a half ago. Long as is the interval, it is not too late to atone for an unparalleled atrocity. And to those whose instinct it is to leave things alone, we would say: In any case the outraged remains of some Englishman still cry out for peaceful burial — it may well be the outraged remains of one of the greatest Englishmen our land ever bore.

The proper resting-place for any remnant of the Protector's bones which chance may have spared is unquestionably the vault in Henry VII.'s Chapel, where the nation laid him. For years past many of us have visited that solemn corner of the Abbey year by year, and rehearsed the tale of ignominy with yearning for some ultimate reparation of the national crime. Our glorious Abbey, unlike St. Denis or the Panthéon in Paris, has no desecrated tombs but these. And the bitter memories they still awaken in us rise, unbidden and irrepressible, in the midst of the pilgrimages we make to our national burying-place of the mighty dead.

In the Abbey should be laid in final rest any relic of Oliver that might conceivably be recovered. Another suggestion has been made, which we need not discuss until it is plain that some obstacle could be raised to this obvious reburial, on behalf of the Abbey or the Crown. Some have thought that the relic itself might be embodied in the pedestal or beneath the statue of Oliver, so that the new effigy would be at once monument and actual tomb. There is something to be said for the idea; but it is one which it is needless to discuss. The proper place for the new statue of Oliver would be Charing Cross, and I should like to see the fine statue of Charles I. removed to the neighbourhood of the beautiful banqueting hall where he died. Oliver himself should have no connection with Parliament, nor should he stand in its environs at all. He belongs to England, and not to the three kingdoms which our Parliament (at least as yet) claims to represent. Let Oliver stand in Charing Cross hard by the very spot where some of his bravest Ironsides shed their blood.

THE CENTENARY OF GIBBON

1894

THE present year is the hundredth anniversary since the death of the greatest of all English historians. Edward Gibbon died in London, in January 1794, in his fifty-seventh year. His reputation has been so perfectly established since the appearance of the first volume of the *Decline and Fall* in 1776, it has been so unbroken, it is so continuously growing, that there is as little need for any formal commemoration of his achievement as there is for that of Shakespeare or Bacon. And his life was so simple, so transparent, and has been told by himself and by his friends with such ingenuous familiarity, that there would seem to be at first sight no occasion for any further research into his labours, or for any special revival of interest in his memory.

There are some circumstances, however, of a rather peculiar kind which make it a genuine concern of English literature to ask for some further light, to review what the great historian left at his premature death, and to bring his personality before the world ere the means of so doing shall have been effaced by time. The National Portrait Gallery (which has likenesses of Peg Woffington and of John Wilkes) has no portrait at all of Edward Gibbon. The only recognised portraits are in private hands, and not accessible to the public. The house at Putney in which he was born, his house at Lausanne, the house in which he died, in St. James's Street, have all been destroyed. There is no record of him in our great burying-places, not even a bust or a tablet. The bones of Edward Gibbon lie in a vault of a small village church in Sussex, a spot with which, except by friendship, he himself had no kind of connection, and where he was merely an occasional visitor. Not one in a thousand, or in ten thousand, of his ardent admirers has ever stood beside his quiet grave, and few of them, perhaps, could say where his body has found rest. The public at large has never seen either portrait, bust, inscription, manuscript, relic, or any visible memento to recall to them the greatest historian of our language, or to give voice to the honour we all feel for one of the most signal triumphs of our literature. We cannot be said to have erred by any excess of hero-worship in the case of our great historian.

But there is something more than this, and that of a practical kind. Gibbon died before he had completed his fifty-seventh year. He was not worn out; his mind had never been in such activity; he still talked of his being "a good life for ten, twelve, or perhaps twenty years." His great work had been completed more than six years before; he was still an indefatigable student, and was preparing his *Antiquities of the House of Brunswick*. Death suddenly cut short this busy career — an end largely due to neglect and imprudence — about a week after his return from his friend's house in Sussex. He made this lifelong friend, John B. Holroyd, Lord Sheffield, his executor, who buried him in the Sheffield mausoleum in the church of Fletching, near East Grinstead in Sussex. Lord Sheffield was the possessor of the well-known portrait by Reynolds and that by Warton dated 1774, and stated by Lord Sheffield to be "by far the best likeness of him that exists." Lord Sheffield also had all Gibbon's manuscripts, his memoirs, essays, diaries and journals, materials for the *House of Brunswick*, and all his other letters.

As is well known, Lord Sheffield issued two quarto volumes in 1796, containing the historian's miscellaneous works; and again, in 1814, he issued a second edition in five octavo volumes, with much additional matter. For what posthumous work of Gibbon's it possesses the world is exclusively indebted to Lord Sheffield, who had also portraits, manuscripts, correspondence, and every other relic of the great historian. He discharged his task with great diligence, discretion, and devotion to the memory of his friend. But after the lapse of a hundred years, and the vast increase in the worldwide fame of Edward Gibbon, it seems reasonable to ask that the present generation should have the means of deciding for itself whether his literary executor has omitted nothing which the world would care to have.

Friendship — constant, pure, generous, and warm friendship — was the ennobling trait in Gibbon's far from heroic nature; and it formed the main beauty of his simple life. His love for his aunt, Catherine Porten, for his step-mother, for Deyverdun, for the Neckers, redeems his biography from commonplace. But, above all, his friendship with Lord Sheffield is a landmark in the history of literature in their age. Nothing is more natural or more honourable than Holroyd's devotion to his great friend's memory. He buried him in his own family tomb, carried off all his remains, edited his memoirs and correspondence, and undertook a careful selection of his manuscripts, essays, and materials for publication. Lord Sheffield made himself more than the Boswell of Gibbon; he not only published his *Life* and remains, but he took effective care that no one else should ever intrude on his own labour of love, or add by one line to the Gibbon literature which he himself judged fit to entrust to the public eye. Such devotion, such zeal, such jealousy for the memory of his illustrious friend, are much to his honour. But now that a century has passed, we may fairly ask to have some review of the execution of this difficult task.

This is not the case of a great writer having made his own selection of his writings, and forbidding publication of whatever he judged unworthy of his reputation. That veto ought, as a general rule, to be religiously respected — though few of us would go so far as to burn the manuscript of the *Æneid*. The detestable trick of publishing any scrap from a great man's pen that an editor can beg, borrow, or steal should be sternly suppressed. There is nothing of the kind here. Gibbon made no selection, put no veto on any publication. Within twenty hours of his death he talked of living for years, and evidently anticipated a new literary career and the completion of his second great work. The selection made of his remains, the veto upon any further publication, was the sole act of his friend, the first Lord Sheffield; and it is now a hundred years old. However judicious the choice, however proper the embargo, it cannot be held conclusive, without fresh examination, by posterity for evermore. Nor can it possibly bind the present representative of the house, who was born long after the death of the first Earl.

There is a strong, perhaps an unreasonable — often it is an unreasoned — prejudice against centenary commemorations in this country. But the practice of other nations, and the growing tendency of the public mind, make something of the kind inevitable; and they certainly have their convenience. The "Services," public officials, Society, and the world in general would greatly miss the suppression of birthdays, jubilees, and anniversaries of royal or public personages and great national events. A centenary is often a convenient occasion for doing some forgotten duty, recalling some fading memory, or repairing some public omission or default. And it is a public default that our national collections contain no likeness of the greatest historian of modern times, that our national monuments contain not a tablet to record his name, that his memory is not kept alive by a single object of any kind in any public place or museum, that not a single living scholar has ever had access to the mass of writings he left, which still remain sealed up in a country house.

There can be no need at the present day for any new eulogium upon Gibbon's work, nor any doubt as to his true place in the world's abiding literature. As the Athenian orator said: "When one is speaking to those who know, there is no occasion for a long harangue." The late Mr. Cotter Morison — who, after so much historical promise, was cut off prematurely — has given us in his admirable *Life of Gibbon* (The Men of Letters Series, 1878) an estimate of our great historian so just, so mature, so sympathetic, so enthusiastic, that it would be in vain to attempt to add to it. Mr. Morison has stated with decision and weight Gibbon's shortcomings and limitations, as well as his supreme merit. The *Decline and Fall* is not the work of a philosopher; it is not altogether scientific history; it is not without very grave misjudgments. But it is a consummate work of art; it unites vast learning with a perfect mastery of lucid narration, superb good sense with unfailing acumen, vivacious wit, and brilliant vitality that irradiates the whole enormous field.

The *Decline and Fall* is the most perfect *book* that English prose (outside its fiction) possesses, meaning by *book* a work perfect in design, *totus, teres, atque rotundus*, symmetrical, complete, final, and executed from beginning to end with the same mastery on one uniform plan. There is no other history extant which can be put beside it, if we reckon all the following qualities and conditions: (1) its immense field, both in extent of area and in epochs of time; (2) its consummate concentration and grasp of view; (3) its amaz-

G

ing range of learning and curious accuracy of detail; (4) its pomp of movement and splendour of style. There have been before and since more subtle observers and more truly enlightened spirits. There have been historians quite as learned, who have made even fewer errors, and some who have written in a purer form. But no historian has ever combined all Gibbon's supreme gifts. And, accordingly, the *Decline and Fall* remains the type of the perfect literary history, just as the Zeus of Pheidias remained the type of the father of gods and men.

As Mr. Cotter Morison has so judiciously explained, Gibbon was the first to give to the world a complete history on the largest scale and with profound original research. And his subject is one so mighty, his scheme so vast, his execution so brilliant, that it still remains in a class by itself — as yet unapproached, gaining by the efflux of time rather than losing in value. His true theme is the complex stormy evolution of the modern world out of the ancient world, the terrible and laboured transition from polytheism and slavery to monotheism and free industry. And this is the most critical and protracted transition in the annals of mankind. The geography of his subject embraces the old world from the Hebrides to the Indus, from the deserts of Tartary to the mountains of Atlas. His topic is the history of civilisation over thirteen centuries. And this vast canvas is filled without confusion, without effort, without discord, by one glowing, distinct, harmonious composition.

This is the supreme merit of Edward Gibbon, that he produced the first perfect literary history on a grand scale — one which still remains the most perfect we know. The only ancient history which in breadth of subject, epical splendour of imagination and beauty of narration, can be compared with his is the Roman history of Livy, of which, alas, we have only fragments. But we can hardly regard the delightful *chansons de gestes* of the glorious Augustan *improvisatore* as history in our sense of the term, for his whole soul turned to rhetorical effect and not to authentic record. But Gibbon fused the pomp and clang of Livy's epic with the conscientious veracity of Cæsar's *Memoirs*. Herodotus has a field as wide almost as Gibbon's, a spirit of inquiry as insatiable, and has painted certain great scenes with an even nobler art. But the Father of History was obviously not equipped with the elaborate historical apparatus of a modern library; and his ever fresh and fascinating muses do not group into an organic composition of the highest art. Each muse in turn takes up her favourite subject — legend, antiquities, voyages and travels, anecdotes, fairy tales, memoirs, and battle scenes — but their inexhaustible encyclopædia does not form one continuous epic. Gibbon has combined the epic unity of Livy with the infinite variety of Herodotus, the vivacity and portraiture of Plutarch, and the punctilious truthfulness of Cæsar. He combined the minute accuracy and vivid detail of the best *memoirs* with the vast survey and poetic transfiguration peculiar to the highest type of *history*. And he was the first, and the greatest, of those who have done this.

The true devotees of Gibbon are the foremost in restraining their admiration within due limits, and in frankly admitting the grave shortcomings of the master. No one has done this more thoroughly than Mr. Morison. He has abundantly shown that Gibbon is in no sense to be judged as a philosophic historian, that he was not a philosopher at all, that he did not penetrate into the deepest truths behind the record of events, that he sadly misjudged some things of prime importance. But in Gibbon's century the philosophy of history was in mere germ, and what are now the commonplaces of every student were truths concealed from them of old time. No one will pretend that Gibbon possessed the profound insight into the human mind of Thucydides, or of Tacitus, of Julius Cæsar; we may add of De Comines, of Bacon, or of Hume. He did not see as deeply behind the veil of the heart and of social movements as any of these. But of all these men, Hume alone wrote history on a really grand canvas, and, as we all know, Hume painted a great historical picture without "studying from the life" at all. He did all that a man of genius and a consummate writer could do with a very cursory knowledge of his facts. But Gibbon, though a great writer, was even greater in research. And though he was not a profound moralist, and wrote before such a science as sociology had been dreamed of, his task was very different from that of keen thinkers who meditate upon men and events of their own age, or on things that passed under the eyes of their own fathers and grandfathers. The writer of *history* has a very different task from that of the writer of *annals* or *memoirs* — and in many ways a much more difficult task.

Let us never pretend that Gibbon was a philosopher. Machiavelli, Bacon, Hobbes, Montesquieu, Leibnitz, Hume, perhaps we may add Vico and Pascal, had yet deeper insight to follow the dynamics of society. Both Montesquieu and Hume, his immediate predecessors, stood on a totally superior level as social philosophers. With all their glaring misconceptions, prejudices, and blunders, even Bossuet, Voltaire, Condorcet, and Burke had a clearer vision into social evolution and the grand battle of ideas and manners than ever Gibbon attained in his fifty years of voracious historical study. Nor need we deny that some of Gibbon's own contemporaries wrote history more in the spirit of philosophy. Voltaire, with all his perversity, was an even superior artist, and had a truer sense of the paramount mastery of ideas. And Robertson's *State of Europe* showed a sounder historical judgment than the *Decline and Fall*. Robertson's best work preceded Gibbon's by some ten or fifteen years; Voltaire's and Hume's both by some twenty-five or thirty years. So that Gibbon was certainly not the earliest real historian of the eighteenth century, and he was certainly by no means the most eminent social thinker. Yet, notwithstanding, given all these qualifications, he was the greatest literary historian.

He was essentially the consummate literary artist who transmutes mountains of exact research into a complex mass, glowing with life in all its parts, and glorious to contemplate as a whole. This is a literary, rather than a philosophical, feat; and as such it must be judged. Its art is akin to that of the epic poet who works out a grand plot in symmetrical order, with episodes, incidents, digressions, but on a consistent scheme, with beauty in each part and memorable form in each line. Now, it is beyond dispute that Gibbon's subject and scheme far transcend in breadth and importance to humanity those of any other historian, even those of Herodotus and Livy, Henri Martin, Grote or Milman, if we put aside such manuals as those of Heeren, Becker, Ranke, and Freeman. This is also beyond doubt, that no historian of ancient or modern times has ever shown the creative and formative imagination triumphing over such transcendent difficulties and working on so grand a scale. Carlyle's *French Revolution* is perhaps a typical example of this power to infuse exact record with poetic vitality, but Carlyle's masterpiece gives us the story of five, or at most of twenty years, and of one country, or, rather, of one city. Gibbon's epic history is the story of mankind over the planet during thirteen centuries. And Gibbon's story is even more accurate, more brilliant, more organic, more truly a work of art than is Carlyle's.

And what vigour, what wit, what a clarion ring in every sentence from the first line of the first volume to the closing phrase of the last! How it holds the attention, how it leaves its imprint on the memory, how it conjures up scenes to the eye. It is like watching some interminable procession, as of a Roman triumph — some Cæsar returning from his Eastern victories, with warriors of all races, costumes, and colours, and the trophies of barbaric peoples, and the roar of many tribes, strange beasts, the pomp of war, and the spoils of cities. We need not insist that it is a perfect style, or a style without grave limitations or defects. It has not the lucid simplicity of Voltaire and of Hume, nor the grace of Addison, nor the pathos of Burke. It is too elaborate, too stiff with jewelry, and too uniform in texture. And perhaps these defects have induced the most versatile of living critics to put on record his memorable saying that he did not care for Gibbon except for his *Memoirs*. This is as if one said that he did not care for Shakespeare except for the *Sonnets*.

A famous authority on the beautiful was disappointed with the Atlantic; but we must not take these purists too literally. The Atlantic becomes rather grandiose, and at last somewhat monotonous; and so, Gibbon's interminable antithesis and unbending majesty do pall upon the constant reader, if he takes in too much at a sitting. But how splendid is the vigour, the point, the precision of the language; and, with all its faults, how well fitted to rehearse these "strange stories of the deaths of kings," how akin to the theme and to the glowing scheme of the painter's colouring! It is impossible to hurry through your Gibbon; you cannot skip; you cannot take in a description at a glance; you cannot leave out the adjectives, or jump the second half of a clause. You may take up your *Decline and Fall*, of which you can repeat pages by heart; you may have read it fifteen times, but the sixteenth reading will give you a phrase of which you had not previously caught the full sense, or throw light on something which has long been a puzzle. And how fixed in the memory are the quips and innuendos, the epigrams and the epithets, with which the page coruscates like a piece of jewelry. It may not be a pure style, it is certainly not a model style, but it is one that gives a gorgeous colour to a supremely organic composition.

Needless, too, now to enlarge on Gibbon's conscientious research, his wonderful accuracy, and the instinct which carries him sure-footed across the rotten and worthless rubbish whereon he had to tread. "That wonderful man monopolised," says Freeman, "the historical genius and the historical learning of a whole generation. . . . The encyclopædic history of 1300 years, as the grandest of historical designs, carried out alike with wonderful power and with wonderful accuracy, must ever keep its place." This from the most scrupulously accurate of modern historians, who so seldom found anything accurate outside of the *Constitutional History of England*, is conclusive. The accuracy of Gibbon's work is only equalled by the vast range of his knowledge; and even this is surpassed by the grandeur of his design and the splendour of his handling. Such accuracy never before went with such brilliancy; such breadth of conception with such literary art. Thucydides, for all his consummate veracity, is often obscure, trivial, and sometimes tedious. Tacitus, with all his insight into character and mastery of phrase, remains always the Roman noble of cast-iron type and limited world. We no more expect critical exactness from Herodotus or Livy than we do from Homer or Virgil. The great painters of historical events are not supposed to be given to laborious research; the great memoir-writers are *ipso facto* confined to their own memory; and the profound antiquarians are almost invariably dull. But we take down our Gibbon time after time, knowing that we can turn up chapter and verse for every sentence, and yet are stirred and delighted by his pictures, as if it were a familiar poem or a work of fiction.

This need not debar us from admitting very serious defects in his work. His perverse misconception of Christianity, his cynical depreciation of its noblest chiefs, his incurable taste for scandal, his disbelief in heroism, in popular enthusiasm, in purity, in self-devotion, and his own epicurean, unromantic, aristocratic habit of mind, very seriously blot his great work and cloud his own memory. Neander, Gfrörer, Von Sybel, Michaud, Lacroix, Guizot, Milman, Michelet, Carlyle, Froude, Freeman, Green, have a far truer conception of the Middle Ages, the Crusades, of Feudalism and its great chiefs, of the Catholic Church and its services to civilisation, than has Gibbon. They are constantly right where he is wrong, and they tell us much of which he is quite uninformed. But, for all that, no one of these excellent men has given us a single work which can compare with the *Decline and Fall* in breadth, in knowledge, in unity of conception, and in splendour of form.

Let us, then, in the hundredth year after its author's death, lay a wreath upon his tomb, for we specially need to keep him as a type before us. The age is one of interminable specialism, colossal research, microscopic minuteness of examination; and our mountains of documents are become very Pelions upon Ossa. All this is right and necessary; and Gibbon was an accomplished specialist, a glutton of research; no man so microscopic, so minute, so documentary, in the true sense and in the right way. But then Edward Gibbon was much more. His gigantic accumulation of facts and indomitable accuracy were not the *ends* of his labour — but the *instru-*

ments.   Research was to him, like grammar or scholarship, not his title to honour, but his raw material for thought and creation.   He did not discharge his note-books in a heap like bricks from the brickyard, and leave us to build them up into a house as we pleased.   He built us the house, and did not ask us to come into it till it was perfect from foundation to roof-ridge, ornamented, elaborated, habitable, and pleasant to dwell in.   His teeming brain disdained the aqueous placidity with which Bavius flows on through one hundred mild and meandering chapters; his creative genius abhorred the rough-hewn masses of stone which year by year Mævius unloads upon us from a thousand quarries.   When we grow weary of histories which are nothing but undigested note-books or copies from the dullest jottings of some contemporary memoir — histories without form, without mind, without imagination, without purpose, without beginning, middle, or end — when we yearn for a book — for a man, an idea within the cover, then, for the tenth or the twentieth time, we take down the *Decline and Fall of the Roman Empire,* and we have one of the greatest dramas of human civilisation, rehearsed with the ordered imagination of a poet and the monumental form of a consummate master of language.

THE CARLYLE HOUSE

1895

THE dedication to the public of the house in Chelsea where Thomas Carlyle lived and died marks an onward step in our growing habit of reverence for the earthly work amongst us of our mighty dead. So far as I know, this is the first time that London has, so to speak, consecrated an entire house to the memory of one of her worthies. Long ago, the house in which Shakespeare was born has been preserved for the nation, and, indeed, for the civilised world. Recently, the little cottage which sheltered Milton at Chalfont whilst he wrote his last poem has been given to the public. The homes of Scott, of Byron, of Shelley, though in private hands, are the object of many a pilgrimage. But London has hitherto been even more chary than England in general to take note of the habitations and haunts of its famous denizens. How few Londoners have even seen the house in Gough Square where Johnson wrote his Dictionary, or the house in which Dryden died, or the gravestone of Goldsmith in the Temple, or the houses where Dickens and Thackeray wrote.

But now the friends and admirers of Carlyle have rescued from decay the house in which he toiled, poured forth his soul, and died; and they have dedicated it to the public as a memorial, just as the followers of Auguste Comte have acquired and preserved the house in which he lived and died in Paris. It is a kind of hero-worship not to be undertaken lightly, not to be pushed too far, apt to degenerate into senti-

mentality, fussiness, cliqueism, and other trivialities and ego-
isms. But with Thomas Carlyle we are safe. Our regard
for his memory, his home, the portraits and relics of him is
genuine, spontaneous, irrepressible. Chelsea — which has
been the residence of Sir Thomas More and Locke, of
Swift and Steele, and Smollett and Walpole, of Leigh Hunt,
Turner, and George Eliot—has long been vocal with memories of Thomas Carlyle. There are Carlyle Square, Carlyle
Mansions, the statue within a few yards of his home, and now
there is a Carlyle House, a public museum, the centre of a
general pilgrimage.

Let no one suppose from the words of qualification, even
of reproach, which are so often used about Carlyle by those
who reverence him most, that such dissent is incompatible
with profound respect. Few of us, indeed, are followers
of the gospel of Carlyle — if there can be a gospel of any
idiosyncrasy so solitary and so fulminant — we are not
followers, but grateful hearers of his words. We cannot
speak of him without breaking out into language that sounds
like criticism, because we do not care to swear allegiance to
his infallibility. He himself has taught all who care to hear
him to be sincere first, to speak out what is in them, and to
take orders from none in the free air of personal beliefs.
Even as we listened to Mr. Morley's eloquent and wise address,
an enthusiast was heard to whisper that the chairman himself seemed at times to take upon him the office of *advocatus
Diaboli*. I have had occasion to speak of Carlyle as an intellectual power in more than one piece, and in each I have
been stirred to disclaim, to qualify, to abate very much in the
homage it was my purpose to offer. It is the peculiar quality
of the great teachers of new truth, especially in the moral
and spiritual realm, to awaken what he so truly called the
"wrestlings of soul," which go down to the depths of defiance

as well as rise to heights of loyalty and trust. All the great inspirers of youth stir these wrestlings. There was no truer prophecy in the Gospel than the words, "I came not to send peace — but a sword." And so Carlyle, like all the deeper moralists, sent a sword into modern society, into each hearer's spirit. It pierced him to the quick, and stung him into many a struggle within him which seldom issued in simple discipleship.

But the dedication to his memory of his home in Chelsea, to be for ever a sort of London cenotaph of his genius, is the season for other thoughts than for "wrestlings of spirits"; it calls for sweeter and more pious recollections. I was one of those who, without being in any sense intimates or friends, were occasionally admitted to his house, and enjoyed the privilege of hearing him talk. In response to sundry messages that he would see me, I called one afternoon in Cheyne Row, and was received with a most gracious and genial courtesy. He made me feel at home at once, and he talked on with a simple and hearty openness of thought, full of drollery, epigram, laughter, and racy deliverance on men and things, with warm kindliness towards his visitor, a manly forgetfulness of himself and his position as acknowledged master in letters, and an utter absence of embarrassment, discontent, or spleen. He rolled forth Latter-Day Pamphlets by the hour together in the very words, with all the nicknames, expletives, and ebullient tropes that were so familiar to us in print, with the full voice, the Dumfries burr, and the kindling eye which all his friends recall. It seemed to me the first time that I sat at his fireside and listened to him that it was an illusion. I seemed to be already in the Elysian fields listening to the spirit rather than to the voice of the mighty "Sartor." Could printed essay and spoken words be so absolutely the same? Was he reciting one of his old pamphlets committed to memory, or was he really speaking impromptu as thoughts passed through his brain? Was this really Thomas Carlyle, or was it some mysterious personation of the man, made up to represent the Sage, and dramatising his familiar speech? No! it was all perfectly spontaneous, frank, and simple; and the generous old man was simply talking freely to a young man who came to hear him talk. And when, after a most memorable afternoon, he rose to bid me farewell, and conducted me to his staircase with a sweet and stately courtesy, I thought I had rarely seen a more simple and genial dignity. How the fierceness and crabbedness which the *Memoirs* seem to attribute to much of his earlier life could ever have dwelt in a nature so urbane, so hearty, so sympathetic as that which I found in his later years, is more than I can unravel. I have seen, and have spoken with, some strong and famous men — with Gambetta, Mazzini, Garibaldi, John S. Mill, Tourgénieff — but I can remember no more intense and impressive personality than that of Thomas Carlyle.

I had seen him in earlier years in public places and in society, walking with Froude and Fitzjames Stephen, or on his historic and "humorous" horse Fritz. I had even seen him receiving with artless gratification, in a great London "crush," the fascinating homage of many a *grande dame* ("the politest and gracefulest kind of woman," we know the Master pronounced her to be) — but it was not till his latest years that I had speech of him in his own house. He once took me as his companion in a walk, and gave me earnest and friendly counsel to betake myself from law to letters — a piece of advice which perhaps came too late in my life to be of any service to me. On another occasion I remember calling upon him at the instance of the widow of my dear and honoured friend, Jules Michelet, the historian. Madame Michelet was then labouring, with all the energy of love and sorrow, to raise a marble monument to her husband in Père la Chaise at Paris, and she was anxious to have the thought and culture of Europe to join in the testimony to the historian-poet of France. I accepted the commission with reluctance and doubt; but Carlyle received the request with readiness, spoke warmly of Michelet as a genuine man, and himself subscribed the sum of five pounds. The gift of these English admirers (amongst whom were also enrolled the names of Charles Darwin, Joseph Chamberlain, and John Morley) was recorded on the beautiful memorial which we see to-day over the grave of the historian in Paris. On this occasion, as on so many others which have come to my notice, the whole nature of Carlyle was inspired by generosity, sympathy, candour, manliness — genial interest in the young and the struggling ones, ungrudging homage to great character and to true genius.

It may have been with some surprise that certain younger men heard Mr. Morley, with all his judicial discrimination of Carlyle's powers, speak of him as "the foremost figure in English literature during the greater part of his life." And I have ventured to call him, "by virtue of his original genius and mass of stroke, the literary dictator of Victorian prose." Many of our younger friends are puzzled by such language. What does it mean? To my mind it means this. Not indeed that Carlyle was ever a critic, an arbiter, a model, as Addison was, or as Johnson was, or as Voltaire in France and Goethe in Germany have been. Macaulay, Hallam, or Southey more nearly filled such a part. But the peculiar power of Carlyle was, by his superb independence and the fiery impact of his genius, to kindle a great variety of movements, and wake into life many active minds. The Victorian age has been one of singular activity, and of erratic and adventurous energy. How many forms of this energy owed inspiration to Carlyle! Ruskin, Froude, Kingsley, the

Stephens, Tyndall, were avowed followers of his, whilst we can see the traces of his mind in Tennyson, in Huxley, in Maurice, in Freeman, in John Morley. And if Browning, Arnold, George Eliot, Swinburne, Morris, Symonds, move in a different world from that of "Sartor," they have all been held spellbound at seasons "by the glittering eye" of that Ancient Mariner. Of whom else, in the era between Byron and Darwin, can the same be said? No one would compare Carlyle to Socrates. But as the Sage of Athens used to call his function simply that of the obstetric physician, who enabled those big with ideas to bring them forth into the living air, so Carlyle had something of this same gift — that of helping ideas to live and to come forth. Socrates, too, disclaimed any system, any philosophy, any school. But a dozen schools of very different kinds rose out of that ferment of original questioning which the great moralist and insatiable cross-examiner had scattered far and wide in the market-place of thought.

Carlyle, too, had "his dæmon," though what his "dæmon" was we know as little as in the case of Socrates. Nor do any two of us agree exactly as to what that dæmon revealed to him or to us. But he set us all thinking; he inspired us with courage; he taught us to be honest, zealous, truthful, reverent. Alas! he was in much the very opposite of Socrates, who lived in the world, with the world, a heroic citizen, a soldier, a public counsellor, tolerant, jovial, great-hearted, and indulgent almost to a fault. Carlyle shut himself up with his books in that little home where his memory is now enshrined, knew nothing of affairs except through books, and was too disdainful of the world outside to sympathise with its troubles or to comprehend its needs. Socrates was a true Sage. Carlyle was preacher, rhapsodist, student. But it will be long before we see his like again.

SCIENTIFIC HISTORY

1906

MR. HERBERT PAUL'S most interesting *Life of Froude* has raised again the unsolved problem of the true method of writing history. As Horace told his friend long ago, it was a business full of peril and chance, like walking over the crust of lava. But in our age its difficulties are greatly increased. Not only has the historian to meet the criticism of rival partisans, but the scientific school and the literary school wage incessant war on each other. And history to-day is being *made* faster than it can be *recorded*. As the greatest of historians put it in immortal words, a strictly historical narrative of facts is wont to disappoint those who want to be interested. Shall history aim at being "a possession for all time," or shall it seek to be "the success of the hour"?

The conspicuous champions of Literary History were, in old days, Livy and Plutarch; in modern times, Clarendon, Hume, Robertson, Alison, Michelet, Thiers. The scientific historians of our own day hold by Mommsen, Freeman, Stubbs, and Gardiner; and, we may add, so do the official representatives of history in our Universities — such as Bury, Firth, and Oman. By common consent, Gibbon combined Research and Literature as nearly as we are ever destined to see them combined. And Macaulay, Froude, Carlyle, we may perhaps add Green, have striven to do the same. All four have a multitude of readers — and long will have them, owing to their brilliant literary power. The question still is, Can we trust them as we trust Mommsen and Stubbs, Gardiner, Bury, and Firth?

Of all the literary historians of our day Froude has been the most fiercely rebuked by the scientific school. And now two warm admirers of his, one English, the other foreign, have given us a studied defence of the Froudian method. Mr. Herbert Paul, in his fascinating *Life*, very properly devotes more than a quarter of his book to examining all that can be said for and against the *History of England*. Froude had "a doctrine to propound, a gospel to preach," says Mr. Paul. And Dr. Sarolea of Brussels, and now of the University of Edinburgh, in an eloquent volume of *Essays*, proclaims Froude to be a great historian, the "national historian of England," on the very ground of his passionate prejudices on behalf of persons and institutions. The historian, says Dr. Sarolea, cannot be impartial, for reasons whether of art, morality, or sociology.

Mr. Paul, as may be expected, takes a much more guarded view. He is eminently aware of the idiosyncrasy and temptations which coloured Froude's splendid narrative. "His besetting sin was a love of paradox." "He was an advocate, an incomparably brilliant advocate." "He was not a chronicler, but an artist, a moralist, and a man of genius." And all through his vigorous fourth chapter Mr. Paul eloquently describes the spirit which sustained Froude in his immense task, and the devotion with which he pursued it over long years of toil. Mr. Paul does not mince matters as to Froude's defects. "He was an advocate rather than a judge." He gave undue prominence to facts which told for his own cause. It is notorious that he was not always accurate in detail. He set out on his task with a polemical purpose. "Misquotation was too frequent a habit with him." Even

H

when gross errors had been pointed out to him, Froude still left them in his text. All this Mr. Paul admits.

In an equally vigorous fifth chapter, Mr. Paul squires Froude in his grand joust with Freeman. And Mr. Paul's citations from Freeman's own copy of *Froude's History*, with marginal notes, are indeed amusing: — "Beast," "vilest brute," "a lie," "may I live to embowel J. A. Froude." It has already been related that when Freeman sat down to attack Froude in a review article he would have played a noisy piece of music which he hated, to give him the needful fit of ill-humour. Mr. Paul does right in showing us the furious prejudice which animated these attacks. But few historians will go with him when he says that, "in patient assuidity of research, Froude was immeasurably Freeman's superior." Mr. Paul has shown ground for hesitating to accept the whole of Freeman's criticism. On the other hand, he has little idea of the extent of Froude's blunders. They may be "mole-hills," as he calls them. But when a meadow ceases to be green, and is turned brown with mole-hills in every square yard, the pasture is sadly to seek for the hungry cattle.

If Mr. Paul would carefully compare the printed text of any one of Froude's books with the authority which is there cited, he would find a mistranslation, a misquotation, or a variation in almost every sentence. What does he say when Froude tells "an apocryphal anecdote," and adds "there is no reason why it should not continue to be believed"? What about his "apocryphal" confession of Queen Catherine on her death-bed — which represents her as doing exactly what she did not do? What about "the most perfect English history which is to be found in the historical plays of Shakespeare"? Mr. Froude was a very great writer and almost a great dramatist. But he, too, often studied his original "sources" in the spirit in which Shakespeare studied his Holinshed. He sought to draw out of the dry bones of the chronicles splendid pictures of moving events, the play of great characters, and the clash of contrasted natures and minds. *C'est magnifique, mais ce n'est pas l'histoire.*

Unfortunately, the habit of misquotation, small slips, inadvertent "mole-hills," form not the serious part of the charge against Froude as an historian of authority. Even "mole-hills" cause nasty falls when they inadvertently turn a negative into an affirmative. The real defect of Froude's history is that, as his friends and apologists agree, he made himself the enthusiastic advocate of certain leading judgments upon the Tudor Sovereigns, undertaking on crucial points to reverse the current view — and in that task has failed. He has given us some splendid narratives, and many powerful portraits of men and women. He has done much to correct popular judgments, and to qualify the prejudices of partisans against whom he argues. But he has quite failed to satisfy independent minds that Henry was a wise and benevolent statesman; that the Reformation was the beneficent work of high-minded and godly patriots; that Mary Stuart was a mere fiend; that Elizabeth was a heartless tyrant. Freeman's vitriol has, perhaps, rather obscured the true case. As Mr. Paul shows us, Freeman was always violent, and often unjust. But Freeman did not touch the serious charge — the essential failure of Froude to reverse accepted conceptions of historic truth.

What are we to say to Dr. Sarolea's ingenious argument that Froude was our great "national historian," not although but because he was a passionate advocate? The Edinburgh Professor tells us that the historian cannot be artist, or moralist, or psychologist — unless he is an enthusiastic partisan; that his text will be colourless, his judgments neutral, and his figures dummies. This is going very far beyond Mr. Paul, or any reasonable friend of literature in history. It is to confound the Judge with the advocate. The historian ought, no doubt, to feel a steady flame of enthusiasm for all great spirits, for all just causes — not for *one* — but for *all*. His merit is to be judicial — to acquit the innocent with honour, to condemn the guilty without fear. But just because he sits in judgment on all parties alike, and because he has to weigh and test every shred of evidence on both sides equally, so he prostitutes his office, when he shows favour towards any single party, or propounds any partial estimate. Even when Carlyle restored Cromwell to his true place in our history, he seriously impaired his work by fanatical hero-worship.

Hero-worship and anathemas are alike false art as well as shallow policy in history — where *Te Deum* and *Commination* Services have no place. The historian holds a kind of mimic rehearsal of the Last Judgment, only he has no Recording Angel to tell him the facts truly. When the ghosts and shadows of the dead rise before his sight from the past, he has before him whole generations at once. None are wholly guilty, none are wholly blameless. His task is to weigh each sinner, not as if he were a saint, nor as if he were a devil — but to strike the true balance, neither devoid of human sympathy with those who have borne much grief, nor sparing of just indignation with those who have lived to be a curse to their age. But the essence of his task is to judge all equally together — to conceive the whole human panorama in its entirety and its true proportions.

The supreme task of the Muse of History — the incalculable difficulty — is to present a broad and glowing picture of a past age in its true proportions. Neither artistic colour nor microscopic accuracy suffice to do this. Literary brilliance is just as inefficient as meticulous research. Both destroy the truth of proportion — literature by misleading us with false lights, research by overwhelming its canvas with trivial details.

The problem has never been better stated than by Lucian in his delightful essay, "How to Compose History." The perfect historian, he says, must start with two indispensable qualifications — "the one is political insight, the other the faculty of expression." You may acquire the gift of expression, he says, by practice and study. But political insight is a rare gift of nature. It is genius for affairs. The most laborious student of documents without this gift is a tedious pedant. The most brilliant advocacy, apart from political insight, is merely a means of perverting the truth. It is too little understood that no amount of grinding old parchments, collating manuscripts, and piling up facts, will outweigh political *flair*, the power of judging men and events with insight.

The great historian is really an unofficial statesman. This insight of his can hardly be attained except by those who have been conversant with affairs, in close touch with those who rule or who advise rulers. All great historians have been statesmen, or in intimate relations with statesmen, in great times. Thucydides, Polybius, Cæsar, Tacitus, De Comines, Machiavelli, Clarendon, Gibbon, Macaulay, Guizot, Thiers — all passed large parts of their lives in public life.

Hear Lucian's test of the great historian. Let him be fearless, incorruptible, independent, a believer in frankness and veracity; one who will yield nothing to his likes or dislikes; nor spare any one through pity and good nature; an impartial judge, kind to all, but too kind to none; not of one nation, but a citizen of the world, owning no hero, no king of men; indifferent to what the public thinks or likes; bent to set down truly things which befell in fact. Thucydides is the eternal model, who wrote, as he says, for all time; not Herodotus, who enchanted the Greeks at their Festivals by eulogies on their noble selves.

THE NEW MOTLEY [1]

1896

MESSRS. Bell and Sons are still energetically pursuing their
task of adding to and improving the famous series of Bohn's
Libraries, which Thomas Carlyle pronounced to be "the
usefulest thing I know." As copyrights expire, Messrs.
Bell are constantly adding to the Libraries, in the new and
certainly pleasanter form, reprints of standard works which
"no gentleman's library should be without." Amongst the
latest additions is a reprint of Motley's *Dutch Republic*, a
book of which it may be said that "no man's reading should
be without." And to this edition they have added a biographical introduction by his countryman and friend, Mr.
Moncure D. Conway, and a good reproduction of the portrait
of Motley after the picture by Bischop, now the property of
the Queen of the Netherlands at The Hague.

To the hundreds of thousands of men and women who
have felt the thrill of a first reading of *The Rise of the Dutch
Republic*, and to those who rejoiced that the great Republic
of the West should be officially represented in England by a
typical man of letters of America, it will be a pleasure to see
the singularly handsome, intellectual, and refined face of the
historian as given in this volume. It is a face little familiar
to the general reader; and, as Motley has now been dead

---

[1] *The Rise of the Dutch Republic.* By John Lothrop Motley. A new
Edition in three volumes, with a Biographical Introduction by Moncure D.
Conway. Bohn's Standard Library.

for nearly twenty years, it can be remembered in life by only
a limited part of modern society. To those who take up this
volume, with its generous notice of the author by his friend
Moncure Conway, it is a welcome frontispiece wherein we can
see with our eyes the grand brow, the delicate features, and
the air of power and resolution in the historian's whole aspect.

John Lothrop Motley was born in Boston, Mass., in 1814,
of an old New England Puritan family, that traced descent
to emigrants for conscience' sake, on the one side from the
North of Ireland, on the other side from the English Midlands.
Mr. Moncure Conway, naturally and very rightly, dwells
on the literary life of the historian. Motley was also diplomatist, politician, and publicist, and for seven years represented his country as Minister in Austria and in England. But
in this volume Mr. Conway gives us almost exclusively a
picture of the historian; and this was the only really important side of Motley's whole career. It is the life of an
ardent man of letters, dominated by a high ideal of a great
historical purpose. This single purpose absorbed his whole
life for more than thirty years, until his death in May 1877.
His design was to describe from contemporary documents
the great struggle for freedom of belief which created a powerful and independent republic in the Netherlands; and no
man ever devoted his life to study with more industry and
patience.

Motley, Mr. Conway tells us, belonged to that inner circle
of culture in New England which produced Emerson, Lowell,
Oliver Wendell Holmes, Wendell Phillips, Longfellow, and
so many others. He spent four years at Harvard College,
1827–31, and then some four years in Germany and other
parts of Europe. At Göttingen he met Prince Bismarck,
and they became fellow-students at Berlin, intimate friends
and fellow-lodgers, sharing their meals and exercise. This

intimacy with the great statesman lasted throughout Motley's life, and must have insensibly reacted on his knowledge of men and affairs. Motley's early studies were somewhat desultory, self-directed, and wholly without academic or early success. Like Gibbon, he was "sent down" by his college. Indeed, it is worth noting how very seldom eminent writers of history have been distinguished by youthful or scholastic triumphs. There seems to be some instinctive opposition between them and their official teachers. Returning to his native country in 1835 — he was then in his twenty-second year — Motley devoted himself to literature — he wrote romances, poems, plays, sketches, essays, articles — but it must be admitted that the first ten years of his literary activity were attended by no success, and, indeed, produced little to deserve it.

But the course of these pieces, which turned so largely on the Pilgrim Fathers and their early history, directed Motley, about the age of thirty-three, to the great struggle of the Dutch for freedom in religion and in government. Motley's own account of the way in which the grand subject took possession of his soul may be set beside Gibbon's famous anecdote of the origin of the *Decline and Fall* in the Church of the Franciscans on the Capitol. "I have not first," said Motley, "made up my mind to write a history, and then cast about to take up a subject: *my subject had taken me up, drawn me on, and absorbed me into itself.*" He was warmly encouraged by Prescott, with whose *Philip the Second* he had feared to come into unfriendly competition or damaging comparison; and after some ten years of labour *The Rise of the Dutch Republic* appeared. He had been incessantly occupied over documents and archives in Holland, Belgium, and Germany. "Whatever may be the result of my labours," he writes to Dr. Holmes in 1853, "nobody can say that I have not worked hard like a brute beast; but I do not care for the result. The labour is itself its own reward, and all I want. I go day after day to the archives here (in Brussels), as I went all summer at The Hague, studying the old letters and documents of the sixteenth century. Here I remain among my fellow-worms, feeding on those musty mulberry leaves of which we are afterwards to spin our silk. . . . The dead men of the place are my intimate friends. I am at home in my cemetery. With the fellows of the sixteenth century I am on the most familiar terms. Any ghost that ever flits by night across the moonlit square is at once hailed by me as a man and a brother. I call him by his Christian name at once." It is a typical picture of original research —

> . . . expertus credes quam gravis iste labor!

Mr. Conway gives us an interesting study of the long labours which produced the work, the obstacles that delayed its publication, and the wearisome search for a publisher. It is one of the curiosities of literature that one firm after another rejected the book, which at last was accepted by John Chapman *at the author's expense and risk*. Motley thought it hardly worth while to incur the expense of travelling from Vevey to England "to secure a copyright which I could not sell for £100." It was deposited in the British Museum, Oct. 20, 1855; but six months later Motley writes from Italy that he supposes very few copies have been sold. His publisher failed soon after, and the receipts do not seem to have been large. As a matter of fact, "*17,000 copies* were sold in England during the first year of publication." Such are the uncertainties of authorship and the mysterious ways of the trade.

This is not the place for any new estimate of so well-known a work as Motley's *Dutch Republic*, which has long passed into the class of standard histories, such as are the handbooks of all historical study. The latest student in that field, Ruth Putnam, in her *William the Silent* (two vols., New York, 1895) very truly describes the care with which Motley has been used by all subsequent historians in Europe, and her own admiration "for the untiring industry of his laborious researches, and for the accuracy and skill of his adaptations from the enormous mass of matter that he examined." The forty years that have passed have seen the publication and careful editing of many of those contemporary records which Motley had to study in manuscript. The Memoirs of Pontus Payen, Renon de France, the correspondence of Cardinal Granvelle, the publications of Gachard and Kervyn de Lettenhove, have now enabled us to follow up this period, without our personally "feeding on the mulberry leaves" in the archives of Brussels and The Hague. But although a vast literature has grown up round the great subject, it can hardly be said that Motley has been corrected on very material points, much less has he been superseded.

Motley's deficiencies, such as they are, certainly do not lie in any want of industry, thoroughness, or accuracy. All of these he had in a supreme degree. But we can now see that he had a somewhat superabundant enthusiasm for his favourite heroes and people, and a somewhat deficient strength of philosophic insight and calm. He can hardly be ranked with the philosophic historians at all; and no one has claimed for him the magnificent power of Gibbon to marshal in close array an enormous host of various incidents and events. Motley's eloquence is not always as chaste and simple as is required by our modern taste; and, though he is almost never tedious, he has given disproportionate bulk to the story of a single generation in so small a corner of Europe.

More serious defects are these. He has treated the great William of Orange too much as a saint and martyr, and too little as a man of his age. Hero, statesman, mighty chief, and founder, as was William of Nassau, he was a man who was always growing; a man who used all the resources familiar to his time; and, like all consummate opportunists, a man who was perpetually foiling his opponents by superior craft and alarming his colleagues by a change of front. He professed in turn three different creeds, and was a member of three successive Churches, without any profound conviction of the minor professions or practices of any one of the three. To Motley he is always too much the spotless ideal and religious enthusiast. Nor does Motley adequately estimate the profound roots of the Catholic reaction in Belgium, or enable us to understand why, and in so short a time after the rule of Alva, the Belgian provinces relapsed to the old faith. We need something more than a partisan of Puritan heroism to explain the revival of Catholicism. I was a short time ago at High Mass on Sunday morning in the Cathedral of Antwerp. As I recalled the tremendous scene of iconoclasm enacted in that very church 330 years ago, so splendidly described by Motley, and then turned to the gorgeous ritual, the noble music, the impassioned sermon, and the vast throng of worshippers, who hour after hour crowded round the many chapels and altars, knelt before the images, gazed at the glorious pictures, and all the statues, decorations, and symbols of the Catholic faith — I asked myself if the New England historian had fully grasped those vast and abiding forces of which Philip and Alva were the satanic incarnation.

Yet let us not call Motley a New England historian, for he belongs to the Old as much as to the New England. The best years of his life were passed in Europe; his last home was in England; he died in England; he and his wife are buried in England; he married his daughters in England, and one of them, as all the world knows, is the wife of the leader of Her Majesty's Opposition. Old England divides the fame of Motley with New England, and Englishmen will thank his American fellow-citizen for giving us this timely account of one who will long live amongst the classics of the English tongue.

MAINE'S "ANCIENT LAW" REVISED

1906

FORTY-FIVE years after its first publication, and three years after the expiry of the original copyright, the famous book which founded in England the study of Comparative Jurisprudence is about to start on a new life. *Ancient Law* was published in 1861, and has long grown to be a classical text. But as all classical texts, especially in matters of law and of historical research, soon become more or less antiquated by discoveries which they themselves have stimulated and partly suggested, so *Ancient Law* was of late years tending to be thought superseded by later learning, or disproved by more recent theories. Nothing of the kind was true. But the book certainly had to be brought up to date, and in sundry points it had to be supplemented, explained, corrected, and justified. This has been thoroughly well done by the man of all others most qualified for such a task. Sir Frederick Pollock, by his masterly "Introduction" and " Notes," appended to each of Maine's ten chapters, gives the student all the explanations and corrections he needs, and in fact launches Maine's first and typical work upon a new career for the students of Comparative Jurisprudence at home and abroad.

I am old enough not only to remember the publication of the book in 1861, but to have attended the course of lectures of which the book consists; and I was myself the pupil of Sir Henry Maine in Lincoln's Inn in 1857. On the publication of the volume with which I was so familiar, and which I had seen in proof-sheets, I wrote in the *Westminster Review* of 1861 one of the earliest tributes to the importance of the work, a paper which I know satisfied the author himself. I remained in close friendship with Sir Henry till his too early death in 1888; and I am still, with Sir Frederick Pollock, one of his executors and trustees. It is needless now to expatiate on the originality and value of *Ancient Law*, but I may give from my own memory some account of the part it has played in the development of legal science.

When Maine first began to lecture at the Temple in 1852, as Professor to the Inns of Court of Roman Law and Jurisprudence, the British ignorance of Roman Law and at any rate of Comparative Jurisprudence was really a unique phenomenon. To the successful case lawyer a "jurist" was a term of reproach, meaning an ignorant impostor. And one of the greatest masters of Real Property learning in Lincoln's Inn would warn his pupils "against that beastly book — Justinian," by which he was believed to mean the Institutes, for he had never heard of Digest, Code, or Novels. The days of Selden and Locke were long past, and even the time when English lawyers sometimes followed a course of study at Leyden. Blackstone, perhaps, would be plucked to-day at Oxford for ignorance of the most familiar rules in the *Institutes*. As to anything like the history of legal ideas, it was hardly thought worthy of notice. Bentham and Austin had brought powers of rare acuteness to the analysis of law; but neither of them had any real historical training, nor, indeed, any historical instincts. And in dealing with the dominant conceptions of sociology — all *ex hypothesi* subject to the law of evolution — the acutest logic is a poor substitute for the study of the facts of progressive development.

It is quite a commonplace with jurists that Maine's *Ancient Law* opened a new era. In the half-century since Maine began to lecture, the systematic study of the "Corpus Juris" has taken its place in the Inns of Court, in the Universities of Oxford, Cambridge, and London. Holland, Poste, Roby, Hunter, Bryce, Muirhead, Clark, Goudy, Moyle, Greenidge have worked systematically on this science; whilst the best works of German and French Civilians are ordinary text-books with our students. In the way of the history of legal and social conceptions such English writers as Tylor, Lubbock, M'Lennan, Spencer, Lang, Pollock, Maitland, have removed from English letters the opprobrium of treating English law as something as sacred and as mysterious in origin as the law of Moses. The movement itself was part of the great tidal wave of Evolution which swept over English thought about the middle of the nineteenth century — of which Darwin and Spencer were the scientific and philosophical protagonists — which produced the school of historical research of Stubbs, Freeman, and Gardiner, the logical school of Mill and Morley, the archæological school of Frazer and Westermarck. It would be extravagant to pretend that Maine founded these movements — but he touched on them all; and he was certainly the first to give them brilliant literary form.

In forty-five years, during which some of the acutest minds and some of the most profound scholars in Europe have made a vast body of research in the origins of human society and the evolution of social institutions, it was, of course, inevitable but that new lights should be thrown on many of the problems discussed in *Ancient Law*, and some of its conclusions be qualified and corrected. In this age, which has a superstitious respect for the "latest" telegram and the "newest" book, students were getting uneasy that Maine did not know everything contained in the last monograph issued in Germany, Russia, France, India, or the Colonies, to say nothing of the indefatigable output from American Universities. They can now trust Sir Frederick Pollock, who knows all these, and is in touch with the best scholarship of all these countries, to point out where Maine's language has to be supplemented, qualified, and revised. There are eighteen "Notes" appended to the ten chapters, which, with the "Introduction," make up about one-third of the volume as new matter. Altogether, *Ancient Law* may now be regarded as much a new work as if it had been recently compiled. There has been, of course, no attempt to interpolate Maine's text or to make such a ridiculous hash as the "modernised" *Blackstones* present, nor is there any pretension in the "Notes" to imitate Maine's brilliant power of casting his apothegms into memorable phrases. But all debatable points have been discussed with a learning at least as wide as Maine's, and with a bibliography of the subject far more complete than any open to the author a generation ago.

The main points now noted are these. Maine's incisive language must not be taken in too absolute a way. He somewhat overrated the antiquity of Roman Law, and gave a rather too systematic shape to the XII. Tables. And we must guard against the Continental use of such terms as "written law," and remember that English lawyers use it in a different sense. The most important corrections needed are in Maine's third and fourth chapters on the "Law of Nature," where he seems to ignore the extent to which the Civil Law continued to influence mediæval jurists and churchmen. Nor is he right in his account of the origin of what we call the "Law of Nations." Maine perhaps placed Montesquieu's constructive work higher than modern historians and sociology would do. Nor need we be disturbed by the

I

ebb and flow of the eternal battle waged between enthusiasts for the Patriarchal and the Matriarchal theories, and around the prostrate forms of the archaic brides as to "Early Forms of Marriage." Victory is not yet declared — if it ever will be. Maine's dictum as to "Status" and "Contract" may require limitation in terms, but in substance it is as sound as it is luminous. On the whole, recent research rather tends to confirm Maine's judgments, if his words are not pressed too absolutely. And of all writers on these obscure topics he clothes them in the most brilliant literary form.

IMPERIAL MANNERS

1906

HISTORY does not repeat itself in periodic cycles, as Vico and the older philosophy of history taught, but it is curious how subtly the dominant ideals of an age are repeated in the current ways and habits of men. The Disraelite and Cecilite age of purple Imperialism, which has happily ended in dust and ashes, has given us some gaudy revivals of Imperial Rome in the first century after Christ.

Nero is now the fashion. The most brilliant (and, indeed, the most erudite) spectacle ever presented to a London audience takes us to the centre of the Neronian world. The Universities exhaust their learning in vivid pictures of Imperial Society. The elaborate work of Professor Dill of Belfast on *Roman Society from Nero to M. Aurelius* was followed by the lectures of Dr. Bigg, Canon of Christ Church and Professor of Ecclesiastical History at Oxford. Both books analyse the influence of the new thought and religion of the first century on habits and manners. Oxford has just given us an admirable translation of Lucian — the Voltaire, the Swift, the Le Sage of antiquity.

And on the top of the wave of Neronian fashions there come two editions and translations of Petronius, Nero's "arbiter of elegance," his Beau Brummel, and victim. "Trimalchio's Supper-Party," with its Rabelaisian buffoonery, its Swiftian grossness, its Thackerayan *Book of Snobs*, has a queer analogy to modern London and Monte Carlo. How near is Petronian Rome to the "smart" London of to-day!

Trimalchio to-day is a self-made millionaire, the son not of a slave, but of an honest workman. He began life, not as an aspiring freed-man, but as an office boy. He brags of his rough beginnings and of his lavish gifts to public charities and deserving friends. His mansion in Hyde Park or Belgravia is stored with curios which Bond Street dealers assure him to be genuine and rare. He holds tight by the Imperial cause, and parades his zeal for Empire with banquets, illuminations, and royal donations. When he invites you to sup, he tells you there will be wild boar's head from the Campagna, cold pheasant in August, or mangostines in ice from Java. He talks grandly about Nero himself, and is intriguing to get His Majesty to try his preserves.

The Trimalchio of Petronius boldly introduced to the supper-table his head-huntsman and his Laconian hounds. We do not have gamekeepers and whips in Park Lane. But our own Trimalchios will show you sport in their own county, and they can never cease to talk of it.

Petronius makes his Trimalchio offer his guests entertainments which are no longer exactly in vogue. The grossness of speech and act, the tomfoolery, the insolence of the Neronian *nouveau riche* are no longer tolerated. And perhaps Petronius, like Swift, overdoes the caricature. But in substance how like they are!

The vulgarity of the adventurer is eternal. The low-bred upstart seeks, by sheer weight of gold, to force himself into the Imperial circles, and, indeed, sometimes succeeds in arriving there. He is surrounded by cosmopolitan parasites, who own no common race, or tongue, religion, or country. The "Kaffir Circus" are the counterpart of Trimalchio's "Græculi esurientes." Trimalchio plays at dice over supper.

Belgravia plays bridge. The table is loaded with eccentric viands, with bedizened dishes made to imitate Dresden porcelain or Chinese monsters. Trimalchio's wife, Fortunata, was a harridan, as low-born as himself, covered with big jewels, and even more extravagant than her lord. The profusion of exotic plants and flowers was as eagerly sought at Rome as it is in London or Paris. There as here, then as now, in the vulgarian's establishment everything was "*de trop — trop de choses — outrè.*" Objects of art, viands, entertainments, were bought, not because they were good, but because they were difficult to buy. Things were valued, not for what they were, but for what they cost. Art, society, manners, literature were coloured with the same purple glare.

It should make us shudder to note the sinister analogies of Imperial Rome and Imperial Britain. There is the same wantonness in extravagance, the pretence of art, refinement, and culture, with the real debasement of all of them by vanity and low tastes. Our English tongue gets vulgarised by foreign slang. As Roman society caught up the vernacular of slaves, British conversation gets infiltrated with costermongers' cant phrases learned in music-hall songs. If Cicero would gasp at Petronius's solecisms, Addison would shrink from the "short story" in slum idiom which adorns half our magazines and newspapers.

A Neronian banquet, such as Mr. Tree provides with such magnificence and such learning, is hardly a caricature of some New York festival of flowers, jewels, delicacies, and entertainments. We imitate New York at a distance. Petronius would smile with pity at the poverty of the wildest debauch Park Lane ever imagined. But we shall come to it in time.

The Imperial "swelled-head" which made Caligula,

Nero, and Domitian crazy, ends in a ghastly ruin. The Neronian age was a resplendent and resounding orgy. But underneath the orgy there was growing up a new society, a new faith, a nobler race, a purer life. The first century showed the old world at its worst. But it was the cradle of the new world which was destined to sweep away the old.

BENJAMIN FRANKLIN

1906

In these days of centenaries hardly enough has been made of the memory of Franklin, who was born in 1706, and died at the ripe age of eighty-four, after one of the most extraordinary careers in modern history. He was at once one of the pioneers of scientific discovery and one of the founders of the great Republic of the West. The arch rebel of King George III. was the idol of the Court of Versailles. Saturated with true literature and absorbed in physical science, he was one of the wisest statesmen, and also one of the most creative revolutionists, even of the eighteenth century, rich in subtle statecraft and organic revolution. The fifteenth child of a humble family of New England, Benjamin was born and reared in poverty, and began a stern life of toil as a boy in a printer's workshop. There, and in England, he managed to give himself a sound and varied knowledge of books, nature, and men. Returning to America, he set up in business as printer, bookseller, publisher, and editor, and in each occupation that he undertook he won wealth, friends, influence, and fame. By the time he had reached the middle of his life this home-spun printer had become the most eminent citizen of his own State, and also a leader of science renowned all over Europe. His "immortal discovery," as a philosopher has called it, by which he founded the modern science of electricity, placed him on such an eminence as was afterwards obtained by the founder of Evolution. Franklin was acknow-

ledged in England and in France as one of the great lights
of modern science.

This typical American patriot passed nearly half his life
in Europe, a large part of it in England, and was regarded
as a great discoverer, as a brilliant man of the world, and
also as the Ambassador of a new nation. In the literary
world he was the peer of Johnson, Burke, Voltaire, and
Turgot; in the social world he was the friend of statesmen,
courtiers, and princes, both at St. James's and at Versailles.
The triumph of his political life was the French alliance,
which at last enabled the United States to defeat the King
and to constitute themselves a nation. Returning to the
Republic he had so largely assisted to create, he became,
with Washington, the organiser of its institutions. In the
later years of his long life, with wealth, influence, and honours
growing up spontaneously around him, he devoted his practical genius to a series of foundations, academic, scientific,
philanthropic, whilst dispersing his own fortune in public
and private benevolence.

From boyhood to old age Franklin remained the same stout
and simple citizen; gracious, social, cool-headed, clear-
sighted, fearless, wise. The Greeks had an admirable
phrase to describe such a character of complete virtue and
cyclopædic capacity. He was — "a man four-square on
all sides, himself without defect," or, as our poet puts it,
"who stood four-square to all the winds that blow." Even
better than to Wellington may we attribute to Franklin the
famous lines:

> Rich in saving common-sense . . .
> In his simplicity sublime.

Franklin was, indeed, one of the most complete intelli-
gences and one of the most all-round personalities of modern
history. It was a character which the eighteenth century

specially produced, as in such men as Priestley and Turgot,
Condorcet and Burke. But Franklin was far more successful in everything he touched than any of these men, happier
in his conditions than any, with a far keener genius for practical affairs, for obtaining permanent results out of intricate
entanglement. Plunged as he was from birth to old age in
circumstances apparently contradictory and hopeless — poor,
untaught, the official agent of an insurgent race accredited to
an obstinate tyrant — a man of science harassed with daily
distractions and business troubles, he remained the same
imperturbable, successful, happy conqueror over all obstacles.

And one of the paradoxes of his career is this. The self-
taught printer's boy, fighting his way in trade, spending time
and money in physical experiments and practical adventures,
incessantly travelling from America to Europe, and immersed
in society, in diplomacy, and in scientific meetings, contrived
to acquire a literary gift of singular effectiveness. He wrote
on all kinds of subjects — his memoirs, essays, letters fill
ten stout volumes. Their form is quite unlike the brilliant
and elaborate style of contemporary Englishmen. Johnson,
Burke, and Gibbon would regard it as trivial. Goldsmith,
Hume, Cowper, and Gray would hardly call it "elegant."
But it has some of the qualities of Swift; homely, pellucid,
easy, incisive. One knows what it means, every word of it.
It arrests attention. It "hits the nail on the head"; it does
its work; it makes one think, and, still more, makes one act.
Franklin had not the imaginative genius and pungency of
phrase that lighted up the masterpieces of the fierce Dean.
But he was a kind of home-spun, practical, benevolent,
large-souled Swift — in simplicity of speech, quiet humour,
and social observation of men and manners. A really solid,
inexhaustible, efficient intellect — always, in every circumstance, master of itself, true to itself.

There has just come to my hands a little volume of *Selections from the Writings of B. Franklin,* which may serve to give those who will not read ten octavo volumes a glimpse of Franklin's mind and style. It ranges from homely hints to a young tradesman to physical experiments, the care of health, economics, slavery and the slave trade, the American rebel cause, Imperialism, grammar, reading, ladies' toilettes, foreign manners, and international alliances. Here one may read the letter to the Royal Society explaining the famous "kite experiment" of 1752, which identified lightning with electricity, and gave an electric shock to the thought of Europe. Here is a pleasant causerie on the game of chess; there a scathing satire on the "Slave trade" in the manner of Swift, which reads to-day like an article on the use of Chinese coolies in the Rand. We are again reminded of Swift in the profoundly wise piece of caustic wit entitled "Rules for reducing a great Empire to a small one." One by one all the acts of folly and oppression committed on the American Colonies by the Georgian rule are laid bare. Paragraph by paragraph these warnings might be addressed to our own transmarine Empire, and I am not sure that some passages might not be put into the mouth of an Irish Nationalist.

Franklin, though a figure less majestic than Washington, less imaginative than Hamilton, remains the typical Republican citizen; and if the feeling of his people for him is less that of reverence, it is more that of affection and fellowship. He is more easily understood as a man, and his origin and life are more akin to those of the average man. He will ever be remembered by the noble verse of Turgot, which embodies a grand tribute to the patriot in an exquisite epigram :

Eripuit cælo fulmen, sceptrumque tyrannis.

He wrested the thunderbolt from the heavens and their

sceptre from tyrants. What remains of eighteenth-century Philadelphia is to-day almost the only historic and antique flotsam in the United States. And I know no corner of that central pile more pathetic than that where, in the roar and bustle of that vast city, we come upon the lowly cemetery and plain slab, as ordered by his testament, inscribed to "Benjamin and Deborah Franklin, 1790."

ALEXANDER HAMILTON

1906

An English study of Alexander Hamilton, in the domain of thought the main Founder of the United States as a cohesive Commonwealth, was urgently needed. His was one of the finest minds of the eighteenth century. For more than a century the great State he did so much to create has been broadening in the lines which he traced for it, and to the ends which his genius foresaw more truly than all his colleagues. His hurried political pamphlets, which brought order out of chaos at the close of the War of Independence, have taken their place amongst the permanent classics of political science. And yet few Englishmen have ever opened the *Federalist*; and many well-read students of history, who know all about his personal scandals and his tragic end, have no very definite convictions as to the share in forming the United States, due to Washington, to Jefferson, Madison, Adams, and to Hamilton. As philosopher, as publicist, as creative genius, Hamilton was far the most important. And it was indeed time that English readers should have the story told them from the English point of view. His own son, Senator Cabot Lodge, and other American writers have amply done him justice. But one fears that standard American works are not assiduously studied in England. Mr. Oliver's work, which is not a biography, but "an essay on American Union," adequately supplies a real want in political history.

Sir Henry Maine, in his work on *Popular Government*, 1885, devoted the fourth essay to the Constitution of the United States, which he truly called "much the most important political instrument of modern times." And throughout this fourth essay Sir Henry does ample justice to the sagacity and foresight of Hamilton. He quotes Chancellor Kent, who compares the *Federalist* (mainly written by Hamilton) with Aristotle, Cicero, Machiavel, Montesquieu, Milton, Locke, and Burke; and Maine declares that such praise is not too high. Talleyrand, a diplomatist and a cynic, spoke of Hamilton with enthusiasm, and Guizot praised his political writings as of consummate wisdom and practical sagacity. Mr. Bryce, in his great work on *The American Commonwealth*, does full justice to Hamilton. Sir George Trevelyan, in his *American Revolution*, calls Hamilton "the most brilliant and most tragic figure in all the historical gallery of American statesmen." In the new *Cambridge Modern History*, vol. vii., Professor Bigelow truly describes Hamilton as "the master spirit of the Convention which framed the Constitution of the United States." "A nation was to be created and established, created of jarring commonwealths and established on the highest level of right." The accomplishment of this stupendous task by the dominant character of George Washington and the piercing genius of Alexander Hamilton places both amongst the great creative statesmen of the world.

Mr. Oliver's book does not profess to be a history or a biography, but "merely an essay on the character and achievements of a man who was the chief figure in a series of striking events." This is perhaps rather too modest a claim. For the years from 1780 to 1796 — the years when Hamilton first contributed to the task of practical statesmanship down to his drafting Washington's "Farewell Address" — the history of the War and of the Settlement during the two Presidencies of Washington is quite adequately sketched. And as to a biography of Hamilton, a living portrait of the man himself is vigorously drawn in the midst of the historical and political chapters. It is quite true that Hamilton and the circumstances of his career are by no means the exclusive subject. Washington, Jefferson, Madison, Adams, Monroe, Burr, and other prominent politicians have sections of the book to themselves. And the aims and principles of the various parties — Federalists, Democrats, State Rights, Republicans, Patriots, Neutralists — so obscure to us at home, are made clear as the story moves.

This is no doubt the true, perhaps the necessary way of recounting the life-work of Hamilton. He was so closely associated with every phase of the American movement for the twenty years after the virtual close of the war at Yorktown, in 1781, that the life of Hamilton is hardly intelligible unless we read it as part of the history of his country. And his relations with his colleagues in government, and with his opponents, rivals, and enemies in controversy and intrigue, are so close and so complex that no true portrait of Hamilton is complete till we have sketches of his contemporaries. On the whole, Mr. Oliver has set Alexander Hamilton in his true place, as next to Washington, the leading founder of the United States — the intellectual creator of the great Commonwealth of which George Washington was the typical father and the moral hero.

Hamilton is the American Burke in his union of literary power with political science. If he falls short of Burke in the majesty of speech and the splendour of many-sided gifts, he was never hurried into the frantic passions and fatal blunders which finally ruined Burke's influence over his age. Hamilton at times exaggerated the dangers he foresaw, was too pessimist and even unjust to the failings he condemned. But on the whole he made no great mistake, and all those ideas for which he struggled with such tenacity and earnestness have in the course of ages come to a triumphant issue. Hamilton, too, reminds us of Burke in the sadness of his personal history, in the poignant disappointments of his career, and in the want of full recognition of his supreme greatness in his lifetime. Colleagues whom we now see to have been his inferiors, both morally and intellectually, men representing lower ideals, came to the first place in the State he had created, a seat to which it was quite impossible that he could have been chosen. Even in America Hamilton has hardly been judged with full honour. He was too conservative, too anti-democratic, of too philosophic a temperament, too much the idealist, and too little the demagogue ever to attain the popularity which wins the votes of a vast majority.

The book has a moral — somewhat startling, and at the present moment charged with lively interest. The concluding book is occupied with general reflections upon Nationality, Empire, Union, and Sovereignty; and the problem of welding the thirteen American States into a single Commonwealth is applied to the present-day problem of reconciling the British Constitution with our transmarine Empire. Mr. Oliver, if I understand him aright, seems afraid that the British Empire is held together by bonds too loose and undefined, and would urge on it the Hamiltonian doctrine of central Sovereignty and resolute Union. He quotes Washington's maxim: "Influence is not government." He says the tie of affection or kinship is not union. He seems, like Hobbes and Austin, to ask for force as the basis of true union and government. Why, the self-governing Colonies would fly into fifty bits at the mere sound of such a thing. The American Civil War of 1863 would be a flea-bite compared to this. For my part, I quite agree with Washington that "influence is not government," and with Mr. Oliver that sentimental ties are not Union. But the casual conglomeration called the British Empire has nothing else to rest on, and the least attempt to bind it with closer ties would mean immediate and final disruption.

THACKERAY

1903

THE appearance of a great contemporary writer's works in various forms, as by the law of copyright his books become, one by one, the property of the public, reminds us that he has now entered into the literary elysium shared only by those who are English *Classics*. A "Classic" is one who, being dead and gone, is read more freely and with more reverence than ever was done in his lifetime; one whose rank is settled and acknowledged; who is found in manifold shapes of type and form, and has a familiar corner in every household.

Thackeray is eminently a classic. It is safe to predict that no prose writer of the nineteenth century will retain a more steady, even, and general popularity, and be for ages one of the typical facts in the history of English letters. The combination of faultless English, at once pure, nervous, and simple, with wit, humour, insight into the human heart, and perfect command of his own genius and knowledge of its resources and its limits — this forms a power so rare that the scholar and the "general reader," the philosopher and the man of the world, the literary *virtuoso* and the novel-trotter, can all enjoy it, and will always enjoy it. Thackeray has been dead now nearly forty years; he became famous nearly sixty years ago; his masterpiece is now fifty-five years old; and his collected works were published thirty-three years ago.

And now Messrs. Dent and Co. are issuing an edition of his prose works in thirty volumes, each with some ten illustrations, at a modest price, in continuation of their standard editions of Old English authors. The form is convenient, the type easy, and the illustrations entirely adequate (which in such a case is saying a good deal). Thackeray will go on and will continue long to be read in a dozen different forms. I have read him in the magnificent large octavo edition, with his own illustrations, of 1883–86 (which cost a small fortune), and also in the twelve-volume edition of 1871–72, and in many more editions, including the handy contraband of foreign reprinters. And now, as I take up the new issue in thirty volumes, I can hardly get on with this article for dipping into my favourite scenes and wasting my time over passages that I know by heart. He is ever fresh, ever welcome, ever racy — dear old "Snob."

As I turn over this issue of thirty volumes of *prose* — and he left us capital ballads, burlesques, and rhyming tags as well — I am amazed at this huge product of a writer who died at the age of fifty-two. It was also the age of Shakespeare at his death. I do not recall the name of any of our great prose writers, except Henry Fielding and Goldsmith, who died at so early an age. Scott and Dickens, who both worked themselves to death, reached a somewhat longer term. Some poets, and two rare women novelists, died even younger. But almost all our great prose writers amongst men lived and wrote to a riper age, some of them into a great age, as Hallam, De Quincey, and Carlyle. But Shakespeare, Fielding, Thackeray, all died in middle life, leaving an immense output. I do not claim Thackeray as the peer of Shakespeare, nor, indeed, of Fielding. But he has a measure of their supreme qualities of insight into the human heart, their zest for life, their broad outlook at the world, and its strange contrasts of manners, ranks, and characters.

There is another quality in which I hold Thackeray to be eminent. I mean his sober evenness of workmanship. He is almost never slovenly, or extravagant, or drivelling. He wrote too much, as they all did, and wrote for money, and not for fame or love of his art. He wrote many pieces that are quite below his best and his true form. But even his worst are written in that faultless and racy English of which he was master; they are never hysterical, bombastic, or farcical; they are never so nonsensical or so tedious that we cannot read them twice. Now, Fielding poured out volumes of dramatic rubbish; Dickens is insufferably maudlin at times, and too often grossly affected; Lytton is sometimes ludicrous, and George Eliot is sometimes pedantic; Trollope gives us stale small beer at times; Kingsley, Charlotte Brontë can be both coarse and sensational. Even Scott and Shakespeare, Olympians as they are, would rattle off what they knew to be rubbish when the printer's boy or the prompter's boy was waiting for copy. But Thackeray, though he ended at last in some very poor stuff, never flung at us rank balderdash or careless gabble.

Thackeray is a special favourite of mine, mainly by reason of his consummate flow of effervescing talk, his inexhaustible wit, and never-failing manly good sense. He is the jolly man-of-the-world who sees the follies and pretences of people about him, holds them up to contempt, but is never morose, sardonic, or peevish. I am quite aware of Thackeray's limitations, and I am not about to ignore them. I do not say he is a Fielding or a Scott, nor a Molière or a Cervantes. But I do say that *Vanity Fair*, as a comedy of modern society, is the best we have had since *Tom Jones*; and, if it be placed on a narrower stage, and inspired with a less generous spirit than *Tom Jones*, it may be put beside it, and will live along with it. Thackeray is not an epic poet like Scott; he has not the deep pathos that Dickens has reached more than once, and Richardson many times; he has not the noble humanity of Fielding; he has not the feminine subtlety of Jane Austen or of Charlotte Brontë. He has not the Gargantuan rage of Swift, nor the idyllic charm of Goldsmith. But his prose, as English style, is superior to any other prose of the nineteenth century. His invention is the least spasmodic and uneasy. And he will long stand with Fielding, Richardson, and Scott as one of our four or five standard romancists.

Years ago, when I tried to make an estimate of Thackeray, I was moved to say that, "of all the Englishmen of his century, he had written the best comedy of manners, the best extravaganza, the best burlesque, the best parody, and the best comic song," and that some of his admirers would add "the best lectures and the best critical essays." This was a parody of Byron's famous eulogy of Sheridan; and I hold that it had as much justification. *Vanity Fair* may be really "the best comedy of manners" without being the greatest romance of the century. It has not the epic poetry of Scott's best, nor the rollicking waggery of Dickens at his best; nor has it the exquisite aroma of Jane Austen's boudoir, nor the intense passion of Jane Eyre's confessions. But as a serious anatomy of social manners in a broad and judicial spirit it has something that none of these have, that nothing has since *Tom Jones*, something Shakespearean in its sane, comprehensive, penetrating survey of human character all round.

Vanity Fair, too, stands out again as far the chief masterpiece of Thackeray. For, to my mind, *Esmond*, with all its beauties and its wonderful mastery of the style and tone of the eighteenth century, is too artificial. And the *Newcomes* and *Pendennis*, for all their minor merits, are too much variations upon one key, and have no such power, no such unforgettable characters, as *Vanity Fair*. This novel also is the only one of all Thackeray's longer romances which has anything that can be called a plot, a drama, and an organic story of action. The plot of *Vanity Fair* is thin and desultory enough — not to be named beside the plots of *Tom Jones* or *Clarissa*, of *The Antiquary* or of *Jane Eyre*. But it has something that can be called a drama of incident worked out to a catastrophe. This cannot be fairly said of any other of Thackeray's longer romances. The story of them wanders on in the manner of serials composed from month to month. I doubt if a reader of the *Virginians*, of *Lovel*, or of *Philip*, could write out from memory a summary of the plot of any of them.

This leads us to another point — that Thackeray is peculiarly at home in his shorter pieces and in detached studies. I always hold the *Hoggarty Diamond* to be in his best vein. The *Snob* papers, again, have every one of his qualities in perfection. Few satires, unless it be *Don Quixote*, *Pantagruel*, *Gil Blas*, and *The Barber of Seville*, have ever killed the affectations they attacked and improved public opinion. But the *Book of Snobs* really killed certain forms of snobbery and reformed social taste. The book has lost much of its interest because it paints to some degree effete types of folly. It was for this that Charlotte Brontë called Thackeray "the first social regenerator of the day." He was hardly that. But, in spite of his turn for painting vulgarity, rascality, meanness, hypocrisy, pretentiousness, base natures, low vices, and pitiful shams, although he is much more at home with a mean character than he is with a noble nature — Thackeray is not a cynical mocker at human goodness. He loved the best in human nature. He did not a little to develop it.

REMINISCENCES OF GEORGE ELIOT

1901

IT is now some years ago that I ventured to make a prediction that "it will be the duty of the more serious criticism of another generation to revive the reputation of George Eliot as an abiding literary force." And the quality which I especially noted was this, that "she raised the whole art of romance into a higher plane of thought, of culture, and of philosophic grasp." I thought that this "noble aim" of hers was being too much overlooked — and I think this is still true in England. Her American admirers have shown more constancy in their affection.

It is more than forty-one years since I first made her acquaintance, on New Year's Day 1860, at the house of her close friends, Dr. and Mrs. Richard Congreve, at Wandsworth. It was twenty-one years later, almost to a day, that I was one of the mourners who followed her body to the grave in Highgate Cemetery on the 29th December 1880. During those twenty-one years I constantly saw her, had much conversation with her on literary and philosophical topics, and received many letters relating to her own writings, and also to her views on art, politics, and religion. Some of these letters have been published by her husband, but the incidents that called them forth are not quite evident to the readers of Mr. Cross's *Life*, and some of the most interesting have not been published at all. I am asked to contribute my own recollections of her conception of life and her methods of work. Having the sanction of those whom she left behind her, I will try, before it is too late, to put down my memories of a friend whom I so profoundly honoured. As I do this, I recall to mind not a few of the most golden days of my past life, and some of the most inspiring "banquets" or *symposia* of high thinking to which it has ever been my fortune to be bidden as a guest.

How well I remember that New Year's Day when I met Mr. and Mrs. Lewes at the dinner table of Mr. and Mrs. Richard Congreve! She was then at the age of forty, in the first outburst of her fame as the author of *Adam Bede*, and was just finishing the second volume of the *Mill on the Floss*. She had no friends at Wandsworth except Mr. and Mrs. Richard Congreve, who had made her acquaintance the year before. Mrs. Congreve, she wrote in her journal (May 3, 1859), "was the chief charm of the place to me." Dr. Congreve had retired for some years from his work at Oxford to give himself up to the study and propaganda of the principles of Auguste Comte. He had just published his translation of the *Positivist Catechism*, which Mrs. Lewes had already read, whilst George Lewes was occupied with the *Politique* of Comte. I was a young man, just called to the bar, who had been the pupil and then as tutor was the successor of Richard Congreve at Oxford, but I had written nothing, and was quite unknown to the public. Though we were all more or less interested in Comte, the talk round the table was quite general, and the small party was nothing but a simple gathering of intimate friends.

I listened with lively interest to the words of one who was already famous, who from the first moment impressed every one with a sense of grave thought, high ideals, and scrupulous courtesy. She had not a grain of self-importance in her manner, and took quite a simple and modest part in the general talk, listening to the brilliant sallies of George Lewes with undisguised delight, respecting Congreve's views as those of a trained historian and scholar, and showing me the kindly welcome of a gracious woman to the friend of her friends. I remember an argument in which she engaged me, wherein I thought, as I still think, she was mistaken. She maintained, *apropos* of a review of troops she had lately seen, that "the pomp and circumstance of glorious war" was more conspicuous in our day than it was in the Middle Ages. Having some knowledge of mediæval art, Italian war-paintings, and illuminated Froissarts, I ventured to doubt. The company seemed to think me bold in venturing to differ from her opinion on a matter of local colour. But she did not think so herself; and nothing could be more graceful than the patience with which she listened to my points.

In the year 1860, at Wandsworth, she was working under severe pressure, having broken with her own family, retaining only one or two women friends, quite unknown to general society. Years afterwards, when she lived in London and at Witley, she had the cultured world at her feet; men and women of rank and reputation crowded her Sunday receptions, and she was surrounded by friends and reverential worshippers of her genius. But she remained still the same quiet, grave, reserved woman that she had been in her retreat and isolation at Wandsworth, always modest in her bearing, almost deferential towards any form of acknowledged reputation, almost morbidly distrustful of herself, and eager to purge out of her soul any germ of arrogance and pride that her fame and the court paid to her by men and women of mark could possibly tend to breed.

It was the foundation of the *Fortnightly Review*, in 1865, which brought me into constant association with Mr. Lewes,

who was then established in the Priory, Regent's Park.   Early
in 1865 George Lewes was chosen as its first editor.   I contributed in that year four articles to the new organ, and
George Eliot wrote in the first number.   I was at that time
a constant visitor at the Priory, where Herbert Spencer,
Thomas Huxley, Anthony Trollope, the Congreves, Deutsch,
and Sir Frederic Burton were frequently found.   I there
learned to estimate at its full value the immense range of
George Eliot's reading, both in poetry and in philosophy,
the high standard of duty, whether personal or social, that
she kept before her own sight and required of others, and the
conscientious labour she devoted to her own art.

George Eliot was occupied on her novel of *Felix Holt*
during 1865 and the first half of 1866; and, as every reader
knows, the plot and *dénouement* in the later part of
the story turn on an intricate legal imbroglio, whereby
an old English family were suddenly dispossessed of their
estates which they had held for many generations.   She had
endeavoured to work out this problem for herself, but found
herself involved in hopeless technicalities of law.   As is
stated by Mr. Cross in the opening of chapter xiii., she had
written me the kind letter of January 5, 1866, to invite me
to join a party consisting of Herbert Spencer, T. Huxley,
and others, and she there imparted to me her difficulties as
to the law of entail and the statutes of limitations.   She wrote
of it in a letter to me of the 9th January that she "must go
sounding on her dim and perilous way through law-books
amidst agonies of doubt."   I offered her text-books, but she
preferred to put to me her difficulties in writing.   The law
case she required to fit her plot in the year 1832 was one which
on the first sight of it seemed impossible in the face of the
statutes of limitations.   She wanted to dispossess a family
which had been in peaceable possession of estates for a century.

This was "the statement of her needs," as she termed it :

It is required to know the longest possible term of years for the existence of the following conditions :

1. That an estate, for lack of a direct heir, should have come into the possession of A (or of a series — A, A', A'' — if that were admissible).

2. That subsequently a claim should have been set up by B, on a valid plea of nearer kinship.

3. That B should have failed in his suit from inability to prove his identity, over which certain circumstances (already fixed) should have cast a doubt, and should have died soon after.

4. That B's daughter, being an infant at the time of his death, should have come to years of discretion and have a legal claim on the estate.

These are the essentials as closely as I can strip them. The last, viz., the legal claim of B's daughter, might be dispensed with, if the adequate stretching of the time is not to be obtained by any formula of conditions. The moral necessities of the situation might be met by the fact of injustice and foul play towards B ; but I should prefer the legal claim, if possible.

You see, I should be glad of as large a slice of a century as you could give me, but I should be resigned if I could get forty years.

I was at first inclined to think the case to be impossible, as contrary to the then existing statutes of limitations. But I presently fell back on the rare, but not impossible, case of a *Base Fee*, under which a settlement might be perfectly valid for the issue of a tenant-in-tail for many generations, but would not bar the rights of the remainder-men. It happened that, before I finally submitted the scheme to George Eliot, I asked the opinion of a colleague at the bar. The man I consulted chanced to be the late Lord Herschell, the ex-Chancellor, who died on a public mission in the United States and who was then a junior barrister. Having his entire concurrence, I carried the scheme to George Eliot, who at once recast her plot, and was enabled to carry back the settlement of the Transome estates not only for forty years, but for more than a century. An attempt was made in a review to throw doubt upon the correctness of the law on which *Felix Holt* was based; but an eminent conveyancer of Lincoln's Inn disposed of this criticism in a conclusive answer in the press.

I have in my possession about sixteen letters written to me in the months from January to May 1866, asking for assistance in legal points relating to *Felix Holt*. And during that period I had many interviews with her thereon, and read large portions of the story in MS. and in proof. The letters and my own recollections testify to the indefatigable pains that she took with every point of local colour, her anxiety about scrupulous accuracy of fact, and the often feeble health under which the book was produced.

I was again consulted on an incidental point of law in the novel of *Daniel Deronda*. The letter of June 1, 1875 (partly printed by Cross, *Life*, iii. 258), begged me to come and talk over a point of difficulty. On the day following I received this letter:

June 2, '75.

DEAR MR. HARRISON — Herewith the statement you have kindly allowed me to send.

It occurs to me that in my brief, fragmentary chat with Mr. Bowen he had gathered Sir H. to be a tenant-in-tail coming of age, so that his Father could make no disposition without his consent. But even then I don't see why he — Sir H. — should have objected to a settlement in the given sense. Do you? This question has reference simply to my alarms about apparent improbabilities. — Yours thankfully,

M. E. LEWES.

This question referred to the desire of Sir Hugo Mallinger as to the settlement of the estates. She had consulted Charles Bowen, then a junior barrister and afterwards Lord Bowen, Lord of Appeal, but only in casual conversation. She then sent me a statement of the case she needed for the plot, and I forwarded to her the sketch of a possible

solution. This satisfied her requirements. She wrote
(June 15, 1875):

> I must write to tell you my joy that on further study of your
> " document " I find in it precisely the case that will suit the conditions
> I had already prepared. I mean the case that " Sir H. might ardently
> desire a particular house and property, locally part of the settled estates
> or not, to leave to his widow and daughters for their home and resi-
> dence, etc." Clearly I have a special Providence to whom my grati-
> tude is due, and he is the able conveyancer who has drawn up said
> document. We are in the pangs of preparation for starting to-morrow
> morning.

Felix Holt and *Daniel Deronda* were the only novels on
which I was consulted, and then simply as to points of law
and legal practice. I wrote the "opinion" of the Attorney-
General, printed in italics in chapter xxxv. of *Felix Holt*,
as a guide to the language used in Lincoln's Inn, and she in-
serted it bodily in the book. I remember telling her that I
should always boast of having written one sentence that was
embodied in English literature. The "opinion" was little
more than "common form," and she took kindly my little
mot. I need hardly say that I had nothing whatever to do
with the composition or scheme of either of these tales, nor
with anything else of her work. I do not think any one else
had. Except that she took pains to be accurate as to legal
subtleties, as to facts of history, and the Jewish rites in *Daniel
Deronda*, I do not believe she took counsel of any one but of
George Lewes. Everything she produced was entirely
original, both in conception and in execution.

My purpose in this paper is to try to clear up such points
as this, and to explain the meaning of some letters of hers
printed by Mr. Cross, but of which he could give no elucidation.
The very long and beautiful letter of August 15, 1866, printed
in chapter xiii. of the *Life and Letters*, headed "Aesthetic
Teaching," is hardly intelligible without some account of the

proposal to which it was an answer.   During her absence at
the German Baths in July of that year I wrote her a long
letter to suggest that she might use her great powers of imagination and her deep interest in social questions to describe an
ideal state of industrial life. It would present a picture of
the relations of all concerned in a great manufacturing industry, under conditions of health, happiness, and beauty,
so as to realise the Utopia of regenerated Industry directed
by an efficient spiritual force and inspired by the providence
of Humanity, as conceived by Auguste Comte. George
Eliot had been a careful student of all his works for many
years, and through the Congreves she was familiar with every
phase of the Positivist ideal, with the general idea of which
she had entire sympathy. I even suggested, as a *milieu*, a
manufacturing village in a beautiful part of northern France,
where the owner of a great factory had reorganised Labour
on humane and social lines, himself an ardent republican and
ex-socialist, whilst the education and worship of the township
were directed by the local physician, who exerted a positive
priesthood on a basis of scientific convictions.

Her long and convincing letter of August 15 was her answer
to this proposal.   She feared (and no doubt with some reason)
that the effort to idealise a social state, consciously imagined
as possible only in the future, would want the life and reality
that she gave to her modern pictures.   She was quite in her
element in painting character.   She did not shrink from treating a past epoch, as in *Romola*, "The Spanish Gypsy," etc.,
etc.   But, as she says in the letter, she was there dealing with
only *some* of the relations, treating of selected characters,
not with a form of society with definite moral problems, nor
with the panorama of a regenerated type of human life.
Furthermore, she adds, her gift for tragic crises would have
no scope in the tableau of a glorified world where virtue and

happiness reigned. She was no doubt quite right. She shrank from any Utopia in which there was danger that "the picture might lapse into the diagram." But the idea, as she said, continued to rest in her mind.

The poem of "The Spanish Gypsy" was one result of the conception that was floating in her mind of presenting in a typical scene some of the phases of a religion of Human Duty. Later on she wrote to me:

Yes, indeed, I not only remember your letter, but have always kept it at hand, and have read it many times. Within these latter months I have seemed to see in the distance a possible poem shaped on your idea. But it would be better for you to encourage the growth towards realisation in your own mind rather than trust to transplantation.

My own faint conception is that of a frankly Utopian construction, freeing the poet from all local embarrassments. Great Epics have always had more or less of this character — only the construction has been of the past, not of the future. Write to me — Poste Restante, Baden-Baden, within the next fortnight. My head will have got clearer then. — CROSS (*Life*, iii. 51).

In the beginning of 1867 George Eliot made the memorable journey to Spain, from which she wrote to me the beautiful letter given by Mr. Cross (iii. 8). She was then meditating her poem; and undoubtedly Positivist ethics supplied her with the conception of Zarca.

The relation of George Eliot towards the ideal of Auguste Comte has been accurately stated by Mr. Cross (vol. iii. 419) as "a limited adherence." "For all Comte's writing she had a feeling of high admiration, intense interest, and very deep sympathy." "But the appreciation was thoroughly selective. Parts of his teaching were accepted and other parts rejected." But her letters to me and her conversation showed something more than sympathy, and not a little practical co-operation. Her life-long friendship with Richard Congreve, the recognised leader of English Positivism, began in

February 1859, and continued until her death in December 1880. From that time she read Comte regularly, and was occupied on him during her last illness. The study of him, she wrote in January 1867, "keeps me in a state of enthusiasm through the day — a moral glow." "My gratitude increases continually for the illumination Comte has contributed to my life." She subscribed to the foundation of the Positivist School in 1870, of which Richard Congreve remained Director until his death in 1899, and also to the foundation of Newton Hall, of which I have been the President since 1881. And I have many letters from her relating to Positivist writings of my own. An interesting letter is that referring to the attack of Matthew Arnold on Comte.

On the publication of my article on "Culture," reprinted in my *Choice of Books*, she wrote to me (November 7, 1867):

I suppose it is rather superfluous for me, as one of the public, to thank you for your article in the *Fortnightly*. But *le superflu* in the matter of expression is *chose si nécessaire* to us women. It seems to me that you have said the serious things most needful to be said in a good-humoured way, easy for everybody to read. I have not been able to find Matthew Arnold's article again, but I remember enough of it to appreciate the force of your criticism. Only on one point I am unable to see as you do. I don't know how far my impressions have been warped by reading German, but I have regarded the word "Culture" as a verbal equivalent for the highest mental result of past and present influences. Dictionary meanings are liable rapidly to fall short of usage. But I am not maintaining an opinion — only stating an impression. My conscience made me a little unhappy after I had been speaking of Browning on Sunday. I ought to have spoken with more of the veneration I feel for him, and to have said that in his best poems — and by these I mean a large number — I do not find him unintelligible, but only peculiar and original. Take no notice of this letter, or else I shall feel that I have made an unwarrantable inroad on your time.

The highly characteristic letter of January 15, 1870, printed by Cross (iii. 103–4), was called out by my article on the

"Positivist Problem" in the *Fortnightly Review* of November 1869. In her letter George Eliot admits that she has "an unreasonable aversion to personal statements"; she "shrinks from decided 'deliverances' on momentous subjects, from the dread of coming to swear by my own deliverances, and sinking into an insistent echo of oneself. That is a horrible destiny — and one cannot help seeing that many of the most powerful men fall into it." All this is not very clear without some explanation, which I will try to give. In reply to various criticisms on Comte by Professor Huxley, Matthew Arnold, and Fitzjames Stephen, I attempted to state the general conditions of the philosophical and religious problems as understood by Positivism. At that date, 1869, I did not at all accept Comte's idea of a Religion of Humanity, and as I was believed to do so, being a colleague of Richard Congreve, I thought it right to state that fact in my article. This was not to the liking of Congreve at all, who would have preferred me to keep silence about my personal opinions. And George Eliot, in her sympathy with the Congreves and her morbid horror of confessions of all kinds, was inclined to remonstrate with me for making any reference to my own beliefs. I never saw, nor do I see, any ground for such reticence, but much the contrary, as leading to false impressions. Those who promote unpopular ideas naturally wish for nothing but whole beliefs in all who go with them. But I repudiate such an attitude. In the thirty-two years since 1869 I have come to adopt the Religion of Humanity, though not in the sense of some followers of Comte, who wish to treat his writings as having a sort of verbal inspiration. I have studied his system now for fifty years, and have never allowed those whom I address in public or in private to be in ignorance from time to time as to the form and extent of my adhesion. And I have no disposition to shrink from "personal deliverances."

There are times when they are an indispensable guarantee of good faith.

Nothing in the shape of a "service" on Positivist lines was attempted in the Positivist chapel for the first years of its foundation. But by degrees the need for the full expression of religious feeling in public and in private made itself felt; and as our own children grew up from infancy, their mother was called upon to supply some equivalent for family prayer. We consulted George Eliot, who, with her deep sympathy with the inmost emotions of humanity, had so great a gift of poetic expression. The letter of June 14, 1877 (given by Cross, *Life*, iii. 311), was the outcome of this appeal. She there said that she was not able to conribute "to the construction of a liturgy," but that she would keep the subject in mind, and "perhaps it might prompt some perfectly unfettered productions." "O may I join the choir invisible" had been composed in 1867, and was published with " Jubal" in 1874; and it was always regarded as a religious embodiment of the Positivist hope of subjective immortality. I continued to urge George Eliot to produce other pieces in prose or in verse with the same devotional feeling.

In the month of July 1877, we drove over from Sutton Place to Witley, and there had long talks with her on the same subject as we strolled about the heather and the pine woods on those Surrey heights. And I sent her a few passages of the kind, which at first she seemed inclined to look on as inappropriate. On consideration, she changed her mind, and wrote to me, December 26, 1877 :

I have now reread more than once the Prayers we spoke of, and withdraw my remark (made under reserve) as not at all applicable. The prayers keep, I think, within the due limit of aspiration and do not pass into beseeching.

Certainly, if just the right words could be found — what Vauvenargues calls *cette splendeur d'expression qui emporte avec elle la preuve des*

L

grandes pensées — a ritual might bring more illumination than sermons and lectures.

The summer of 1878 was partly occupied by George Eliot in writing *Theophrastus Such* — perhaps the only one of her books which was not a success. I have a guilty conscience as to this book, as I may have contributed to induce her to write it. I pointed out to her that our English literature, so rich and splendid in almost every field of poetry and prose, was deficient in those collections of Thoughts which the French call *Pensées* — pregnant apothegms embedded in terse and memorable phrase, which could be remembered like fine lines of poetry, and be cited as readily as a familiar proverb. It seemed to me — it seems to me still — that she was eminently fitted to produce such a book, and indeed the *Wit and Wisdom of George Eliot* was a volume culled from her writings. But *Theophrastus Such* — where the queer title came from I know not — was not an adequate expression of her powers. She was in very poor health all the time, and George Lewes was then stricken with his last illness. His death delayed publication, and when she read *Theophrastus* in revise, she had serious thoughts of suppressing it (Cross, iii. 352). Would she had done so! Her life was ebbing away when it was actually published.

After the death of George Lewes, November 28, 1878, we saw little of George Eliot for some time. "Here I and sorrow sit," she wrote in her diary, January 1, 1879; and she devoted herself to the publication of his posthumous works, and to founding a studentship in his memory, to be called after his name. This necessitated interviews with friends; and in the spring she began to see a few intimate callers again. She wrote, April 8, 1879:

DEAR FRIENDS — Will you come to see me some day? Though I have been so long without making any sign, my heart has been continually moved with gratitude towards you.

And on May 25, 1879, she writes:

I fell ill last week I was in town, and was obliged to leave much undone, else I should have written to you. I have not yet recovered my former level, but I hope soon to do so under country influences. I keep by me two letters, and sometimes reread them when I feel in need of a moral stimulus which is half rebuke, half encouragement.

In May 1879 George Eliot published a work which George Lewes had left in MS. — *The Study of Psychology, its Object, Scope, and Method.* It was an elaborate treatise on the relation of psychology to physiology, and treated in turn the views of Comte, Mill, and Herbert Spencer. Lewes, without entirely agreeing with any of these theories, tends rather to place the science of psychology on the same basis as Comte, whilst denying Comte's doctrine that the Introspective method was wholly illusory. George Eliot sent me a presentation copy of this book, which I read with deep interest. And I made it the basis of a paper I read to the Metaphysical Society on June 10, 1879, entitled the "Social Factor in Psychology," which was based on Lewes's chapter iv. I submitted the paper to George Eliot, who sent me the following letter. The term "Factor," by the way, was the word used as headline to chapter iv. of Lewes's book:

June 10, '79.

I am greatly obliged to you for sending me the paper you are to read to-day, and I appreciate it the more highly because your diligence is in contrast with the general sluggishness of readers about any but idle reading. It is melancholy enough that to most of our polite readers the Social Factor in Psychology would be a dull subject. For it is certainly no conceit of ours which pronounces it to be the supremely interesting element in the thinking of our time.

I confess the word Factor has always been distasteful to me as the name for the grandest of forces. If it were only mathematical I should not mind, but it has many other associated flavours which spoil it for me.

Once more — evermore — thanks. — Yours most truly,

M. E. Lewes.

I trust your whole household is blooming again now.   I am a little better.

The fine letter of April 19, 1880 (printed by Cross, iii. 388), is the last that I received.   It was written a few weeks before her marriage to Mr. John Cross, on May 6, and a few months only before her death.   In it her warm admiration for Wordsworth comes out very strongly.   When she writes, "I think you would find much to suit your purpose in 'The Prelude' such as,

> There is
> One great society alone on earth :
> The noble Living and the noble Dead,"

she was referring to my "purpose," which was to find suitable passages of poetry to read as introductions to the courses of Positivist lectures which were then being given.

It will be noticed how largely George Eliot's thoughts and her correspondence with myself turned upon the Positivist ideal of an organised Religion of Humanity.   This was only natural, inasmuch as I had been introduced to her by Dr. Richard Congreve, and with him I was, during our intimacy, one of the leaders of the Positivist movement, in which she deeply sympathised.   We were all anxious to see this sympathy develop into full adhesion, which it never did, and perhaps was never likely to have done.   When a separate group was formed, which met in Newton Hall, George Eliot gave to its funds an annual subscription, without withdrawing that which she had contributed to an earlier movement.

But it must not be supposed that she was entirely wrapped up in deep problems of metaphysics and ethics.   Far from it !   She was the most courteous and considerate of friends, delighting in lively conversation and good-natured gossip. She was an admirable housewife, and very proud of her practical accomplishments as a sensible and kindly mistress. She interested herself much in finding a comfortable situation for any young woman whom she judged to be in need of a friend. We have letters she addressed to my wife recommending a girl as a nurse. "I have reason to believe," she wrote, "that her habits of feeling and conduct are much above the average in young women offering themselves for domestic service." The girl in question was leaving her place, as George Eliot suspected, owing to "a cabal against Mary in the kitchen as 'the proud house-maid.' Her underclothing was thought arrogantly good, and her bearing towards the men had a little too much dignity."

Her zeal to help those who were in trouble was always active. I remember once seeing her spring to her feet, and stretching up her arms with that passionate gesture she sometimes would display, she said, "Yes! the day will come when it will be a natural instinct to stretch out a hand to help one who needs support, as automatic and irresistible as it is now to use our hands to keep ourselves from a fall."

There was much of Dinah Morris that was studied, not from Aunt Samuel Evans, but from the depths of the heart of George Eliot herself.

THE COMPLETE RUSKIN

1906

THE new Library Edition of Ruskin's Works is now before
the world; and to every one who values pure English, original
genius, and many-sided Art, it must be an inexhaustible
mine of study and delight. Let no one suppose that this
collection is mere reprint — "that we knew it all before";
that it "gives us nothing new." It gives us much that is
new, and it gives us the old under new forms. Though I
am myself saturated with the writings of John Ruskin,
whom I began to read fifty-six years ago, and though I have
read every one of his books as they came out, between 1849
and 1899, I am amazed at the freshness and the richness of
this monumental work. What miracles of labour, thought,
invention are crowded in these thirty-seven big volumes!
What microscopic delicacy of observation! What subtlety
of hand! What glowing enthusiasm for beauty, truth,
goodness! It is the perennial fertility of the writer, the encyclopædic variety of the ideas, which holds me spell-bound.

Has any English writer poured out such masses of pregnant prose, such varied thoughts about nature, poetry, art,
society, history, religion? We pass on in these volumes from
mountains to rivers, to the sea, to the lakes; to trees, rocks,
gems, clouds, sunsets — to the buildings of Athens, of Italy,
of France, and England — antique, mediæval, renascent;
then to pictures, Giotto and the Primitives, Bellini, Tintoretto,
Veronese; to Claude and Turner, Prout and Millais; to

Phidias, Michael Angelo, Florentine reliefs and medallions; and then to the Dismal Science, Social Economy, a new Heaven and a new Earth. It is an encyclopædia of homily, criticism, analysis, poetry, and passion. I am not the man to value quantity in lieu of quality. The rare bits we have of Sappho, Vauvenargues, or Lovelace, are worth whole libraries. But when I count up the contents of these thirty-seven volumes of Ruskin to contain some seven or eight millions of words, I confess I am amazed at such productive energy and inexhaustible eloquence. And in all these eight million words in some 18,000 pages there is not one page that any other but Ruskin could have written.

Though I am *fanatico per il Giovanni Ruskin*, as the Venetians say, I am quite alive to his blunders, his nonsense, his delirious loves and hates. Alas! there are ignorance, babyism, and perversity scattered broadcast, not a little extravagant rhetoric, and some cruel injustice. But withal, what geysers of noble feeling! What an Ithuriel spear to unmask the lurking toads of falsehood! What patience! What subtlety! What refinement in the drawings! What a sense of a pure and exquisite spirit pervades these "sermons in stone," as Carlyle said — these sermons in colours, in drawings, in landscapes, in cathedrals, in the eternal hills, and in the smoky factories of crowded cities! These thirty-seven volumes contain enough teaching about buildings to equip a leading authority in Architecture; enough teaching about Painting to found a school; enough material to base a general history of Art; enough history to give a new reading to the Middle Ages; enough about Poetry to make a master in criticism; enough of Economy to create a special type of Socialism; enough verse to rival an average minor poet; enough of perfect prose to place him beside Bacon and Burke for his inimitable style.

And withal, this man — so often from boyhood prostrated by physical maladies, and then by despair and cerebral affliction; who spent years and years in travelling over Europe, in lonely meditation on mountains, moors, lakes, and sea; who gave up days and nights to schools, classes, and college lectures; who poured out his thoughts daily to unknown correspondents; who flung away the whole of his paternal inheritance with lavish, and indeed reckless, generosity — found time, as this collection shows us, to produce hundreds of exquisite studies of buildings, landscapes, pictures, statues, and natural objects — from Mont Blanc to a boulder or a tuft of grass — all of them full of suggestion to the artist and the naturalist, unique in their method, and some few so subtle, so lovely, that they might pass at a first glance for the work of Prout or of Turner. Truly, it is only now when we see in one uniform collection these eighty different works, these 1400 plates, with all the new biographical matter, the diaries, the notes, the letters which serve to elucidate and illumine the text — it is only now that we can judge how largely bulks in the glorious Victorian age the name of Ruskin — whose publications from 1837 to 1900 exactly cover the whole reign of the late Queen.

I said there is a great deal that is new in this collection, and what is old is given under new forms and with fresh illustrations. In the first place, there are more than 100 drawings by Ruskin himself, which have never been published. All students of his work and life have seen many of the originals — wonderful in their subtlety and precision, now and then really lovely in cloud and air effects. As an old Alpinist, I make bold to say that no other man has ever drawn the Alps with absolute truth, not even Turner, who idealised and glorified the mountains as he did the rivers, the sea, and the palaces of Venice. Ruskin alone of draftsmen has drawn the Alps as they are — as Tyndall might have drawn them if he had been an artist, as Turner might have drawn them if he had been a geologist. And in this collection we have in one set the whole series, singular in their variety, but all marked with the same intense patience and meticulous pains. Ruskin often declares that he could only copy — not compose. But there are some of his larger studies of distant landscapes in France and Switzerland which make one think he might have been a real painter, if he had not chosen to be a Professor of universal Art — as he might have been a great Social Reformer, if he had not chosen to be a lonely Prophet in the wilderness.

But there is much besides the drawings which is new. The nineteenth volume contains no fewer than three unpublished Lectures, which together give the essence of Ruskin teaching on his central idea: the dependence of all great Art on moral and spiritual enthusiasm. It was a noble message, to which his whole life was devoted — in some ways, a true message, however much he misunderstood the hard facts of history and overrated his own power to solve one of the most complex problems of social science. Almost every volume yet issued contains matter more or less new even to diligent students of Ruskiniana. And apart from new appendices, the body of extracts from diaries, letters, memoranda, and criticisms give life and meaning to the essays in the text. But the elaborate introductions to each volume, mainly the work of Mr. E. T. Cook, running at times to 50 or 100 close pages, describe the circumstances, in Ruskin's long and chequered life, under which each book, essay, or lecture was produced. This biographical commentary is at times a revelation of a mind — one of the most marvellously endowed and certainly one of the most vividly interesting in the whole of the nineteenth century.

I am a Ruskinian myself — but with a difference. There

are still people who accept the pure milk of the Ruskinite word, just as there are people who still believe in Christian science or other mysteries. But I am free to confess that John Ruskin, in his long life, his encyclopædic range of study, his restless search for new ideas, and his deluge of writing, maintained continuously for sixty years, did emit much wild guesswork, some arrant nonsense as he often confessed, and changed his point of view backwards and forwards, as passion, love, indignation, pity, and sorrow moved him. What man of eager spirit and piercing inspiration, who for sixty years flung himself into every problem of art, of poetry, of morals, of religion — even of science — could avoid inconsistencies, contradictions, absurdities, and cruel injustice to those whom he could not understand? And yet I find fascination in all these outbursts. Nay, more; even when Ruskin is most wrong, unjust, intolerant, I find food for reflection and care. His view may be one-sided, but it is always the view of a side which has to be taken into account — a view which can only be met by thoughts which force us down to the very roots of moral, social, and religious questions.

Take as an example the famous lecture of 1870 on Michael Angelo and Tintoret (vol. xxii. 75–110), which so "fluttered the Volscians" of the Academies and the art critics. As the world has done now for 400 years (the cartoon of the Pisan war was of 1506, I hold by the supreme greatness of Buonarroti myself; and in a little sketch of his life I wrote that "in nobility of character, in sublimity of imagination, and in stupendous achievements, Michael Angelo may rank with the greatest sons of Humanity." And yet I find much that is true, a great deal that is most instructive, in Ruskin's furious onslaught, his denunciations of "the ostentatious display of strength and science." How true is his wrath with all "stage decoration," with the fatal effect of the gigantic powers of the master, whose influence, as I said in my sketch, was "disastrous to his contemporary followers." Ruskin's tirade against Michael Angelo is not the whole truth — far from it — but it has truths which we cannot shut out. How fine are Ruskin's "four essentials of the greatest art": 1, faultless workmanship; 2, serenity; 3, the human face first; 4, freedom from vice and pain. The famous (or infamous) lecture on Michael Angelo should be read again in vol. xxii., with the notes, criticisms, letters, and personal reminiscences, for the first time included in this series. It forms a typical example of Ruskin's moods, ideas, and limitations. We find him therein not so much the student and critic of art, as the perfervid poet, moralist, preacher, *censor morum*, and social reformer.

He himself regarded his lectures as the most careful and important part of his life-work. The energy and labour he gave to his museum and his art collections are perfectly amazing. His first professorship at Oxford dated from 1870–78. These years were "the busiest period of his busy life." He delivered eleven courses of lectures at Oxford. He wrote guide-books, works on botany, geology, drawing; he started a library of standard literature; he catalogued and annotated his art collection; he founded a museum at Sheffield; he engaged in a series of social experiments; he founded the Company of St. George; he wrote incessantly to newspapers; he issued that wonderful medley called *Fors Clavigera* month by month. That it all ended in a dreadful brain collapse is not wonderful. It is a subject of wonder that he ever recovered the lucidity and activity of his powers at all. But it is not at all wonderful if, in the course of production, so miscellaneous and so passionate, he was hurried into many false judgments, and laid down the law in many things, of which he could have no really scientific knowledge. And yet in all this torrent of poetry, homily, keen vision, and rapturous enthusiasm, there are for some of us imperishable charms and exquisite sympathies with beauty and goodness.

These volumes of lectures, read with the mass of illustrations printed and pictorial, the notes and letters made public for the first time in this series, display the man, Ruskin, in more living reality than do his greater works. They explain much that is latent in *Modern Painters* and in *The Stones of Venice*, often qualifying and correcting his earlier judgments. All through his long life, from the childhood when he wrote poetry at nine, till he finished *Præterita* just before his death, Ruskin was perpetually learning, as Michael Angelo said of himself, *ancora impara*. His theme was the whole world of art, of nature, of history, of man, of earth, of sky: and none of these could present a problem which he did not burst to solve. Often, as we know, he egregiously failed to solve them. But how suggestive, how fascinating, often how wonderful were his guesses, his insight, his intense earnestness of soul!

When it comes to me to find myself unable to work and but faintly to enjoy sights of the world and to read anything new, as I saw him in the last years of his life, in his study, softly gazing at Coniston Old Man, as he sat in a bower of roses, and turning over a volume of pictures, I think I would wish to have these thirty-seven volumes of the Library Ruskin by my side, and gently read a favourite passage here and there, or turn from one lovely drawing to another, trying to recall a past vision of beauty.

It is the inexhaustible prodigality of this collection of thoughts and suggestions which ever strikes me with fresh wonder. It may sound a wild paradox, but I ask myself if any other of our famous men of genius, since Shakespeare,

has poured out such a world of original fancies about everything visible in Nature, or in the handiwork of Man, about
the literature of the ancient and the modern poets, about
the regeneration of society, the inner meaning of religion,
about the duties of man, the prerogatives of woman, the
training of children, the dignity of Labour — in the indomitable search of that Sangreal of the true knight — a new
Heaven and a new Earth.

Mr. Cook's introductions will be found to have singular
interest for all lovers of the Professor, enriched with many
private letters of his, entries in diaries, personal and biographical pictures from intimate friends, and a vivid presentment of his life at Coniston, as those who know it will bear
witness. Surely no genius of the Victorian age, hardly
Carlyle or Tennyson, has ever been revealed to us so faithfully and so lovingly, in every detail of his life, and mind,
and inmost feeling. And assuredly no English writer, unless
it be Shakespeare himself, has ever had his writings edited,
annotated, and illustrated with such zeal, labour, and ample
knowledge.

A volume which will have special interest for Ruskinian
students will be the unpublished lectures given at Oxford in
1874 — "The Æsthetic and Mathematic Schools of Art in
Florence." The eight lectures were thus classified : — I.
The Æsthetic Schools of 1300: Arnolfo, Cimabue, Giotto
(the lecture on Giotto being incorporated in the "Mornings
in Florence" and "The Shepherd's Tower"). II. The
Mathematic Schools of 1400 — Brunelleschi, Quercia, Ghiberti. III. The Christian Romantic Schools of 1500 —
Angelico, Botticelli. This section is illustrated by twelve
drawings and photogravures. These lectures contained some
of Ruskin's most vigorous and characteristic thoughts. He
was himself pleased with them, and he tells us that the lecture

on Arnolfo was considered the best he had ever given in Oxford. Twelve lectures were written, he says, in six weeks "from hand to mouth." They were delivered to a great extent extempore from notes. And for that reason they were not published, and now are only recovered from a rough MS., with the assistance of the notes taken by Mr. Wedderburn and others. Though they still remain fragmentary, this only adds to their lifelike form and effect. As we read them we seem to hear the eager, masterful, irrepressible tone of the speaker as he poured out his passionate ideas and glanced from grave to gay, from poetry to science, from morals to religion.

The analysis of Florentine Art into the three schools — æsthetic, mathematic, and romantic, typified respectively in Giotto, Michael Angelo, and Botticelli — goes down to the roots of Ruskin's whole conception of Art and of Society, and with him Art and Society were indissolubly bound together. The distinction between Imagination and Science, between spiritual ideals and accomplished knowledge, between Angelico and Buonarroti, is profoundly instructive, and explains much in Ruskin's darkest sayings, his rapture in the archaic limitations of Cimabue, and his indignation with the academic megalomania of Michael Angelo. Nothing has injured Ruskin's credit with students of Art more than his violent repudiation of Michael Angelo as a supreme type. In these lectures one sees more clearly what Ruskin meant, and why, recognising as he does the unapproachable power and knowledge of the mighty sculptor, he turns from the man who defies all the Christian spiritualities and revolts the Catholic graces. But this judgment assumes that no power and no knowledge, no tragic intensity or inimitable skill of hand, can outweigh a want of spiritual convictions. At Oxford this assumption thirty years ago might pass unchallenged. But to those who have parted with the spiritual convictions of Cimabue and Angelico, the tirades of the Professor are sounding brass. Half of Ruskin's doctrines and precepts about Art rest upon his own very fervid and quite personal beliefs as to things social and religious. And, as his beliefs were in constant flux, and not quite intelligible at all times, his Art judgment is open to eternal controversy. To accept him as final arbiter in Art we must accept him as infallible master in theology and in sociology. The judicious accept him as an inspiration, but not as a judge. And yet, how rich in suggestion and in light are even his most daring paradoxes and fantasies!

Nothing can be more instructive than all these volumes contain about Giotto. The force of Ruskin's artistic instincts leads him direct to understand the great Florentine who united profound intellect to exquisite sense of beauty. Buonarroti had the intellect, though less sane and less lucid. Angelico and Botticelli had the sense of beauty, but not the brain power. At first sight Giotto would not seem to satisfy Ruskin's ideal; and in this book we learn that he did not satisfy it at first sight. But at last Giotto is felt to be supreme in all but such technical knowledge as was impossible in the age of Dante. As I pointed out in 1902, Ruskin has taught us to "rank Giotto as one of the greatest forces in the entire history of art." These "Mornings in Florence," these views of the Campanile, justify even such language of admiration. We know it is disputed how much Giotto did for the Campanile. If he did not conceive its form, and the motifs of the reliefs round its base, there must have been two Giottos in Florence.

The Complete Works of John Ruskin will ever be read, as the Sixth Article tells us the Apocrypha are read, for example and instruction, yet not so as to establish any doctrine. They may never become "canonical" books, and yet how beautiful, how wise, how illuminating they are!

For my own part, I am free to confess that with all the means I have had for understanding Ruskin's temperament and methods, I have gained a new insight from the material here collected for the first time. Although I knew him and heard him during the last forty years of his life, had read, as I fondly supposed, all that he had ever written, and had myself compiled a biography, I have learnt much in the new volume.

The chief interest of the new biographical matter lies in the fresh light thrown by it on the very painful and obscure part of Ruskin's life from 1874 to 1877. It was the period of his worst illness and greatest moral trial. As his editor tells us, "The work is broken, scattered, incomplete, and marked by irritability of tone." He truly says "the fire now becomes fitful and feverish." As Carlyle wrote, a little earlier: "He has fallen into thick, quiet despair again on the personal question; and meant all the more to go ahead with fire and sword upon the universal one." He was suffering personal disappointment. In 1875 he wrote: "The woman I hoped would have been my wife is dying." She died in May, having steadily refused to see him. The death deeply affected Ruskin's mind and nature, and coloured with gloom and mysticism his whole after-career. How it shook and over-shadowed his mind, how strangely it worked itself into his art studies and his inmost musings and fantasies, can be learned, I think, most faithfully and at first hand from the letters and impressions now given to the world.

These years were a period of great but restless activity. The "great fountain of sorrow," he wrote, "can never ebb away. Meanwhile I live in the outside of me and can still work." He did work at Oxford Lectures, the Drawing

School, St. George's Company, *Fors Clavigera*, month by month, the *Guide to Venice*, and other undertakings. And we now learn how deeply at this time Ruskin became interested in vague forms of spiritualism and hypochondria, which floated about his mind, giving it no rest, but rather, as he said, a "quite terrible languor." The effects of this sorrow, malady, and mysticism combined, more or less darkened the rest of his life, and clouded the balance of his thoughts. I can now better understand the tone of mind which induced his denunciation of Darwin, Mill, Spencer, Miss Cobbe, Liberals, and Agnostics, and his appeal to me, which led to our controversy in 1876. When I wrote the reply reprinted in my *Choice of Books* I had no idea of the morbid condition of his mind or of the causes of his affliction, though his private letters to me betrayed a strange excitability. Ruskin's writing after the year 1874 was never quite the same thing, until perhaps in the calm of *Præterita* (1885–89). We may enter more fully into his state of mind by reading the forty pages of Introduction that Mr. Cook has compiled. It is a fascinating chapter in the psychology of genius. The way in which Saint Ursula and Rose La Touche are blended into a sort of Dantesque Vision is a strange episode in a many-sided nature.

The elaborate study of Giotto's frescoes at Padua belong to 1853 and 1860. I believe no sounder or more illuminating art criticism was ever composed. We may even say that truly right understanding of Italian Primitive Art dates from this epoch, for Englishmen at least, and largely by means of Ruskin. Giotto, we now know, was one of the profoundest men of genius whom the modern world produced. His pre-eminence was obscured to our grandfathers by the technical ignorance inevitable in his age. No one has ever explained so well as Ruskin why Giotto's artistic imagination

M

should in no respect suffer by his defects in manipulation and scientific training. "Giotto was not one of the most accomplished painters, but he was one of the greatest men who ever lived," cries our Professor in his enthusiasm. These frescoes do not teach us drawing, but they expound to us "the history of the human mind." The whole power of Giotto's work rests on "pure Colour, noble Form, noble Thoughts." Giotto made no attempt to give complete details, nor any laborious realism. His was "a symbolical art which addresses the imagination, not the realist art which supersedes it." The entire series of these studies of Giotto forms a masterly type of fine art judgment and analysis.

The *Guide to the Academy at Venice* (of 1877) and *St. Mark's Rest* (of 1884) have been, and long will be, the handbooks of innumerable travellers. But the copious notes of the editors and the plates in the new edition will force most readers of the original manuals to look at them again. One of the most interesting studies in *St. Mark's Rest* is the subtle analysis of Carpaccio's works, and of these the most new and ingenious is the mystical meaning of the symbolical St. Jerome. Here we have Ruskin with his lynx-eye, his subtlety, his love of symbolism, and his mediæval passion. The St. Jerome is a typical example of the way in which the early Venetians could blend intense realism, the most precise representation of minute facts as they saw them, with an enthusiastic idealism of spiritual mysteries.

As we read and enjoy Ruskin's rhapsodies over the faithful precision with which Giotto and Carpaccio saw with the mind's eye miracles and transfigurations exactly as scripture and legend recorded them, and when he raves at Raphael and Michael Angelo, who use these scriptures and legends merely as the texts whereon they could dilate on their own delight in all forms of human nature and of earthly grace

— careless of the words of evangelist or father — the question arises in the mind: Why were Raphael and Michael Angelo and the men of the New Learning bound by any literalism of Holy Writ? They were painters, whose business it was to show us noble men and lovely women in picturesque and moving incidents. They were not the handicraftsmen of monks, bidden to produce illustrations of homilies and sermons. Michael Angelo did not take the Last Judgment seriously in the vein of the Book of Revelation. Nor do we to-day. Nor, for that matter, did Ruskin himself. Giotto's Bible at Padua is most impressive Art — but it is Primitive Art. Its profound interest is historical — not theological, not religious. Or if it teach us religion, it is the religion of human nature and of human genius.

MAURICE HEWLETT

1906

TEN years have passed since a new writer came forward in English letters with a vein of his own so subtle that, for the moment, it delighted the thoughtful rather than the casual reader, who is slow to accept any unfamiliar note. But in these few years the wider public has learnt that, amongst the two or three living prose writers of the first rank stands Maurice Hewlett, who in a decade has given them, almost year by year, a series of romances of rare imagination and power. In the quality of fantastic idealism, indeed, he remains alone without a rival. Now that novels tend to become coloured photographs of commonplace life, the gift of exuberant imagination is as precious as it is rare. And when to inexhaustible fancy is added the charm of curious felicity of form, we all feel that something has been done to redeem our literature of to-day from the charge of monotonous mediocrity and patient copying of obvious fact.

Even yet, amidst the brilliant success of these romances, the world has hardly recognised how rare a gift is that of Hewlett; and even his early admirers do not always grasp the sum total of his original creations. I am only too conscious that in points of substance, as well as of form, I am not the best fitted to do him justice, for my own pursuits lead me to historical facts, social and ethical problems;

whilst in language, my taste is ever for the plain and direct words, such as the average man can grasp. As this essay is an attempt to explain Hewlett, not to praise him, I shall not hesitate to say squarely where I cannot go with him in matters of ethic and in mannerism of phrase — admitting that prose can never be an adequate measure of any poetry — least of all of the poetry of imagery, fancy, and mysticism. But, bound over to prose realism as I am, and by temperament alien to all innuendo, euphuism, and forms of trope, I am carried away by the fantastic magic of these masques, fairy tales, and *chansons de geste*, whilst, in spite of my cooler judgment, I am charmed by the artful mosaic of word-painting and word-conundrums with which each page dances and scintillates.

The peculiar note of fantastic idealism (in which I make bold to say Hewlett has no living rival) was struck in his first romance; and the *Forest Lovers* (1898) still remains the typical Hewlett. Later books show historical insight, brilliant colour, subtle psychology, a wider grasp of human life, of the genius of various epochs and races. But the fantastic imagery, the sympathy between man and nature, the wild passion of adventure — all glow in the dissolving fairy scenes of Morgraunt Forest; and these same qualities run through the whole series of these "Gestes." This is their proper title, as Ben Jonson says:

> The gestes of kings, great captains, and sad wars.

Rather, perhaps, they are romances of adventure, as Chaucer has it:

> The halle was al ful, I wis,
> Of hem that writen olde gestes.

Hewlett's books, even his historical and topographical pieces, are "olde gestes" — that is, romances in prose as to form, but in essence poetry, as were the *Decameron* or the *Morte Darthur*.

These "Gestes" of his have often an ideal world of their own, wholly unconscious of time, place, or reality. They have no known country, take place in no recorded age, and are not bound by laws of material nature or crude common sense. You might as well ask when and where the Nibelungs came to King Etzel's land — search museums of archæology for Cinderella's slipper — and show us in ruins the castle of Uther Pendragon. The overture to the *Forest Lovers* sounds the dominant note. "My story," says our Troubadour, "will take you into times and spaces alike rude and uncivil. Blood will be spilt, virgins suffer distresses; the horn will sound through woodland glades; dogs, wolves, deer, and men, Beauty and the Beasts will tumble each other, seeking life or death with their proper tools. There should be mad work, not devoid of entertainment." Yes! In these tales there is almost always "mad work," but it is never "devoid of entertainment."

The author of these "masques," "extravaganzas," "visions," or allegories begs us "not to ask him what it all means, or what the moral of it is." "Leave everything to me," he says. So we do. We would as lief ask him to explain Isoult la Desirous as we would ask Spenser what were the other six virtues, and what became of them, or in what order of Mammalia the Blatant Beast was classed. We do not cross-examine poets. As Browning said, "God knows what I meant!"

The *Forest Lovers* was the first of his books I saw, and I still think it his true type. It was the rapid improvising of an omnivorous reader of poems, romances, old ballads; Provençal "Chansons"; "Fabliaux," French, German, Italian; Decameronic "Novelle"; Orlandic epics; sagas,

folk-songs; Spenser's *Faërie Queene,* and Sidney's *Arcadia.*
It was more mediæval than Elizabethan; more Italian than
English; more redolent of Malory and Ariosto than of Spenser
and Tasso. He calls out in his first lines — "blood will be
spilt"; "there will be mad work":

> Le donne, i cavalier, l' arme, gli amori,
> Le cortesie, l' audaci imprese io canto.

Our Maurice must have a foreign strain in his pedigree.
There is a touch of the *diavolo incarnato* in this Inglese
Italianato, with his "mad work," his taste for "bloody
work."

What we are to make of *Pan and the Young Shepherd*
(of the same year 1898), I will not venture to say. This is
clearly poetry, a masque, an extravaganza, or what not —
something made out of echoes of Aristophanes and Ben
Jonson. As we see it as a play, we try to solve its mysteries,
but anything less dramatic can hardly be conceived as the
book stands. The *Dramatis Personæ* are the great god Pan,
who talks like a tipsy tramp, seven immortal daughters of
earth, Aglae and her sisters, who sing Shelleyan stanzas,
shepherds and carters with Greek names: — Geron, Teucer,
Mopsus, who talk north-country brogue — "Gi' us a snack,
wenches; this Piphany Eve." The wench calls Pan "gaffer,"
"jail-bird," "rope-ripe villain," "old knave." She boxes his
ears as an "old gallus-bird," when Pan makes rustic love,
but she is ready to marry him at last, as Parson "Sir Topas
would christianise a he-goat." And the masque ends in a
carol with the true country-side ring. What it all means,
in what vein of ideas this medley of Hellenic mythe, plough-
boy roystering, and moorland witchery took form in verse
and drama, we need not inquire. The old shepherd believes
not in God, but "in sheep, and a bulging stocking 'gainst the
rheumatics." The young Shepherd believes in the seven

sisters — trees by the tarn — who sing o' nights. The immortal and arboreal sisters *do* sing thus:

> We ride at our will o'er the bonny wild moor,
> Air is our fee, and the deep brake our demesne.

The god Pan falls in love "with the sinew and tan of a country wench," who cuffs him soundly. And the yokels chaff him in true ale-house style. We do not often get such a medley of old and new, ethereal and coarse; but the Renascence often made it so, and loved it so. Nor can I deny that the thing has in it poetry, humour, learning, mother earth, and human nature.

If the *Forest Lovers* and *Pan* have no possible date or local colour, this cannot be said of the later tales, some of which, like the *Little Novels of Italy*, *Richard*, *Queen's Quair*, and the *Fool Errant*, are dated to a year, or a decade, and have very vivid and exact painting both of place and race. One of the interesting gifts of this writer is his power to take us first into a fairy world full of goblins, wonders, and mysteries, and then to whirl us into scenes alive with the historical fidelity of Macaulay or Carlyle. And these two worlds are never far apart. The vein of weird fantasy and historical realism runs through all the tales. The yokels who heckle the god Pan over their ale might have come out of Thomas Hardy's Wessex. Brother Bon-Accord in Morgraunt tells another Canterbury Tale in perfect good faith. When Hewlett leaves fairies, sorceresses, and knights-errant, he can be as grim and sanguinary as the *Nibelungen Lied* or the Elizabethan dramatists. He calls his hearers round him, crying:

> For God's sake, let us sit upon the ground
> And tell sad stories of the death of kings: —
> How some have been deposed, some slain in war,
> Some haunted by the ghosts they have deposed:
> Some poison'd by their wives, some sleeping kill'd.

The fierce passions and catastrophes of kings and queens, lords and ladies, captains, dare-devil swordsmen, lovely beggar-maids whom King Cophetua raises to a throne and generally strangles — these are the puppets of the show. They are almost all from the south; Italians, Provençals, or French — usually living in Italy itself —never in our own England in any modern era. Hewlett is ever *Inglese italianato*, even if he is painting an English man or woman.

His special field is Italian life in the age of the Renascence. He has painted its beauty, its intense life, its poetry, its delirium of lust and blood, with a colour and a glow that we hardly get from the laborious learning of Symonds, Sismondi, and Burckhardt all together. It has the fascinating vitality of Cellini's *Memoirs*. I take the *Little Novels of Italy* to be as true a tableau of the *quatrocento* as an oil painting by Pinturicchio or a fresco by Signorelli. Indeed, I hold the "Madonna of the Peach Tree" to be as perfect a short story as we have had in our time. Its local colouring charms all who love Verona and have lingered in the moonlight round the tombs of the Scalas, or chaffered for fruit in the market-place. It has humour, poetry, pathos, mystery, imaginative history, and a pure humanity. In Hewlett's gallery of portraits I remember no woman so sweet as the lowly Vanna Dardicozzo, nor do I know a more finished tale in contemporary romance.

Hewlett knows Italy, and its story from Dante down to Tasso and Alfieri, as hardly another Englishman since Symonds does. Each Italian city and province, nay, each castle, cathedral, or palace, seems to him to have its own history, temperament, patriotism. Each kindles in him a new dominant note. Verona, Padua, Romagna, Pistoja, Ferrara, are to him as different as Oxford, York, and Edinburgh to us. Each has its proper record. The tyranny of the

Despot, the intrigues of Monks, the affectation of Academics, the ruffianism of the Condottieri, the conceits of the Sonneteer, the pomp of the Palace — furnish in turn the themes of a novel which may be far too gruesome to suit the lovers in the *Decameron*, but which paints to the life the times of Sforzas, Baglionis, and Borgias.

There was so much of historical insight, antiquarian realism, in Hewlett's earlier legends that it was inevitable but that he should set himself the task of reproducing an elaborate picture of a past epoch. This he has done twice on a great scale — with, perhaps, over-much elaboration. I said so much about *Richard Yea-and-Nay* when it first appeared (*Fortnightly Review*, January 1901) that I need not discuss it again. Five years have only deepened my conviction that it is a fine and original romance in the great style. It is a true historical picture of a wonderful epoch, with archæological realism, with learning sound and wide, and insight into the nature of its typical men and women. As I said, "such historic imagination, such glowing colour, such crashing speed, set forth in such pregnant form, carry us away." It pictures to us the wild times and the wilder heroes of the twelfth century, with more living force than we find in contemporary chronicles, or in "standard" histories. It makes us understand the glamour which for seven centuries has hung round the memory of the Lion-Heart, in spite of the savage vices with which sober history has stamped him.

I need not enlarge on matters wherein I could not follow the method employed — the incessant change of scene, country, type of society, manners, and religion; the fantastic improbabilities in the action; the bewildering adventures of knights-errant, troubadours, and disguised damsels. Nor am I a convert to all the archaisms, conceits, and tropes which make some passages as hard to read as a chorus of

Æschylus. Much as I enjoy quaint old words, the tooth-some phrase, the classicalisms, mediævalisms, italianisms, which bestar the page (it is a catching trick of speech!), I draw the line at such Osricism as an altar lamp "that hinted at the Son of God," — "flying flags" for blushing; the "sun putting the air to the sword," *e.g.* a hot day. Not only are these forced conundrums of speech impertinent in a long narrative, but they disturb the attention from the story, and make it halt and limp.

The second great historical novel, *The Queen's Quair*, has the same features as the *Richard* — the same historical elaboration, the same vivid realism, the same ingenuity of phrase. I shall say less about it, for it is less to my taste, perhaps because Mary Stuart has always been to me an odious minx, interesting only in the moment of her death. The story seems to me more complicated, crowded, and bewildering than that of *Richard* — whilst the age is far less romantic, and the persons far more coarse. The Hewlettisms of phrase, if rather less profuse, are not so much in keeping as they seem in the chronicle of Abbot Milo. The story of the Queen of Scots has had a splendid success with the public, and if I find her less romantic than Richard it is my own fault. But Hewlett is at his best in the Middle Ages and the Italian Renascence. His imagination is so singularly hot and fanciful that the banality of modern life repels him. For that reason I wish the fascinating adventures of the *Fool Errant* had befallen an ancestor of Francis Strelley in 1521 rather than a young squire in 1721. The Georgian age, even in Italy, had but a languid turn for extravagant peregrinations; and there is incongruity in an English gentleman of the times of Swift leading the life of Benvenuto Cellini. But all the same, no living Englishman could have painted such a Fool as Francis or such a Queen as Mary.

Now that I am in a warning mood I would advise him to stick to the age of Plantagenets, the Cinquecentists, and the Humanists — to indulge his genius for the legendary and fantastic — to produce "Fabliaux" rather than histories. His short stories are perfect: his simpler style inimitable. In romantic colouring of Italian Humanism he has no living rival — even if he ever had an equal. He should choose no canvas of an encyclopædic scale — no world-history, no panorama of whole epochs. Some day he will give us the picture of an adorable woman, who is neither a beggar-maid bred in a hovel, nor a high-born dame who defies all the decencies of her station. It has become almost a mannerism of our troubadour that his heroines are starvelings in rags, who follow the hero about like lap-dogs, and are never happy till their lover brutalises them. It is then discovered that these Cinderellas and Griseldas are noble ladies ready to die for "their masters."

His theme is ever spasmodic Love and homicidal Death as conceived in the Italian Renascence. It is high time to give us some less passionate and less sanguinary scenes. The Hypnerotomachia of the fifteenth century alarms too many readers in the twentieth. Mudie's subscribers must have books that they can read without a dictionary, and will not ask for books of which the very titles puzzle them. They read him with avidity, as it is. But how few of them know that English literature has now a writer who may yet reach a place in the front rank of that illustrious band which for five centuries has carried on the torch from age to age.

IMPRESSIONS OF AMERICA

1901

IF you would fully grasp all that the geographical conditions of the American continent imply, you should cross the Atlantic in its winter gales, and travel far to the west with the thermometer sinking down towards zero. No imagination can bring home to you this vast isolation and this boundless expanse, until, for some eight days, you have watched your great ship as it ploughs across these inexhaustible waters at the rate of a South-Eastern Railway train, seeing nothing but waves, clouds and sky, so that the lonely monotony of this enormous ocean seems to try the nerves at last. And then, when the express train thunders on, day and night, across the Allegheny mountains to the west, a journey that would suffice to cross Europe just brings you over but a moiety of the space that divides the Atlantic from the Pacific.

Make this voyage and try to conceive what it must mean to the ordinary emigrant rather than to the luxurious tourist, and you will begin to understand how far outside of Europe is this American continent; how completely it offers a new life, a fresh start, a world detached, on a virgin soil unencumbered with our antique civilisation and its burdens. Again, make this westward journey by rail, and watch how the emigrant has to make it, and you feel an awakening sense of the boundless area, the inexhaustible resources, the infinite varieties of the transatlantic hemisphere, which for practical purposes has only just begun to take its place in these latter days in the secular life of humanity as a whole.

America is detached from Europe by a gulf which, however trivial it seems to the summer tourist in his luxurious state-room and saloon, has been a veritable "middle passage" to millions and millions of American citizens and their parents — a gulf which the "Upper Ten thousand" cross backwards and forwards as we go to Paris or Rome, but which seventy millions of American citizens never cross or recross. To them our Europe is a far-away world, of which but faint echoes reach them, which they will never see more, which can never directly touch their lives; whilst the vast expanses and inexhaustible resources of their own continent are brought home to them, day by day, in a thousand practical and visible ways.

And yet the paradox strikes my mind that American life, such as a passing visitor finds it in the great cities, is essentially the same as our own; that, in spite of the geographical isolation and the physical conditions, the citizen of the United States is at heart much the same man as the subject of King Edward; that life is the same, *mutatis mutandis*; that the intellectual, social, and religious tone is nearly identical; that the proverbial differences we hear of have been absurdly exaggerated. Put aside trivial peculiarities of language, manners, habit or climate, admit a certain air of Paris in New York, and a certain European tone in Washington — and these only concern small sections in both cities — for my part I noticed no radical difference between Americans and Englishmen. Physically, they are the same race, with the same strength, energy, and beauty; except for superficial things, they live the same lives, have the same interests, aims, and standards of opinion; and in literature, science, art and philosophy, the Atlantic is no more a barrier between our two peoples than is St. George's Channel or the Tweed in the British Isles. The citizen of the United States seems to me very much what the citizen of the United Kingdom is — only rather more accentuated. The differences are really on the surface, or in mere form.

I do not forget all that we are told about the vast proportion of non-American people in the United States: that New York and Chicago contain "more Germans than any city but Berlin, more Irishmen than Dublin, more Italians than Venice, more Scandinavians than Stockholm, and" (they sometimes add) "more sinners than any place on earth." Statistics give us the facts, and of course there is no sort of doubt about the immense degree in which the States are peopled by a race of foreign birth or origin. In the eastern slums of New York, in the yards and docks of the great cities, one sees them by myriads: Germans, Irish, Italians, Swedes, Russians, Orientals, and negroes. But those who direct the State, who administer the cities, control the legislatures, the financiers, merchants, professors, journalists, men of letters — those whom I met in society — were nearly all of American birth, and all of marked American type. I rarely heard a foreign accent or saw a foreign countenance. The American world is practically "run" by genuine Americans. Foreigners are more *en évidence* in London or Manchester, it seemed to me, than they are in New York, Philadelphia, or Boston. The reason is that foreigners are not so easily assimilated here.

It is my own impression (of course, I can pretend to nothing but an *impression* at a first glance) that in spite of the vast proportion of immigrant population, the language, character, habits of native Americans rapidly absorb and incorporate all foreign elements. In the second or third generation all exotic differences are merged. In one sense the United

States seemed to me more homogeneous than the United Kingdom. There is no State, city, or large area which has a distinct race of its own, as Ireland, Wales, and Scotland have, and of course there is nothing analogous to the diverse nationalities of the British Empire. From Long Island to San Francisco, from Florida Bay to Vancouver's Island, there is one dominant race and civilisation, one language, one type of law, one sense of nationality. That race, that nationality, is American to the core. And the consciousness of its vast expansion and collective force fills the mind of American citizens, as nothing can do to this degree in the nations of western Europe.

Vast expansion, collective force, inexhaustible energy — these are the impressions forced on the visitor, beyond all that he could have conceived or had expected to find. It is borne in on him that he has come, not so much to another nation as to a new continent, inhabited by a people soon to be more numerous than any two of the greater nations of western Europe, having within their own limits every climate and product between the Tropics and the Pole, with natural resources superior to those of all Europe put together, and an almost boundless field for development in the future. Europeans, being in touch with the eastern seaboard, do not easily grasp the idea how fast the population, wealth, and energy of the United States are ever sweeping to the west. It is an amusing "catch" when one is told that the central point of population of the United States is now at Indianapolis, nearly a thousand miles west of Boston; that the geographical centre of the United States since the acquisition of Alaska is now west of San Francisco. It is [1901] long since an Eastern State man has been elected President, and we are told that there will never be another. The political centre of gravity is now said to lie in the Mississippi Valley. And the destined metropolis of the United States will soon be Chicago or St. Louis. Chicago, with its unlimited area for expansion north, west, and south, and its marvellous site on the vast inland seas, may prove to be, in a generation, the largest, richest, and most powerful city in the world.

CHICAGO

Chicago, to which I was invited to give the annual address in commemoration of George Washington, was the first city in the United States in which I sojourned; and it naturally interested me much It did so, amongst other things, because I am older than the city itself. At my own birth, I learn, it was a village in a swamp with 100 inhabitants, and I heard of a man now living who has killed bear on the site of the Central Lake Park. Although it is said to extend over a space of some thirty miles, it has vast edifices of twenty stories, and its banks, offices, public buildings and halls show a lavish profusion of marbles, granite, and carved stone. It is not a beautiful city, though it has great natural opportunities on its level lake shore; and perhaps, as whole streets have been bodily raised upwards by machinery many feet, it is conceivable that it may be made a fine city in time.

Chicago struck me as being somewhat unfairly condemned as devoted to nothing but Mammon and pork. Certainly, during my visit, I heard of nothing but the progress of education, university endowments, people's institutes, libraries, museums, art schools, workmen's model dwellings and farms, literary culture, and scientific foundations. I saw there one of the best equipped and most vigorous art schools in America, one of the best Toynbee Hall settlements in the world, and perhaps the most rapidly developed university in existence. My friends of the Union League, themselves men of business

N

proud of their city, strongly urged me to dispense with the usual visit to the grain elevators and the stockyards, where hogs and oxen are slaughtered by millions and consigned to Europe, but to spend my time in inspecting libraries, schools, and museums. No city in the world can show such enormous endowments for educational, scientific, and charitable purposes lavished within ten years, and still unlimited in supply.

In a country like the United States, where every principal city is struggling to become the first, and every second-rate town is struggling to reach the front rank, there is much jealousy between the competing cities. And Chicago, the youngest of the great cities of the world, is the butt of the wits of New York and Washington. I was, no doubt, fortunate in the conditions under which I saw it, but the impression left on my mind was that the citizens of Chicago were bringing their extraordinary enterprise to bear quite as much on social, intellectual, and artistic interests as they confessedly do on grain, ham, steel, and lumber. They will have to dispel and outlive the evil character their food "rings" and syndicates have acquired, if they are to hold their own in the future of civilisation. For the manifest destiny of Chicago is to be the heart of the American continent.

For energy, audacity, and enterprise, the Chicago people are famous even in the Western States of America. "When I come to London," said a leading man of business, "I find your bankers and merchants stroll into their offices between ten and eleven in the morning. I am at my desk at seven," said he, "and by noon I have completed fifty transactions by telephone." Telegrams, in fact, are no longer up to date in the United States, and few busy men ever use a pen except to sign their names. They do not even dictate their letters. They speak into a phonograph, and have their message type-written from the instrument. Life in the States is one perpetual whirl of telephones, telesemes, phonographs, electric bells, motors, lifts, and automatic instruments. To me such a life would not be worth living, and the mere sight of it is incompatible with continuous thought. But business seems to be done in that way. And I did not learn that the percentage of suicide or insanity was very seriously increased by these truly maddening inventions.

No competent observer can doubt that in wealth, manufactures, material progress of all kinds, the United States, in a very few years, must hold the first place in the world without dispute. Its population will soon double that of any nation of western Europe. That population will have an education second only to that of Germany and Switzerland, and superior to that of any other European nation. The natural resources of their country exceed those of all Europe put together. Their energy exceeds that of the British; their intelligence is hardly second to that of Germany and France. And their social and political system is more favourable to material development than any other society ever devised by man. This extraordinary combination of national and social qualities, with vast numbers and unbounded physical resources, cannot fail to give America the undisputed lead in all material things. It is a curious instance of the power of national egotism that Europe fails to grasp this truth — that Germans, with their wretchedly poor country, narrow seaboard, and scanty rivers, ports, and minerals, still aspire to the first place; that Frenchmen fail to see how their passion for art, rest, and home has handicapped them in the race for supremacy in things material; that Britons, in their narrow island and their comfortable traditions, will not recognise that the industrial prizes must ultimately go to numbers, national unity, physical resources, geographical opportunities, trained intelligence, and restless ambition.

Enormous material triumphs obviously have their moral and intellectual evils. And one is constantly led to fancy some parallels between modern America and old Rome at the close of the Republic and the rise of the Empire. The sudden possession of vast areas to be exploited, the control of enormous masses of skilled workers, the rapid acquisition of all the resources the world can offer by men bred in hard work and having unbounded energy and ambition — these are common to the Rome of Cicero and Julius, and to the United States of Grover Cleveland and William M'Kinley. Paradox as it sounds, I was constantly reminded of the old stories of Crassus, Lucullus, and the Cæsars when I saw the lavish profusion of marbles, carvings, and mosaics in public and private buildings — so many a *porticus metata decempedis* — the wanton luxury which seems inspired by a mania of rapidly squandering the riches that have been so rapidly acquired. Wealth is acquired in Europe by slow stages and usually in more than one generation. In America it comes in a few years to men whose boyhood was usually passed in hardship or severe effort. The sudden mastery of enormous sources of power is the peculiar fact of American society — and its special form of temptation. It is often said, "From shirt sleeves to shirt-sleeves needs only three generations." Such power is not seldom used well, generously, and with public spirit. Very often it is used ill, with vulgarity, cruelty, folly, and selfishness. In any case, it knows nothing of the social conventions, habits, and traditions which, for good and for evil, control the use of wealth in modern Europe.

DEMOCRACY

The characteristic note of the United States is to be found in this freedom of the individual — the *carrière ouverte aux talents* — in a sense which is unknown to Europeans and can hardly be conceived by them. Every one of these seventy millions — at least of whites — has an "equal chance" in life. A first-rate education, comfort, and "betterment" are within the reach of every youth and girl of average capacity and industry. Most of the men eminent in business, politics, or literature began life by " teaching school." Every messenger boy or machine-hand may be an embryo President of the United States, of a railroad, or a bank, a powerful journalist, or a millionaire. Every lad seems conscious that this is open to him, and most of them live and work as if they meant to try for this end. Every girl at a type-desk or a telegraph office may live to reside in Fifth Avenue, or — who knows? — in the White House. And the ease with which the youth and girl adapt themselves to new careers and wider functions is one of the wonders of American life. Europe, even France, is organised more or less on the caste system, where only the rare exceptions pass from one social rank or office to another from time to time. America is the only land on earth where caste has never had a footing, nor has left a trace. But this (be it said) is true of the white race alone.

Rare as the prizes are, though the chances are millions to one against the winning, the possibility is ever before man, woman, and child. And this infinitesimal chance, this not absolutely impossible hope, colours life in the New World; so that, in spite of all the slum horrors of New York and Chicago, and all the industrial pressure of this furious competition, populist agitation, and anarchist outbreaks, the proletariat of Europe has good ground for looking to the United States as the paradise of Labour. New York, San Francisco, Chicago, and Philadelphia may swarm with the disinherited of other continents, but the standard of material well-being in the United States for highly-trained artisans reaches a far higher point than has ever yet been attained by the labouring mass of civilised men.

The ease with which men can pass from one locality to another, from one climate to another, from one business to another, the entire absence of social barriers or class distinctions, the abundant means of technical and scientific education, leave it open to each man and woman to make their own lives. The vast continent, with its varieties of climate and soil, produces almost everything except champagne, diamonds, and ancient buildings. With New York and San Francisco, the two grandest natural ports in the world, open to the ships of the Atlantic and the Pacific, with Chicago or St. Louis as the centre of traffic, the clearing-house of this boundless trade, the material prosperity of the American continent must reach in the twentieth century a height of which the nineteen centuries before it never dreamed. When the Englishman talks about the evils of Protection and the benefits of Free Trade, he is reminded that the United States occupies a continent self-sufficing, except for a few luxuries, which has its own Free Trade on a gigantic scale, over an area far larger than all Western Europe. It seems impertinent to lecture men about their neglect of Free Trade, when in their own country they can travel in every direction thousands of miles without ever meeting a Customs frontier. They insist that they are the greatest Free Trade people on earth.

Of course, for the American citizen and the thoughtful visitor, the real problem is whether this vast prosperity, this boundless future of theirs, rests upon an equal expansion in the social, intellectual, and moral sphere. They would be bold critics who should maintain it, and few thinking men in the United States do so without qualifications and misgivings. As to the universal diffusion of education, the energy which is thrown into it, and the wealth lavished on it from sources public and private, no doubt can exist. Universities, richly endowed, exist by scores, colleges by many hundreds, in every part of the Union. Art schools, training colleges, technical schools, laboratories, polytechnics, and libraries are met with in every thriving town. The impression left on my mind is that the whole educational machinery must be at least tenfold that of the United Kingdom. That open to women must be at least twentyfold greater than with us, and it is rapidly advancing to meet that of men, both in numbers and in quality. Nor can I resist the impression that the education in all grades is less perfunctory, amateurish, and casual than is too often our own experience at home. The libraries, laboratories, museums, and gymnasia of the best universities and colleges are models of equipment and organisation. The "pious founder" has long died out in Europe. He is alive in America, and seems to possess some magic source of inexhaustible munificence.

Libraries, of course, are not *learning*; museums and laboratories are not *knowledge*; much less is an enormous reading public *literature*. And, however much libraries may be crowded with readers, however spacious and lavish are the mountings of technical schools, and though seventy millions of articulate men and women can pass the seventh standard of a board school, the question of the fruit of all this remains to be answered. The passing visitor to the United States forms his own impression as to the bulk and the diffusion of the *instruments* of education; but he is in no better position than any one else to measure the *product*. The sight of such a vast apparatus of education, such demand for education, and that emphatically by both sexes, must create a profound impression. The *Cooper Institute* of New York, one of the earliest of these popular endowments, still managed and developed by three generations of the family descended from its venerable founder, the Jeremy Bentham of New York, is a typical example of a people's palace where science, art, and literature are offered absolutely free to all comers. But what is the result? Few Americans pretend that, with all the immense diffusion of elementary knowledge of science in the United States, the higher science is quite abreast of that of Europe. Of scholarship, in the technical sense of the word, in spite of the vast numbers of "graduates," the same thing may be said. And no one pretends that American literature rivals that of France in its finer forms — or indeed that of England.

The reason for this is not obscure, and it is hardly covered by the ordinary suggestion that the American people are absorbed in the pursuit of gain and material improvement. However much this may react on the intellectual world, the numbers of the American people are so great that numerically, if not proportionately, those who are devoted to science, art, and literature are at least as many as they are in England. The vast development of material interest is rather a stimulus to the pursuit of science than a hindrance, as the vast multiplication of books is a stimulus to authorship. But why suppose that a general interest in practical science conduces to high scientific culture, or that millions of readers tend to foster a pure taste in letters? The contrary result would be natural. Practical mechanics is not the same thing as scientific genius. And the wider the reading public becomes, the lower is the average of literary culture.

But other things combine to the same result. The absence of any capital city, any acknowledged literary centre, in a country of vast area with scattered towns, the want of a large society exclusively occupied with culture and forming a world of its own, the uniformity of American life, and the little scope it gives to the refined ease and the graceful *dolce far niente* of European *beaux mondes*, all these have something to do with a low average of lettered genius.

The lighter American literature has little of the charm and sparkle that mark the best writing of France, because, apart from national gifts of *esprit*, American society does not lend itself to the daily practice of polished conversation. After all, it is *conversation*, the spoken thought of groups of men and women in familiar and easy intercourse, which gives the aroma of literature to written ideas. And where the arts of conversation have but a moderate scope and value, the literature will be solid but seldom brilliant.

But all these conditions, if they tend in the same direction, are perhaps of minor importance. The essential point is that literature of a high order is the product of long tradition and of a definite social environment. Millions of readers do not make it, nor myriads of writers, though they read the same books and use the same language and think the same thoughts. A distinctive literature is the typical expression of some organised society, cultivated by long user and moulded on accepted standards. It would be as unreasonable to look for a formed and classical style in a young, inorganic, and fluid society, however large it may be and however voracious of printed matter, as to look in such a land for Westminster Abbeys and Windsor Castles. America will no doubt in the centuries to come produce a national literature of its own, when it has had time to create a typical society of its own, and intellectual traditions of its own.

Literature, politics, manners and habits, all bear the same impress of the dominant idea of American society — the sense of *equality*. It has its great side, its conspicuous advantages, and it has also its limitations and its weakness. It struck me that the sense of equality is far more national and universal

in America than it is in France, for all the pæans to equality
that the French pour forth and their fierce protestations to
claim it. "Liberty, equality, and fraternity" is not inscribed
on public edifices in the United States, because no American
citizen—or, rather, no white citizen—can conceive of anything else. The shoeblack shakes hands with the President,
and (in the absence of a Pullman) travels in the same car with
the millionaire. The millionaire has a very restricted household of servants, and they are more or less his masters, because the true-born American will not accept domestic service on any wages, and the Irish "helps" are the despair of
the housekeeper. The owner of a splendid mansion has to
ascend ten steps to his own door, because all Americans, and
even Irish helps, decline to live in rooms below the level of
the street. Thus the ground floor belongs to the domestic
"auxiliaries." The middle-class American citizen has to
black his own boots or walk out to a blacking stand, because
white American citizens will not perform so menial an office.
All this has its fine side, though perhaps the reaction from
European servility is carried to needless lengths. Is it natural, they say, that a lad who may live to be a senator or a
President, to found a university, or to control a railroad, should
black another citizen's boots? Should a cookmaid who may
live to drive her own carriage in Central Park put up with a
cellar-kitchen below the level of the street? Every soldier of
Napoleon carried a marshal's *bâton* in his knapsack. And
every American citizen has a Fortunatus' cap in his pocket,
if he only knew how to fit it on his head. And this he is
perpetually trying to do.

But this ingrained sense of the absolute equality of all
white citizens reacts on all things. The Congressman is, at
Washington, a successful politician; but, outside Congress,
he is one of seventy millions. A senator, a cabinet minister,

or a President, is merely a prominent citizen raised by ballot from the ranks, to return to the ranks when his term of office is up. The reaction from the divine right and hereditary privileges of the monarchies and aristocracies of Europe has led to slipshod habits in public affairs which scandalise the Old World and go much deeper than mere outsides.

Men who manage affairs of state in their shirt-sleeves are too apt to take a rough and ready view of life and of that which is becoming and right. The dominant social maxim seems to be *caveat emptor*. The paramount political maxim is *quod populus vult Deus vult*, or it may be *populus vult decipi, et decipiatur*. As Mr. Bryce has so well said, the sense of *noblesse oblige*, which still survives in Europe as a force constraining men in high office or in great social position, has hardly any equivalent in American life. The want of commanding social influence by men of great reputation and acknowledged standing makes itself felt in national and municipal affairs, in manners, in business, and in literature. A certain French philosopher who comes to England is wont to say at once, "You have an organised society; our society is inorganic, and no class or group exercises any social influence." All this has its bad side as well as its good side. So, in crossing the Atlantic, the observer finds that he has left a world more or less "organised" for good or for ill, and has come to a society which, for good or for evil, is organised only as a huge electoral machine. Public men in America are commonly accused of accepting the moral standards of the mass and of tamely yielding to the voice of majorities. Their excuse is that their fellow-citizens would resent their setting up superior standards of their own, and flatly refuse to accept any leadership from them. Where in England a man of ambition is constantly aiming to gain "influence," and is constantly considering "what is due to his own position," in

America he has little need to consider anything but what will satisfy the electors, and what is the average conscience of the larger number. He has no "position" to maintain.

The Capital

The ceremony of the Inauguration of the President and Vice-President at Washington on the 4th of March is, indeed, a characteristic and suggestive function. I had the good fortune to witness it this year [1901] under the most favourable conditions, and I was deeply impressed with all it represented. It summed up the vast extent and power of the United States, its absolute democracy, the simplicity, ease, and homeliness of its government, its contempt of forms, its entire confidence in itself and perfect satisfaction with its own ways. In the grand Capitol of the noble city of Washington, than which no finer edifice or city exists in the Old World, were gathered the men chosen by the adult citizens of a nation of some seventy millions, scattered over a vast continent. The President, Vice-President, senators, and representatives elected on this enormous ballot, entrusted with this stupendous power and wealth, sate indistinguishable from the ordinary citizens around them — clerks, secretaries, journalists, and casual friends, who were crowded pell-mell on the floor of the Senate House itself.

To this miscellaneous body, which might be any average county council or borough board, there entered a long file of ambassadors and Ministers in all the finery of European and Oriental courts; uniforms blazing with gold lace, plumes, velvet or fur, swords, sabres, and helmets; the Austro-Hungarian magnate, the stately ambassadors of Great Britain, Germany, France, and Russia, in their court uniforms, stars, crosses, and ribbons; Mr. Wu Ting-fang, the accomplished

Minister of China, in his buttoned head-dress and embroidered silks; the Japanese Minister, in European court uniform; the envoys of the smaller Powers of Europe, and then the diplomatists of the South American and Central American and West Indian States; black men, brown men, whity-brown men, in various gaudy uniforms; the Minister of the Sultan in his fez, those of Siam and Korea in their national dress — more than thirty in all, in every colour, adornment, and style representing men of every race, from every part of the planet.

This brilliant and motley group may be seen at St. Stephen's, or at the functions of Berlin and St. Petersburg, where it is only a natural part of similar bravery and feudal splendour. But here, in a hall crowded with sober citizens in broadcloth, without a star, a ribbon, or a sword between them, the effect was almost comic. Siam, Korea, Hungary, and Portugal as gay as butterflies! M'Kinley and Roosevelt matter-of-fact civilians, as if they were Chairman and Vice-Chairman of the London County Council! And around them were the chosen delegates of the great Republic, jostled in their own hall by pressmen, secretaries, and curious strangers like myself. The shirt-sleeve theory of government could hardly go farther, and, perhaps, need not go quite so far. My own republican soul was stirred when I set myself to think which of the two forms would prevail in the centuries to come. I thought first of the Roman Senate (according to the old myth), sitting immovable as statues in their white togas, when the Gauls of Brennus, in their torques and war-paint, dashed into the Senate House; and then I began to think, Were these quiet citizens seated there to see a comic opera at the Savoy Theatre?

Not that the representatives of the Republic are wanting in personal bearing. The President sate through the ceremonies with placid dignity, his fine features, in their stern repose, looking like a bronze figure of the Elder Brutus or Cato the Censor. At a personal reception in the White House Mr. M'Kinley will show as much grace and courtesy of demeanour as any Sovereign by divine right, and his smile and his voice are pronounced (not only by women) to be perfectly winning. The diplomatists of Europe agree in assuring us that nothing can exceed the tact and "correctness" which distinguish Mr. Hay, the accomplished Secretary of State. It is true that Congressmen (in their shirtsleeves) have not that repose of manner which marks the caste of Vere de Vere. But the men who are charged to speak in the name of the State will usually be found to rise to the occasion with that facility which enables every genuine American to adapt himself to play a new part, and to fulfil an unaccustomed duty.

It is no easy task to combine the conduct of vast interests, the representation of enormous power, with the ultra-democratic traditions of the absolute equality of all citizens. No sooner had the President summoned before him the splendiferous envoys of the whole world, than he passed out to the historic steps of the Capitol, to pronounce his Inaugural Address. As I stood near him and listened to the clear and keenly-balanced sentences, which the cables and telegraphs of the civilised world were carrying to expectant nations, I noticed how the crowd, a few feet only below him, was a miscellaneous gathering from the streets, like a knot in the Park listening to a Salvation preacher or a socialist orator on a Sunday, negroes and lads not the least vociferous in their applause, whilst on a platform fifty yards off there were mounted a dozen batteries of photographers, from kodaks to life-size lenses. The American public man — even the private man and woman — has always to reckon with the man in the street, journalists, and kodaks.

It is needless to point the moral of the difference between the Inaugural Address of a President, delivered in the open air to a miscellaneous crowd, and the speech of an European Sovereign opening Parliament. The one is an elaborate State paper, spoken by a citizen in frock-coat to a mob of his fellow-citizens in the street; the other is usually conventional platitudes, pronounced in a gorgeous palace with a scene of mediæval pageantry. It is the contrast between the monarchical survival and Republican realism. Kodaks, mobs, and vociferous negroes are not a necessary part of the government of a State. But the Presidential address from the steps of the Capitol is certainly more like that of Pericles on the Pnyx, or of Scipio and Marius on the Rostra, than our House of Lords; and it is conceivable that it may prove more agreeable to the practice of future republics in the ages to come. The President of the United States expounds his policy in a reasoned argument to all citizens who choose to hear him. The European monarch performs a traditional ceremonial to a crowd of stage courtiers who possess office without power and honour without responsibility.

The White House, as the executive mansion is called, is interesting for its historic associations, which exactly cover the nineteenth century, with its portraits and reminiscences of Presidents and statesmen, and its characteristic simplicity and modest appointments. It is not a convenient residence for a President with such great responsibilities. But, as a term of residence is usually so short, and the associations of the house are so rich, it would be a pity to change it for a pretentious modern palace. In the meantime the quiet old mansion, merely a fine Georgian country house in a pleasant park, serves to remind the American citizen of the democratic origin of his Chief Magistrate, who is certainly not yet an emperor. The White House was a residence suitable for men like Jefferson, Lincoln, and Grant; and it seems a not unfitting office for their successors.

The Capitol at Washington struck me as being the most effective mass of public buildings in the world, especially when viewed at some distance, and from the park in which it stands. I am well aware of certain constructive defects which have been insisted on by Ferguson and other critics; and no one pretends that it is a perfect design of the highest order either in originality or style. It will have one day to be entirely refaced with white stone. But as an *effective* public edifice of a grandiose kind, I doubt if any capital city can show its equal. This is largely due to the admirable proportions of its central dome group, which I hold to be, from the pictorial point of view, more successful than those of St. Peter's, the Cathedral of Florence, Agia Sophia, St. Isaac's, the Panthéon, St. Paul's, or the new Cathedral of Berlin. But the unique effect is still more due to the magnificent *site* which the Capitol at Washington enjoys. I have no hesitation in saying that the *site* of the Capitol is the noblest in the world, if we exclude that of the Parthenon in its pristine glory. Neither Rome nor Constantinople, nor Florence, nor Paris, nor Berlin nor London possesses any central eminence with broad open spaces on all sides, crowned by a vast pile covering nearly four acres and rising to a height of nearly three hundred feet, which seems to dominate the whole city. Washington is the only capital city which has this colossal centre or crown. And Londoners can imagine the effect if their St. Paul's stood in an open park reaching from the Temple to Finsbury Circus, and the great creation of Wren were dazzling white marble, and soared into an atmosphere of sunny light.

Washington, the youngest capital city of the world, bids fair to become, before the twentieth century is ended, the most beautiful and certainly the most commodious. It is the only capital which has been laid out from the first entirely on modern lines, with organic unity of plan, unencumbered with any antique limitations and confusions. The spacious avenues, intersected by very broad streets, all lined with maple and elm, and radiating from a multitude of "circles," its numerous parks and squares, with fountains, monuments, and equestrian statues at each available junction, its semi-tropical climate, for it is in the latitude of Lisbon and Palermo, its freedom from the disfigurements of smoke, trade, and manufactures, its singular form of government under a State autocracy without any municipal representation, give it unique opportunities to develop. As yet it is but half completed, owing to local difficulties as to rights of property; and it still has the air of an artificial experiment in city architecture. But within two or three generations, when its vacant sites are filled up, and public buildings, monuments, and statues continue to be raised with all the wealth, resources, and energy of the Republic, if the artists of the future can be restrained within the limits of good sense and fine taste, Washington may look more like the Rome of the Antonines than any city of the old world.

Mount Vernon

Of all that I saw in America, I look back with most emotion to my visit to Mount Vernon, the home and burial-place of George Washington. I saw it on a lovely spring day, amidst thousands of pilgrims, in the Inauguration week. On a finely-wooded bluff, rising above the grand Potomac river, stands the plain but spacious wooden house of the Founder of the Republic. It has been preserved and partly restored with perfect taste, the original furniture, pictures,

o

and ornaments supplemented by fit contemporary pieces. It enables one perfectly to conjure up an image of the homely, large, and generous life of the President before the war called him to the field, and after he had retired from all cares of state. We fancy him sitting under the spacious eastern portico, with its eight tall columns, looking out over the broad landscape of forest and river, or lying in his last sleep in the simple bed, with its dimity coverlet, and then laid to rest in the rural tomb below the house, which he ordered himself, and in which his descendants have insisted on keeping his remains. General Grant lies beside the Hudson at New York, in a magnificent mausoleum palpably imitated from the tomb of Napoleon in the Invalides. How infinitely more fitting and more touching is the Spartan simplicity of Washington's burial-place — an austere cell within his own ancestral ground; yet not a morning's drive from the splendid capital which the nation has named after its heroic founder — how much more fitting and more touching is this than is the pompous mausoleum to which they have carried the bones of the tyrant who ruined France ! It has been frequently attempted to remove from Mount Vernon, his home, the sarcophagus in which Washington lies, in order to place it under the dome of the Capitol. But as yet it has been wisely decided to do nothing which can impair the unique legend which has gathered round the memory of the western Cincinnatus.

In a country so flagrantly new as America, with every town and building striving to show its intense modernity, the few remnants even of eighteenth-century antiquity have a rare charm and a special value. They awaken an interest far beyond that of their actual beauty or quaintness, for they represent the only history of a country which has grown to be so vast and so different. Such relics as Mount Vernon, Independence Hall and Carpenter's Hall at Philadelphia, the

Common of Boston, the Green at Newhaven, and a few bits at Baltimore and old New York may still attract a traveller sated with the most picturesque corners of Europe. The history of the American soil is a very short record. But, such as it is, the American people seem very keen to cherish it in perpetuity. If the preservation of Mount Vernon and of Independence Hall as national monuments is the finest example of this, the most amusing instance is the rescue of the wooden cottage of Betsy Ross in Arch Street, Philadelphia, where the original "star-spangled banner" was constructed in 1777 and approved by General Washington.

Few Englishmen seem to know the history of the "Stars and Stripes." In its original form it was a not ungainly device, adapted from the undoubted arms of the English family of Washington. These were: *argent*, two bars *gules*, on a chief *azure* three *mullets* [stars] of the first [argent]. When the thirteen States of the Union resolved to adapt a national flag from the ancestral coat of their chief, this became "barry of thirteen, *gules* and *argent*, on a chief *azure* thirteen mullets of the second arranged in circlet." But when the other States were added, the "stars" began to be increased, until to-day the flag displays, on a canton *azure*, forty-five mullets *argent* in monotonous rows. Nothing more artless, confused, and unheraldic can be conceived.

An unlucky question was once put to me by a patriot, whether the "star-spangled banner" was not beautiful as a work of art. I was obliged to answer that, with all my veneration for the banner of the Republic, in my humble judgment it was (heraldically speaking) both awkward and ugly, unbalanced, undecipherable, and mechanical. It may be well to distinguish the Republican emblem from the feudal heraldry of the Old World, but it is a pity that the invention of the New World could not have devised an emblem with some claim to be clearly read and to look graceful. The thirteen *bars*, or stripes, have now lost their significance, and might in time disappear. A plain field, *semée* of "stars," would not be unsightly nor too difficult to distinguish. Forty-five mullets on a canton (*i.e.* a corner) in six regular rows are not easily visible at all, and, when perceived, are hardly elegant.

PROBLEMS TO BE SOLVED

America is making violent efforts to evolve a national architecture; but as yet it has produced little but miscellaneous imitations of European types and some wonderful constructive devices. A walk along the Broadway and Fifth Avenue of New York leaves the impression of an extraordinary medley of incongruous styles, highly ingenious adaptations, admirable artistic workmanship, triumphs of mechanics, the lavish use of splendid materials, and an architectural *pot pourri* which almost rivals the *Rue des Nations* at the Paris exhibition of 1900. There are some excellent copies of European buildings, such as the Giralda of Seville, Venetian palaces, Châteaux from Touraine, Palladian *loggie*, and here and there a German schloss. There are some beautiful revivals of fine art, such as the thirteenth-century Gothic of St. Patrick's, the Italian palaces of the Metropolitan and University Clubs, the Renaissance palaces of the Vanderbilts. Facing the Central Park, each millionaire seems to have commissioned his architect to build him a mansion of any ancient style from Byzantine to the last French Empire, provided only it was in contrast to the style of his neighbours. So commissioned, the artist has lavished skilful carving, singular ingenuity, and noble material in stone, marble, and mosaic. Many of these are interesting experiments and some are beautiful; but the general effect of such rampant eclecticism is rather bewildering.

In constructive novelties the American builder is consummate. Amongst these are the Brobdingnagian piles of twenty stories, the substitution of lifts for staircases, the construction of edifices of steel, the profuse use of stone and marble as ornaments rather than as material, the multiplication of baths, heating apparatus, electric and other mechanical devices, and the intensely modern and up-to-date contrivances which put to shame the clumsy conservatism of the Old World. Nothing in Europe since the fall of old Rome and Byzantium, not even Genoa in its prime, has equalled the lavish use of magnificent marble columns, granite blocks, and ornamental stone as we see it to-day in the United States. The Illinois Trust Bank of Chicago — a vast marble palace — is, I suppose, the most sumptuous and one of the most beautiful commercial edifices in the world; and its safety deposit vaults are among the sights of that city — magically opening as with an "Open Sesame."

The reckless use of precious marbles seems to threaten exhaustion of the quarries, but one is assured that they are ample for all demands. Why more use is not made in Europe of the magnificent marbles of America is not very obvious. But we certainly might easily adopt some of the constructive devices of their builders. Not, one trusts, the outrageous towers of Babel, in twenty or twenty-four floors and five hundred rooms, built of steel, and faced with granite as a veneer, which are seen in New York and Chicago, and hopelessly disfigure both cities. If these became general, the streets would become dark and windy cañons, and human nature would call out for their suppression. But the British architect has much to learn from modern American builders. In matters of construction, contrivance, the free use of new kinds of stone and wood, of plumbing, heating, and the minor arts of fitting, the belated European in America feels himself a Rip Van Winkle, whirled into a new century and a later civilisation.

As to the two burning problems of American society — the Labour question and the Negro question — it would be idle for a passing tourist to pretend to an opinion of his own. Certainly, there is not visible in the United States, even in the slums of New York, Chicago, or Philadelphia, anything approaching the acuteness and extent of the destitution to be seen in London, Liverpool, or Glasgow. The slums of American cities are filled, it is true, with the waifs and strays, failures and outcasts, from Europe, and are not of native American origin. But those who have made a comparative study of the life of the poor assure us that nowhere in the United States are the general conditions of the workman so threatening as they are too often in Europe, and the evils are certainly less difficult to cure. An influx of cosmopolitan misery has filled America with embarrassing problems, but the enormous resources of its continent, and the vast opportunities which its development affords, give Industry a free hand such as is elsewhere impossible and unknown.

The future of the Negro has always seemed to us in Europe the gravest of all American problems. And though I saw nothing to justify the extravagant stories we are told as to race antipathy and the ostracism of the negro, I was surprised and shocked to hear from men of great cultivation and humanity such sweeping condemnation of the negro race, such cool indifference to the continual reports of barbarous lynchings which appear almost daily in the public prints, and that in other than old Slave States. I should come to look on the race problem as incapable of any satisfactory solution were it not for such examples as that of Tuskegee and similar foundations. The life of Booker Washington, as told in his autobiography called *Up from Slavery*, is one of the most wonderful of our age. The story of the success in the education of the Negro achieved by this ex-slave, one of the most remarkable of living men, and by the white and coloured friends by whom he was assisted, may serve to convince us that the Negro problem may yet find a happy end.

About the prodigious luxury, extravagance, and money-making of the United States, of which we hear so much, a passing visitor has no right to dogmatise. America is a very rich country, where everything but raw material is very dear, where fortunes are made very rapidly, and where the scale of everything is raised in proportion. The sudden acquisition of wealth is more often the result of the vast numbers of those who deal in any market or buy any commodity, rather than of any abnormal development of the acquisitive instinct. The railroad, or corn, or oil "boss" becomes a multi-millionaire in a decade owing to the colossal scale of the railroad, corn, and oil trades. There are perhaps more rich men in America than there are in Europe, but then there are not so many poor men. There are costly mansions in New York city, though none on the scale of Stafford House, Bridgewater House, and Dorchester House. And there are no such royal palaces as Arundel Castle, Castle Howard, Longleat, and Mentmore. American millionaires do not own spacious parks, racing-studs, and deer-forests, nor are they surrounded by armies of tenants, dependants, servants, and equipages as are described in *Lothair*. They roll up fortunes, often automatically, owing to the wealth and numbers of the population in which their capital operates. And they lavish their rapid gains sometimes in houses, paintings, yachts, and banquets, and not seldom in schools, observatories, and museums. But I saw nothing to suggest that

wealth in America is worse acquired or worse applied than
it is in Europe.

I must repeat that I am giving nothing but the first impressions of a passing visitor who spent two months in the
United States for the first time in his life. Though I had
special opportunities to see from the central point the official
world, the universities, the literary and the commercial society, I am well aware that I brought away nothing more than
the thumb-nail sketches of an impressionist. But my impression is that the accounts we too often get of American life
are ridiculous exaggerations. English journalism distorts
and magnifies the caricatures it presents, just as American
journalism distorts and magnifies the traits of English life.

There are, no doubt, vices, blots, follies, and social diseases
on both sides of the Atlantic, but the proportion these bear
to the nation is grossly overstated by sensational literature.
As to the worship of the "Almighty Dollar," I neither saw it
nor heard of it; hardly as much as we do at home. I may
say the same as to official corruption and political intrigue.
Congress, ministers, magistrates in the United States seemed
to me to be a good deal of the same stuff as parliaments, cabi-
nets, and judges with us. There are a few good journals;
but the average Press seemed to me dull, trivial, provincial,
and harmless, however insipid. The yellow Press, the brutal
and gutter Press, I never saw nor heard of, nor did I meet any
one who read it. New York, of course, has the vices of great
cities, but they are not visible to the eye, and they are a drop
in the ocean of the American people. Even the passing tourist must note the entire freedom of American towns from the
indecencies that are paraded in European cities. The youngest girls go about the streets of New York alone; and a lady
travels unattended from San Francisco to Washington. I
received a deep impression that in America the relations of

the sexes are in a state far more sound and pure than they are in the Old World; that the original feeling of the Pilgrim Fathers about woman and about man has sufficed to colour the mental and moral atmosphere, and to give all sexual problems a new and clear field to develop in normal ways.

I close my impressions with a sense that the New World offers a great field, both moral and intellectual, to the peaceful development of an industrial society; that this society is in the main sound, honest, and wholesome; that vast numbers and the passion of equality tend to low averages in thought, in manners, and in public opinion, which the zeal of the devoted minority tends gradually to raise to higher planes of thought and conduct; that manners, if more boisterous, are more hearty than with us, and, if less refined, are free from some conventional *morgue* and hypocrisy; that in casting off many of the bonds of European tradition and feudal survivals, the American democracy has cast off also much of the æsthetic and moral inheritance left in the Old World; that the zeal for learning, justice, and humanity lies so deep in the American heart that it will in the end solve the two grave problems which face the future of their citizens — the eternal struggle between capital and labour — the gulf between people of colour and the people of European blood.

THE TRUE COSMOPOLIS

1896

THOUGHTFUL and patriotic men in all parts of Europe and America have welcomed various attempts to found some inter-communion of ideas between the nations of the West. All the chief tongues of Europe and all the leading minds of both continents may one day find a common ground for interchange of thought. Italian and Spanish are closely akin. As to Russia, so few of us read the Russian language, and educated Russians themselves read and write the chief European languages so freely, that they are always at home. The Hollander, the Dane, the Scandinavian, are usually familiar with German, French, or English — if not with all three. And much the same is true of the cultured world of South Eastern Europe. For practical purposes, then, an ideal COSMOPOLIS should from time to time unite the five chief languages of Western Europe.

There have been found some to doubt if there is any room or need for an international organ in these days of incessant travel and rapid diffusion over the civilised world of everything produced by the Press, whether permanent or fugitive. Of course, in this age of telegraphs, accelerated post, "trains rapides," "trains express," and the myriad-tongued journalism that circulates in every village, we *know* more of what is being done and said in European countries than our ancestors *knew*. Do we *understand* each other as well, do we *feel* the same joy in the art, literature, movements, and aspirations of foreign nations as was common enough in the age of Shakespeare, or the age of Voltaire, or of Hume, or of Goethe? It is no paradox to say that we do not. We *hear* about our neighbours far more than ever. We have less *sympathy* with foreign thought, we have far less of the Cosmopolitan genius, than was common in the most fertile epochs of the human mind.

One need not go back to the Middle Ages, when there was a learned language, a religion, a church, a system of education common to Europe, so that all men of superior culture were citizens of an intellectual commonwealth apart from any national distinctions. The great Universities had their "nations" who sometimes proceeded to contests even keener than our own inter-University "Sports"; but the superior minds could pass from one school to another and find themselves perfectly at home, irrespective of country. Let us recall for a moment what the University of Paris contained when the famous Dr. Sigier taught in the *Rue du Fouarre*, and a haggard Italian exile from Florence, whom we call Dante, listened to his lectures. When Albert the Great, Aquinas, John of Salisbury, Alighieri, Roger Bacon, Alexander of Hales, Ockham, Bonaventura, Raymond Lully, met, taught, or exchanged ideas, no man dreamed of asking if the professor or the pupil were German, or French, or English, or Italian, or Spaniard. That was a detail as unimportant as his native county or his local patois.

They all talked and wrote in Latin, pronouncing it in the same way, and they accepted one type of culture, regarding their civil allegiance to any sovereign lord at home as subordinate to their spiritual allegiance to Church and School. And so, when Petrarch left Florence for the valley of the Rhone or the valley of the Po; or when Chaucer travelled in

Italy and came home with the glow of the *Decameron* colouring his soul; or when Froissart travelled from castle to abbey round Europe, and was at home in every hall amongst knights, ladies, squires, and men-at-arms, wherever chivalry was a bond of intimacy, from the Grampians to the Pyrenees and the Apennines; when the Troubadours in Western or Meistersingers in Central Europe were welcomed in every barony; when the same Romances, the same Legends, the same Miracle Plays enchanted the audiences throughout all Europe in hall, town, abbey, or court — there was a fellowship of Thought and of Art that we have lost to-day.

We know very well that all this is dead and buried, and we know why it is gone, and that none but a few *codini* and Jesuits want to restore it. But we need not accentuate the national jealousies which make such an inter-citizenship impossible to-day. It was a vast gain to intellectual progress, to philosophy, and to art, to have a common language intelligible and familiar to all educated men. A great jurist remarked recently that the crucial difficulty in the way of a Code of English Law lay in the want of a strict legal tongue, and in the indistinct and various senses with which the same phrase was used in English decisions and commentaries. This is true of philosophy, of theology, of art amongst us now, especially for the English and the Teutonic races. A common language to-day is impossible, if for no other reason than that each of the great nations of Europe thinks its own national tongue ought to prevail, and in any case declines to admit the primacy of any other tongue. So we learn to read each others' languages, though we suffer grievously from wanting the precision and scientific terminology of Latin. Anyway, the cosmopolitan citizenship of the Mediæval University is gone for ever, for the same reasons that Mediæval Churchmanship and manners are gone. We cannot help it, and we cannot have it back. Since the age of Louis XI. and Charles V., the Emperor, we have been settling into *national*, and not European lines, and in the present age more than ever. The enormous increase of inter-communication due to steam, electricity, railways, and the press does not at all counterbalance the great increase of national pride, jealousy, and self-assertion fanned by patriotic dreams of Empire, Victory, and Leadership of the World. This is the ideal Culture of our martial and aggressive age, and it is *ex hypothesi* a national and not an European culture.

Then let such of us as do not care to be for ever bowing down the knee in the Temple of Nike Apteros, or of the Athene Pandemos of our own national tribe, offer up a prayer from time to time before the altar of the true and general Athene, Goddess of Wisdom and of healthy Knowledge, above all tribes or tongues. We are as true patriots as any: we will suffer no man's hand to be raised against our Fatherland, nor endure a word against its honour. But there is something more than Fatherland and wider than Patriotism. The supreme development of Humanity in all forms of civilisation needs the joint co-operation of many countries, and would languish under any narrow type of national self-sufficiency. The civilisation of Europe was assuredly not made by one nation, and it cannot be developed by one nation alone. It knows nothing of nations, of national tongues, of national schools. In one department of thought this is abundantly recognised. The physical sciences are European. A Darwin, a Helmholtz, a Pasteur, are of all nations, all schools, all languages. With the moral sciences, with philosophy, with politics, with criticism, with art, it is far otherwise. We have a philosophy far too local in its language and in its methods and aims; a theology and an ethic which are full of mere tribal antagonisms; a literature, an art, a romance, which are often so hide-bound in sectional and not human conventions and interests — that they are either unintelligible, insipid, or grotesque to readers belonging to some other party, school, or sect, and seem to come from another race familiar with different types.

THE RENASCENCE

When the Mediæval Church, language, education, had passed away, there arose a new general movement of ideas; the Renascence of the sixteenth century, which is so absurdly known by the French form of its name, though it was Italian in origin and European in result. Shakespeare and his contemporaries were saturated with Italian romance. Marlowe and *Faustus*, Spenser and Ariosto, Rabelais and Cervantes, remind us how far into modern times extended the freemasonry of the common genius of Europe. Benvenuto Cellini, the very much spoilt child of the Renascence, was as free of every great house in Europe as a German fiddler or an American globe-trotter is to-day. No doubt Shakespeare knew far less of Italian than an average girl in a high school, and even Erasmus or the Admirable Crichton — nay, Milton himself — were infants in cosmopolitan information when compared with Doctor Garnett or the editors of *The Athenæum* and the *Revue des Deux Mondes*. That is a very different thing. We are crammed with special erudition. We have on our library tables the *Transactions* of a hundred learned associations in eight or ten different languages. But I doubt if any living man to-day, whatever his genius or his learning, feels within his veins the throb of the European life-blood as did Shakespeare or Rubens, Cellini, Columbus, or Raleigh.

In spite of all the national and religious wars of the sixteenth and seventeenth centuries, philosophy at any rate managed to be neither national nor sectarian, and Bruno, Descartes, Hobbes, Spinoza, Grotius, and Leibnitz rose into the empyrean of an European point of view. The intellectual commerce between Voltaire and his eminent countrymen, with England on the one hand and Germany on the other hand, is one of the great landmarks in the history of modern progress. Trace the way in which the ideas of Hume, Gibbon, Adam Smith, and Bentham were received in France; the effect upon England of the ideas of Montesquieu, of Diderot, Rousseau, Voltaire, and Buffon; the union between Germany and Italy accomplished by Winckelmann, Lessing, and Goethe; the effect upon Italy and Greece of Byron and his fellow-enthusiasts; the effect upon Europe in general of Newton, of Pascal, of Kant, of Vico, of Leibnitz, of Hegel, of Comte — and we must admit that, with infinitely less *knowledge* of each others' books and discoveries, our forefathers in great epochs of human progress had a greater effective *communion* of ideas, a greater intellectual *solidarity*, than we see to-day in Europe.

One department of thought we must certainly except from this judgment — that of the exact and physical sciences. The European influence of a Darwin, a Helmholtz, a Pasteur, is in its way almost equal to that of a Newton, a Leibnitz, a Lagrange. Physical science has now no native country, and the true European communion of ideas is paramount in that sphere of thought. There may be rivalry of persons, of schools, of methods in physical science; this is at times most shamefully noisy and bitter; but there is practically in physical science no antagonism of nationality. The solidarity of work is almost perfect. Every man of exact science is bound to read the principal European tongues, and to follow the records of advance in all the chief European

Transactions. The Röntgen rays of physical science pierce the boundaries of nations as easily as they pass through the flesh of the hand or a wooden box. Exact science has gained enormously by the diffusion of books, papers, and instruments, and all the cosmopolitan appliances of the Press. This alone of all the departments of modern thought has won great success from our material civilisation, and yet has lost nothing by our national rivalries.

Now, why is it that in philosophy, in the moral and social sciences, in art, we fail to find the same solidarity, the same European *consensus* of thought? The answer is plain. Philosophy, moral and social science, even art, touch our pride, our passions, our ideals of life, in a manner that exact science does not. Exact science, with its dry light, does not stir emotions, disturb habits of conduct and standards of judgment, appeal to national ambitions or foibles. The discovery of the cholera bacillus or the geography of Mars cannot possibly kindle the fires of theological and political animosity. But a new theory of the Synoptic Gospels, an original view in the philosophy of Economics, a history of the French Revolution, or of Europe in the Nineteenth Century, instantly appeals either to *odium theologicum*, to the claims of the Churches and the hopes of their rivals, to the perennial war between Labour and Capital, or to the rancour of parties and the glorification of national triumphs. Take Mr. Ruskin to the *Salon* in Paris, and show him the colossal "Massacres," "Slave Markets," "Temptations of St. Anthony," and similar canvases with acres of gore and nudity, and we should have him deliver a prophetic homily worthy of Jeremiah at the Court of Jehoiakim. Ask Mr. Lecky to write us a review of Karl Marx, or the Bishop of Peterborough to write the history of the Papacy during the last half-century, or beg the Académie Française to explain why they did not elect M. Zola — we should then have something that would be highly entertaining, but would not tend to consolidate opinions in any European *eirenicon* of the higher criticism. We think, we teach, we write, we paint too much on sectional lines; and in our very philosophy, our history, our art, we are thinking first of our national Flag, and only secondly of the vanguard of human civilisation.

There can be as little doubt that this is so to-day, in a measure which some fortunate ages have been without, as there can be doubt to what it may be ascribed as a cause. The tremendous national wars that have been waged in Europe in the last forty-three years were on a scale more vast than anything known in Europe except in the age of Napoleon. It is true that most of these wars have been comparatively short. But they have called to arms so large a proportion of the entire population; they have led to such vast material efforts and changes; they have caused such intense spasms of patriotism and humiliation down to the very depths of the national feeling, that they have affected the temper of the nations of Europe perhaps in a degree hardly ever before known. The fact of war is far the least part of the phenomenon. The wars have not been long; and even the material losses and ravages of war have been replaced in five or ten years at the most. But they have led, even in time of unbroken peace and *entente cordiale*, to such huge and increasing armaments, they have stimulated national ambitions so fiercely, and they have so deeply infected the minds of all citizens alike with ideas of national aggrandisement or defence as the primary concern of a patriot, that they have inevitably tended to accentuate the national point of view and to weaken the European *consensus* of ideas — always, as I have said, with the exception of physical science.

I am old enough to remember the time when influential

P

schools of opinion and eminent men in England were deeply influenced by French thought, especially in things social, historical, political, and critical. They were the days of Guizot, De Tocqueville, Hugo, and Sainte-Beuve. In those days there still was a similar movement in France towards England, and many men of great mark were foolishly nick-named "Anglomanes." I remember dear old M. Barthélémy St. Hilaire telling me in 1895 — the last year of his long life — that he now stood alone in his desire for cordial relations and common sympathies between our two peoples. In the time when Bismarck was carving, not the map of Europe, but his fellow-students' cheeks and noses, there were "Gallomanes" in the Fatherland, where now no German can eat his dinner with a menu in French. Englishmen, Frenchmen, and Germans of course still read each other's books; correspond, meet, and discuss as much as ever, and perhaps more. But the Englishman who is in admiring sympathy with French ideas, or the Frenchman who loves to steep his spirit in German ideas, or the German who is "Gallomane" or "Anglomane," or the educated Englishman, or Frenchman, or German whose intellectual *Alma Mater* is the "Cosmopolis" of European thought — is, I firmly believe, far more rare than ever he was.

This is not the place to suggest any doubts as to the necessity for our mighty armaments on land and sea; and I for one claim to be as fervent a patriot as any of my neighbours. To pretend to be "Cosmopolitan," and superior to Country, is a puerile affectation for which I have neither sympathy nor mercy. As a Nationalist by conviction, I hold that Governments and States cannot be too entirely national for all political purposes, or too absolutely capable of defending their own nationality. But the interests of intellectual Progress are not confined within any boundaries of nation, and will assuredly be atrophied by any such narrow limitations. It deeply concerns all those who have at heart the true interests of intellectual Progress to strive to counteract the tendencies towards national jealousy and depreciation fomented by an age of gigantic preparations for war and the passion for commercial and political supremacy. Our knowledge of the literature of Europe, and our elaborate study of the last new work of the foreign Press, have too much of the character expressed by the old saying that "Familiarity breeds contempt." We need somewhat more of that sacred light of sympathy which inspired Diderot, Voltaire, and Montesquieu, and made them more than Frenchmen; which inspired Locke, Hume, and Gibbon, and made them more than Englishmen; which inspired Leibnitz, Lessing, and Goethe, and made them more than Germans.

It is true that very great mistakes were made in former ages by hollow or premature enthusiasms, and we do not wish to have them repeated. We want no "Anglomanes" nor "Gallomanes," nor "Inglesi Italianati," nor Teutonic "Welt-Geist" of any kind. The spurious and spasmodic fashion which suddenly discovers in another country a man of genius or a new school of thought or art is a very short-lived thing; it does nothing but harm to the country whence it is imported as to the country which adopts it. Ibsen, Tolstoi, and Zola are undoubtedly men of genius; but their reputation would be both more solid and more enduring if they had not been acclaimed by fanatical schools of followers as the evangelists of some new gospel that was to revolutionise human art. Ibsen suffers from his Ibsenites, Zola from his Zolaists, and Tolstoi from Tolstoyans.

We are often told that the wonderful development of travel in these days is a sovereign specific to make people of different nations understand each other better, and that the multiplication of railways, telegraphs, excursion tours, and postal facilities must end in establishing a family feeling — the true solidarity and fraternity of peoples.   It is a pleasing hope; but after a generation of Cooke's and Gaze's and other tourist companies, after "World Exhibitions" and "Cosmopolitan Fairs" in every capital of the East and the West, and a series of the "Greatest Shows on Earth" in every ambitious town of Europe and America, the jaded excursionist comes home rather to grumble than to praise; and, somewhat poorer both in purse and good nature, he is just in the mood to increase his armaments at home.   The American globe-trotter who bragged that, in his voyage round the Mediterranean, "he had given seven hours to the Eternal City," brought away but few new ideas as to the Quirinal or the Vatican.   And the English millionaire who reminded his courier "that they must not leave Rome without seeing the Colosseum" did not really assimilate much of the true genius of Italy.

It is no paradox to maintain that the great labour and slow course of travel in former ages really promoted a more thorough and intimate knowledge of the country and the people where the traveller — as distinct from the tourist — chose to wend his way.   Travelling went out with railways.   We are all tourists now, and tourists who come home with tales of the *chef* at the "Metropole" and the rifling of one's boxes on those Mediterranean lines.   When Dante and Chaucer, Froissart or Cellini, travelled in Europe, they had a far harder task; but they really lived amongst the people they visited.   Milton only travelled once in Italy, and Voltaire only came once to England; and Goethe, Byron, and Shelley never saw a tenth part of the countries that any Oxford tutor scampers across in a few vacations.   But these men took time, took pains, found means to be admitted into the societies they met, and lived long enough in each place to saturate them-

selves with its spirit.   Nowadays we have journalists, diplo-
mats, book-makers (in both senses of the word), miscellaneous men-about-town, who live in railway trains, like the
stokers or the guards, and who know as much of the countries
they "travel in" as if they had crossed them in balloons, getting up "Baedeker" as they sailed along.

When we read an old book of real "travels," such as
Goethe's *Italian Journey*, or Gibbon's *Memoir of my Life*, or
even, of our own age, those exquisite pictures of foreign life
in Ruskin's *Præterita* and his *Modern Painters* or *Stones of
Venice*, we see how the incessant whirl of locomotion that we
absurdly call "travelling" has actually robbed us of all real
intercourse with foreign nations.   Parcels forwarded by the
post do not "travel."   An active man of means and leisure
(some of them even without either means or leisure) will
make twenty, thirty, or forty "tours abroad" of a month or
two at a time, yet he will know less of other nations at the end
of his life than if, with fit introductions, he had spent one six
months rationally in any European centre.   He will *know*
less; but what is worse, he will come back with feelings more
akin to antipathy than sympathy — a more violent Jingo
than he went forth.   He has seen enough to despise, to pity,
or to dislike.   He has not seen enough to know, to understand, to enjoy.   He likes mountains, pictures, promenades,
and casinos.   "He never took to the queer ways of the
natives !"

We have just been celebrating (with trumpets attuned to a
somewhat minor key) the Jubilee of Free Trade; and the
rare foreign Abdiels, still faithful to that great economic
cause, have crossed the Channel to record their loyalty to the
faith.   Rational Englishmen are as staunch to the creed as
ever.   But they mournfully admit that they stand alone.
They have, with pain, to confess how strange were the illu-

sions that floated before Richard Cobden and his fellow-apostles when they looked to an increase in trade relations as certain to reduce armaments, and diminish international animosities. It was a dream from the ivory gate. Commerce, trade, and international intercourse have been multiplied threefold; but they have brought neither Free Trade nor Peace into the world. Yet by all the rules of logic, of common sense, and of obvious interests, they should have brought both. Cobden and Bright were right in their facts and correct in their reasoning. Free Trade is our true interest — the true interest of all settled peoples. And common material interests infallibly favour a policy of peace and of friendship. It is as certain and universal as the Law of Gravitation. Yet the predicted result did not follow.

Cobden and Bright and the apostles of Free Trade did not foresee — no man could foresee — other and stronger forces which neutralised the influence of material interests and overrode the communion of business relations. Charles Kingsley, and some men of greater genius, have gravely informed us that the Law of Gravitation is at times "suspended" by some occult power that desires to impress us. The advent of Free Trade and its beneficial issue in a millennium of Peace was not indeed "suspended," but it really was adjourned by the direct operation of a higher and stronger law. That law was the passion of national ascendancy and the glory of military triumphs. Mankind are governed more by their passions, sentiments, traditions, than by their interests and even their well-being. The great cause of International Free Trade, the far greater cause of International Sympathy, has been postponed into the centuries to come by a recrudescence of the warlike energies and the fierce race for primacy amongst the nations. The interests of Trade are even become the bar to Peace, the stimulus to War.

IMPERIALISM

It would be a long story to trace the rise, growth, and culmination of this mighty power over a period now of some fifty years, till it led to a renewal of European wars after a long peace of nearly forty years. The revival of material prosperity that the era of Free Trade opened did not a little to stimulate the growth of military and national ambition. The revolutionary upheaval of 1848–49 was at bottom the uprising of wealth and of labour against the worm-eaten absolutisms of Europe. Free Trade, no doubt, saved England from the violent struggles which went round Europe. The monarchies, the aristocracies, the governments of the Continent made a desperate rally, and entirely recast their civil and military organisation. The arts, and even the engines and machinery of war by land and sea, took a fresh departure soon after the revolutionary epoch and the reorganisation of governments and armaments which was represented by the Third Empire in France. Rifled guns, breech-loading guns, large and small, the concentration of armies by railways, rapid "mobilisation," steamships of battle, armoured vessels, the marine screw-propeller, big cannon, shell projectiles, machine guns, and all the scientific appliances of modern fortresses and modern ships of war, began to be in use soon after this epoch. Those of us who can remember *Brown Bess*, the old solid column of attack, men-of-war propelled by sails, having seventy-four guns muzzle-loading with round shot, — these have seen, as compared with the armies and fleets of to-day, perhaps the greatest, and certainly the most sudden, change in the arts of war that the world has ever witnessed, at any rate since the introduction of gunpowder. A single first-rate ship to-day would sink in an hour the entire fleet commanded in the Crimean War by

Napier or Lord Lyons, and Napier and Lyons would be less able to command such a ship than the lowest lieutenant in the navy.

From the middle of the nineteenth century the reorganisation of civil administration and the adoption of modern scientific methods went on nearly as fast, so that at the date of the Crimean War the Powers of Western Europe, with Italy added to their circle, found themselves in possession of vast organised forces, both military, marine, and civil, which had been rusting in store, as it were, for the long peace of forty years from the fall of the First Napoleon. The command of such tremendous armies, fleets, and budgets, and the knitting up of the nerves of national cohesion everywhere, roused new ambitions and led to distant adventures. The formidable mutiny and resettlement of India, the opening of Burmah, China, and Japan to Western arms and commerce, gave a warlike turn to commercial enterprise. The revival of Imperialism and the splendid armies of France led directly to the war with Austria and kindled the natural jealousies and ambition of Prussia. The Danish war, the Austrian war, the French war, followed in the next decade. And throughout the generation that succeeded the Franco-German war of 1870–71, the nations of Europe have been industriously augmenting their already tremendous military resources, whilst fiercely competing in a race with each other, half military, half commercial, to extend their Empires and their markets in Asia, in Africa, and in the seas of both Hemispheres. It is little cause for wonder, then, if, in the array of such rival forces, the cause of Free Trade stagnates, the cause of International Friendship wanes.

The key to all rational estimate of European, and even domestic politics, is to recognise that the dominant factor in politics to-day is the passion of national self-assertion, the struggle for national primacy. For right or for wrong, the great nations were all resolved to make themselves, without more delay, as big as they can be made; as formidable, as extensive, as rich as science or energy can make them; or at least to tolerate no other nation bigger than themselves. For this they are ready to sacrifice everything at home or abroad — their traditions, their safety, their credit, and almost their honour. This, and this alone, has planted in England the most powerful Conservative Government ever seen in our age. This has made the Republic in France frantically acclaim the fleets and servants of a despotic Tsar. This has made Prussia aspire to be a great naval power — a great African power. This has made Italy the enemy of France, Austria the friend of the Turk, and Russia the indifferent witness to the massacre of Armenian Christians. The private seeker of fortune may say, *Rem, quocunque modo rem.* The cry of the Nations is rather, "Empire, at whatever cost, at whatever risk, by whatever folly!"

There are, therefore, deep down in the heart of the great nations of Europe, overwhelming national tendencies which foster international jealousies and neutralise cordial relations, even in matters of intellect and taste. Physical science alone, with its appeal to material fact, is exempt from the effect of prejudice. The moral sciences, opinions, art, are far too liable to suffer from the contamination of political rivalry. And it behoves all those who (apart from the strife of politics) devote their lives to the moral sciences, to history, philosophy, criticism, or art, to clear their own field, their own minds, from the narrow prejudices of national chauvinism. Philosophy, social and moral science, the pursuit of truth, the creation of the beautiful, have no exclusive country; and they are often conspicuously fostered in the smallest countries, as far removed as possible from the roar of big capitals and the passions of dominant empires. How many of the best minds, how much of the immortal work of the world, came from solitary retreats into which no passion of national vainglory and jealousy was suffered to enter. Dante, Petrarch, Tasso, Byron, Shelley, were exiles, or sojourners in homes not their own. Erasmus, Descartes, Hobbes, Locke, Diderot, Voltaire, Priestley, Gibbon, did much of their best work in foreign lands or in distant retreats. The philosopher, the historian, the poet, the romancer, the artist, need always to have before them an ideal of *the best* — the best that ever has been — the best that they can give. And this *best* never is, never can be, in a narrow sense, *national*. This is the true COSMOPOLIS!

THE REGRETS OF A VETERAN
TRAVELLER

1887

WE are wont to smile over the fantastic but exquisite egoism with which Mr. Ruskin in *Præterita* records his boyish reminiscences of travel; but to any one who can remember what Europe was some forty years ago there come similar hours of despondency and keen regret. Railways, telegraphs, and circular tours in twenty days have opened to the million the wonders of foreign parts. But have they not sown broadcast disfigurement, vulgarity, stupidity, demoralisation? Europe is changed indeed since the unprogressive forties! Is it all for the better? I have no theories, no parable to take up, as Mr. Ruskin has; nor do I doubt that Watt, Stephenson, and Wheatstone were benefactors of mankind. But as I sit here, penned in my Alpine nest by a snowstorm, a few vain regrets will thrust themselves on the mind.

It is a moral change no less than a material change. True, one goes by steam in place of coach or boat; and lovers of the beautiful and the characteristic may well regret all that they lose thereby. But this loss is not a moral evil, nor is it compulsory. Mr. Ruskin can still drive (if it pleases him) in his own carriage from Calais to Venice. I go myself not unwillingly by rail; even though I can remember how delightfully one used to drive by the high road into Rouen, Geneva, Milan, or Florence. Ah! for the crack of the whip as one galloped down those Norman glades that shelve into the Seine, and for the sight of the sun rising in gorgeous wrath over the chain of Mont Blanc, as we toiled up the crest of the Jura in the twilight; for the white oxen who tugged as leaders up the steep slopes of the Apennines, and the chat with the village gossips at each post station; the midday halt, where one dived into castle, church, or old courtyard, the postillion lore of many countries, the chaffering for some local trifle, the queer but not untoothsome supper, the antique furniture of the *salon*, the early walk before the horses were harnessed, the local colour at every turn from morn till night — it is all gone. And we are carried now to Geneva or Milan like a box of game from Aberdeen to London. But there are changes far more profound.

Those who remember Europe before the Third Empire and the great wars of the last five-and-thirty years, know how deeply the outward intercourse of nations has been altered by all that has happened since '48. The Englishman who travelled then did not feel himself as in a mere time of truce in the midst of a war of races. The Frenchman was chatty, gay, outwardly courteous to all, and inwardly full of bright views of himself and his great nation. The German gave himself no airs, being perfectly happy if he could save some thalers by his superior information, and willing at all times to impart to all he met his inexhaustible stores of erudition and original views on things human and divine. The Italian was not a traveller. But the Italian or the Russian, if we met him, was the easiest and most versatile of travelling companions. Time was when travellers who supped at the same table could talk quite naturally to each other in any language that served best, when Englishmen did not stare at their countrymen much as undergraduates stare at "an out-college man"; when Frenchmen and Germans discussed the beau-

ties of the Rhine, and when it was not an impertinence to
address to a stranger a remark about the weather. All that
is over. Wars, annexations, revolutions, race jealousies,
railways, circular tours, Harry and Betsy Jane, have made
an end of that. We consort with those of our own nation
only, and with much hesitation and doubt even with them.
Germans, Frenchmen, English, Russians, or Italians take
their pleasure sadly in foreign parts, and in strict national
lines. There are English, German, and French resorts; English, German, and French hotels in the same place; English,
German, and French tables in the same room. You may
see English, German, and French families pass many weeks
together in the same house, eat thrice a day at the same table,
and sit for hours in the same *salons* without ever exchanging
a chance word. This is not from want of a common language; for, as we all know, Germans are usually as much
at home in our language as in any other, and most people
who travel habitually speak at least some French. No, it is
national and political jealousy, a deep consciousness that
neither sympathy nor fair judgment exists any longer between
the nations of Europe. Forty years ago an Englishman, a
German, a Frenchman, and a Russian, who passed twelve
hours together in the same carriage or inn, were rather willing than otherwise to exchange a few impressions. And such
to this day is the tone of the average American. While all
his European contemporaries have good reasons for keeping their own counsel, our American fellow-traveller is as
good-tempered as ever; affable, self-satisfied, and buoyantly
at home. He has no disasters in wars or in diplomacy to forget, no pretensions to assert, and no enemies to fear. He has
annexed no provinces, paid no *milliards*, fought no battles
except with his own dear brothers at home; he is building
no fortresses, forging no guns, nor running amuck through

the Press of Europe. He is perfectly satisfied with his own national position, nor does he doubt a moment that any one can misunderstand it. He is consequently as completely at his ease with foreigners of every nation as a rational traveller ought to be, and as forty years ago an English traveller used to be; and, as far as his meagre linguistic attainments carry him, he is, nationally and socially, open to converse with all whom he meets.

It is hardly in human nature to expect such ease from a Frenchman. Sedan, Metz, Strasburg, and *milliards* are eternally on his soul; revolutions, communes, proscriptions, and party animosities make him as silent with his own nation as with others. Political causes have led to a singular change. The average Frenchman has lost his manners, and with his manners his liveliness, his happy opinion of himself, and his flow of speech. Out of his own set or party he is morose, taciturn, uneasy, and ill-bred. Hazard a few words about the weather, and his second sentence will relate to the fogs of London (of which he has read in his pet *feuilleton*); ask him to pass you the mustard, and he will inquire if the favourite dish of the English is still raw beef. If a German sits down at the same table, you are almost glad to observe that the knives and forks abroad are so blunt. In short, the Frenchman conducts himself generally like a man who has been declared a defaulter at his club. The consequence is that the Frenchman abroad is too often a melancholy, silent, uncompanionable man.

The German abroad is almost as reserved as the Frenchman; but it is not, at any rate, from *wounded* pride. He is aware that by many he is not loved, and he gently enjoys the sensation. He is quite sure that intellectually, materially, and artistically he stands before all the nations on earth, and, as he knows that his claims are beyond dispute, he needs no pretensions of his to assert them. The inexplicable *verve* of the Frenchman, the versatile energy of the Englishman, are very well in their way, but as nations they are both second-rate. If they decline to associate with him on this understanding he declines to associate at all. The war with France and the reconstitution of the German social economy have produced a great change in German society. The German middle class is no longer poor, and not at all disposed to put up with anything second best. It is more enterprising, more lavish, more cultivated than the corresponding class in France; and if not quite so numerous, or so wealthy, or so restless as that of England, it has far more real education, taste, and industry.

The Germans, therefore, with their newly-acquired wealth, their skill and general enterprise, are in neutral countries like the Alps almost the rivals in travel of the English. They spend nearly as much, they are almost as numerous, they have everything almost as good, and they are far more really accomplished travellers. It must be admitted that their manners are not yet equal to their essential culture. The German of the higher class is poor, he travels little, and he does not form the manners of the mercantile and professional class. The middle-class Englishman, whose horror is the knife to the mouth, the spittoon in the *salon*, and sundry eccentricities of habit and dress, is too often disposed to undervalue his German fellow-traveller, though in knowledge, culture, and just self-respect the German is much his superior. Now the middle-class German is far too acute not to feel that, in refinement of manner and person, both he and she have still something to learn, but as a member of the nation which leads the van of European civilisation he and she are far too proud to acknowledge it. On the other hand, the Englishman of the middle class, who is apt to take the conventional habits of his own aristocracy for real good breeding, very much exaggerates such superiority in refinement as he may happen to possess with respect to his German neighbour. Wealth, power, knowledge of all sorts, the German knows that he has. He is not at all disposed to be snubbed by living man or woman, nor in any place or way will he now be relegated to the second class. The Englishman too often has silly schoolboy prejudices about what he calls "Continental habits," sometimes things perfectly innocent and natural in themselves. Very properly, Continentals decline to recognise the schoolboy standard of manners, and the general code of what is, and what is not, "swagger." Hence comes it that travelling is very much less sociable and cheerful than it was. Germans, French, and English practically hold no intercourse. The Frenchman's tongue is tied; the German no longer instructs us with his vast erudition and complacent affability; the Englishman no longer comports himself as if every one were glad to meet him, and as if it were every one's duty to answer his questions and supply his wants. Frenchmen, Germans, and English live side by side in the same house, walk in the same paths, lounge in the same verandah, and sit round the same fire as though utterly unconscious of the presence of each other, without betraying by a word, look, or gesture that they observe fellow-creatures around them. When we travel now we all put "invisible caps" in our bags, caps which make, not us invisible to others, but all our fellow-travellers invisible to us. At any rate, all persons of different nationality are not in focus at all. We walk, talk, eat, and drink as if they were mere Banquo's ghosts, invisible to the company generally. A British peer at a race-course could not seem more absolutely unconscious of the presence of his fellow-beings.

The Italian used to be, if one met him out of Italy, the

prince of travelling companions. He was usually a very
superior type of his nation, and his urbanity, grace, and
sweetness of temper were a constant consolation and charm.
The better specimens of Italian gentlemen are still, perhaps,
the most agreeable of the European races.   But one may have
too much of a good thing; and the hordes of Italian middle
class who now pour across the Alps are not always beautiful
or good.   The great Alpine railway tunnels have opened a
new world to the untravelled millions of Northern Italy.   No
people in Europe have felt the opening more certainly, as
none are so close to it; and week after week the middle
classes of Milan, Genoa, Turin, Lombardy, and Piedmont
pour across the Alpine passes and through the tunnels by
tens of thousands.   The districts bordering on the great
Alpine railways are now the main haunts of Italian *villeg-
giatura*, and the neighbourhood of Lucerne and St. Gothard
is an Italian summer colony.   It could hardly be expected
that, with such a vast increase in numbers, Italy could maintain the high standard of the Italian traveller of old.   *Italian-
issimo*, as I always profess myself, I confess that I am a little
tried by the vacuous garrulity of these Milanese burghers,
their taste for colour in costume, now, alas! descended to the
level of a Jamaica negress, and the vapid *insouciance* of man,
woman, and child.   As on the deck of the Lucerne steamboats, amid scenes perhaps the most exquisite and sublime
in Europe, I listen to the eternal grasshopper's chirrup of these
bulbous, plain, black-eyed *signorine*, perpetually sucking cara-
mels and lozenges, with their oleaginous mamma, a bundle
of ill-assorted *chiffons*, their obese papa with a big bad cigar
in his blackened teeth, and the *fainéant* young men with
gewgaw jewelry, vile tobacco, and almost every accessory of
a tourist, except books, information, enthusiasm, and interest, I confess I wonder if the "Administration of Italian Rail-

Q

ways" have really benefited their countrymen by organising "no less than fifty-one circular tours." But these Milanese and Turinese happy families, if they carry little out of the Alps either in mind or body, do no more harm than the grasshoppers; and one can only trust that here and there in their crowds there yet lingers the charming Italian fellow-traveller of our youth, with far finer manner than the Frenchman, far more grace than the German, and far more repose than the Englishman, who was not without enthusiasm, knowledge, and energy, all infused with a certain sympathetic sweetness which was his own peculiar note.

And our own dear countrymen, have they, in these thirty or forty years, gained as much intellectually and morally as they certainly have in material opportunity? Let us trust so. Foreign, and especially Alpine, touring has become a highly organised institution, brought to perfection by everything that administrative genius, capital, and science can give. Steam, electricity, human energy and ambition can hardly add another touch to the mechanism of travel. The development of the circular tour system, of the *pension* system, of the coupon system, the patience and genius which now transport all the joys of Scarborough, Trouville, or Homburg up to the snow level, have indeed transformed the Continent to the tourist. Morally, we Britons plant the British flag on every peak and pass; and wherever the Union Jack floats there we place the cardinal British institutions — tea, tubs, sanitary appliances, lawn tennis, and churches; all of them excellent things in season. But the missionary zeal of our people is not always according to knowledge and discretion. We are now planting also in these foreign *pensions* that other English institution, of which we are so justly proud — our beautiful family life. Thousands of charming British children now make gay the foreign *pension* with their innocent prattle and engaging frolics. But a word in season to the judicious parent. The *pension*, comfortable as it is, is not absolutely home; the foreign visitors who surround us there, though by a fiction of international comity invisible to each other, really have human eyes and ears. The innocence of youth is but too apt to mistake conventional fictions for facts; and encouraged by the social attitude of their elders, the children and youth of both sexes are ready to treat the *pension* as their own particular home, and themselves as its sole inmates. They romp, shout, giggle, sing, and indulge in every sweet domestic gambol with as much spirit as if they were really in the dear old rectory or grange in Loamshire — nay, they add an extra touch of *abandon* and dash to their romps. A family party who have been a week or two in a *pension* are apt to take themselves to be the little masters and mistresses of the whole establishment, and any recent arrivals as mere intruders. They "go on," as children say, not wholly unconscious perhaps of our presence, but sweetly indifferent to our observant eyes. In these Alpine *châlets* the floors are mere decks and the chambers simple cabins. Every giggle, scream, or laugh is audible from stem to stern, and the whole house rings with these young voices and the merry thumps of those young limbs. A particularly engaging family of girls lodged exactly over my head would play leap-frog with their brothers every morning from 5 to 7 A.M. and every evening from 9 to 11 P.M. with many a shriek of delight and much rough-and-tumble tussling, like a scrimmage "at the wall." Perhaps it a little shortened our night's rest; some of us had just arrived straight from London; others were busy with letters; and some were to start at daybreak. But what mattered it so long as the sweet things had a good romp and a loud laugh? And then how engaging it is to hear them chuckling and screaming till the *salon de lecture* rings with their innocent mirth, or to watch them purloin the English newspapers for papa and mamma, and to listen to them by the hour strumming their exercises in B flat or variations on the "Carnival de Venise." And such is the artless confidence of childhood, such its naïve unconsciousness, that these dear babes will rattle off their simple waltzes and marches in presence of a score of Germans, of whom each third man and woman is a trained musician. I confess that, when after some hours of this schoolroom banging of the keys the piano is at last free, and I have heard a German *virtuoso* sit down, and with a few subtle touches of a master-hand, even on that ill-used *pension* instrument, remind us of what music really is, I feel some patriotic shame at this practice of carrying the whole schoolroom abroad.

And how refreshing it is to see our British lads stalking about with their ice-axes like conquerors in a subject race, for all the world looking like young Goths at Rome in one of the colossal historical tableaux in the Paris Salon, or the Varangians at Byzantium in *Count Robert of Paris*. What lofty scorn gleams from their young calves for man, woman, and child not British by birth, and for every man who has never carried an ice-axe. The bowler in the great school match is not a more superb sight at Lord's nor the stroke of a winning eight at Henley. In this matter of ice-axes perhaps the glorious practice of glacier walking is being a little discredited. An English lad nowadays can no more venture to be seen in Switzerland without an axe than he could show at Henley without flannels, or at Cowes without his deck shoes and yachting cap. But of the thousands of striplings who now carry about these cumbrous and murderous looking weapons not all know how to use them properly, and perhaps not one in three has ever seriously tried them. Those who have tried it know well that it takes no little practice

before the axe is anything but a danger and a nuisance to the
young climber.   There is, we may be sure, a certain amount
of "swagger" about this ice-axe shop.   Mere lads call themselves "mountaineers" and chatter about "*arêtes*" and
"*couloirs*" as if they were each Melchior Anderegg or Christian Almer.   At evening and in bad weather they stalk and
lounge about the hotel terrace, moody, terrible, and statuesque
as "Red Shirt" and "Yellow Tail" at the Wild West camp.
They speak to none but to other young braves, with whom
they perpetually mutter dark things about bad places,
bergschrunds, and cutting the record by seventeen minutes.
To call raw lads out for a month's walk "mountaineers" is a
misuse of terms.   The instinctive foothold on rock or ice
acquired by real mountaineers is the education of a lifetime
begun in childhood.   Not one Englishman in fifty ever attains
to it, even after long training; but not one in a hundred
comes near to it without a good season or two.   Real skill on
a glacier or a peak, such as every decent guide possesses, is
only acquired now and then by an Englishman after long
years of labour and practice.   A good many English climbers
come in time to be nearly as steady as a third-rate "porter."
But the mere beginner, who sees a bad *arête* for the first time,
is about as helpful as a "sleeping-bag."   Nay, he is no more
a "mountaineer" than his own boots are.   Good guides and
stout porters take him up peaks and passes fairly well, and
usually bring him safely down.   An average healthy English
lad, with his four limbs well exercised, a sound constitution,
a perfectly steady head, and the nerve and handiness which
most English lads have got, can usually be trained in a season
or two to go safely over most places with a good guide to lead
and another good guide in rear.   It is a glorious and health-
ful exercise, by all means to be encouraged.   But to call
them "mountaineers" is an abuse of terms.   The common

cowherd boy on the pastures is an expert in comparison to them, and they would break down in a few hours if they tried to do the work of their own porters. The mountaineer's instinct on rock and ice is an art quite as subtle and complex as the art of the seaman or the horseman. From the nature of the case an ordinary English lad cannot have made, in his season or two, more than a score or so of difficult ice expeditions. To call oneself a mountaineer on the strength of twenty days' practice is as ludicrous as it would be to call oneself a seaman after a month's yachting in the Channel, or to call oneself a horseman after twenty or thirty mounts in one's whole life. How would our tennis-players and cricketers smile at a young Frenchman who wished to enter himself in a county match because "he had practised for six weeks last season at Wimbledon or Lord's!" *Punch* once gave us a portrait of the foreign sportsman who had never caught a fox, "but would try, *mon ami*, would try." I think of it as I see some of our young heroes crossing the Channel with unsullied axe to face a glacier peak for the first time in their lives and to try if they also are not mountaineers.

A very melancholy abuse of a splendid pastime is the common practice of forcing the pace. Climbing mountains is perhaps of all forms of exercise the one most closely associated with the sublime impressions of nature, and with majestic and inspiring ideas. To degrade it to mere muscular exercise, like boating on the Cam, or running on the measured track, is the part of a simpleton. Morally, poetically, and intellectually a great Alpine expedition stands far above all other forms of athletic enterprise. To think about "cutting the record" is to show that one has no soul for any but its lowest and most animal accompaniments. If we go on thus we shall have gate-money and handicaps introduced into this most noble of pastimes. The young athlete who is sweating

upon a snow slope in hopes of beating "Tomkins's time" has
not a glance for one of the noblest visions this earth contains.
On the summit of his peak he is gasping for breath, or else
he is fretting to be back at the hut ten minutes before Brown.
It is a wretched affair to waste poetry, beauty, and nature
in a common race which is far more in place at Lillie Bridge
racing-ground.   In the glorious days of old, when we carried our axes and did our passes and peaks, we took our own
time, stayed as long as we could see anything, and drained
to the last drop the cup of inspiration which the Witch of the
Alps holds forth to him who seeks her humbly on her topmost throne.   But it is only now, as I potter about slowly
with a walking-stick, and no expeditions or passes more, to
the infinite contempt of my young ice-axe friends — it is only
now, in the late autumn of my travelling life, that I come to
see all the infinite glories of these Alpine crests, the untrodden
regions of poetry that yet lie round them to be known, the
mystery of these heaven-descending veils of cloud and mist,
the majesty of these towering masses, the unfolding drama
which is played round us night and day of man and nature,
for ever in contrast, for ever at war, for ever in alliance.

Another wonderful development of the *pension* system is
the vast multiplication of English churches.   Forty years
ago there were English churches in some principal towns,
and an impromptu service was often arranged for a clergyman who chanced to be present on a Sunday morning.   Now
the chapel or church is almost as much a requisite of an hotel
as a *table d'hôte*.   Nay, every mountain *châlet* inn pretends
to its "chapel" and its "chaplain."   It is very natural that
English tourists should desire a regular service on Sunday;
and no one could blame Church people for seeking to secure
it.   But, like all other things, this laudable desire has its
own dangers of being spoiled by over-organisation.   The

congregations do not always remember the very peculiar conditions under which they exist. They are not a real "congregation" at all — they have no corporate existence, no local duties or interests, no social cohesion, no poor, no charities, no parish. They are mere chance visitors, unknown to each other, and with no common sentiment or interest. The "chaplain" is not a real priest of a real parish. He is merely a tourist out for a holiday, who gets his board and lodging for his Sunday services. He knows nothing of his flock, has no parochial duties, no poor to help, and no local interests. Any attempt to plant a sort of *quasi*-congregational system, any tendency of the "chaplain" to regard the hotel and its inmates as the parish of which he is the spiritual pastor, any effort on the part of the *habitués* and *pensionnaires* to make themselves a society for the guarantee of moral and religious order in the *pension*, would rest upon a thoroughly false basis and lead to nothing but disappointment. It is to be hoped that the bishops who license these chapels make stringent inquiries as to the feeling of the people among whom they are placed. To the natives and to the civil and spiritual authorities of the country these chapels are too often centres of schism and heresy, and not seldom are symbols of bitterness and offence. The irritation of the local churches and congregations is often stifled by the eagerness of the landlord to secure British custom. But we must hope that the bishops in licensing these *primâ facie* schismatical chapels will carefully remove every cause of offence, and will satisfy themselves that they do nothing to add a new anti-Christian feud. At all times congregation and chaplain should remember that they exist on sufferance, and that their *raison d'être* is peculiar. They ought certainly to be centres of good works and charity to the poor and to the parish in which they stand, and in all things seek the good will of the Churches against which their mere existence is a protest. It would carry one very far if one tried to explain how it comes that the Church of England alone of all religious bodies in Europe fills almost every village on the Continent and crowns every Alp with its own rite and place of worship. Tourists of all other nations can exist without their national service. Catholics in a Protestant canton, Americans in Europe, Lutherans, Presbyterians, and Orthodox Greeks worship God in their own way without special chapels. But where there is an English *pension* there beside it is an English church. Is it that we English are the only religious people in Europe?

In things spiritual and things temporal alike our modern mania abroad is to carry with us our own life, instead of accepting that which we find on the spot. The generation which planted London-on-the-Sea is succeeded by the generation which has planted Paris-on-the-Alps, Paris-on-the-Riviera, and Paris-on-the-Bay-of-Naples. Long lines of mules file up the Alps, carrying Saratoga trunks and cases of Veuve-Clicquot to the level of the eternal snows. In every little village inn we expect to be supplied with five courses at the *table d'hôte* — tinned salmon, bottled peas, preserved soups, and all the other horrors of the dear-and-nasty sham Paris *menu*. It was pleasant of old, when one reached a mountain *châlet* after a day's walk, to see how the good-humoured host welcomed one to his quaint *salon*, with pictures of Napoleon, Tell, and Winkelried, and his wife prepared a *potage bonne femme*, a *kalbsbraten* with potatoes, a *mehl-speise*, or the like, and a bottle of *vin du pays*. One touched at those moments on the native life of the place, one tasted the local fare, and saw the homes of the people. It is all over now. At 7000 feet above the sea, or in some village of 500 thrifty peasants, we sit down in Grand Hotels to a dinner which is a poor imitation of the Palais Royal *cuisine*. What is the good of these mirrors, gilt cornices, and plated centre-pieces, filled with paste-board flowers, on the top of a mountain, or in a valley swept twice a year by avalanches? What mortal can care for *cotelettes d'agneau à la jardinière* when he knows that lamb, sauce, vegetables, cook, and dish are all sent in by contract from a foreign country hundreds of miles off? After a month of foreign hotels we sicken of tinned vegetables, bottled sauces, packed meat, spurious wines, canned fruits, gaudy *menus*, and the whole apparatus of pretending to mimic the Café Riche on the tops of the Alps or the shores of the Mediterranean. We were far better off when we had to put up every now and then with the overdose of oil of the Italian *albergo* or the rough-and-ready roast veal of the Swiss *gasthaus*. Nowadays it is the horrid sameness of one bad standard which haunts us from Calais to Palermo. *Cœlum non vitam mutant qui trans mare currunt.* We go abroad, but we travel no longer. We see nothing really of the people among whom we sojourn. We never touch their lives. They are not even our caterers or our servants. We lodge in sham Grand Hotels, we take our meals of sham Paris dishes, our food is a foreign import, we are served by sham French waiters, and supplied by sham French cooks. Everything we touch, or see, or eat is a horrid kind of patent "notion" for making a thing look what it is not. And all this fraud, pretence, and artificiality in the midst of scenes the most lovely and sublime which earth contains, among a people who can barely keep off hunger, cold, and want by incessant labour and unsparing self-denial. In a month or two we shall have returned home to the weary round of our *cotelettes à la financière*, and these frugal peasants will be battling for life with the elements and their ungenial soil, huddled in dark and fetid huts, watching the rare visits of the sun above their gorge, fearing the avalanche and the storm, wending through the wreaths of snow to the village mass, wearing out their hard, dull, dark lives, which we travellers no longer care to touch even with the tips of our fingers.

THE RIVIERA DI LEVANTE

1898

I OFTEN wonder how people of taste and sense can continue to crowd into the Frenchified, vulgarised, and stuffy western end of the Riviera, when they can find health, beauty, and quiet in the Riviera east of Genoa, from which I write a few stray notes. It is true that, on this side, there are no spots so warm and sheltered as are many to be found between Nice and San Remo. Nor are there the promenades, hotels, gardens, and villas of Cannes, Monte Carlo, and Mentone. Invalids and votaries of society and fashion keep strictly to the brilliant modern Baiæ, which within the last forty years has spread itself out from the Gulf of La Napoule to the Capo Verde that screens San Remo. Those who have delicate lungs, or who cannot live without the luxuries of Paris and the gaieties of New York, naturally keep westward of the Green Headland. But some people are rather bored by Métropole Caravanserais of the latest pattern, and find no charm in cosmopolitan gamblers and bedizened *mondaines* from all parts of the world, rolling along dusty boulevards in showy barouches. We can see all this in the season in the Champs Elysées, and it brings us no abiding joy. Those who have sound lungs, good legs, and an eye for history and art should seek a little rest and enjoyment in the true Italian Riviera, east of Genoa, which is still what Italy was in the days of our grandfathers — picturesque, historic, old-world, sunny, and natural.

Forty or fifty years ago, before the great transformation took place on the French Riviera, when Nizza, Villafranca, and Mentone were antique Italian towns, and when it was one of the eccentricities of Lord Brougham to like Cannes, all that seaboard was a delightful land. Only a hundred years ago Arthur Young had trouble to get an old woman and a donkey to carry his portmanteau from Cannes to Antibes. I can myself remember Cannes in 1853, a small fishing village with a quiet beach, and Mentone, a walled town with mediæval gates and a castle, a few humble villas, and the old Posta to give supper to any passing traveller. It was one of the loveliest bits of Italy, and the road from Nizza to Genoa was one long procession for four days of glorious scenery, historic remnants, Italian colour, and picturesque ports. From the Estrelles to San Remo this has all been ruined by the horde of northern barbarians who have made it a sort of Trouville, Brighton, or Biarritz, with American hotels and Parisian boulevards on every headland and bay. First came the half-underground railway, a long tunnel with lucid intervals, which destroyed the road, by blocking up its finest views and making it practically useless. Then miles of unsightly caravanserais, high walls, pompous villas, and Parisian *grandes rues* crushed out every trace of Italy, of history, and pictorial charm. No vulgarity of modern luxury can wholly destroy the loveliness of the country itself; and there are still to be found some bits round Mentone, Bordighera, and San Remo where the old Italian charm survives. But these have to be sought out and detached from the sea of pompous commonplace, as it is understood by the smart managers of French and American hotels.

Those who care to know what the Riviera was once must come east of Genoa; where, though something of the same process is beginning, the old Italian character is still to be seen. I quite admit that forty years ago the road from Nice to Bordighera was the most beautiful and romantic in Italy, perhaps in Europe. Since that coast has been Frenchified and Americanised, it is so no more. The seaboard from Nervi to Sestri di Levante (or, to put narrower limits, from Camogli to Chiavari) has now taken the first rank. I have known Italy now for five-and-forty years, and have seen every part of it from Bellinzona to Syracuse. But I know no district which in natural loveliness, variety, and Italian local colouring surpasses the country which lies round the promontory of Porto Fino — say that between Camogli and Zoagli. Here are no "Métropoles" and "Continentals," with "electric lights, lifts, and 600 beds," no circular boulevards, clubs, concerts, or races. But, in a rocky seaboard clothed with profuse vegetation and rising up into fine mountains, one finds a succession of quaint old-world Italian ports and townships, strewn with remnants of antiquity, Roman, Saracenic, Mediæval and Renascence, every hamlet glowing with colour and luxuriant vegetation, winding streets with arcades, loggias, and sanctuaries at every turn, Genoese forts and Lombard campanili, and all the picturesque confusion and luscious glow of an ancient Italian town that has hardly changed for a century or two.

The contrast between the climate of Mentone or San Remo and that of the Eastern Riviera is something extraordinary. Pulmonary cases are, of course, more safe in the west. Yet for an active man in good health almost every "health resort" between Saint Raphael and Alassio has a somewhat enervating effect. But the hillsides between Genoa and Spezia, though much more open to cold winds, have a thoroughly bracing air. I have walked over the Highlands and the Alps, and I know almost every part of the coast from the Estrelles to Spezia; but no air that I have ever tried surpasses in its dry briskness the winter climate of the rocky promontories that abut on the great Porto Fino headland. The climate in good seasons has the double quality of singular dryness with perfect lucidity and buoyancy. It has that elastic effervescent tone which is so common on the Grampians and the Alps, combined with entire absence of moisture and a far more blazing and continuous sun. Those who know the top of a snow mountain in a hot summer noon have experienced the same union of radiant heat with cool draughts of pellucid air. And for an active man in sound health this combination of sunlight and ozone is not only the most health-giving of all climates, but one of the balmiest sensations that Nature offers to the human frame.

From Porto Maurizio round to Spezia — a distance of nearly 130 miles — the Italian Riviera exists still, not seriously modernised by the *fin de siècle*, but as it was seen by "Doctor Antonio," by Ruskin, Byron, and Shelley, and our forefathers in the last century. It has the Italian colour, the free-and-easy, disorderly, picturesque grouping of outline, still innocent of modern "improvements" and the geometric architecture of the *grande rue*. The irregular narrow streets, with no two houses of the same shape, height, or colour; the portici, or arcades, with their mediæval columns and dark cellarage; the frescoes on the walls, the shrines and pictures of saints at every corner, lit with lamps and decorated with flowers; the chapels, belfries, piazze, palazzi, and loggie; the balconies and terraces, adorned with aloes, myrtle, roses, oranges, and cactus; the brown fisherfolk in red berette, the bare-legged venders of maccaroni and fruit — all that makes Italy so dear to the painter and the man of taste — may still be found at its best in this Eastern Riviera. The cosmopolitan luxury which worships at Monte Carlo has practically improved away all this in the Western Riviera between Cannes and San Remo.

The broad and lofty headland of Porto Fino is far the most important promontory between Nice and Spezia; it stands many miles due south into the sea, and, with the headland beyond Sestri, about ten or twelve miles to the east, it forms a bay which has much the look of a lake. The scenery both east and west of Porto Fino has thus very much the sky outline of the fiords of Norway, or the western coast of Scotland, not that of the open sea, as seen from Monaco or Cap Martin. And, as the larger bays are broken with a series of innumerable coves, the variety of view is endless. Nor does any heavy sea, even in tempestuous weather, break into these sheltered nooks. There are few weeks, even in winter, when it is not perfectly easy to boat about Porto Fino, but when boating would be quite impracticable between Monaco and San Remo. The famous Dolphin Harbour, which gives its ancient name to the lofty promontory, still confers a special character on the Riviera around it, by varying the scenery, forming a vast natural breakwater, and multiplying the points of access both by land and water.

In the extreme cove at the end of the eastern bay lies Rapallo, once a walled republic with an ancient history, which is pronounced by Mr. Augustus Hare now to be "incontestably by far the most beautiful place on either Riviera. It is thoroughly Italian in the character of its campaniles, cypresses, and little rocky bays. Its natives are kind, civil, and respectable. Its walks are inexhaustible." Every word of this description is strictly accurate. In the town, and in the walks and drives within an hour or two around it, are certainly to be found the most interesting and lovely views on the entire Riviera, since the ruin of the French side after annexation. The old road from Nice to Mentone doubtless once surpassed it, with the "Trophy" of Augustus, Eza, and mediæval Monaco; but the charm of that wonderful district has been boulevarded and casinoed out of all memory; and the *genius loci* has fled before the horde of unclean punters and the painted fribbles who represent the upper crust of Europe.

Jam pridem in Tiberim Syrius defluxit Orontes.

East of Genoa, as we approach towards Tuscany and Rome, the historic record is more deeply graven on rock, city, and tower, and it has been far less obliterated and disfigured by the rage of vulgar luxury and display. Here, for more than 2000 years, a long succession of ages have left the marks of their civilisation, their religion, and their art; and there are few out of all those twenty centuries which have not left visible traces. All along the coast we come on continual fragments of the Roman Via Aurelia, which was the highway from Rome to the Rhone. The lines of this long and important road, with here and there a bit of bridge, of embankment, of pavement, are continually cropping up, often for only a few yards, sometimes for half a mile or more.

The great road was kept up all through the Middle Ages, and it may be said never to have been abandoned even for a century since the first construction. The configuration of the seaboard, where mountains leave hardly a ledge of ground between them and the sea, made it practically impossible to change its course, or to make a new road, as was the case with so many of the Roman roads in other parts of Europe. The necessities of the day compelled many repairs and renewals. And he would be a bold man who could assign precise dates to these antique and foot-worn fragments of black limestone and marble. But for essential purposes the patches of old road which are seen so often are the actual remnants of the memorable track, along which for 2000 years have tramped consuls, cohorts, and armies of Rome, Spaniards, Gauls, and Britons to the Eternal City, pilgrims from

R

the far West to the tombs of the Apostles, the Northern invaders of Italy, Lombards, Saracens, Byzantines, and Normans, Petrarch and Dante, and the wayfarers from Provence to Tuscany all through the Middle Ages, and so on throughout the French and Italian wars down to the age of Napoleon. The noble road from Nice to Spezia, along which we used to travel in the present century, until the amphibious railroad in turn superseded it, made havoc of the old Aurelian road of Roman and mediæval times, has crushed out much of it, and has thrust more of it into olive grounds and vineyards out of sight. But here and there bits of it crop up still. Oh! that those black stones could speak, and tell us what they have seen.

All round the headland of Porto Fino the rocks are studded with remains of Genoese towers, which have defied Saracens, Pisans, and Normans, and almost every bay in the last 2000 years must have been the scene of a sea-fight, a raid of pirates, or a border tussle. The most picturesque of these forts is that which defends Rapallo on the east, which still has its dungeons and its prisoners and guards. The ancient republic of Rapallo has left some remnants of its mediæval structure even in the busy, cheerful, and orderly little port into which it has shrunk. Fragments of the city gate, transformed into a rococo sanctuary, the base of the old Palazzo Publico, monasteries and nunneries, an old palace or two, the arcades with the earliest pointed arch, and four campanili of Renascence style, which, however horrific to the whole Seven Lamps of Architecture, make up a group that only Turner could paint. Over the portal of the principal church is a long inscription of the sixteenth century, recording the finding of an older inscription, which records the conversion of the people in the first century, and the founding of the church on the site of a temple of Pallas. The inscription, like most of such things, can as little be held worthy of a place in a genuine *Corpus Inscriptionum* as we can believe that the great Carthaginian led his army over "Hannibal's Bridge," a mile off, though they serve to suggest to a simple and imaginative people the vast layers of antiquity upon which their lives are cast.

Every mile or two on this historic ground may be found traces of the growth and battles of nations, creeds, and rival civilisations. Hill-forts built by Romans when they garrisoned their Chitrals and Ali Musjids to curb the Afridis of old Liguria — rocky fastnesses which sought to stem the Lombard invaders — mountain strongholds wherein the scared population of the seaboard took refuge on the sight of Saracen and Turkish pirates — the arsenals of petty republics which fought first against Genoa and then as members of the Genoese Empire. Again, it is some ancient monastery or hospice, sanatorium or refuge, of an order of monks, mendicant or military — some secluded convent of early Lombardic structure in a woody glen — now and then a fragment of quaint Byzantine work — or the pilgrimage sanctuary on a mountain spur that commemorates a gracious visit of the Mother of God. And on each commanding point a rococo Jesuit church in the debased manner of the seventeenth century, or a palace of a Genoese noble, built in the days of Rubens and Vandyke. Of all these remnants of past glory and strife none can compare in pathos with the ancient cloister of San Fruttuoso, where lie in their solemn sarcophagi centuries of Dorias, facing the city they served, surrounded by the waters they were wont to sweep, and guarded by tremendous precipices, deep in the recesses of a wooded glen.

Here around Genoa, itself one of the grandest and most fascinating cities of Europe, are spread out in one of the richest and loveliest landscapes in the world a series of historic remnants which suggest a thousand memories and a crowd of problems yet unsolved. And though the monumental record of the Riviera is almost continuous from palæolithic times to Victor Emmanuel, there is no confusion or discord in it; nor has it yet been submerged by modern hotels, villas, and boulevards. The only inns are old-fashioned houses of a century or two ago. The people are hardy, laborious, courteous, and honest. What vital religion survives in Italy may be seen here at its best. Cleanliness, comfort, and decency are the rule and not the exception. It knows not the penury of Lombard rice grounds, the horrors of Sicilian mines, nor the mendicity and thievery of the Neapolitan slums. Poor as is all kind of classical music in Italy, one feels that the gift of vocal melody is still not dead, but dormant and hibernating in the mass of the people. And however vulgar are the more pretentious forms of Italian art, and garish as is the modern taste with its bourgeois thirst for colour — still, one can see that of the Western nations of Europe, the soil of Italy is yet the true and natural nidus of fruitful and spontaneous Art.

POSTSCRIPT, 1906

Alas! alas! this corner, too, of old Italy is going the way of all else that was lovely, sacred, and historic in Europe. American Grand Hotels, Monte Carlo villas, Parisian boulevards have already invaded this peaceful retreat of our old age; and I am told that my own praises of it have helped to swell the incursion of our Northern barbarians. And now that new disease, the pestilent *motoritis*, has begun to make the Riviera di Levante as foul, as noisy, and as dusty as is the Riviera di Ponente at the height of its orgies.

ECCO LA TOSCANA!

1904

A FASCINATING book has just appeared which has stirred in me a thousand memories of pleasure, such as can be but little known to men and women of the present generation. The delights of the old Italian *vettura* as a method of travelling are an experience only possessed by those who are far past middle life. Yet Mr. Maurice Hewlett, in his new book, *The Road in Tuscany*,[1] though not a veteran, has given us a set of vivid pictures of what real travelling was before railroads, trams, Métropole hotels, and Mr. Cook's tours had modernised, barbarised, and cockneyfied Central Italy. In a delicious passage in one of his sweetest books (*Præterita*, ch. vi.) John Ruskin describes the joys of travelling by road exactly seventy years ago: in the glorious times before "the poor modern slaves and simpletons let themselves be dragged like cattle, or felled timber, through the countries they imagine themselves visiting."

Sono anch' io vetturino. At least I have descended upon Italy along every one of the great Alpine roads — have driven along the Riviera from Cannes to Spezia long before the railway blocked out the view from the road — when Cannes was a sleepy fishing village, Mentone a machicolated, gated, and

---

[1] *The Road in Tuscany*: a Commentary. By Maurice Hewlett. 2 vols., 8vo, profusely illustrated by Joseph Pennell. London: Macmillan and Co., 21s.

walled city with a mediæval castle, and Genoa the most romantic of seaports. I have driven over the Simplon to Milan and thence to Verona; from Bologna to Florence; from Parma to Ravenna; from Leghorn to Rome, across that weird Maremma. Ah! it was fifty years ago and more — before you were born or thought of, my friend Maurice — and yet you have brought back to me the full sense of glorious exaltation in the Italian travel by road — *trasumanar significar per verba non si porria.*

I remember how a dear old lady said to me when I was about to start on the most memorable tour of my whole life, "Take care," she said, "to go by road. There is no happiness in life to compare with an Italian *vettura*, drawn by four horses, and the one you love best by your side!" I was more modest in my equipage. But I remember, as we crossed the Simplon and opened on the valley of Domo D'Ossola, how our *vetturino* sprang up on his box, cracked his whip, and shouted "*Ecco l'Italia!*"

I had thought the supreme joy of the Italian *vettura*, as Ruskin says, that which was "virtually one's home," day after day, was an irrecoverable sensation, to be reckoned with the few memories which only threescore years and ten can give — such as those other memories, to have heard in their prime Rachel, Grisi, and Lablache; to have read *David Copperfield* and *Vanity Fair* month by month in their early shilling numbers; to have seen the British fleet under sails; to have seen French cathedrals yet unrestored; and Rome as it was seen by Byron, as it was drawn by Piranesi. Yet Maurice Hewlett now shows us how, if we care and are not "pressed for time," nor slaves to Baedeker or Cook, we may see Tuscany still in the way that Milton and Goethe, Rogers and Turner, Shelley and Ruskin, saw it: when men travelled to see the country and the people, and were not shot like luggage through tunnels from one museum to another, from one Grand Hotel to the next, with hardly anything to remind them that they had quitted Charing Cross. There are the Tuscan roads, the hill villages, the towns of the plain, the *vetture* still — more likely now with two horses than four or five — but the *vetturino* is there, the Tuscan folk are there still. And Maurice Hewlett will show you how to find them.

Hewlett has some special qualifications for a book like this. Ten years ago he published his first books upon Tuscany. Ever since he has been a close student of Italian history, poetry, art, topography, and national character. And he is one of the first living masters of the entire Dantesque cycle in all its breadth and its depth. He calls his book *The Road*. It is a whim of Maurice to give us conceits on his title-page, and sometimes, I fear, inside as well. But there is a great deal more than the *Road* in this book. First, there is history — not drum and trumpet or Heralds' College history — but the memories which have moulded races, families, cities, and lands. Then there is very acute and searching race history, what they call anthropology or demology, ingenious musing upon local and generic types, often, we fancy, too ingenious and fine-spun, as the demology of local types usually becomes. Then there is topographical realism about what you see and do and hear on the road, as you may find it in Horace Walpole, Boswell, Eustace, and Laurence Sterne.

Our "carriage-gentleman" has the same horror of rail-roads as Ruskin himself. Pierre Loti wrote an elaborate book about India from Benares to Ceylon without having met a trace of anything British. And Maurice Hewlett trots leisurely along the highways and bye-ways of Italy, from Ventimiglia to Orbetello, without once having seen or heard of a railroad in those parts. This is how some of us saw Italy fifty years ago. But it can be done to-day "in the mind's eye," Maurizio! Dante and the Dantesque legend meet us in almost every page. Though he rails at museums, galleries, and art critics in general, Hewlett has a good deal to say about pictures, statues, tombs, and more about baptistries, campanili, and cloisters. But the essential aim of the book is to paint for us the roads, the wayside humours, the hostelries, the calvaries, the gardens, the rivers, bridges, castles, and abbeys, the old world stories of romance and crime, the garrulous peasants, and the bathycolpous glaucopid Tuscan girls who make our roadster amorous and poetic. What is the authority for giving to Dante's Beatrice green eyes? The only green-eyed charmer we ever heard of was Becky Sharp in *Vanity Fair*. But by these green eyes hangs a tale.

Hewlett seizes, reiterates, and illustrates that which is no doubt the true key of Italian character, the real explanation of Italian history — the fierce local patriotism, that flame of pride, jealousy, egoism, that *politica del campanile*, which from the age of Boëthius to that of Pio X. has coloured the art, the manners, the language, and the annals of the Peninsula. No observer has ever gone more truly home to the intense burgher jealousy of the Italian townsman than does Hewlett. And I know no other witness who can testify to the same municipal pride in a petty hill village, and in the wards of a decaying city. Few travellers can tell such experiences in centres so small and insignificant. We all know how the possession of a single picture made one ward of Florence to be called the Gay Borough. I remember the scorn of the true Trasteverini for the populace of the Left Bank, in days before modern Rome had again become a new *colluvies gentium*. And I have heard a Syracusan, proud of his ruins, call the people of Palermo *quei Saraceni*. But few of us have witnessed the feuds of Siena between Giraffa and the Goose: the Snail and the Dragon. But then few of us have ever known Livia, "The most vividly beautiful girl I have ever seen," says this enthusiast after beauty, whose effect "was that of a moonlight night, compact as that is, of ivory pallors and velvet darks, at once clear and cold, severe and calm." This is poetic but vague: all about a girl in the streets of Siena, who may have been clear and calm, but was certainly neither cold nor severe, who had no hat, white stockings with loose slippers, a green skirt, and green eyes. Well! if she had green eyes, I should not care a fig for her myself. And Dante's Beatrice, I know, had dark eyes — not green.

The history in this book is continuous and masterly. It is history of the right sort — the unlocking of social and intellectual movements, the unearthing the roots of that which we can see to-day, that compound of languor and passion; of love of beauty and tolerance of squalor; that intellectual subtlety and that proneness to grovel in the petty, the childish, and the mean. How often Hewlett's tales of mediæval Tuscany remind us of Greek life in our old classics, of the scuffles between rival towns in Thucydides, the wild games in Aristophanes, the religious festivals, the materialist worship, the local deities, the poetry, the fissiparous and dispersive genius, the restlessness and the sloth, the desperate burgher passion, the incapacity for national cohesion.

The appendices resume in a more regular and continuous form the flashes of historical insight which scintillate along every page of Hewlett's book, touching as with deep sunset glow the ruined tower, the smoke-stained and bedaubed tomb of a saint, the mediæval *municipio*, the gloomy and ordurous lane in a rotting hill town. In smaller type at the end of the chapter it has pleased our author to paint many an episode of the old times, and here and there a new "Little Novel of Italy." Especially to be noted are the following:

the history of Florence, of Siena, of Arezzo; the biographies of Castruccio Castracane, of Ser Martino and Donna Berta, types of the mediæval tyrant and the Florentine burgher. But it is not history as we find it in Guicciardini, Sismondi, Roscoe, Ranke, Symonds, or Creighton. It is history according to Maurice Hewlett, which is a different thing, a singularly idiosyncratic thing, very fascinating and very edifying I find it.

The distinctive and rare note of this book is its intensely *personal* point of view. No writer, unless it be Ruskin, has ever taken us to a country, so bent on making us see what he sees, knowing what he knows, enjoying what he enjoys, scorning what he scorns. The two volumes are saturated with personal tastes, fancies, dreams, loves, and whimsies. That is what a book of travel ought to be, as were the *Sentimental Journey, Childe Harold, Corinne, Reisebilde, Præterita.* Else we had better have a mere gazetteer or Herr Baedeker's truly exact, careful, and useful handbooks. It is all very well to sneer at Baedeker; but I am certain that Hewlett has carried a red book at some time or other. I can remember the days before Baedeker, and how many a sight we missed, how much time we lost for want of knowing distances, times, and where to find the key. It is this personal note in every line of this book which makes it so delightful to read—so troublesome to "review." He puzzles his critics, just as Ruskin did. They "don't know where to have him." Exactly so! It is not a history of Tuscany; nor a guide-book to Tuscany; nor a Tuscan romance; nor a study of Tuscan art; it is simply — Maurice Hewlett in Tuscany.

This personal note reaches its acme in the two chapters, "The World is a Garden" and "Thoughts in Church," devoted to the passionate humanism of the *quattrocento* and to the gross paganism in the worship of the Renascence and ever since. Why Hewlett should go out of his way to describe the Renascence as "the theory that the world is a garden" we will not inquire. The Renascence is simply Humanism — *i.e.* the sense, or the discovery, that the proper business of mankind is man; the essential knowledge is to know himself and the world in which he finds himself; the true aim of human life is to make the best of man and of the world. That is a perfectly reasonable creed, leading, by its emancipating force, to glorious results, and ending, for want of a true philosophy and an adequate faith, in horrible corruptions. But why use the weak French term — *Renaissance* — for a movement which was essentially European, but began in Italy, and was promulgated by Italians? Years ago I insisted that *Renascence* is the proper term — nearer to the Italian origin, and free from the suggestion of outlandish, petty, and affected meaning which a French word implies.

It is a welcome relief to find this book almost free from the excessive Hewlettism — that modern variant of euphuism — of which we were getting somewhat weary. The intensely vivid and pictorial speech which has made him one of the very first prose writers of this age is now being mellowed and refined. Nothing is lost in brilliancy by softening the more violent tropes. Santa Maria Novella has a façade "bitingly personal"; San Michele is "a church of delirium"; Orvieto is "naked"; Siena is "a tiger-moth swooning on a rock." How a church can bite, can swoon, strip, and go mad, we have to imagine. I know these venerable fanes pretty well; but I never saw them at these gambols, nor do I see the analogy between one of the vastest cathedrals in Italy and a moth. They were all rather unsuccessful attempts of Italians to acclimatise an architecture for which they had no real genius. And so, I gather, does Hewlett think. But where

does the mad dog or the tiger-moth come in? My dear
Maurice, if you would only be a little less cryptic, you would
be the finest writer of English prose of this age.

One of the most charming — most important — chapters
is the last, "The Heart of the Country." It is concerned
with the folk songs, the people's poetry, still as pure, as
native, as pathetic as ever. The people's poetry of Tuscany
is not only one of the most beautiful forms of living art, but
by its union of delicacy and tenderness it is one of the most
piercing revelations of national character. Alone it serves
to redeem the taint of so much blood, lust, treachery, affectation, meanness, which stain Italian annals and manners.
These *rispetti* I have known and loved ever since I first read
Dante with Aurelio Saffi once Triumvir in Rome, in the
year 1850. Hewlett is right in finding in this truly indigenous
poetry "the heart of the country."

One must not overlook the wonderful realism and vitality
of the illustrations by Joseph Pennell. Their profusion
illumines and explains almost every page. Every aspect of
Tuscany is recorded here — cities, towers, churches, roads,
rivers, bridges, gardens, villas, foliage, landscapes, ruins,
lanes, and porticoes. I know not which to admire more, the
refined pen-and-ink sketches of buildings, gardens, and hill-
crests, or the powerful chalk drawings of vaulted interiors
and sombre alleys. They have the gift of truly depicting
the architecture, a gift which so few painters, not even
Turner, chose to cultivate, which they leave to scientific
architects such as Ruskin. To my eye, these drawings, with
all their photographic truth of form, too often magnify the
scale, by Prout's artifice of diminishing the figures which
measure the buildings. But on the whole they reproduce
Tuscan sights with marvellous truth and force.

A PILGRIMAGE TO LOURDES

1896

AFTER my visit in last September to Paris and to Monsieur Laffitte at Cadillac, I went on to Pau to perform a pilgrimage at the birthplace and ancestral home of Henri IV.; and thence to Lourdes, which I saw on two occasions during the autumn pilgrimages. A visit to Lourdes is very much to be recommended to those who care to understand France of to-day and Catholicism as it is. I cannot pretend to have studied the matter very deeply — I do not believe that there is anything deep to study. I give my impressions of a *coup d'œil* for what they may be worth — premising only that I have known the French peasant for fifty years, and I think I am entirely clear of any Protestant or anti-Catholic bias.

Any one who goes to Lourdes expecting to see anything like what M. Zola saw, or, at least, what he paints in his sensational book, will be rudely disillusioned. I saw no trains loaded with the sick and the dying, the halt and the blind, the ecstatic and the paralytic: I saw no spasmodic emotion, and heard no agonising prayers and hymns. The priests and monks, the "sisters" and "mothers" — of whom there were thousands, were very much the same quiet and businesslike people we see in any Catholic country, or even in the Isle of Thanet or round Arundel in Sussex. The great mass of the "pilgrims" were ordinary holiday-makers in their best suits, enjoying a few days' trip in a lovely country, and steadily working round the various devotional functions with entire satisfaction, with a determination to do it all thoroughly, and see all that was to be seen, and hear all that was to be heard.

I do not at all mean that there were no sick, no lame, no excitement, no ecstatic prostrations, no church-going, no hymn-singing. The various churches were crammed; the services were continual; the congregations heartily and reverently joined. But the sight-seeing, the booths, the shows of the fair were quite as well attended; the picnics were as gay and as many as the booths; and the prevailing air was that of a Bank-holiday crowd enjoying a very pretty scene in an exquisite spot. Some sick, halt, and afflicted I saw, but they were rare exceptions. Out of 20,000 happy and healthy people whom I noticed, I could not count more than ten visibly marked with disease, and about as many who could not walk without crutches or help. Out of some thousand or so seated in quiet meditation round the grotto of the Madonna, but two or three behaved otherwise than as reverent persons ordinarily behave in church. One group interested me much.

Two brothers and two sisters all in deep mourning, the girls very young, in a paroxysm of distress and spiritual exaltation flung themselves on the pavement, fervently praying with arms extended in the form of a cross, until the exhausted body fell forward prostrate in the dust which they kissed with passionate veneration. The worshippers round the grotto, bright with a gilt image of Mary, but itself blackened with the smoke of a thousand candles, and hung round with votive offerings, seemed like ordinary worshippers in any Catholic church. Nearly a thousand crutches were hung upon the miracle-haunted rock, which the resident physician assured a friend of mine to his certain knowledge were the crutches of lame persons who had been healed at the grotto. We visited the sacred spots and duly drank of the healing water, in spite of a somewhat sinister smell of carbolic round the well. Some pilgrims duly bathed in the bath — where "swimming was strictly forbidden" — and one young girl, ecstatically declaring herself healed as she came out, was fervently kissed by those present in spite of her dripping gown.

It was a delightful scene. Lourdes itself is a spot exquisitely beautiful, standing at the mouth of two grand valleys which run up to the Pyrenean mountains, and crowned by the donjon keep of an ancient feudal castle. The rushing Gave, in two lucent torrents, sweeps round the precipitous rocks on which stand village and churches; and all round are fine hills clothed with green pasture and woods, and topped with craggy pinnacles. Beyond the grotto are delicious avenues of shady chestnut trees beside the swift river, with grassy banks and mossy knolls, wherein were hundreds of picnic parties, who having done the round of churches and holy places were refreshing themselves with wine and cold meat. The whole town and the country round it were bright and gay with summer visitors and pleasure parties. The streets were lined with thousands of shops, booths, open-air stands and sheds for the sale of relics, mementoes, images, models of the grotto and the churches, copies of the Madonna, rosaries, photographs of Bernadette, and all the myriad trumpery of a religious fair. I am bound to say that more tasteless trash was never collected together. I looked with a sinking heart in vain for a single article that was other than mere conventional and machine-made rubbish; and I could not help remembering that our word *tawdry* comes from the cheap finery that used to be bought at the fair of St. Etheldreda. A fair the whole thing was. Hotels, eating-houses, wine-shops, drinking-gardens and saloons, lodging-houses, stalls for confectionery or various viands and drinks, itinerant venders, toys, panoramas, dioramas, vehicles, landaus, omnibuses and bath chairs crowded the streets and lanes. The whole scene was like Margate or Brighton on Whit Monday, though very much prettier and not quite so rowdy. I see nothing to blame in this. If 20,000 hard-working men and women are taken to a mountain village for forty-eight hours, they must eat and drink and be housed. They can't be in church or grotto the whole time. They will naturally need to be occupied and amused, and they will wish to carry home some trifling record of their visit.

Protestants to whom religion means silent communing of the Soul with its Maker, are wont to treat scenes like this as somewhat profane, or, at least, unspiritual. But Catholics, we know, take a much more genial, sociable, spectacular, and all-in-the-day's work conception of religion — as they certainly did in the Ages of Faith. The scene at Lourdes recalled to me the mediæval pilgrimages and sacred fairs at which trade, society, amusement, art, and literature made up quite half of the attraction. So it is with the pilgrimages to Benares, and so it was with the festival at Olympia. The dioramas, panoramas, shows, and trinkets at Lourdes vividly reproduce the miracle-plays, the gaieties, gossip, and fairings of Canterbury, Reims, Loretto, or Rome. The interest of Lourdes lies in a spontaneous revival of a mediæval pilgrimage — of course without the heroic enthusiasm and unreasoning passion of a pilgrimage to Jerusalem or Rome in the eleventh century, but far less worldly and unholy than pilgrimages were wont to be about the sixteenth century.

The pilgrims had come from every part of France, almost of Europe — from the farthest coast of Brittany, from the seafaring people of Normandy, Belgium, and Holland, from the plains of Lombardy, and the mountains of Auvergne, from the Basque seaboard, and the valleys of Northern Spain. Huge caravans in four heavy trains came from Tours and the Loire; others from Lyons and the Rhone; others from Toulouse, Carcassonne, and the Mediterranean coast. Fishermen, shepherds, ploughmen, vine-dressers, with the miscellaneous crowds of towns big and small. Nineteen out of twenty were peasants, most of them from very rude districts; and not one man and woman in a hundred seemed to belong to the cultivated classes. It was the most motley, picturesque, and old-world gathering I ever beheld, even in Italy or the Tyrol of thirty years ago.

The three memorial churches were crowded to suffocation, and the various functions were continued hour by hour. Each excursion party had its own hours; sometimes the church was reserved for men, sometimes for women; at other times for all comers alike. The worshippers showed great zeal and devoutness; and the hymns and chants were shouted out from a thousand throats with pious but unmusical energy. Every fourth or fifth man or woman seemed to have some ecclesiastical function, or to belong to some sacerdotal or monastic order; and all the parties and groups were carefully piloted by religious guides.

The pilgrimage to Lourdes has now become an institution of a very mixed kind — organised on business and professional lines, and naturally becoming more and more a summer holiday. To a great extent it is a gigantic Cook's Tour, admirably managed and carried on with immense energy by curés and devout persons in every corner of France. We have seen our Anglican canons and priests get up successful religious holiday-tours and turn their clerical societies into excursion agencies. The French priesthood has done this on a far larger scale. From every corner of France they send

s

up excursion trains of parishioners, whom the railways convey at fabulously low rates, and whom the canny Béarnais
are delighted to house, feed, and supply. The Bishop of
Tarbes has poured a veritable Pactolus through his simple
diocese with the usual results; and the Lourdes pilgrimage has
now become one of the biggest excursion businesses on record.

But it is far from being even yet a mere Crystal Palace or
Margate at holiday time. It has given an immense stimulus
to Catholic ceremonial throughout France; and it has been
a real fillip to the Church. It is evidently quite spontaneous
and has worked up from below. The higher ecclesiastical
authorities did their best to damp it down, and for nearly
twenty years they succeeded in doing so. The present generation has seen in France a recrudescence of theological
ardour, and it has forced the Church to give official sanction
to the pilgrim business at Lourdes. Those who fancy France
to be utterly Voltairean would be rudely undeceived if they
saw Lourdes. At least half the excursionists are visibly
believers; and the fishermen of Brittany and Belgium and
the herdsmen of the Cevennes and the Pyrenees are fervent
and devoted Churchmen. About half of the excursionists
are no doubt ordinary holiday trippers, most of them having
no objection to wear an emblem or to listen to a mass. Here
and there are scattered a few fanatical pilgrims who expect
to be cured or who believe in a cure. And here and there
are a few tourists on cycles or a few curious observers as I
was myself. Altogether, I came away with the impression
that a pilgrimage to Lourdes was a sight from which one
might learn many things, both of the past and the present;
and that he who thinks the Catholic Church to be decrepit
or the Catholic Faith to be moribund in France is very much
in error. As to one half, Lourdes is a glorified Cook's excursion office for rural France. As to the other half, it is a
very solid and thriving phase of the revived Catholic Church.

L'ESPRIT FRANÇAIS

[*Reply to a request from the Gaulois of Paris to classify the writers who best express the French esprit.*]

LONDRES, *Janvier 1899.*

MONSIEUR — En recevant votre gracieuse invitation je réponds à la question : — Quels sont les écrivains du passé qui ont le mieux exprimé le vrai esprit français ? Je m'amuse à compiler une Académie de trente "Immortels" véritables, rangés en trois décades. Les auteurs du premier ordre sont déjà couronnés par le jugement des siècles, et l'opinion éclairée en Angleterre est en pleine harmonie avec celle de la France.

I

1. Molière. — 2. Voltaire. — 3. Corneille. — 4. Racine. — 5. Rabelais. — 6. Buffon. — 7. Bossuet. — 8. Montesquieu. — 9. Diderot. — 10. Pascal.

II

1. Fabliaux du Moyen-Age. — 2. Froissart. — 3. Montaigne. — 4. Vauvenargues. — 5. Fénelon. — 6. Madame de Sévigné. — 7. La Fontaine. — 8. Le Sage. — 9. Rousseau. — 10. Balzac.

III

1. Victor Hugo. — 2. Béranger. — 3. Duc de Saint-Simon. — 4. P.-L. Courrier. — 5. A. de Musset. — 6. George Sand. — 7. Théophile Gautier. — 8. Alexandre Dumas père. — 9. Sainte-Beuve. — 10. Jules Michelet.

Agréez, Monsieur, mes meilleures salutations.

FRÉDÉRIC HARRISON.

A WORD FOR ENGLAND

1898

As a real patriot, I grieve to see how the ancient and beloved name of my Fatherland is being driven out of use by the incessant advance of Imperial ideas. A politician nowadays hardly ventures to speak of his own country by its historic name. When Mr. Morley, or Sir William Harcourt, or Mr. Asquith — true Englishmen if any men are — go down to address their constituents, they are corrected by an angry roar if they chance to speak of England or of Englishmen. And they hasten to apologise to the electors who send them to Parliament for the *slip of the tongue* which led them into the blunder of calling our country "England," and of referring with pride to the deeds of our countrymen by the style of "Englishmen." It has come then to this. It is a "slip of the tongue" — a "blunder" — to speak of our country by the name which it has made glorious for a thousand years, or to call oneself a countryman of Cromwell, Shakespeare, Elizabeth, the Henrys, the Edwards, of Harold, of Alfred. One of the curious results of the late schism has been the driving of Liberal politicians out of England, with the melancholy consequence that they are warned off calling themselves Englishmen at all. Lord Rosebery, Sir H. Campbell-Bannerman, and Mr. Bryce were brought up as Scots, in the habit of calling themselves "Britons"; though why Home-Rulers should call the United Kingdom "Britain," I fail to see. One always expects Scots to call themselves

"Britons," if they cannot well say "Scots." They can hardly apply the term "Briton" to Nelson and Wellington, to the two Pitts, to Walpole, Cromwell, and Wolsey. If they think it finer to talk of "Britain" rather than England, they must do so. They cannot help being Scots, as Dr. Johnson said. I should think the term "Scot" was better than "Briton," if they must assert the race tradition. But I very much object to their forcing us to drop the venerable name of "England," and the proud title of "Englishmen." England is my native land, and the name is good enough for me. Irishmen and Scots can call themselves what they like. So may Canadians, Australians, New Zealanders, and Rhodesians. But, in spite of all temptations to belong to these mighty nations, I remain an Englishman. I am proud of the name and of its 1300 years of record. And I pity the Englishman who is ready to drop it, like a Smith or a Brown who has inherited a family estate, and takes on a name which suggests broader acres and more baronial pretensions.

What are we, citizens of no mean country, to call ourselves, if we give up the style of Englishmen? I object most positively to "Briton." I am not willing to call my native land "Britain." Why "Briton" and "Britain"? These terms are wrong on every ground — whether of history, of constitutional right, of language, or of justice. They deliberately exclude Ireland and Irishmen. They are even used in order to exclude Ireland and Irishmen. The style "England" no more excludes Ireland than it excludes Scotland, or Canada, or Australia. The use of the style "Great Britain" — a truly silly and almost comic compound name of our small island — was invented to appease the jealousy of Scots when they accepted the Union. And it was acquiesced in by Englishmen in a spirit of good-nature and almost as a joke. It was used in diplomacy, in Georgian poetry, and in tall kinds of rhetoric. But we Englishmen never seriously took to "Britain"—great or small—in the stress of life. Nelson would have scorned to signal — "*Great Britain* expects every man to do his duty." The poet never said — "Britain, with all thy faults I love thee well!" Let us imagine the bathos of correcting the "slips of tongue" in the Laureate's "Ode to Wellington." Try this: "The last great *Briton* is low." "For this is *Britain's* greatest son." If the Wesleys were Irish, this would be ridiculous. But "Englishman" and "England" may properly describe every subject of our Queen, and every part of her dominions.

Ever since the Union of Ireland, through the whole of this century, the use of the style "Britain" to describe the United Kingdom has been a misnomer. It has been bad in law, false in history, unjust to one of the three nations, and utterly anomalous in any point of view. Scots have insisted on it, because it gratifies Scotch pride and snubs Irish pride. It is a real offence in a politician, whether he be Home-Ruler or Unionist, to allow Scotch pawkiness to jockey both England and Ireland out of the running. One cannot say whether Home-Rulers or Unionists are the greater sinners against their own principles, when they use the terms "Britain" and "Britons," though they mean the United Kingdom of England, Scotland, and Ireland, and all the subjects of Her Majesty. "Britain," which is supposed to include both Wales and Scotland, most distinctly shuts out Ireland; and every time they use the term "Britain" to denote the Three Kingdoms, politicians are giving fresh offence — and just offence — to Irishmen, and justify the claim for a full recognition of Irish nationality. If English Home-Rulers do this, they are plainly minimising the claim of Ireland to be an equal member of the composite State. If Unionists do this, they are treating as a nullity the Act of Union with Ireland.

Irishmen may very fairly say — "Whilst politicians, whether Liberal or Conservative, combine to ignore Ireland in speaking of the United Kingdom, we shall continue to cry out that Ireland is treated as a dependency, and not as a constituent part of the Crown!" There is no answer to this. And it is a great deal more than an accident of speech. It is too true that not a few of those who talk about Britain, when they mean the United Kingdom, deliberately choose to give a prerogative vote to England and Scotland. But that Mr. A. J. Balfour, or Mr. John Morley, should talk of "Britain" when they mean the Queen's Realm, is enough to make the blood of a patriotic Irishman tingle in his veins.

It makes my blood tingle, as a patriotic Englishman, when I see the silly, unhistoric, and bombastic term "Briton" supplanting the ancient and grand name of "Englishman." All that is truly great in our poetry, in our history, in our language, and our household words centres in "England." England is the home of our Monarchy, our Parliament, our Government. In England is the centre of finance, commerce, army, navy, art, and literature, almost as much as Paris is the centre of France, far more than Prussia is the centre of Germany, or Rome the centre of Italy. I do not assert that this fact is enough to compel other nations under the Crown to accept "England" as their common title, if they refuse to do so. But it shows how absurdly inadequate is "Britain" to give that common title. If "England" is to be tabooed what are we going to call our country? It is ridiculous to say "The United Kingdom of Great Britain and Ireland," every time we wish to describe the Queen's Realm. It is a pitiful case for a people if they cannot agree upon a handy name for their own Fatherland. Frenchmen can speak of France, Germans of Germany, Italians of Italy, Russians of Russia. It is a sound and noble form of national pride.

Are we to be forbidden to speak of "England," or else to be driven to the cumbrous periphrasis of the "United Kingdom, and so forth"? Germany, Italy, and Russia are made up of many composite states and nationalities, having different histories, habits, and even dialects and laws. But they can all consent to be known by the common style of Germany, Italy, or Russia. If the subjects of our Queen cannot accept a common style, there must be something ominously wrong in our aggregate realm.

Even if we could use in practice the preposterous sentence which is the legal and formal style of the Three Kingdoms, what about England over the ocean? We have lately been told how important and vast a part of the whole nation is Canada, Australia, South Africa, and scores of lands in both hemispheres. Great Britain is a speck on the vast area of the lands which acknowledge Victoria. Why are these little islands to give their name to the huge congeries of lands and peoples which obey our Queen? If Scots cannot accept "England" as the national style, just as Welshmen have done, and Canadians and Australians have done, by what right can Scots force on Canadians, Australians, and the rest a new-fangled name which exclusively belongs to these islands? The hundred nations, races, and tongues which formed the Roman Empire, all called themselves Romans, and were proud of that name. It was a perpetual source of strength. Even Byzantine Greeks for ten centuries called themselves Romans, and Mussulmans still call Constantinople "Roum." That was a real Empire, and a signal example of a national nucleus giving its historic name to a composite realm. If our Empire refuses to do the same I shall doubt its reality and its vitality. There is in Europe a very ominous type. The subjects of the Emperor who sits so uneasily in Vienna refuse to call themselves "Austrians."

The Dual Monarchy has no common name. And publicists are now discussing "the breaking-up of the Austrian Empire." An empire, to which its own subjects cannot agree to give a national name, is not in a sound and abiding state.

Of course the Imperialists of the Forward school desire to sink "England" in "Empire." But what is the national name of this Empire to be? Why British any more than Pictish or Jutish? It is a thing like Napoleon's Empire or that of Philip II., an accident, a passing anomaly. How does one feel a common patriotism with Klondike and Mashonaland? England has had a thousand years of organic life and glorious record. The Empire of Pathans, Klondikes, Mashonalands, and Ugandas is a thing of yesterday. Who can say where it will be to-morrow? I want something more definite, more organic, more permanent to satisfy my ideas of a Fatherland. I have that in England, in my birthright as Englishman. I will let no Scot, no Australian, no Rhodesian, swagger me out of that name. Who says "Little England"? I say Great England. It is great enough for me, and for all true Englishmen.

ON A SCOTCH REPLY

1898

ON returning from Italy I have been amused to learn that a sect of Scotch patriots have taken seriously to heart a little plea for England which I shot off homewards one day when I felt unusually exhilarated by the glow of the Southern Sun. I was indulging in a gentle jest at some of my Sassenach friends; but the last thing I expected was to be charged with want of sympathy for Scottish nationality. It has always filled me with the liveliest interest and affection. I am myself *Scottis ipsis Scottior*. Ever since, as a schoolboy fifty years ago, I spent some months in the Highlands and every part of Scotland, I have felt the most hearty enthusiasm for Scottish history, poetry, nature, and traditions; I know every corner of Scotland, I have dear Scottish friends, and have entire faith in the indestructibility of Scottish nationality. If blood had anything to do with sentiments, it so happens that I am anything but a mere "Saxon churl." On the father's side I descend from Angles of the Midlands; by women I happen to have Welsh, Irish, and Scotch blood in my veins. I am a nationalist *pur sang*. And the *Positivist Review* in which I wrote is in a special sense the advocate of true nationalist patriotism; and its Editor, Professor Beesly, like myself, is continually insisting that Patriotism is one of the first of public virtues, and that real patriotism must be national, local, and historic. My "Word for England" was a protest against swamping our ancient fatherland in a congeries of boundless tracts without any national cohesion. And one might as well call Mr. Chamberlain a "Little Englander" as think me to be afflicted with any English arrogance.

I fear that it was imprudent on my part to drop a little friendly banter into a discussion which arouses such heat, but of course there is a very serious and complicated question underlying the point which I raised, perhaps in too light a heart. The constant use of the name "Britain," I said, is ending in robbing us of the name of "England." But, quite apart from that, "Britain," as now used, is both inaccurate and inadequate. It is inaccurate because it displaces the legal, official, and constitutional title of these realms. And it is inadequate because it ignores — and not seldom purposely ignores — the other constituent nations and peoples of the Queen's dominions. I am the last man living to wish to force on these nations and peoples the style of "Englishman" and "England," if they object to it. But in like manner I protest against forcing on them the style of "Briton" and "Britain." I should have thought that my "Word for England" would entirely appeal to such hearty Scots as the Reverend David Macrae and his friends. We both plead that England should be English and Scotland should be Scottish. I have the warmest sympathy with these excellent patriots in their gallant efforts to keep alive the sentiment of Scottish nationality, Scottish individuality, and Scottish sentiment. Our cause is the same. But when they seek to sink both Scotland and England in "Britain," when they wish to swamp this island in traditions of mere savages, when they clamour to impose this barbarous style on the English-speaking subjects of our Queen all over the globe — then I say that national patriotism is carrying them too far — into what is both offensive and absurd.

I have seen the use of "Britain" defended by arguments

which are false in history, bad in law, wrong in philosophy, and ridiculous in common-sense. It is said that by Treaty and Act of Parliament this Realm is properly described as "Great Britain." That is untrue. It was true from A.D. 1707 until 1801. Since 1801, the proper title of this Realm is the "United Kingdom of Great Britain and Ireland." That is by Article 1 of the Act of Union, 39 and 40, Geo. III. c. 67. For ninety-eight years this latter style has been the legal title of Her Majesty's dominion. The style "Great Britain" had a shorter currency, and it was legally surrendered by the Scottish representatives in the two Houses at the Union with Ireland. Having by the Act of Union with Ireland in 1801 surrendered the title assumed in the Act of Union with Scotland in 1707, the Scottish people have no claim whatever to impose the obsolete style on England and on Ireland. Those who appeal to international Treaties and Acts of Parliament are flagrantly defying the last Treaty and Act which is still in full vigour. The people of Wessex or Strathclyde might as well appeal to their ancient history, and ask us to tear up the latest great Constitutional settlement.

It is said that "Great Britain" includes Ireland. That is untrue. Every single article of the Act of Union with Ireland (1800) speaks of the "United Kingdom of Great Britain and Ireland," of the "Parliament of the United Kingdom," of his "Majesty's subjects in Ireland" and his "Majesty's subjects in Great Britain." In no single article does this Act use the term "Great Britain" to include Ireland. And the Act of Union with Scotland, 1706, in no single article uses "Great Britain" to include Ireland. The Act 9 Anne, c. 6, speaks of "exports from Great Britain into Ireland." The official title of the Sovereign after the union with Scotland was "Queen (or King) of Great Britain, France, and

Ireland." Ever since the union with Ireland in 1801, it has been "King (or Queen) of the United Kingdom of Great Britain and Ireland." It may be said that this is official, legal, constitutional language. But the plea for "Great Britain" is itself official, legal, and constitutional, or rather it pretends to be. If we turn to scientific nomenclature we may read in Dr. Murray's *New Dictionary* that "Britain" is the proper name for "the whole island containing England, Wales, and Scotland with their dependencies." Neither in law nor in correct language does "Great Britain" include Ireland. And my point is that it is too often used to exclude Ireland.

We have been told that the ancients included Ireland in "Britain." That is untrue. The Greeks and the Romans called Ireland Ierne and Hibernia; and the whole current of ancient geography limited "Britain" to our own island and often opposed it to Caledonia, as any one can see who will turn to Sir E. Bunbury's *History of Ancient Geography* or W. Smith's *Dictionary of Geography*. But the true question is, not what style is used by the Greeks and Romans, by poets, or in popular talk, but what is the legal, official, and Parliamentary title of our country. Most certainly it is not "Britain" nor "Great Britain," for which there is no basis except in loose habits of speech. To appeal to Treaties and to Acts of Parliament is absurd, for they tell the other way. By what Treaty, by what Act, by what international or public agreement, did Englishmen, Welshmen, Scots, and Irishmen ever agree that the formal style of their country should be "Britain," or agree to call themselves "Britons"? Yet the Petitioners talk of Treaties, Acts, and Rights!

What is so laughable is that this appeal to formal styles, rights, and laws comes from those who are habitually violating all these at once.   Mr. Macrae says that "*the proper title* of the United Kingdom is Britain." He might just as well say that "the proper title of Edinburgh is 'Auld Reekie.'" The proper title of the United Kingdom is stated in 39 and 40 Geo. III. c. 67, and it is not "Britain." Even before that Act, from 1707 until 1801, it was not "Britain" — but "Great Britain," and these sticklers for official titles should not clip the Queen's English. If we are always to speak by the card and any equivocation in national titles is to undo us, we ought to talk of the "Great British Army," which our foreign rivals would find rather comical, and always refer to Mr. Balfour as the "Leader of the House of Commons of the United Kingdom of Great Britain and Ireland." That is a mouthful, but it is strictly official, and these gentlemen appeal to Acts of Parliament. If it is to be a matter of loose talk, who made the term "British" the "proper title"? We Englishmen, Welshmen, and Irishmen have never agreed to it; and even Scots, if they insist on using it, ought to say "Great British," and not British. They can use any cant nickname they like, but "British" to my ear is a silly nickname. It suggests painted savages, scythed chariots, and Queen Boadicea.

Happily, the mass of sensible Scots in 1800 consented to surrender the term "Great Britain," or rather to merge it in a new title, the legal and official authority of which is unimpeachable. Unluckily, that legal title is rather awkward and cumbrous for ordinary use. It is no doubt true that a convenient common name for our vast Empire is rather a want, and my object when I first wrote was to point this out. Whether all the peoples within it across the seas can agree to call it "English," as all our neighbours do and will do, I am not greatly concerned. But with the most lively sympathy for Scottish nationality, and hearty approval of its patriotic champions, I cannot consent to their forcing on us Englishmen and on all the many millions of subjects of our Queen the term "British," which to my ear connotes something barbarous, something tribal and local, and which at times has an almost comic suggestion.

THE SCOTTISH PETITION TO THE QUEEN

1898

I HAVE been favoured with sundry copies of a Petition to the Queen from her Scottish subjects, dated 13th November last, signed by David Macrae and others. I had not previously heard of this document nor of its signatories; but as I suppose the first name to it is that of the reverend gentleman who has recently mistaken a few words of my own in so curious a way, I venture to submit to him some remarks thereon. I need not repeat that with the wish of patriotic Scotsmen to cherish their ancient nationality, to be extremely jealous that the historic name and individuality of Scotland should not be merged and smothered in any other nationality and name, I am in most hearty sympathy. And my simple "Word for England" was put forth in a kindred sense; and, without wishing to impose the name of England on others, I asked merely that it should not be merged and smothered by Englishmen at home.

The Petition to the Queen relates to a formal title as defined by public law, and consequently must be worthless if it be itself inaccurate and loose in its own language and references. Now English publicists are amazed to find how little this Petition corresponds with the legal learning, the precision, the common sense which we always expect from public men in Scotland. The Petition asserts that in 1707 the official title of the Sovereign and the Realm was changed by law, and was settled for ever; and it prays that this official title may now be strictly observed. It calmly ignores the notorious fact that in 1801 by the same law, and in the same constitutional way, the official title of the Sovereign and the Realm was again changed by law and was settled for ever in a new way. Do the Petitioners mean to tell us that the Act of Union of 1801 was mere waste paper? They demand the revival of an official title which was superseded 98 years ago, and pray for the abrogation of that title which has never been challenged during the present century? Queen Anne is dead: and a good many things have happened since — so that the Titles and Acts of Her Sacred Majesty have been somewhat amended and modified.

The first sentence of the Petition professes to cite the Union of 1707. I turn to the *Revised Statutes* (2nd edition, 1888) i. 787, for we have nothing to do with Preliminaries and Treaties: the Act of Union of 1707, as amended and now in force, to the understanding of a lawyer, governs the whole, and so far as official titles extend, is final and decisive. Now, I find that the first sentence of the Petition is a slovenly and quite inaccurate paraphrase of the First Article of the Act of Union of 1707. That Act was amended and modified so far as the official title of the Sovereign and the Realm is concerned by the Act of Union of 1801. I have both Acts and the Petition before me as I write. And I assert that the Petition wholly ignores the later Act and wholly misquotes the earlier Act. It is a pity that, in approaching the Throne on so solemn an occasion, the reverend gentleman and his friends could not have secured the help of that accurate learning and scrupulous precision for which Scottish jurisprudence is justly famous.

The petitioners are wont to claim the Act of Union of 1707 for the official use of the term "Britain" and "British." It so happens that the Act, even supposing that it had not been superseded on this head by the Act of 1801, does not once contain the term "British" from beginning to end, nor does

T

it use the term "Britain" apart from "Great Britain." "Oh, but," they say, "we use the terms 'Britain' and 'British' for short in everyday speech, and every one knows what we mean!" Yes, but the Petition is not dealing with short names or everyday speech, but with formal titles as strictly defined by constitutional law. That is just the slipshod way in which the whole Petition is drawn. It cites an Act of Parliament without noticing another Act by which it was modified and superseded; and it misquotes the language of the Act itself, though the sole point in dispute is a matter of strict language.

I come to a point on which I will try to be serious, though it is too funny for words. The Petition as sent to me bears on the cover a grand woodcut that professes to be a new and improved version of the Royal Coat of Arms and so forth. I am no herald, but I have had, in pursuit of history, to dabble a little in that abstruse science. Anything more comic than this work of art I never saw. It blazons "over all, on an Inescutcheon of Pretence," the Arms of Hanover! Prodigious! as Dominie Sampson would shout. Do the Petitioners assert that Her Majesty is now Queen of Hanover? Have they not heard that, from June 1837, the Arms of Hanover were (very naturally) removed from the Royal Shield? Do they pretend that our Sovereign is to this day a feudatory of the German Emperor, or a Pretender to the Crown of Hanover? What do they mean? Do they know the elementary rule of Heraldry that all minor titles are merged in Royalty, and that no subordinate arms can be quartered or mingled with Arms of Dominion? And these sticklers for Heraldic titles perpetrate a blunder which makes the very Unicorn turn round and grin "like a Cheshire cat"!

I come to the chief point of the whole Coat as amended, on which I confess that I tread as if *incedens per ignes sup-*

positos — I mean the grand coat of Scotland — *or*, the lion rampant *gules*, within a double treasure flory counter-flory of the last.   I have such genuine admiration for this beautiful creation of the herald's art, and such a fascination for its historic traditions, that I would not seem to smile at that noble beast, caged as he is in a double tressure flory counter-flory.   But what on earth do the Petitioners mean by doubling this royal carnivore, by setting him in the first and fourth quarters, and by kicking the poor, half-starved lions of England into a back seat in the second quarter?   No doubt it is meant to assert that Scotland is the "predominant partner" in the United Kingdom of Great Britain and Ireland.   I shall not attempt to dispute it.   But heraldry in the art of quartering has to deal with legal inheritances and not with the wealth, acreage, or achievements of families.   What then is meant by the claim of the double *Lion rampant gules*?   And what is meant by setting the Scottish Unicorn as *dexter* supporter and banishing to the *sinister* side the English lion, who looks grumpy enough?   One can only suppose, from the herald's point of view, that it means that the Sovereign represents primarily and directly a Scottish family, and tacks on the coats of her English and Irish inheritances as subordinate quarterings.

Was there ever such childish nonsense in a schoolboy's caricature?   Does it mean that Her Majesty represents the House of Stuart and not the House of Hanover?   Let the Reverend David Macrae take care.   He is dabbling in treason.   Does he mean to lead the Clan Macrae again to Derby?   Does he mean to chuck over the Act of Settlement as well as the Act of Union with Ireland?   Is this Petition another phase of that tomfoolery about the rightful heir to the throne being a foreign Prince who claims Stuart descent?   The throne of these realms is settled upon the descendants of the

Electress Sophia. The Electress Sophia was the daughter of the King of Bohemia, and the wife of the Elector of Hanover. She was not a Stuart, except in blood, as were scores of men and women. In law, in heraldry, and in common sense, a woman who marries, and certainly one who marries a foreign prince, cannot represent the family from which she descends, but only the family into which she marries. The Electress Sophia was not, legally and heraldically, a Stuart, either by birth or by marriage. The Crown has been settled on her descendants, and consequently is not settled on a Stuart.

Supposing that she had been a Stuart by birth, would that make Queen Victoria a Stuart, or chief of the House of Stuart? How came James Stuart to have any claim to the throne of England? Well, because his great-grandmother was a Tudor — daughter of Henry VII., and descended from Plantagenets, Kings of England. The throne of these islands has descended since the Conquest to one House after another through married women, who on entering a new House have entered a new family and borne a new name. The same devolution which took the royal title to the Scottish Stuarts, took it from them to the Hanoverian House (vulgarly called Guelph) — just as the Scottish Stuarts took it through women from Welsh Tudors, and they from English Plantagenets, and they from Normans and Angevins. There is therefore not the smallest reason to pretend that Her Majesty represents Stuarts or any Scottish family more than she represents Welsh Tudors, or English Plantagenets, Normans and Angevins. By descent she traces her family through them all; but by law and the constitution she represents the House of Hanover. And if Mr. Macrae attempts to dispute it, he may end yet, like some of his Highland cousins, on Tower Hill.

They died for Scotland, true to the memories of that ancient kingdom. He will die for "Britain," and with his last gasp will forswear the land of his fathers, and claim allegiance to a lot of painted savages. We are the true patriots. We stand up for England and its ancient name and glorious memories. I am sorry to learn that Scotsmen can be found who wish to sink Scotland and its grand traditions in a style which is too often used in the way of swagger or the way of mockery.

IDEAL LONDON

ADDRESS GIVEN AT LONDON UNIVERSITY, 1898

Now that you have heard so much of London in the past and in the present, of London a thousand years ago, and of London and its new County Council, of the art, the science, the poetry, the schools, the churches of London, I am bidden to speak to you of "Ideal London," which I understand is — London as it *might* be, as it *should* be, as it *shall* be.

Neither the subject nor the title of this lecture is of my choosing, but I willingly accept the task. And I can imagine that some of you may be saying — Ideal London is an impossible London; an unpractical, unreal, visionary thing; of no use to man or woman; an idle day-dream, which need not be intruded on serious students and laborious research. Do not be too sure of that. An ideal is a standard at which we aim, the hope of things not seen, that which we yearn to make ourselves and our lives, for the things we see are temporal (saith the Apostle), the things not seen are eternal. Without ideals we grow into fossils, drones, brutes. What is the good of study, what is the need of research, unless it be to know, in order to improve, to leave the world better than we found it, to attain to a true and well-grounded progress? And can there be progress unless we see clearly some goal at which we ought to arrive, however slow be our course, however laborious the study with which we prepare it and forecast it. As the poet says:

> We live by admiration, hope, and love.

Morality, religion are based on ideals. Without ideals there would be no hope, and without hope, neither religion, nor

278

aspiration, nor energy, nor good work. A true ideal is no dream, no idle fantasy. It is the justification of study, and the motive of all useful endeavour.

If I am asked to speak of London as it might be, my only claim to occupy your attention may be that London is my birthplace, and for nearly sixty years has been my home; that I have watched the growth and rebuilding of London for two generations, whilst it has increased its area four or five times and its population two or three times. I have seen the rise of the Houses of Parliament, the Royal Exchange, the National Gallery, the British Museum, the whole of the new towns at Paddington, Kensington, Chelsea, and Maida and Notting Hills, the covering with houses of the vast area west of Belgrave Square and the Edgware Road and the area north of the Euston Road. I have seen begun the embankment of the Thames and the whole of the railway system out of London. My memory of London goes back to the time of the first epoch of policemen, omnibuses, and cabs, to a time when Tyburnia, Chelsea, and South Kensington were market-gardens, when there was not a single railroad out of London, no penny post or telegraph, when no man or woman in working clothes was admitted into Kensington Gardens, and when the people were still buried in city churches and in urban graveyards. May I add that for some years I worked hard in the service of the government of London, as a member of the first and second County Councils, an experience which brought home to me the incessant needs of London reorganisation and the enormous difficulties which in practice it has to overcome? I come before you, therefore, as a rather "old London hand," who knows something of the greatest city on this earth, who longs to see it live up to its marvellous history, and one, too, who knows something of the practical difficulties that beset its reform.

Now, in speaking to you of Ideal London, or rather of London as it might be made, I shall keep within the limits of practical statesmanship and possible reform. I put aside any fancy picture of an unsubstantial city in the air — what the Greek dramatist called a Cloud-cuckoo-land. I know something of the difficulties which await the Municipal Reformer — difficulties of the legislature, of finance, of vested interests, of law, of opinion, of habit, and indifference. I know these obstacles, and I shall not pretend to ignore them. But I am not bound by limits of time, or by the legislation of this or that Parliament, the prejudices of the present generation, or the tone and customs of to-day, no, nor of to-morrow. London is far older than the Empire, or the monarchy, or the constitution, or the Church, or our actual stage of civilisation in any form — and I think it will outlive them all. And Ideal London is not to be "cribb'd, cabin'd, and confin'd" within this or that generation, this or that habit of life, this or that social organisation. It should be a city that develops all that ever was good in city life, and all that we can imagine to belong to pure and perfect citizenship.

It is the weak side of modern civilisation that it has failed to carry on some of the fine elements of city life as known to the ancient and mediæval world; and, of all Europeans, we English of to-day take the least pride in our cities, and receive from them the least of inspiration and culture. The historic cities of the world — Jerusalem, Athens, Rome, Byzantium — sum up entire epochs of civilisation in themselves. To the ancients, the very idea of a nation, with a national system of life, implied a mother-city as its home and type. And in the modern world the citizens of Florence, Venice, Paris, Seville, Bern, Nuremberg, Cologne, and Ghent have all had far deeper sympathy with their native cities than the Londoner has with his city, at least within the last two or three cen-

turies of its life. This is a definite loss to London and to
England. For if we truly estimate the indispensable need
to a nation of a great capital worthy of itself, as a seat of its
highest culture, energy, organisation, and capacity for the
multiform sides of civic organism, we shall see that England
and the British race are all the poorer in that it still fails to
inspire the Englishman with that sense of sympathy, pride,
and example which Rome gave to the Roman world and
which Paris gives to the French and the whole Latin race.

   To the poor countryman London is too often a place where
he may get bare life, variety, and cheap amusement. To the
rich countryman it is a place where he goes to buy all things
that money can furnish; where Vanity Fair lasts for some
three months; and from which he rushes off when his pur-
chases are made, and when the Fair is over. To the dull
provincial it is a place where he hopes to pick up "the last
thing out" — in the peculiar vernacular he affects. To the
ambitious man of business and the aspiring professional it is
a place where toil and energy and skill may enable him to
make a fortune, and in old age to retire to a rural retreat with
an adequate "pile." And the city suffers, both within and
without, from these unworthy aims; and it has the aspect of
a place which is valued mainly as a market, an exchange, a
warehouse, an office, and a playground. It was not thus that
Athens, Rome, Florence, and Venice were looked on by their
citizens — nor was London so looked on in the age of Norman
and Plantagenet, of Tudors and Stuarts.

   Now "Ideal London," to which I personally conduct you,
covers in buildings barely one-third of the London we know
— a city which measures on an average some ten miles across,
and covers 120 square miles of houses, with streets which
end on end would reach straight across Europe, from the
centre of which you must walk for many hours before you

can see a green field — this is not a city, but a wilderness of houses. It is an old saying that "one cannot see the forest for the trees." So we may say, "in London we cannot see the city for the houses." City life is impossible for a crowd of four or five millions of people, and with a hundred square miles of buildings. The city of Edward I.'s time, the legal "city," still occupied about one square mile; and twenty or thirty such cities is surely the utmost possible area for continuous buildings to cover if true life is to be lived within them. No inventions in locomotion, trams, railways, or bicycles, can do away with legs and feet for ordinary use. And, until science has invented wings to fly with, or seven-leagued boots to jump with, men, women, and children will have to walk on their ten toes. And, unless their ten toes can carry them in an hour out into the open, where they may hear the lark, and smell the hay, and feel the open sky above them — the town is no city: it is a prison.

So I hold that the London that is to be will not exceed two millions of inhabitants, and would be a happier city if it did not exceed one million, and if its area was less than one-third of what it is to-day. You may ask me, what arbitrary limits are there to put bounds to a city? I reply, the arbitrary limits are those which Creation has imposed on ordinary men and women who cannot comfortably walk more than three miles in an hour, not more than three hours at a stretch, and children, old and delicate persons, not half of that. Whilst our size is limited to some five or six feet, and our powers of physical exertion to a few hours out of the twenty-four, any ideal city life for men must be limited by the physical conditions of human nature; and if men are to live in cities with the highest conditions of civic life, those cities must be controlled by limits of numbers and area.

You may ask me by what means can so vast a change be

effected.   And I answer that this involves a big set of practical problems which neither time nor my own powers enable me to deal with.   I am not here to enter on a series of political and economic problems, nor have I a patented body of devices, bills, and projects to effect such change.   As I said at the outset, an "Ideal" is not bound by time, nor by the legislation, prejudices, habits of to-day.   It is bound only by the possibilities of human nature and the wide laws of English civilisation.   All I maintain is, that this change is possible, practicable, within the conditions of modern civilised habits.   The population of London at the opening of this century was under one million.   At my birth it did not exceed a million and a half.   At that date its area was barely one quarter of what it is to-day.   Why need I think these limits are impossible in the future?   Such cities as Rome, Athens, Milan, Marseilles, Lyons, Paris, and London have lived through enormous changes in their population and their area — in some cases exceeding changes of increase by tenfold and of decrease to one-tenth.   Why need we regard as hopeless in an unknown future a state of things which existed in London at my own lifetime?

Those who have studied the topography and history of such cities as Paris, London, Rome, Constantinople, Chicago, Vienna, Alexandria, and Cairo — those who can remember, as I can, the London, the Paris, the Rome, the Florence, of some forty or even fifty years ago — can hardly see what bounds need be placed on the physical transformation of great cities under adequate efforts.   We have witnessed the densest hives of the mediæval cities of London, Paris, Rome, and Florence swept away to make magnificent avenues or vast open sites, or huge palaces, or public structures.   We have seen in London and elsewhere overcrowded centres rapidly depleted, and straggling quarters of small houses replaced by vast blocks of aggregate tenements. This radical series of changes — the emptying of the old effete cores of our cities and the gathering of the population into immense blocks of tenements — is going on at a great pace, and is already beginning to transform London. I am no lover of the "flat" system in itself; I am a warm lover of the old private house system as the normal home of a family. But I see this — that if millions of persons insist on living together in a city, and if they are to live there in a high state of civilised life, some form of the tenement system must be adopted. It is universal in all great European and American cities, and it is unavoidable in all great cities unless they are to grow to unmanageable bulk. It is being done here rapidly. I am far from saying that our actual tenements are what they should be — London, indeed, has no "ideal" tenements. I do not like tenements; I regret the necessity. But if persons will live in a city of some millions and desire to live a civilised life, to the tenement system they must come. Those who cannot endure a tenement life must be content with the country, and with smaller towns. As it is, nine-tenths of the dwellers in London do to-day live in tenements — only the lodgings they have are in small, rotten, ill-kept, unwholesome, old houses. On an average there are ten persons to a house, whilst there might well be fifty or a hundred. Ideal London will give the mass of its citizens spacious, airy, lofty, clean, and healthy blocks, provided with common baths, kitchens, lifts, libraries, play-rooms, sick-rooms, and even mortuaries. All that the few now provide for themselves in their private mansions will be available for the many by the aid of wise co-operation.

London properly housed on a scientific system of tenements would occupy one-third or one-quarter of the area now loosely covered with small houses. And this would give an enormous area of new room for gardens, parks, boulevards, and playgrounds, even if the population continued to exceed four millions of souls. But the causes which within this century have raised the population from one to four or five millions, and the area of buildings from 5 square miles to 120 square miles, are really temporary and incidental. Political, economic, and international changes will react in another way within measurable time; and if this fabulous and unnatural growth has taken place in a single century, it will need but a few centuries to undo it. I wholly repudiate the dismal forecast that London is to go on increasing in size and numbers at the rate of the last fifty years; I will not believe Mother Shipton's prophecy that Hampstead Heath is to be the centre of London, or that its population at the end of the next century is to be ten millions of souls. But if its population is to be even two or three millions, and these are to live a human life, the present parks, avenues, and open places ought at least to be doubled or trebled. With a park, a playground, and a great open ground within one mile at most of every citizen's home, civic life of a high order is possible. Without these things it is impossible.

We have done much in the way of parks within twenty years; but it is only a corner of what we have to do. In the four or five miles of dreary streets which separate Regent's Park from Victoria Park, and in those four or five miles of blackened streets which separate Battersea Park from Rotherhithe, there is a cruel want of fresh air, trees, greenery, and free space. One of the greatest of all wants is good playgrounds, I mean such turf and space as are to be seen at Lord's and at the Oval. A city is not habitable by highly civilised men unless it can offer adequate playgrounds to men, children, and young women within an easy walk of their own homes. The last few years have witnessed a great move in that direction, and what has already been done in Battersea, Regent's, and Victoria parks, as well as the more outlying greens, is enough to show what we can do. But we do not half use our actual opportunities. No man values more than I do the peace and freedom of Kensington Gardens, few men resort to it more. But I still demand that in all the Royal parks and all possible public spaces there should be regularly opened playgrounds, with proper regulations and conditions — to keep the youth of our citizens in health — until such time at least as it shall be possible to provide even better playgrounds within a mile or two of every man's doorstep. A city fails to fulfil its functions completely unless it has as much fresh air as Edinburgh, and playgrounds, walks, and gardens as plentiful and close at hand as Oxford or Cambridge.

In those good days the Thames will again run as clear and fresh as it does now at Henley, and it will be, as of old, the great highway of passage from east to west. The bridges over it and the tunnels under it will be just double of what they are now, and the railway viaducts and termini which disfigure it will be suitably treated. The embankment, finely wooded, will be carried along both sides of the river for the whole length of the city; and where it is necessary to have wharves for unloading, these will be carried into docks, whilst leaving the embankment clear for traffic, and our noble river at London will be as much in use for healthy exercises by men and women as the Thames is to-day at Richmond and Maidenhead. No doubt we shall be carried up and down the river in electric launches — not in smoky, noisome, puffing, and snorting steamboats. Steam engines of all kinds will be excluded from the City — power being obtained from electric and other non-infecting sources. I need hardly say that in the good time to come no smoke will pollute the air and ruin the vegetation of London. That some millions of house chimneys and ten thousand factory chimneys should be suffered to pour out into the pure air of heaven their poisonous fumes, so that we are all to be choked with soot, our flowers and shrubs stunted, our public buildings, statues, and carvings begrimed with a sulphurous deposit — this to our descendants will seem an abomination and a public crime, to be sternly suppressed by law and opinion. They will hardly believe what they read in history that such things were in the nineteenth century. It will seem to them as strange as it does to us when we read that our savage ancestors ate their dinners with their fingers, wore sheepskin clothes for a lifetime, and went to bed between foul rugs, without any clothes at all.

No doubt the reformers of those days were asked with sneers how the people were to procure so many forks and nightgowns, just as we are asked to-day how we are going to abolish smoking chimneys. Our answer is that it *can* be done — it can be done by science, labour, economy, and public opinion. And therefore it must be done, and the sooner the better. When we stand on the Capitol or the Pincian Hill at Rome, or look down over Florence from the Boboli Terrace; when we survey Paris from Notre Dame, or Genoa from the Church of Carignans; when we see how glorious and happy is the look of a smokeless city in a bright sky, how refreshing are the terraces, housetops, and balconies bright with flowers and laid out with summer arbours and garden retreats — it makes one boil with indignation to think that in our own cities at home neither house gardens nor arbours are possible, from the gross indifference with which we suffer preventable nuisances to choke us.

In the good time coming rivers of pure mountain water will be carried into London by gigantic aqueducts, as at ancient Rome. We shall no longer run the risk of poison from polluted drains, or of a water famine from the shrinking of a petty river. Our water supply will come from inexhaustible lakes and reservoirs. Ancient Rome, with its fourteen aqueducts, is the true type; it has never yet been surpassed, or even equalled. Already some northern cities are fairly supplied in a similar way. It would have been done for London long ago, but for commercial self-interest, political intrigue, and administrative jealousy and confusion. It is a blot on our modern civilisation that the water supply of London is still so scanty, so impure, so uncertain, and so dear.

In the good time coming we shall not buy water of money-making speculators any more than we now buy fresh air, or a ticket for Hyde Park, or a pass across London Bridge. Water, like air, highways, and parks, is a prime necessity of civilised life, and it is the business of the State to supply it to citizens freely, in absolute purity and unlimited abundance. I can remember a time when several bridges over the Thames exacted tolls, and when London was surrounded with turnpikes. It sounds incredible to us that our fathers could endure such a drag on civilisation. And it will sound incredible to our descendants that we suffered water to be bought and sold and haggled for in the market. We must go back to the standard of Rome with free and unlimited water, with baths and public wash-houses in every main thoroughfare.

Pure water, unlimited in quantity, accessible to all, fresh air, spacious highways, ample recreation grounds — these things are a necessity of health, and the *health* of the citizens is a primary public concern. It has been the pride of the last half-century that vast sanitary reform has been accomplished. And the proof of it is found in the diminishing death-rate of most great cities, and in the highest degree of London.

There are cities in Europe to-day where the death-rate is double that of London — nay, where it is three times what the death-rate of London has been for whole months within the last year. The normal death-rate of Cairo is nearly three times that of London; 80,000 lives per annum at least are saved in London which would be sacrificed but for the advance of sanitary science and municipal reform. But we are only at the beginning of our task. The rate in London may now be said to be brought well below 20 per 1000. In the good time to come it will be brought down to ten. At this moment there are squares and terraces in the West where the rate is not so high as this. The death-rate of Derby this very week is under ten. And to this ideal limit it must be brought before sanitary reform has said its last word.

That word will not be said until every sewer is as free from poisonous gas and deadly ferments as a scullery sink in a well-found house, until the suspicion of preventable infection and contagion is entirely removed, until the infants of the poor are no more destroyed by unintentional infanticide than are the infants of the rich, until birth, measles, whooping-cough, and scarlatina have ceased to decimate the homes of the careless, the ignorant, and the indigent. As it is, at least a quarter of our present death-rate is due to conditions which if those responsible were not so helpless and so ignorant would amount to manslaughter and even murder. And perhaps a fifth of the death-rate over and above this is due to conditions which are distinctly preventible by science and by organisation. In the good time to come the 50,000 or 60,000 lives we slaughter annually in London alone by our stupidity and misman-agement will be told by our descendants as an abnormal barbarism such as caused the Plague and the Black Death of old.

I am speaking, I trust you will believe, by no means at

U

random and by a vague guess, but from long and careful comparison of various statistics. I will give you one striking example. Rome, having become the capital of Italy, set about a vigorous reform of its sanitary condition. Now, the climate around Rome is one of the most dangerous and uncertain in Europe, and the physical conditions of Rome, except for its grand water supply, offer many peculiar difficulties. Yet in twenty years Rome has reduced its death-rate by one-third, in spite of doubling its population. In 100 years the death-rate of London has been reduced by one-half, in spite of its enormous increase. Within the last ten years the deaths in many great cities of North Europe, even under the very difficult conditions of such countries as Holland and Belgium, have been reduced by 10 and 20 per cent. It is a question entirely of science, organisation, education. There are spots even now where a death-rate of 8 per thousand has been known. London, when it has a clean Thames and abundant and pure water, will be naturally one of the healthiest places in Europe. Why should its death-rate be 18 instead of 8? For no reason but for bad government, ignorance, and indifference, public as well as private.

The problem of health will take a foremost place in the municipal organisation of the future; and a large part of the problem concerns the treatment of disease and death. The hospitals of Ideal London will not be imposing palaces, filling the best sites and endangering the health of the city. All that is a mediæval tradition, maintained for the convenience of the doctors in large practice, and with the advertising aim of being always in public view. Small accident and emergency wards will be multiplied at convenient spots. But the great standing hospitals will be removed to airy suburbs, reached by special rail and tram lines with ambulance cars of wonderful ingenuity, the hospitals themselves being constantly disinfected, pulled to pieces, and rebuilt, so as at last to get rid of hospital pyæmia and the melancholy death-rate of our actual clumsy pest-houses.

The disposal of the dead is an even more urgent problem. I am old enough to remember the dark ages when the population of London was interred in graveyards within the City itself. One of my memories as a child was that of occasional residence in a house which actually abutted on such a burial-ground, and my leisure hours were much absorbed in watching the funerals hour by hour. I am one of those who survived this atrocious custom, which still endangers the health of our city, and for generations to come will continue to be a source of infection. Some fifty years ago the intra-mural graveyards were closed and the suburban cemeteries were formed. But, alas! they are suburban no longer. The ever advancing city has begun to encircle them, and they are again becoming a new source of infection and nuisance. They are driving us to more and more outlying cemeteries, which can only be reached by a long railway journey, and are to all of us difficult to visit.

The result is this. A city which requires its 80,000 interments year by year is compelled to bury its dead either in cemeteries, overcrowded and practically within the city of the living, or else in cemeteries so far from its city that each funeral involves a fatiguing and costly journey, and visits to the tomb of the departed loved ones become rare or impracticable. If the population of London continues to increase it will soon need year by year 100,000 burials — equal to the whole population of famous cities in old times. Where can these be disposed of with safety, so as not to be put away from us for ever, and that only after a wearisome and expensive travel? In this dilemma I do not doubt that London will largely return to the ancient and honoured practice of cremation. Cremation affords to the living absolute protection from infection and poison; to the survivors it spares them the horrible associations of the decaying remains; it solves the problem which awaits us — the appalling accumulation of some millions of corpses in one city in each decade; and it enables the family to place the inurned ashes of those they cherish in a church, or in a cloister, or in a city graveyard, or in any spot, above ground or under ground, public or private, close at hand, and yet entirely void of offence, where the sacred remains may be visited from time to time with perfect ease and peace. It is too much forgotten that cremation is a scientific process for preparing the remains of the dead for such permanent disposal as we please to select, and whether by interment or not. The calcined residuum of the body is no longer a horror and pollution to the living, but may be preserved for ages either in a visible urn in some consecrated spot, or buried in a grave or vault precisely like a coffin. All the sacred associations of the tomb, all the *genius loci* of the grave, are retained when the purified ashes are shrined in their urn and set up in monument or niche. So in my visions I see the London that is to be filled with mausoleums and chapels and cloisters, wherein the dust of generations will lie in perfect peace yet in the midst of the living, far from all possible danger or offence, yet always before their sight and present to their memory, be it in some consecrated urn, or beneath the sod in their midst, or underneath the pavement that is trodden by generations to come.

The problem of reorganising London has taken a new phase since the division into sixty parliamentary boroughs. London is being gradually broken up into manageable parts, each of which is a large and rich municipality with its own administration and local institutions and buildings. Some of these, such as Battersea, Chelsea, Poplar, and Westminster, are beginning to show real municipal life. The movement is still in formation. But it opens a vision of the future when, with an adequate central government and a real unity of London as a whole, its component parts may have their own local institutions, life, and character; their own halls, libraries, schools, museums, playgrounds, parks, and public centres, so that the life of a great city may be offered to all citizens within a mile of their own homes and within reach of their own influence.

The London that is to be, if, indeed, it is to remain with a population counted by millions, will be an aggregate of many cities, each equal in area to Nottingham or Edinburgh, and each possessing a complete city organisation of its own, but all uniting in one central civic constitution. The great arteries of communication will be broad and stately boulevards, without the artificial monotony of the new avenues in Paris, and without the makeshift meanness of Shaftesbury Avenue and the Charing Cross Road. The traveller who lingers with delight round the Hôtel de Ville and the Fountain of the Innocents in Paris; in the Via Balbi and round San Lorenzo at Genoa; in the old Piazzas of Florence and Venice; who strolls along the Corso at Rome, feels his heart sink within him as he returns to the biggest and richest city of the world, and marks how grimy, and filthy, and inconvenient are the streets and open spaces and public buildings of London. Neither breadth, nor dignity, nor permanence, nor self-respect (to say nothing of art and beauty) seem ever to have suggested themselves to the tasteless tradesmen who (we suppose) ordered from ignorant carpenters the cheapest and commonest sort of road or hall which contractors could erect. But it is not to last for ever. Ideal London will far surpass actual Paris in natural conditions, and I think in free play of thought and aim. The race which built the Abbey, and Westminster Hall, St. Paul's, the Banqueting Hall, and laid out Piccadilly and the parks cannot be wholly incapable of a noble building. Even now the energy and individuality of our character is asserting itself through the pall of convention and frivolity which, since the Reformation and the civil wars, has afflicted us as a nation. London has magnificent opportunities, and carries within it the germs of noble art. The Ideal London of our dreams — nay, of our descendants — will be one of the noblest cities of Europe, a model of healthfulness, dignity, and convenience.

We want no Haussmanns and emperors here to drive uniform boulevards or rectangular squares through the old City, on the plan of a chess-board or a figure in geometry. The mechanical planning of a city, so dear to transatlantic fancy and to the vanity of an autocrat in Europe, does not fall in with English habits and our secular traditions. I hope that the historic streets of London will ever be maintained, and the associations of the Strand, Ludgate Hill, Charing Cross, Bishopsgate and Aldgate, Holborn and Piccadilly, may live for centuries yet. I incline to think that it is as well that Wren's magnificent, but too geometric and revolutionary, scheme for rebuilding London after the Fire was never carried out. It was magnificent, but it was not practical. It was not practical, in that it would have swept away the history and traditions of London, just as the history and traditions of the old City of Paris in the Island have been swept away by the Imperial demolitions. No! let us keep the history and the traditions of London, even at the cost of some irregularity, narrowness, and inconveniences in the old streets, retaining infinite variety in the form and style of the buildings along them. Tradition and variety in an ancient city outweigh all the regularity and symmetry of modern reconstruction.

If any one desires to see what has been done of late years, and what it was hoped to do in London improvements, let him study an important new work issued by the London County Council, and prepared by Mr. Percy Edwards, the able clerk of the Improvements Committee. They will see what Wren desired to make of London in 1666, what London was in 1855, what it is to-day, and all the changes made in it these forty-three years. It is a record of many improvements, not a few blunders, many fine schemes ruined by a cheese-paring economy, by political conflicts, by interested intrigues, by local jealousies, stupidity, bad taste, and lethargy. But, as we study that record of the edility of London for forty-three years, we need not despair of the London that is to be.

We shall not destroy the old historic lines and landmarks of London, which, as an organised city, has an unbroken record of a thousand years since Alfred rebuilt it after rescuing it from the Danes. We shall not sweep away the great lines and landmarks of mediæval London; but the hopelessly rotten and festering slums of the old crowded areas will have to be purified and rebuilt, and the inhabitants replaced in airy and commodious dwellings, at least half of them in fresh and healthy suburbs. But the old lines and lanes of mediæval London are hopelessly congested and need a vigorous treatment. We shall not abolish Fleet Street and the Strand, Cornhill, Gracechurch Street, Holborn, and Chancery Lane; but we shall add on new lines of communication that will relieve the arterial traffic. The heavy traffic of merchandise, stores, and plant passing across London, or along it from line to line, will be carried by deep electric railways underground, and also some light conveyance will be effected by new aërostatic modes of transit. It will be considered ridiculous to send machinery, coals, or heavy goods by the ordinary streets, which will be immensely relieved by the almost uni-

versal adoption of automobile cars in place of horse-carriages.
I do not mean the horrid, stinking, rattling motor-cars we see
to-day, but beautiful and elegant vehicles, which will run
quietly and silently by mechanical power.   The main needs
of London are easy and open avenues of communication
from north to south, and across the Thames from Middlesex
to Surrey.   These in the good times to come will be doubled
or trebled, partly by new bridges across our noble river and
partly by sub-aqueous tunnels, fit for both rail, horse, and
foot traffic.   Especially there will be adequate avenues from
the main northern, or Middlesex, railway termini to the main
termini on the south, or Surrey side.   Of these the proposed
street from Holborn to the Strand (the most urgent of all the
London problems) will form but a part.   It is a most cheering
and curious fact that this indispensable improvement can now
be carried out, when treated on lines sufficiently bold and
thorough, at a positive profit to the ratepayer, and without
any ultimate expense to him at all.   This also was done when
Northumberland Avenue was made.   And these examples
prove that a wise and bold improvement in our city is a
commercial success, and not a burden to the public purse.
The great triumph of war, said the Conqueror, is to make
war support itself.   And the triumph of the City ædile, who
wars on decay and obstruction, is so to make his improvements that, whilst they immensely promote the health and
comfort of the citizen, they shall actually fill his budget
instead of laying on him burdens.

In the good days to come, then, our Ideal London, our
glorious city of Alfred and the Conqueror, of Chaucer and
Milton, of Inigo Jones and Wren, of Johnson and Goldsmith,
of Dickens and Lamb and Thackeray, will be as bright and
gay, as full of foliage and flowers, fountains and statues, as
Paris or Florence, but without the monotony and the con-

ventional boulevard-driving which ruined Paris and have begun to ruin both Florence and Rome. Our vast city will then raise up its towers and steeples into a sky as bright and pure as that of Richmond Park. Coal smoke will be abolished as an intolerable nuisance, as unpardonable as a cess-pit or an open sewer. And I dream in my dreams that Science in the good days to come will invent a new tobacco, which, whilst appeasing the craving of the smoker, will not be poisonous and offensive to those about him. In these days we should need no smoking cars in the trains, and could even sit on the garden seat of an omnibus without the risk of being choked by a very foul pipe. It would be ridiculous, if we abolish the nuisance of chimneys, that we should retain the still more noxious effluvia of the pipe. Women, who, I suppose, in those days will form the working majority of Parliament, if not of the Ministry, will, no doubt, in good time see to all this.

Be this as it may, in the good time to come our city will be as pleasant to live in as are Oxford or Leamington or Bath to-day. The Tower of London, the most impressive and most venerable civic building in Europe, will be cleared and freed from intrusive and dangerous lodgers, and will be occupied only by a military guard. Wren's glorious temple at St. Paul's will rise, white and majestic as the St. Peter's of Michael Angelo, and much more beautiful, thrusting its radiant colonnade and dome into a blue sky, where the golden cross will glitter in the pure air like the spires of Chichester and Salisbury to-day. The pile of shops and ignoble ware-houses around it will have disappeared like a bad dream, and the great Cathedral will stand in a vast open space, approached on four sides by stately avenues. So with the British Museum and our few other fine buildings.

The silver Thames, without a trace of sewage or of mud,

will flow brightly between its double line of embankments covered with shady trees and adorned with statues and fountains. The vast concave curve of the Middlesex side of the River, from Chelsea to the Tower, will give scope to new and varied forms of architectural development. The old intra-mural graveyards will serve as sites for lovely cloisters wherein will rest in graceful urns the ashes of the City ancestors. And around the venerable Abbey — when its thousandth anniversary comes to pass in the twenty-third century — will be a new consecrated temple of peace, reconciliation, and honour, where a grateful people will enshrine the remains of the great dead ones whom it resolves to bury "to the noise of the mourning of a mighty nation."

POSTSCRIPT, 1906

In these last eight years not a little has been done on the long upward march towards an Ideal London — a good deal too in the lines adumbrated above. Sanitation in all its forms, water-supply, parks, museums, libraries, playgrounds, open spaces, arterial new streets, flats and tenement lodgings, removal of hospitals, schools, prisons, mechanical locomotives, smoke abatement, cremation — all are beginning to stir in the dry bones of old-world London.

MUSIC IN GREAT CITIES

1898

ONE of the leading features of the reorganisation of London, as I can conceive it in the future, will be the formation of permanent centres of musical culture. Music is the most social, the most affecting, the purest of the arts; the one most deeply connected with the moral side of civilisation. It stands alone in the arts as hardly capable of being distorted to minister to luxury, evil, or ostentation. One can hardly imagine vicious music, or purse-proud music, or selfish music. It is by its very nature social, emotional, and humanising. Hence I hold music to be the art which specially concerns all social reformers and popular teachers. And, as we have pointed out to Mr. Ruskin and the æsthetic pessimists, these latter ages cannot be called deficient in art, since they have immensely magnified the most human of all the arts of sense.

I am no musician, and do not pretend to say a word about music as an art. But, as one who delights in music, and who has long sought to bring out its social and civilising mission, I have been very much struck with the fact that music is dependent in a curious degree on the material conditions of our civic life. Pictures, statues, poems, can be sent about and multiplied in various forms *ad infinitum*. The poorest home can contain a Shakespeare, a cast, or an engraving. A great cathedral may impress the spirit of millions, even as they walk to their business under its shadow. But music of a high kind, though it knows no limitations of country, age, or material — though it is free of time, space, and matter —

does need trained powers of execution, the combination of suitable hearers and performers, and above all, a place exactly corresponding to the kind of art performed.

Music is peculiarly dependent, both for its artistic and social value, on the material conditions of social organisation. It needs three things: (1) highly trained executants; (2) a permanent and duly trained audience; (3) a *place* of performance, convenient to the audience, and suitable to the artistic conditions.

Now London easily gives us the first. But by its enormous inorganic bulk it makes the second condition very rare and difficult. And strangely enough, in spite of its wealth and energy, perhaps by reason of its wealth and energy, it does not give us the third. I have been from my youth a diligent attendant at many of our best series of concerts; and in days when I had more leisure, I made great sacrifices and underwent great trouble to do so. But the huge floating mobs of London, and the rage of "undertakers" to collect mobs, have almost driven me out and make me nearly hopeless. I have watched scores of times how all serious music and all serious artists have to educate their audience gradually by a long and conscientious work of cultivation. A great musician has, I hold, more to do to train his audience than to train his orchestra. No audience can become worthy to listen to great music fitly performed, unless it is a permanent and painstaking audience; unless it labours honestly to understand the master and his interpreters. And it is just this permanence and this self-educating spirit that the floating mob of London chokes. Just as the audience is pulling itself together and becoming fit to be played to, the series of concerts becomes fashionable, or the season begins; the mob breaks in, and all goes wrong. How delightful the —— day concerts used to be till fine people took them up, and till the balls began. Who can listen to a *chaconne* whilst a bare-shouldered dowager and her three daughters are hurrying past one to the first dance! No, a permanent self-respecting, art-respecting audience must consist of quiet people, living within a moderate distance of each other and of the concert-hall. And this we cannot have till London is grouped into smaller social units.

Besides, London with all its wealth and size does not give us suitable concert-halls. They are all either too big, ill-shaped for musical purposes, inconveniently placed, or repulsively like a schoolroom. I cannot call to mind one concert-hall in London which does not sin in one or other of these four conditions. To ask us to listen to a great violin in company with 3000 others (some of them talking German, American, or Cockney; some of them hurrying out to a "crush") is mere torment. No, I will no longer go to hear the finest violin solo on earth with more than four or five hundred of my fellow-beings; and I should greatly prefer three hundred. To give what is facetiously called "a concert" in a colosseum which holds fifteen thousand people is an impertinence. Time was when I never missed an oratorio. But I have never heard one yet, in an arena which seems designed for a bull-fight or a hippodrome. And much as I honour Mr. Manns, I cannot now spend a day in going to Sydenham in order to hear three pieces, the utmost that I care for at the same sitting. There is not one perfect concert-hall in London. The —— and the —— are only fit for public meetings; the —— will do for a symphony, but it is too big for a solo or a quartet. The —— is pretty; but its proper purpose is a fancy ball. In the —— and the —— one can hear a quartet to advantage; but then they look like a class-room in a board-school, and the seats are as bad as a third-class box on the South-Eastern Railway. The ideal concert-hall should hold 500 persons comfortably; it should be within an easy walk of their homes; it should have ample passages, exits, cloak-rooms, artists' and committee-rooms; it should have pure air, cool temperature, no gas, no noise, and no suggestions either of Mohawk Minstrels or fried fish. Lastly, it should be beautiful: architecture, decoration, and fittings should be of an art worthy to invite us to the high art we meet to cultivate. London has no such concert-hall; and it is a burning shame.

Mobs, money-seeking managers, fashionable people, and the wilderness of a city that we live in, make all this as yet impossible. Musical art, more than other art, needs an organised social life, within permanent and moderate limits. Leeds, Manchester, Birmingham, the Crystal Palace, and other provincial centres teach us the same lesson. Even in Germany, where the capitals are not so vast and inorganic as London, the true life of music is in the lesser towns. Music absolutely needs an organised civic society, neither too vast nor too petty. For the Rubinsteins, Joachims, Pattis, and Reeveses, for the highest typical examples of what voice and hand can reach in art, whole populations and continents may be ransacked for an audience. But the blubbery immensity of London adds nothing, even to them. The great social and civilising uses of music can be built up but slowly out of many local centres of art.

POSTSCRIPT, 1906

Things, they say, are even worse now. The very Minstrels and fish are gone. London prefers to have its music while it is eating.

HISTORIC PARIS

1894

OF all the millions of visitors who throng into Paris, how few attempt to learn anything about the history of the venerable city, which they treat as if it were a summer watering-place or a fashionable lounge.   These very same people, when they go on to Venice, Florence, or Rome, devote themselves with zeal to the ancient buildings, to the historical associations, and to the local art of these beautiful remnants of antiquity. At least, the more cultivated section of travellers ransack the churches, dive into ruins, listen to learned disquisitions, and profess for a time quite a passion for antiquarian research, and for any fragment of historic survival which their guides, ciceroni, and books of travel can point out.   There is for Paris no Ruskin, no Browning, no Lanciani or Hawthorne.

Yet Paris was a famous and cultivated city ages before Venice; its history is far richer and older and more instructive than that of Florence; it has more remnants of mediæval art, and even a deeper mediæval interest, than Rome itself. And if we search for them we may find in it historical associations that may vie with those of any city in the world except Rome and Constantinople; and even its antiquarian and artistic remains are seldom equalled or surpassed.   At Rome, Florence, or Venice, the tourist talks of old churches, palaces, and remains: at Paris he gives himself up to the boulevards, the theatres, shops, and races.   The profoundly instructive history, the profuse antiquarian remains of the great city, are forgotten — *carent quia vate sacro*.

No doubt there is fascination on the boulevards; and the

miles of luxurious places that the Vanity Fair of Europe offers to the pilgrim form a huge screen behind which the busy pleasure-seeker has no inclination to penetrate. He stares at Nôtre Dame and the Sainte Chapelle, plods through the long gallery of the Louvre, sees the tomb of Napoleon and Versailles, and is then ready for the Bois, the opera, or Durand. But any cultivated traveller, who chose to make a study of Paris with the same historical interest and love of art that he takes to the cities of Italy, would find inexhaustible material for thought. The minor historical remains of Paris do not lie so much *en evidence* as the Ducal Palace, the Palazzo Vecchio, or the Colosseum, and no one pretends that any of them have the charm and eternal interest of these. But they are easy enough to find, and not very difficult to disentangle from later accretions. On the other hand, the books, drawings, and illustrations, by the help of which they may be studied, are more complete and numerous than they are for any other city but Rome. It is true that old Paris is not so imposing a city as old Rome. It has suffered much more mutilation, disfigurement, and modernisation than old Venice, or old Florence. But then it is a much more accessible and familiar place : and, Rome and Constantinople apart, its historical associations are second to none in Europe.

It is worth noting that Paris is now, in 1894, at last complete and practically uniform as a city, and this can hardly be said of it at any moment before, in all the four hundred years since Louis XII. Down to the reign of this gallant king, Paris remained very much what it had been since Charles V. and the English wars, a vast feudal fortress with walls, moats, gate-towers, and drawbridges, immense castles within the city having lofty machicolated towers, narrow, winding, gloomy lanes, and one or two bridges crowded with wooden houses. There were two or three enormous royal castles, on the scale and in the general plan of the Tower of London, an almost countless number of beautiful Gothic churches, chapels, and oratories, one moderate-sized open place, the Place de Grève, and two or three very small and irregular open spaces, such as the Parvis de Nôtre Dame or the Place Maubert, some cemeteries, markets, and fountains, of a kind to make the sanitary reformer shudder, in the most densely crowded quarters; and then, all over the packed area within the walls, rose huge fortresses of great lords, and monastic domains, each covering many acres with gardens, cemeteries, halls, and sick-houses, all strongly defended by crenellated towers, portcullis, and bartizan. A miniature city of the kind may still be seen entire in some of the remote mountain districts of Italy and Germany.

But about the time of Louis XII., and early in the sixteenth century, the Renascence arose, and architecture and all the habits and arts of modern life began to take the place of the mediæval life. Castles were transmuted into palaces, towers and battlemented walls began to fall, the Italian taste for terraces, colonnades, domes, and square courts slowly drove out the Gothic fortress, and first the Hôtel de Ville, then the original part of the Louvre, then the Tuileries, then the Luxembourg, arose in the course of a century; until, in the middle of the seventeenth century, Louis XIV., the great destroyer, builder, transformer of Paris, began to make the city something like what it was within the memory of living men. But during the two hundred years that separate François I. from Louis XIV., the transformation went on very gradually, so that even when Henri IV. had completed his work on the Louvre and the Tuileries, lofty feudal towers still frowned down on Palladian palaces, and gigantic mediæval convents or fortresses crowded out the new streets, the Italian hôtels, and even the royal mansions.

x

For three centuries the battle raged between the old cas-
tellated buildings and the modern palatial style, and the
result was a strange and unsightly confusion. By the end of
the last century Paris had almost acquired a modern aspect,
but Louis XVI., and then Napoleon, and after him the
Restoration, undertook new works on a vast scale, which
none of them ever completed. The second Empire, in 1852,
began the most gigantic and ruthless schemes of transformation ever attempted in any great city. Mighty boulevards
were driven backwards and forwards from barrier to barrier;
whole quarters of the old city were cleared; and Haussmann
ruled supreme, like Satan in Pandemonium, thirsting for new
worlds to conquer, and resolute to storm Heaven itself. The
Empire fell in the great war of 1870, whilst many of these
ambitious schemes were half-finished, and whilst Paris was
still covered with the dust of the insatiable *démolisseur*.

After the war of 1870 came the Commune and second Siege
of Paris in 1871; and in this perished Tuileries Palace, Hôtel
de Ville, many ministries and public buildings, with whole
streets and blocks of houses. The havoc of 1871, and the
gigantic schemes bequeathed to the Republic by the Empire,
have only just now been made good, after some twenty-three
years of incessant work. Few new schemes of reconstruction
have been undertaken by the Republic, which has had enough
to do to repair the ravages of civil war and to complete the
grandiose avenues of Haussmann. The result is that Paris
at last looks like a city *finished* by its builders — and built
on an organic, consistent, harmonious, and modern scheme.
For some four hundred years it has always looked more or
less like a city in the act of building, or in course of transformation.

Those who will go and look at M. Hoffbauer's ingenious
panoramic picture of Paris, as it appeared in 1588, now in the

Musée Carnavalet, and will study his other drawings there, or in his great work, *Paris à travers les âges*, who will follow out the series of contemporary views of old Paris from the sixteenth to the nineteenth centuries, now in the Municipal Museum, may easily get a clear idea of this prolonged and extraordinary process of transformation, by which, throughout Europe, the cities of the mediæval world very slowly, and bit by bit, arrayed themselves in the forms and arts of the modern world. This study must have peculiar interest for American travellers, because their own continent presents them with hardly any examples of this process. Their magnificent cities have been built direct from the prairie with modern conceptions of art and of life, and with no other conceptions. But in Europe this very laborious and complex evolution has required four stormy centuries to work through. Now it is true that the mediæval plan, type, and architecture are not so visible in Paris as in London, Rouen, Cologne, Prague, or Florence; yet in Paris the modernisation of the mediæval plan has been far more trenchant and is more instructive to the transatlantic student.

To the antiquarian it is painful to reflect how many beautiful and historic remnants of old Paris have been swept away within living memory, or at least within the present century. The two Empires have been perhaps the most cruel enemies of mediæval architecture. In M. Guilhermy's pleasant book, *Itinéraire Archéologique de Paris*, 1855, there is a plan of Paris showing the ancient monuments by Roguet, in which some two hundred buildings, anterior to Louis XIV., are marked. How many of these have disappeared: a large proportion of them since 1852! The new Boulevard St. Germain is a magnificent thoroughfare; so is the Boulevard St. Michel, and the Rue Monge, and the Rue de l'École de Médecine, but what a holocaust of old churches and convents, historic colleges, refectories, halls, towers, and gateways, has been made in the forming them! What exquisite traceries of the thirteenth century, what pathetic ruins of statues and portals, have been carted away to make a Boulevard de Sebastopol, a Rue de Rivoli, and the new edifices in the island *cité*! In my own memory, St. Jean, St. Benoît, the Bernardins, the Collège de Beauvais, have gone, and the tower of St. Jacques, and the façade of Nôtre Dame, have been "restored" out of all knowledge. It is quite true that Paris required new streets, new halls, new colleges, hospitals, barracks, and open spaces. These had to be; but it must be admitted that the *démolisseur* has been a little rough and unsympathetic.

It is an idle occupation for the æsthetic foreigner to grumble when he knows nothing of the practical necessities and the everyday facts which are thrust into the face of the inhabitant. A much more sensible line is open to the tourist to-day, if he will try and find out for himself what still remains to be seen. Not one traveller in a hundred ever goes near the beautiful Hôtel Carnavalet or has explored all the vaults, traceries, and columns of the Conciergerie, or has unearthed that curious and noble fragment of the twelfth century, the Church of St. Julien le Pauvre, formerly attached to the Hôtel Dieu, and now buried in some back streets. It may compare with the Chapel of St. John in our Tower of London, though it is somewhat later in date. Few care to search for the Hôtel de Sens, and the old staircase and tower of the Hôtel de Bourgogne. Fragments of two famous convents remain embedded in modern structures. The Conservatoire des Arts et Métiers, in the Rue St. Martin, occupies the site of the venerable and vast abbey of St. Martin des Champs; and it has incorporated within its immense range of buildings both the church and the Refectory of the Abbey, beautiful remains of the best thirteenth-century work. And so the Refectory of the Cordeliers monks, the scene of the Cordelier Club in the Revolution, which has rung with the big voice of Danton and the eager periods of Camille Desmoulins, is still visible as the Musée Dupuytren, attached to the École de Médecine. Its gruesome contents need not deter men from visiting one of the most interesting historical remains in Paris.

A real history of the city of Paris would prove to be one of the most instructive episodes to which the student of manners and art in Europe from the time of the Crusades could possibly devote his attention. And although some cities in Italy present more vivid and fascinating periods or examples, there is perhaps no other city in Europe where the *continuity* of modern civilisation for at least seven centuries can be traced so fully in its visible record. From the time of Louis the Stout, A.D. 1108, Paris has been the rich and powerful metropolis of a rich and enlarging State; and from that day to this there is hardly a single decade which has not left some fragment or other of its work for our eyes. The history of each of its great foundations, civil and ecclesiastical, would fill a volume, and indeed almost every one of them has had many volumes devoted to its gradual development, final disappearance, or transformation to modern uses.

The history of the Cathedral of Nôtre Dame, from the laying of the first stone by Pope Alexander III., in the age of our Henry II. and Becket, down to the final "restoration" by M. Viollet-le-Duc, and the history of all its *annexes* and *dépendences*, Archevêché, Hôtel Dieu, together with an exact account of all its carvings, glass, reliefs, etc., etc., would be a history of art in itself. The same would be true if one followed out the history of the foundations of St. Germain des Près, of St. Victor, of St. Martin des Champs, of the Temple, and of St. Geneviève. Two or three of these enormous domains would together occupy a space equal to the whole area of the original *cité*. They contained magnificent churches, halls, libraries, refectories, and other buildings, and down to the last century were more or less in a state of fair preservation or active existence. Of them all it seems that St. Victor, on the site of the Halle aux Vins, and the Temple, on the site of the square of that name, have entirely disappeared. But of the others interesting parts still remain. Of the eleven great abbeys and twenty minor convents which Paris still had at the Revolution none remain complete, and the great majority have left nothing but names for the new streets.

It would be no less instructive to follow up the history of the great civil edifices, the Hôtel de Ville, the Louvre, the Tuileries, the Hôtel de Cluny, the Luxembourg, the Palais Royal, the Palais de Justice. Of these, of course the most notable are the transformation and gradual enlargement of the Hôtel de Ville, the Louvre and Tuileries, and the Palais de Justice, including in that the Conciergerie and all the subordinate buildings of the old Palace of the Kings, which occupied the western end of the original island *cité*. The learning, the ingenuity, the art, which have gone to build up the Hôtel de Ville of to-day out of the exquisite *pavillon* that was designed under François I., form a real chapter in the history of European architecture; as the story of the Town Hall for nearly four centuries is the heart of the history of Paris. But even this is surpassed by the history of the Louvre and its final consolidation with the Tuileries, an operation of which the difficulties were much less successfully overcome. The entire mass of buildings, the most elaborate and ambitious of modern construction in Europe, is an extraordinary *tour de force* which provokes incessant study, even when it fails to satisfy very critical examination.

Those of us who can remember Paris before the second

Empire of 1852 have seen not a few quarters of the city much
in the state in which they were at the Revolution, and even
in the days of the Grand Monarque. The sky-line was
infinitely broken and varied, instead of being a geometric
and uniform line of cornice, as we now for the most part
observe it. And the streets had a frontage-line as irregular
as the sky-line; they went meandering about or gently sway-
ing to and fro, in a highly picturesque and inconvenient way.
There was hardly a single street with a strictly geometric
straight line in all Paris down to the first Empire. Now the
ground plan of Paris looks as if an autocrat had laid it out
in equal parallelograms from an open plain. What old Paris
was down to the end of the last century we may gather from
bits of Silvestre, Chastillon, Méryon, Martial, Gavarni, and
others; but not much of it can still be seen extant.

If the curious traveller would follow up the Rue St. Denis
or the Rue St. Martin, two of the oldest streets in Europe,
from their intersection by the Rue de Rivoli to the circular
boulevard, where they are terminated by the Porte St. Denis
and the Porte St. Martin respectively, he would get some idea
of the look of Paris at the Revolution of 1789. The grand
new Boulevard de Sebastopol, one of Haussmann's boldest,
and perhaps most useful, creations, opens a vast thoroughfare
between the old streets of St. Denis and St. Martin, and by
diverting the traffic, has no doubt prevented or delayed their
transformation. Hence these two streets, which date from
the earliest age of the city, have partially retained their
original lines, when they were country lanes through woods
and meadows, and to some extent they keep their old sky-
line and façade. There are corners in them still where the
old street aspect of Paris may be seen almost intact. And
the student of antiquities who cared to follow up the remnants
of these mediæval thoroughfares in the spirit in which he

explores the canals of Venice and the *vicoli* of Florence, who would trace back the history of St. Jacques and St. Merri, St. Leu, St. Nicolas des Champs, the Place des Innocents, and the vast convent of St. Martin, all of which he would meet in his walk, would have a most suggestive insight into the mediæval state of the city. And it would be well to add to the walk by following up such streets as those of Rue Vieille du Temple, Rue des Francs Bourgeois, and its collateral streets, with the Hôtels Barbette, de Béthune, de Soubise, and Carnavalet, ending with the old Place Royale. A few days thus spent, with adequate histories such as those of Guilhermy, Fournier, Viollet-le-Duc, Dulaure, Hamerton, Lacroix, Hoffbauer, or the popular guides of Miss Beale, Hare, or Joanne, would be rewarded by pleasure and instruction.

To the thoughtful traveller the question is continually presenting itself, if the wonderful transformation which Paris has undergone in three centuries, and especially in the last half of the present century, has been a success on the balance of loss and gain; if it might have been better done; if it could not have been done without such evident signs of autocratic imperialism and gigantic jobbery. The enthusiastic admirers of Paris as it is, and the irreconcilable mourners over Paris as it was, are alike somewhat unreasonable. One need hardly waste a thought upon the triflers to whom the great city is a mere centre of luxury, excitement, and pleasure, given up to clothes, food, and spectacles. But the superior spirits whom the modernisation of Paris in the present century afflicts or disgusts are hardly less open to a charge of impracticable pedantry. The Revolution found Paris as unwholesome, as inconvenient, as ill-ordered, as obsolete, as inorganic a survival from mediæval confusion as any city in Europe. It boasts to-day that it is the most brilliant, the best ordered, the most artistic city of men, and one of the most sanitary and convenient for civilised life. And no reasonable man can deny that the substantial part of this boast is just.

The primary business of great cities is to be centres where masses of men can live healthy and pleasant lives, where their day's work can be carried on with the minimum of waste and friction, and where their spirits may be constantly stirred by grand and ennobling monuments. Now a mediæval city, though crowded with beautiful and impressive objects at every corner, was charged with disease, discomfort, and impediments. It choked and oppressed men's daily life to such a point that, about the sixteenth century, a violent reaction against the mediæval type set in. And when this began the civil and religious institutions of the middle ages had fallen into decay, had ceased to be of use or to command respect, whilst their ruins or their disfigured carcases encumbered the ground. The Monarchy led the way in the revolt and the inauguration of the new city; and the Revolution and the Empire added to the work of destruction and renovation with tremendous rapidity and resistless force. If modern Frenchmen were to live in Paris, to feel at home in it, to love it, then the transformation must take place. And one cannot deny that it has been done with consummate energy, skill, and artistic invention.

But a city which deliberately effaces its own past, which mutilates its ancient masterpieces, and carts away exquisite works of art wholesale, which is filled with hatred, not only of what is unwholesome and troublesome, but of what is venerable and ancient, is committing suicide of its own noblest traditions. It is sacrificing the most powerful influences it possesses to kindle that sense of its own dignity and love for its own history, which is really the basis of all civic patriotism. A great city which has no past must do its best to look modern.

But an ancient city which deliberately seeks to appear as if it had not known more than two generations of inhabitants is depriving itself of its own noblest title to respect. Now, too much of modern Paris looks as if its principal object had been to hide away old Paris, as some mischievous remnant of the *Ancien Régime*, unworthy to exist in the nineteenth century. It is true that Nôtre Dame, the Sainte Chapelle, St. Germain, and a few remnants of Gothic art have been "restored." But one of the leading ideas of the Haussmannic renovation has evidently been this — to produce the effect of a brand-new city as completely "up to date" and with as little of the antique about it as San Francisco or Chicago.

It cannot be denied that, however gay, airy, spacious, and convenient are the new boulevards, they have been immensely overdone in numbers, and are now become a new source of monotony in themselves. We see that, at last, boulevard-constructing became a trade; these vast avenues were made first and foremost for speculative builders, enterprising tradesmen, and ambitious architects. It is not so much that Paris needed the boulevards, as that certain syndicates thirsted for the job. Assuming that such main arteries as the Boulevards de Sebastopol and St. Michel, such streets as the R. de Rivoli, 4 Septembre, and Turbigo were indispensable, it does not appear certain that the Boulevards Haussmann or St. Germain were inevitable, or even the latest of all, the Avenue de l'Opéra. These streets are convenient, of course, very "handsome," and profitable to those who knew how to profit by them; but the question is whether they were worth the enormous burdens on the city budget, the tremendous disturbance and destruction involved, and the wholesale demolition of interesting old structures which could never be replaced. As the royal and imperial palaces of Paris bear on them indelible marks of autocratic tyranny and pride, so the new municipal

works of the city too often betray their origin in the syndicates
of the Bourse and Municipal Council.

It seems to be a natural law that an evil moral taint in the
constructors of great buildings or great cities shows itself on
the face of them for ever, just as it is impossible to study the
façade of a mediæval cathedral without seeing by what devout
spirits and by what faithful and honest labour it was raised.
The domineering and inflated temper of a great autocrat
breaks out in the monotony and rigidity of his palaces, and
in his manifest desire to display power rather than life, and
vastness rather than beauty.   The palace of a tyrant is made
to look like an interminable line of troops in uniform mechanically dressed for a review.   The master of big battalions must
have a big palace, and then a bigger palace, a copy and an
extension of the former one.   If his predecessor built a
beautiful palace he must crush it with something that dwarfs
and overpowers it, for is he not an even grander potentate
than the "grand monarque" deceased?   The Louvre is a
perfect study in stone of moral degeneration on the throne.
François I., who, with all his faults, loved France and loved
beauty, began the Italianised Louvre of Pierre Lescot : it is
one of the most lovely conceptions of the Renascence, and
has no superior of its order in Europe.   We see it in the south-
western angle of the inner quadrangle.   The inner quadrangle was not completed for more than a hundred years —
each king caring more for power than he did for art, and
adding a less and less beautiful piece; until at last, under
Louis XIV., the exquisite design of the early Renascence has
sunk into a dull and pompous classicalism.

But the crown of false taste was placed when, in 1665,
Louis XIV. was seduced by the ingenious amateur, Dr.
Perrault, to reface the Louvre of Levau, and to set up the
huge sham screen, known as the famous Colonnade, on the

eastern façade facing St. Germain l'Auxerrois. Its twenty-
eight immense Corinthian columns, carrying nothing but a
common balustrade, are a monument of imbecile pomp.
Directly the trained eye perceives that this vast and stately
façade consists of *two* parallel faces within a few feet of each
other, the mind turns from such a senseless parade of magnificence. It is quite true that the façade is itself very imposing,
well-proportioned, and certain to impress itself as noble on
those who do not perceive its fraudulent construction. It
was just the thing to inflame the imagination of the brilliant
young *Roi-Soleil*: it debauched the courtly taste and ruined
the architecture of Paris. It was more or less imitated in the
grand public offices flanking the Rue Royale, which face
the Place de la Concorde. Thenceforward splendour took
the place of grace; and interminable orders of columns and
windows in long regiments took the place of art.

The first Empire, which had a genius of its own, and even
an imitated art that at times was pleasing and usually intellectual, adopted and even exaggerated the passion of the
Grand Monarque for the grandiose and the uniform. And
the second Empire, which had more ambition than genius,
and more brilliancy than taste, adopted and even exaggerated
the designs of the first Napoleon — but alas! without the
refined learning and the massive dignity which marked his
best work. Louis, accordingly, mauled about the old Louvre
and set up some singularly ingenious but rather inartistic
adjuncts to the Tuileries. He made the disastrous mistake
of prolonging the Rue de Rivoli with a monotonous rigidity
which has positively discredited French taste in the eyes of
all Europe. He insisted on sweeping away the old *cité* of the
island, in order to make sites for the enormous barrack and
the vast hospital — neither of which would be required on
that particular spot by a wisely organised Government.

Nor did Louis stop here; for his courtly, clerical, and Bourse influences drove him to turn the Cathedral of Nôtre Dame into a detached show, standing by itself in a bare clearing, to set up more boulevards, more monotonous Rues de Rivoli in every part, and to gut the interesting old quarter of the University, the Schools, and Colleges, teeming with historical associations and mediæval relics, in order to make it as close a copy of the Boulevard des Italiens as it was possible to produce on the south side of the Seine. Even more than all the sovereigns of France, from Louis XIV. downwards, Louis Napoleon seemed bent on hiding away or carting away the ancient Paris, and turning the whole of the vast and venerable city into a monotonous copy of the Anglo-American quarter round the Madeleine and the Grand Opera.

The Republic succeeded in 1870 to a number of unfinished schemes and to the awful ravages of civil war. And, after almost a quarter of a century of indefatigable effort, it has at length brought the reorganisation of the city to a practical close and has repaired the ruin of the two sieges. Happily, the Republic, with such fearful trials and cruel lessons, has had no desire to plan new schemes for eviscerating the city, and has had other things to do instead of building pompous palaces. It has wisely declined to rebuild the Tuileries, and has made perhaps the best that it could have made of the vast constructions that connected Louvre and Tuileries. In spite of the ambitious and offensive failure in the midst — the noisy monument to a great patriot who deserved something nobler — the palatial pile has not been surpassed in modern Europe; and by cosnent of the world the spacious area between the Champs-Élysées and the Pont Neuf contains the most brilliant city prospect in Northern Europe. But the glory of the Republic is the renewed Hôtel de Ville, the most beautiful building that has been raised in Paris since the original Louvre of Pierre Lescot. The trade of the building speculator and the mania of a despotic uniformity have now received a death-blow. The ingenuity and artistic instinct of France are acquiring again a free hand; the Revolutionary hatred of antiquity is dying out, and the historic spirit is enlarging its scope. When the Eiffel folly has come down, and the *mesquinerie* and *chinoiserie* of sundry big works of the *fin de siècle* have been replaced, Paris may face the twentieth century with the proud consciousness not only of being the most brilliant and pleasant of cities, but also that she bears on her the record of twenty memorable centuries of the Past.

OUR CATHEDRALS

1895

I SHOULD like to support the plea for some national control over local Restoration Committees by my own reminiscences of French cathedrals and the cruel mangling they have suffered in the last forty-five years. I am old enough to remember some of the noblest of them before the advent of Napoleon III. in 1851. One of the disasters of the third Empire was the buying the support of the Church by enabling it to "restore" the cathedrals and churches of the middle ages. The result has been to ruin, disguise, and travesty almost every fragment of the thirteenth and fourteenth century work throughout France. To those who knew the great cathedrals of France, before the murderous hand of the restorer had been at work on them, they look like that ghastly picture of Murillo — "St. Bonaventura writing the Memoirs of St. Francis after his own death." The Seraphic Doctor is a corpse, who sits stiffly in his chair, holding the pen in his blue-cold fingers and tracing the words with his mummy-like limbs. The seraphic churches of mediæval France are to-day such corpses, "restored" to life for a space, and pretending to be alive with a rigid mockery of health. Men might as well drag from their graves Robert de Luzarches and Pierre de Montereau, and show us their skeletons adorned with brand-new robes designed by a learned antiquarian as present to us their churches transformed into modern machine-cut stone.

I can remember the profound impression produced on me

as a school-boy when I first saw the great buildings of Rouen
and the churches and castles of Normandy and along the
Seine in the distant days of Louis Philippe fifty years ago.
What the cathedral of Rouen was then may be faintly imagined by those who know the fragments of it which Ruskin
drew for his "Seven Lamps." It was a mountain of crumbling and pathetic imagery which perhaps in all those centuries had never looked so truly grand and produced so deep
an impression. Time and decay had amalgamated the styles
and harmonised all that was incongruous or corrupt. One
after another almost every great church in the pointed style
throughout France has undergone the same transformation,
until now it is rather their skeletons or their mummies which
remain, and not the living work of the great mediæval artists.

No man now dreams of "restoring" — *i.e.* repainting — a
famous picture, or an antique statue, or the lost books of a
great poem; nor of bringing the Twelfth Mass up to date.
Nobody proposes to "restore" the Parthenon, or to put a new
nose on the Sphinx, or new arms to the Melian Aphrodite,
and it would be absurd to talk of "restoring" the Colosseum
with strict attention to the Flavian "period," or the Pantheon
according to the canons of Vitruvius. But a church is considered fair game for all ecclesiastical personages of æsthetic
proclivities, and every type of local busybody, "munificent
donor," or archæological prig. They revel in it. They fall
upon the poor crumbling ruin like vultures on a dying camel
in the desert. They form rival committees and bitter cliques
about it; they wrangle, sneer, and foam at the mouth in
savage pamphlets and letters to the Press. We know how
all æsthetic persons of leisure and culture interpret the great
motto — *de gustibus est disputandum*; and we all know that
there are no controversies so ferocious as those of the *odium
theologicum*. But the "restoration" of a church combines

the ferocity of the æsthete with that of the theologian, and the poor *corpus vile* of mediæval sculpture has to suffer the knives of a double army of vivisectionists.

The Church cannot be safely entrusted with the sole care of the great remnants of mediæval architecture. The clergy are their most dangerous destroyers. And the example of France, where the Church has had a free hand, is really decisive. Not, of course, that clergymen are either indifferent to the state of their churches, or have any wish to injure them. Quite the contrary. It is that *trop de zèle* which is so mischievous in diplomacy and in archæology. The clergy very naturally wish to see their churches look smart, new, zealously cared for, and handsomely furnished. To the clergy the church is a place for daily worship, preaching, and teaching, and it is as natural for the rector to like a "bright" church as to like a bright rectory house and garden. But to the mass of the public these ancient churches are primarily public monuments, sacred relics, national glories; and it is of infinitely more moment to the great public to preserve their ancient sanctity in its original truth (even in decay) than it is to have them warm, comfortable, bright, and spick-and-span. The clergy, in their natural and almost excusable zeal to show the people that Anglicanism is very much alive, active, cultured, and up-to-date, have really ruined and mauled almost every fine old church in this country with their contractors' machine mason work, their horrid Birmingham mediævalisms, and all the intensely pointed (and silly) gimcrackery which is thought to bring down the peculiar blessing of Heaven.

The rectors and munificent squires have ruined our churches. But the Dean and Chapter have not yet ruined our cathedrals — or not all of them. And I see no chance of saving our English cathedrals from the catholic vandalism which has

Y

ruined the French, except by placing them under a national administration with strictly limited funds, and legislative restriction to *preserve*, but never to *restore*, to shore up buildings which are actually falling, to replace plain stone where it is inevitable, but never under any pretext to copy, imitate, or modify ornamental work. That is to say, to keep old work of all kinds from falling to pieces if possible, but never to try and replace old carving by new, or make a mediæval edifice look as if it had been finished in our own generation.

As to replacing old figures by new, they might as well tell us that the plaster cast of the "Hermes" of Praxiteles in the British Museum is quite as good a statue as the original at Olympia — I dare say they will tell us that it is better, for it is not so dingy, and altogether "smarter." I have no doubt that a servant-girl going out for her Sunday walk with her young man thinks herself much "smarter" in Mr. Whiteley's clean net veil at 11¾d. than she would be in her mistress's real Venice point collar which has been exhibited at the New Gallery, and looks "as if it had been dipped in coffee," says Mary Jane. And perhaps the parsons think their new church looks "smarter" than anything the fourteenth century could turn out — especially as they have got to pay for their last "spring cleaning."

But I have a practical suggestion to make. When an old building gets shaky call in an engineer — not an architect. Let no architect offer an opinion, touch it, or come near it. An architect will naturally want to *renew*. We don't want any *renewing* — we want preservation. An architect will have "taste," "ideas of beauty," and, above all, theories about "epochs" and "styles." Now we don't want taste or epochs or styles — not even if the eminent F.R.I.B.A. were Sir Christopher Wren, Ictinus, and Anthemius of Tralles all in one. We want nothing but the building as it is, the stones as they are, the carvings as time has left them — scarred, blurred, worn to mere blocks it may be, but the original stones as ages have made them. All we want is to keep them together, to prop them up, to prevent their falling — nothing else. This is often an exceedingly difficult job, requiring all the delicacy of an American dentist saving an old tooth, and all the ingenuity that goes to make a railway-bridge. But it is the task of the Engineer, not of the Architect.

It is not a question of Art; it is a question of mechanical skill. An artist is out of place; is worse than *de trop*; he is the most dangerous man you could consult. He wants to be trying "variations" on the old blocks, just as ambitious fiddlers want to show off their own variations on the *Carnival de Venise*. I remember a famous poet, who could often use strong language, noticing how a beautiful English girl, just arrived in Florence, was stared at by a notorious old flower-woman, whose reputation for intrigue was evil. "Why!" cried our poet, "she looks at the girl as a butcher stares at a calf!" Well, I say, the architect who respects himself looks at a Gothic building in bad repair "as a butcher stares at a calf." He is quite right; his trade is butchering, and to serve the gentry with the best new meat. He sees all the mistakes made by Wren or Gibbs two centuries ago; he knows what the old thirteenth-century masonry really meant — or ought to have meant. And as he gazes wistfully at the beautiful old wreck — he sees what lovely *veal* the calf will make.

There is no paradox in my maxim that the work is that of an engineer, that an artist is out of place. It is not an affair of *art* — it is an affair of *mechanics*, if we honestly mean conservation — not renovation. Take any kindred matter. Suppose that Nelson's coat were tumbling to pieces — should we give it to a Court tailor to "renovate," or to a mere workman to darn? If we gave it to a Court tailor, he would furbish it up with new facings and fresh gold lace, as if it were going to be worn at the next levée. If we heard that Domesday Book were falling to fragments, should we hand it over to Lord Acton to repair, with instructions "to bring it up to date," or would the sacred leaves be handed over to a mere palæographic expert? If Raffaelle's cartoons were coming to bits in strips and rents, should we call in Sir Everett Millais and beg him to repaint the damaged parts? No; we should send for a picture-cleaner, and tell him he would be crucified if he dared to add a brushful of fresh colour.

Ah, we cannot crucify Deans and Chapters, and Restoration Committees! As Sydney Smith said, they have neither souls to be damned, nor (worse luck to them) anything that we can kick. We cannot crucify, nor damn, nor kick them, except in a metaphorical and Pickwickian sense. But we still have the privilege of every freeborn Briton to summon them to stop in their career of vulgarity, ignorance, and outrage. There is one infallible test. If, when an ancient monument, delivered into their mercy, needs repair, they call in an engineer to do what is mechanically inevitable, they mean *preservation* — and they mean right. If they call in an architect, an artist, or any one with "taste," or æsthetic views, they mean *renovation* — and they mean wrong. Half of the repairs of our old cathedrals are needed underground; perhaps two-thirds of it. Architects are not wanted underground. Engineers are — and engineers are the only people to be trusted for repairs above ground. Call in the ablest engineers we have, the men who build Forth Bridges and Blackwall Tunnels, and limit them strictly to preservation of the old, with absolute *veto* on adding anything new. Let us avoid architects, artists, and æsthetes as the very Devil. "Some demon whispers — Dean, now show your taste!"

PICTURE EXHIBITIONS

1888

IN spring time we are all much occupied with galleries, exhibitions, and high art in many forms; and we hear incessant discourse, from men and women more or less competent to direct our taste, as to the merits of painters, schools, and styles, as to good and bad *technique*, as to the true and the false, the "precious" and the "foul" in art. I sometimes ask myself, a plain layman who presumes not to have an opinion in these difficult matters, whether we reflect enough upon the limits, sphere, and subjects of painting, on the relations of painting to life, to thought, to religion; whether our painters are as clear as they ought to be on these great antecedent problems: — What can be painted, what ought to be the end of a picture, what, in great ages of art, did the artist regard as his business and function?

Is it clear, to begin with, that the custom of holding *Exhibitions* of paintings really tends to the advancement of art? With very few exceptions, all modern pictures are painted on the assumption that they will be, or may be, ultimately *exhibited*. An immense number of modern works seem painted solely in order to be *exhibited*: and one hopes at the close of the *Exhibition* they are at once painted out. We are so familiar with the institution of art exhibitions that we take them to be as necessary to the painter's art as his canvas and brush. And we seldom reflect that in no great epoch of art were Exhibitions ever imagined.

Can we conceive of Pheidias and Lysippus, Zeuxis and Apelles, carting their works into a gallery, as the month of April came round, and all the young æsthetes in town, in new cheiton and chlamys, noisily criticising the folds of "Nike's" drapery, the curves of "Ilissus'" ribs, the soft limbs of "Aphrodite," and the proud glances of "Athene"? Fancy Giotto, Angelico, Bellini, and Giorgione closely crammed into long galleries, numbered 3785 and so forth, and catalogued with little snippets from Dante, Petrarch, and Boccaccio! And did ingenious youths in the *Gazetta di Firenze*, or the *Giornale di Roma*, publish vehement attacks or insidious puffs of the School that each affected? Was the "Sposalizio" skied by the Hanging Committee; was the "Madonna di San Sisto" jammed between a "Storm at Sea" and a "Portrait of a Gentleman"? Were Titian's "Assumption" and Tintoretto's "Paradiso" ever rejected by the Academy of Venice as unsuited for exhibition and difficult to hang?

A picture, like every work of visual art, is, or ought to be, designed to fill some suitable space and to be seen with harmonious surroundings. An altar-piece has to fill and dignify a chapel. A battle-piece may be in place in a public hall. A portrait, according to its scale and style, may suit an ancestral corridor or a domestic parlour. A vignette from the "West Coast" or "Kittens at Play" may give sweetness and light to the cottage boudoir. But an Annual Exhibition is almost the only spot conceivable where no picture ever can be in its place, where the local environment of every picture is turned upside down, where every note in the gamut of art is sounded in discord. Suppose an Exhibition of musical instruments where from eight till dusk the makers continuously played on their own instruments such airs as each thought best to bring out the tone of the piece! To one who had studied painting only in the Campo Santo of Pisa, in the Arena Chapel, in Santa Maria Novella and Santa Croce, in the Sistine and the Vatican, in the School of San Rocco and the Doge's Palace, to be thrust into a modern exhibition and told to judge the works there, would seem as strange and as painful as to be asked to judge of musical instruments when all were being played upon together in the same room but with different airs.

How vastly does *genius loci*, the placing and the setting of a picture, deepen the impression, when we gaze on the portraits of Titian, Veronese, and Tintoretto in the Doge's Palace, or on the Vandykes in the Genoese palaces, or on the prophets and Sibyls who keep eternal watch in the vaults of the Sistine, or on the "Mantegna" in San Zenone, or the last rays of the "Cenacolo" in the Refectory of San Lorenzo! How utterly different are Pisano's "Pulpit" or Michael Angelo's "Notte," or Ghiberti's "Gates," as we see them in Pisa or in San Lorenzo or the Baptistery, and as we see them in the Crystal Palace at Sydenham, or the South Kensington Museum! And yet year by year we cram side by side, as close as frames can be set, in a wild *pot-pourri* of pictorial discord, Holy Virgins, washerwomen, rapes of the Sabines, scenes from Pickwick, Ledas, Dr. Johnson with Boswell, and Lord Mayors in robes of office. And on the first Monday in May we rush to Burlington House and expect to find new Titians and Raphaels cheek by jowl with a crowd of works which deliberately aim at the kind of success attained by a popular music-hall song or a penny dreadful.

No really great picture can be seen in an Exhibition, and the greater the picture the more it loses. Nearly all pictures are nowadays painted with a view to possible exhibition. But some are not; and we all know how much in these very rare instances the painter gains. A large part of Rossetti's

reputation was no doubt due to the fact that he never exhibited; and promiscuous exhibitions of his works, even in
the absence of discordant surroundings, have hardly enhanced
his peculiar vogue. Those who have seen the pensive fancies
of Burne-Jones or Leighton's bright visions of Greek poetry
in the studios or saloons where they are at home, or for which
they were designed, can hardly believe that they are the same
works when they are seen jammed into a gallery between a
portrait of His Royal Highness and an "arrangement in ultra-
marine." We might as well expect to find Andromache,
Phryne, and Galatea looking natural, goddess-like, and
Greek if they mixed with the public on a crowded Saturday
afternoon.

But it is more the moral effect on the painter's mind than
the discordant effect on his exhibited work which is the real
evil of Exhibitions. Some painters are strong enough and
honest enough to withstand temptation. But the tempter is
always at work. An Exhibition is necessarily more or less a
competition, and a competition where for the most part the
conspicuous alone catches the public eye. *Il faut sauter aux
yeux*, and that in the eyes of the silly, the careless, the vulgar,
in order to be popular. And the painter who never becomes
popular runs great risk of ceasing to paint at all. The diapason tends always to grow higher, and unless an air is given
at concert pitch, and something more, it is in danger of
sounding somewhat flat. Every device that colour, size,
form, title, subject, frame, can give to attract the eye, has
been exhausted by the ingenious painter, and not always by
the worst. No man who respects his art stoops to such an
artifice, and the honourable artist rejects it with scorn. But
it is unworthy of us to subject men to competition with
such degraded rivals, and to expect that we can make new
Titians and Raphaels by a process which, like that of Exhibi-

tions, smothers the great qualities by discordant surroundings and stimulates the activity of the vulgar qualities.

In far other modes were works of art "exhibited" to the public in all great ages of art. They were shown in the studio in which they were produced, or in the place for which they were designed; in the first to the few whom the artist chose to admit, in the second on the public and ceremonial completion of the work. Were Pheidias' Athene of the Parthenon, the gods and heroes of the pediments, and the Panathenaic procession, Centaurs and Lapithæ, sent about from gallery to gallery, and jammed between "Scenes from Aristophanes," "Geese on a Common," and a presentation portrait of the Right Worshipful the Archon Basileus? When the chryselephantine Athene was finally set up in her Parthenon a great festival was made, and the citizens, magistrates, and priests, with youths and maidens in procession, went up to the Acropolis and gazed on the Goddess; and there, amidst hymns, sacrifices, and solemn offerings, the whole city rejoiced and wondered at the marvellous handiwork of the god-like sculptor. And when Cimabue had finished his "Madonna" all Florence attended the ceremony wherewith it was set up above the altar as we see it still; and Florence that day kept holiday as at the Feast of the Annunciation. And when Raphael lay dead in state, his "Transfiguration" stood above the bier; and all Rome came and gazed in wonder and reverence at the dead painter and at his last work on earth. Such were Art Exhibitions in the great ages of art.

This brings us to what is really the key of the matter. The discordant hubbub of modern Picture Exhibitions is the least part of the evil. It is the divorce of art from the highest religious, social, intellectual movement of the age which is the root of decadence in art. It is the substitution of democratic license and personal caprice for grand traditions and loyal service in the larger forces of life. Here is the root of feebleness, far more than in deficient training, crude *technique*, and picture Barnums. In all great epochs of art the painter frankly accepted certain great canons of religious, social, or artistic convention. He thoroughly felt his art to be the expression of the religious, social, and intellectual movement of his time. He took it to be his business to give to that movement colour and form. His art was not at all self-sufficing and detached. It was simply one of the artistic modes of expressing what was deepest and most commanding in the spiritual world. The painter was the servant; the free, willing, creative servant, but the servant of the priest, the thinker, the poet and the statesman. Pericles, Ictinus, and Pheidias laboured at the Parthenon in one common conception: a work by Leucippus, Polycleitus, or Zeuxis was an affair of State: a great statesman of Rome, it was supposed, identified his name with the Pantheon, one of the most original conceptions in the history of art. Giotto worked in the Arena Chapel under the eye of Dante, and apparently under his inspiration. Ghiberti, Brunelleschi, and Mantegna lived on the topmost wave of one of the most wonderful outbursts of the human intellect. Leonardo and Michael Angelo were two of its mightiest forces, even had neither ever touched a pencil. Raphael, Benvenuto, Titian, Velasquez, Jean Goujon, Rubens, Reynolds, were the intimates and the equals of all that their ages possessed of brain, of knowledge, of force.

Painting, which is a secondary and not a primary form of human skill, cannot sever itself from power, from religion, from thought, without becoming at once feeble and wayward. The note of too much of modern painting is to be at once silly and *bizarre*. It has flung off all guides, teachers, and traditions; repudiates any sort of connection with religion, thought, or rule; decides everything out of its own head; and regards everything and anything a proper subject for a picture, from the Day of Judgment to a mushroom. Individual whims, any crude hobby, is thought to be quite enough to enable a man to choose a good subject for a painting, and to emancipate him from the conventions which condemned Raphael to eternal "Madonnas," Titian to perpetual "Europas," "Ariadnes," and "Aphrodites," and Murillo to innumerable cherubs. The modern painter holds himself to be as absolutely free to invent his own subject, to improvise his own canons of art, to humour his own fancy, as Mr. Gilbert when he makes a new burlesque, or Mr. Rider Haggard when he sketches a new novel.

But a picture is not a novel; for the painter's art is immeasurably less fertile and elastic than the written art of the poet or romancer. No genius can enable the painter to compete with the story-teller in versatility, in subtlety, in profusion and continuity of effect. The painter has his own resources in vividness, in colour, in harmony, in suddenness and unity of his blow on the imagination — it may be also in beauty. But of course he buys these resources at the price that he cannot, by the conditions of his art, touch anything but what *is seen*, that he is rigorously limited to one *moment of time*, that he cannot possibly *impart anything which is not known*, that he *can never explain*, never *continue a story*, tell nothing *which it requires words to tell*, and by the very instrument he uses he is forbidden, except in partial and exceptional ways, to touch the loathsome, the horrible, and the spasmodic.

These obvious truisms are trampled under foot in our modern Exhibitions, where half the figure subjects are painted *novelettes*, whereas these conditions were strictly respected in all great ages of art. The necessity for respecting them, and the instinctive sense that the painter's art is a corollary of larger forms of human power, and not a substantive and self-sufficing force, compelled the painter, in all great ages of art, to limit himself to a definite range of subjects, to follow loyally the current ideals in religion, in poetry, and in manners, to use perfectly simple and familiar *motifs*, to shun whims, conundrums, eccentricities and *fantasias*, very seldom indeed to be comic, and almost never to be disgusting. The great painters painted only a few score of subjects — absolutely familiar to all who saw them — and these almost without exception grand, ennobling, obvious types of religious, mythological, and social ideals. Nine-tenths of the painter's aim was, as it should be, beauty.

Nowadays a large part of the modern Exhibition seems to have no other end but to raise a laugh, to invent a *rebus*, to puzzle, to disgust, or, mainly in France, to excite the animal taste for blood and lust. When we walk through a gallery of fine old masters, we need no catalogue to describe to us the subjects. We do not require to read half a page from Boswell's *Johnson* or Macaulay's *History of England*, it may be from Coventry Patmore or Ouida, before we can conceive what it all means. No ancient master would have tried to paint Shelley's *Skylark* or Swinburne's *Songs before Sunrise*. In the whole gallery of old masters there are perhaps not more than a score of different subjects, and all of these obvious to every eye at a glance. Titian and Holbein painted portraits as their sitters were, and did not turn them into ladies and gentlemen dressed up for a fancy ball. Although the subjects are so few, so obvious, so conventional, there is no monotony. All looks noble, solemn, beautiful; for the aim of the painter then was to show how much beauty could be shed over the old ideals of faith, poetry, and manners.

It is quite true that the old ideals in faith, poetry, and

manners have proved insufficient. They have failed us; and
we must make new ones. No sensible man wishes to recall
them; nor does he wish to bind art again in limits so narrow.
Three centuries ago modern Europe got rid of its old standards. The faith which inspired Madonnas and Saints, the
poetry which was limited to a crude mythology and a few
romances, the manners which were essentially based on aristocratic display, indolence, battle, and luxury, were too narrow,
too shallow, and too anti-social to be permanent. Art, like
modern civilisation, has cast them off. And it is idle to dream
that they can ever return.

But it does not follow at all, because the old ideals and
sources of art are gone, that painting is to have no ideals, no
sources, no guide: that every painter is to be a law to himself; and that every hobby, every accident of any painter's
life, can equally supply a subject for a picture. What has
happened is this. So far as modern art is concerned, religion
has almost disappeared; every tradition of great art has been
wiped out; and the old subordination of painting to intellect
and poetry is put aside. The reign of universal democracy
has set in for painting with greater virulence even than in
politics and in manners. Painters, apparently by their fond-
ness for the Stuarts, Marie Antoinette, and the Royal Family,
ought, one would think, to be Tories and loyalists. But in
the practice of their art they recognise the wildest license of
individual judgment, the entire equality of all men to lay
down the law in art, and the trenchant abolition of every great
and historic tradition.

In all great ages of art the artist's subject was expected to
conform to given conditions. It must be simple, familiar,
noble, traditional, and beautiful. Nowadays it is too often
enigmatical, eccentric, mean, whimsical, or disgusting. Pheidias and the great Greeks represented the gods and heroes of

whom Homer sang, the great memories of national history,
the beings in whom centred the worship, reverence, and admiration of men, the loveliest women known to the city, the
finest champions in the games. Raphael and his fellows
painted the great types of religious adoration, the familiar
mythologies, great men and great events in history. But in
all cases, whether the subject was sacred or secular, old or
new, it was always simple, familiar, noble, traditional, and
beautiful. Nowadays a painter seems to consider that his
business is to invent something absolutely new, if possible
queer, accidental, personal, comic, namby-pamby, or *bizarre.*
He seems to imagine that his duty is to compose a mild
original sonnet, a snippety original novel, or a watery anecdote, grave or gay. Now painters are not poets, romancers,
nor literary craftsmen. The result is that, when they try to
paint sonnets, stories, or essays, the work is, intellectually,
too often on a level of that which goes into the columns of a
county newspaper, and is headed "Our Poet's Corner," and
"Curious or Entertaining." How can painters suppose that
cultivated men and women care for their japes, their puns,
their snippings from stale *Elegant Extracts*, or for their own
poetical and moral maunderings on canvas? A painter who
invents a new subject is almost certain to insert something
that is either silly or *bizarre.* Almost all the anecdotes which
fill half a page of the Academy catalogues, as subjects of so-
called historical pictures, scandal about Queen Elizabeth,
the gallantries of some Stuart prince (understanding *gallantry*
in all its various senses), the oddities of Swift, Johnson, or
Walter Scott, anecdotes of the Reign of Terror, etc., are
either quite unauthentic or utterly trivial; nay, not seldom
they are grossly libellous and horribly mean. So long as a
subject offers a medium for sheeny stuffs, quaint costume,
and Wardour Street *bric-à-brac*, none seem to be too silly,

too scurrilous, or too petty for some painters. It is not the
business of painters to become very minor poets and tenth-
rate serial novelists. They have, as we say, to paint the
simple, the familiar, the noble, the traditional, the beautiful
— so as to put new beauty into the old types of our deepest
adoration, love, reverence, and delight. Their business is to
add glow, intensity, charm, to what is best in the faith, in
the memory, in the intellect of their age: — not to puzzle, to
startle, much less to sicken us.

It is the honour of our older Academicians steadily to up-
hold the great traditions of the noble style, as to the subjects
proper for painting. First and foremost in this matter comes
Leighton himself. And in nothing does his culture, taste,
and training in the great schools tell more than in the example
he sets his contemporaries as to the field, limits, and aim of
their art. Never was this shown more finely than in the
subject of the first picture with which he came upon the
world, "The Procession at Florence" to escort Cimabue's
Madonna to Santa Maria Novella. Here was an almost perfect subject for a modern painter. It was simple, obvious,
noble, and beautiful. Though the idea was new, it presented
a touching and dignified incident in the history of art, in a
form familiar and interesting to all cultivated people. It was
like a chapter out of *Modern Painters* in colour and form.
I confine myself strictly to the subject, to the painter's *motif*,
and do not touch upon any point in the execution. As a
subject it was perfect. For some forty years he has continued
to present a series of subjects, almost equally happy —
Greek, mythological, or historical — but all simple, familiar,
noble, traditional, and beautiful. To understand such pictures as the "Daphnephoria," "Phryne," "Cimon," or the
"Hemicycle" at Kensington, it is not necessary to read a
page out of some historian, or to consult Dictionaries of

Antiquities. Every cultivated man at once recognises the subject, and sees at a glance that it is simple, impressive, beautiful. So, too, the *Andromache* is equally happy in its subject. Every cultivated man, without reading the lines from the *Iliad*, can recognise the incident; can see its beauty, its pathos, its tragic and lyric dignity; and so he is drawn on to study in detail the Hellenicism, the refinement of knowledge and taste, the subtle convolutions of grace, with which the painter illustrates the poet. We are dealing now solely with the subject of a painting. And here surely is the painter's art seeking to express the grandest poetry, in high and pure traditional types.

So, too, Mr. Watts has maintained a noble choice of subject in the grand and true vein of the old schools. In his "Dawn," "Death," "Love," "Hope," "Faith," and like symbolical fancies, he is usually within the limits of the simple and the intelligible. At times he, too, wanders off into the abstruse and the fantastic — never into that of the trivial or the repulsive. A poet may be mystical, obscure, even wild for a space; but a painter cannot be so without infinite risk. The definiteness, the fixity, the simplicity of his instrument bind him. No man less than Michael Angelo can venture to be Apocalyptic; nor can painter born of woman be mystical without ceasing to be intelligible; and an unintelligible picture is a *rebus*.

These sound traditions as to subject for the most part are sufficiently preserved by such men as Mr. Poynter, Mr. Armitage, Mr. Long, Mr. Richmond — to mention no others. For the most part the subjects they paint are simple, familiar, dignified, and beautiful. So far as Mr. Long shows a tendency to plunge into learned antiquities, and oddities of archæology, needing, to explain them, long passages from Diodorus Siculus — apparently his favourite author — so far he is leaving the

ground of familiar and simple art. Of Mr. Alma Tadema
and Sir John Millais a few words must be said. Sir John is
only on rare occasions a painter of historical and imaginative
incidents; and his greatest admirers will hardly think that
he best displays in them his wonderful gifts as a painter.
A man who tries to write the chapters of a novel on a canvas
three feet by two is on perilous ground. The "Huguenot,"
the "Order for Release" achieved that feat. It may be
doubted if the "Fireman" and some others did not overstep
the line. The business of a painter is not to tell a thrilling
story, or to paint spasms — we cannot bear thrilling moments
eternally prolonged in one strain. His business is to present
a subject which is simple, familiar, noble, and beautiful.

Still less can it be the business of a painter elaborately,
lovingly, and learnedly to paint a childish practical joke.
From the point of view of subject and *motif*, Mr. Alma
Tadema's "Heliogabalus," in spite of its pictorial skill, is
itself a bad joke. The subject has every vice that a subject
can have. It is at once silly, *bizarre*, incomprehensible,
whimsical, and mean. It is bad enough to commemorate at
all one of the most pitiful animals whom accident ever thrust
into a throne; but to choose a childish anecdote out of some
chronique scabreuse, and one which it is physically impossible
to paint, is really to sin against art and sense. This is all
the more to be regretted because Mr. Alma Tadema's astonishing powers as a painter have been long united with real learning, singular instinct for antique life, and a delightful zest
for the aroma of classical ages. Mr. Alma Tadema is one of
the few living men who can don the *cheiton* and the *toga* with
the air of a true ancient. But he has too often shown a
dangerous turn for archæological eccentricities, and trivial
bypaths and alleys of the antique world; when, with all his
mastery of hand and stores of knowledge, his business is to

z

show us its temples, palaces, life, and thought, its power, its splendour, its beauty — it may be its vices and its weakness, but not its tricks and tomfooleries.

No painter in any age has ever shown more loyal regard for noble traditions in selecting his subjects than has Mr. Burne-Jones. A certain field of romantic mythology he has made all his own — the old tales of Hellas conceived in the spirit of a Renascence mystic. Burne-Jones' studio, full of a long mythological series, looks as if Sir Thomas Malory had made us a volume of Greek myths, "translated out of the Greke boke." These solemn fugues on the theme of "Penseroso" are simple, noble, traditional, and beautiful. It is a question if they are familiar, if they do not verge on the mystical, if they are not at times occult and cryptogrammic. A man who dwells so much alone in a dreamland of his own is necessarily appealing to a select audience. And it has been Burne-Jones' noble aim through life to pray ever for "audience fit, though few." As to Rossetti, he withdrew into a dreamland infinitely less accessible to the public, a dreamland almost confined to one great poet and to one set of types. It required a special study in itself to know what Rossetti was dreaming about at all. No painter ever took such pains to dream for himself, by himself, and within himself alone. To the poet — and Rossetti was certainly a poet — the claim is legitimate enough. But a painter, as he quits the simple and the familiar, is making for the enigmatical and the artificial. And in any case he is deliberately restricting the power of his work to a special circle of *cognoscenti* and *illuminati*.

It is of course in the Salon at Paris that conspicuous examples are seen of the modern craving for new and startling subjects. Not that there is any real "French school," as some persons fancy. For the Salon contains examples of fifty schools, the works of painters from almost every civilised nation, representing a score of very different ideals of art. But in the Salon, with the audacity, license, versatility, and power it collects, are seen examples of the best and worst types of modern aim in art. Humanity, pathos, imagination, tenderness, bestiality, lust, ferocity, impudence, and tomfoolery jostle each other in the fierce struggle to attract the notice of the public. All is wild democratic license. Filth, disease, death, carnage, torture, prurient prying into things which decency and self-respect keep covered, the secrets of the dissecting-room, of the consulting-room, of the studio, of the dressing-room, of the slums and the sewers, form the inspiration of pictures equally with devotion, poetry, sympathy, and dignity. Every man fights for his own hand, paints in his own method, chooses his own subject, and tells his own story. And the result is an unimaginable *pôt-pourri*. Huge canvases seem designed solely on the principle so well understood by the venders of "Pears' soap." They are not pictures, but gigantic *posters*, to let the world know that there is such a painter as *M. Tel* much at your service. No human being could buy, much less live beside, these enormities. And the greater the enormity, the more is the public forced to stare.

Of all infamies on canvas I ever saw the worst is "The Maniac." Here, in a bare room, with every sign of a recent struggle, the furniture smashed to fragments, stove, mirror, chairs, door, and crockery in bits, on the edge of a deal table, sits, in his shirt, a wretched maniac, grinning in ghastly triumph. At his feet lies extended, in a pool of blood, with clothes torn to shreds, the dead body of a woman, common, coarse, and prosaic. Even had the picture power and terror, which it has not, it would be loathsome. But the cold, hard, dry, photographic presentment of a vulgar madman committing a brutal murder is as foul a subject as ever painter imagined. Zolaism is indeed rampant in art when this is possible. But in literature even a ghastly murder does not stand out in such visible crude brutality. And no one is obliged to read Zola unless he deliberately choose. To expose on a life-size canvas to the public gaze Zolaism in its crudest shape is an offence against civilisation, which every decent man and woman ought to treat as an unpardonable outrage.

Or what shall we say to a "Rape in the Stone Age," by Jamin? Here a sort of naked Polyphemus has seized and is carrying off a nude, very white studio model, who is posed as the female of the Stone Age. In her fury this elegant nymph has rammed her thumb into Polyphemus' right eye, which she is just gouging out. Polyphemus, howling with pain, clutches the graceful girl in his huge fist, and is just crushing in her ribs, she yelling in agony. To them come Polyphemus No. 2, a sort of Porte St. Martin torturer; who, seizing his rival behind, is garrotting him by strangling him round the throat. Conceive the man who shall purchase this work of art, and sit down to dinner daily in presence of the last yells of palæolithic man and pre-metallic woman.

A new *motif* for art has also been discovered in death, disease, and lechery, treated in its most prosaic, photographic, and vulgar side. Some dozen corpses laid out with candles, wreaths, and satin pillows, a surgeon examining a girl's bared chest, the painter's model playing pranks without any clothing, everything put on to canvas which Zola puts into print. One picture indeed is a melancholy sight, for it has power, skill, even pathos of a certain kind: on a long, stiff bench, in the ante-room of a hospital, sit a row of women, waiting for their turn to be admitted — disease in all its shapes stamped on their faces and forms. All of them are dull, commonplace, colourless, and weary. No one of them tells her story; no ray of grace, cheerfulness, or imagination lights the composition. No canvas can tell such a story. They sit there tired, faint, and sickly — and that is all. It is a simple study of disease — of disease apparently hopeless; for not a touch is there to show us humanity, goodness, science, or love. There is not even tragedy; for the poor creatures are simply a-weary, without dignity, without strength to suffer even with each other. It is a bald study of disease. But disease is not a subject for the painter's skill. Such is the truly infernal influence of Zola upon modern art.

Happily amidst these horrors start up, like flowers blooming among the grinning skulls of a charnel-house, here and there a noble subject nobly conceived. Cheek by jowl with bestialities such as "L'esclave blanche," "Elle râlait en sanglots sourds . . .," "Le repos du modèle," "Turpe senilis amor," "The Duel between Women," etc., etc., stand such fine conceptions as Detaille's "Dream," J. Lefebvre's "Orphan Girl with her Grandmother at Prayer," Humbert's "Three Stages of Motherhood," Bougereau's "First Death — Abel," Henner's "Saint Sebastian," Aimé Perret's "Golden Wedding," Hébert's "Nameless Heroes." We are dealing now with these pictures, as throughout this paper, with all pictures, solely from the point of view of their subject, as it might be understood from description and a rough sketch. The composition, colour, execution, and the like belong to another field. But these, with some splendid portraits and excellent landscapes, are enough to prove that modern art has yet before it a great future, when it shall have cleared itself from filth, bombast, putrefaction, and gore; and shall have settled the primary problem — What can be painted, what cannot be painted, and what is the painter's function?

The resources open to modern art can be no better seen

than in the scheme of Detaille's "Dream." A regiment in mid campaign is bivouacked by night on the open field, in the first streaks of the dawn which are to bring in a few hours the day of battle, glory, and death. Young and old, veteran and conscript, officer and soldier, lie stretched in long lines beside their piled arms — watchfulness, hope, eagerness, anxiety, indifference, bull-dog courage, and young ambition seem to quiver over the upturned faces and the prostrate limbs. Dimly in the driving clouds overhead may be traced a dreamlike and cloudy army in the air, the ghost or vision of some imperial host, with eagles and arms waving mistily in the sky, filling the heavens with the weird and silent clang of the charge, the rally, and the crash of the heroes of the Grande Armée. Now here is a *motif* wholly new and inconceivable by ancient master, which yet is simple, obvious, imaginative, noble, and solemn. Here for once is a subject wholly within the reach of the painter and yet full of modern poetry. All things are yet possible to an art which can so strike forth a new and noble strain.

J. Lefebvre's solemn and fine picture of the aged "Widow with her Orphan Grandchild in Church," and Humbert's "Mother in Three Ages," belong to a school in which the French are still almost supreme — the majestic simple pathos of the humblest, saddest life — without elegances, without weakness, without puerile sentimentalism; not without a certain severe and restrained beauty, but with no trace of concession to prettiness. In this form of massive tenderness, in this profound simplicity of the human, the Salon stands forth unrivalled. And yet why, alas! in so rare an example? How in the same gallery with works so nobly conceived, beside such exquisite refinement as we see in Bougereau's "Bather," and Henner's "Daphne," such grand landscape subjects as J. Breton's "Shepherd's Star," such pure and touching scenes of peasant life, such *verve* everywhere, such knowledge of antiquity, of the East and the South, such invention, such diabolical cleverness and enterprise, how there can be painted year by year monstrous grotesques, rampant idiocies, satanic obscenities, huge follies, such as "St. Denis," calmly walking along a high road with his decapitated head in his hands, bleeding down his headless trunk, to the terror of the very dull peasants at work, the "Titans tumbling out of Heaven," "The Milky Way" (or "Milk Street," as the official catalogue Englishes it), "Pluto and Proserpine," abominations like "The Minotaur in the Labyrinth," and the like — this is indeed barely intelligible. Perhaps Maignan's "Voices of the Tocsin" may be said to touch the border-line. In a mediæval belfry we see a huge bell swinging madly in the alarum; burning roofs, smoke, and flame in the streets below. And, as the vast bell roars out its awakening peal, weird forms of terror, havoc, despair, courage, hate, and death whirl like vultures through the air, clutching and tearing the bell-ropes in their mad dance, and rocking the very tower to its foundations in their fury. It is a strange Victor Hugoish conception, not without grandeur and poetry; paintable perhaps by an artist who combined in himself Michael Angelo, Tintoretto, and Turner. As it is, though in one way still a striking picture, it is too much of a "*salmi* of frog's legs," as they said of Correggio's famous dome at Parma. It is plain that at the root of modern art lies the primary question: which is this. All canons, and limits, and subjects, of the painter, as understood of old, being gone, what new canons, what new limits, and what new subjects can we find to replace them?

Now this is not an artist's problem, or at least not a problem for the artist to solve alone. It is a problem for the best philosophy and judgment of our age. It is for the best brains amongst us to settle some practical canons of the limits of the art of painting, to indicate the barrier between paintable and unpaintable things, to tell us, and to tell our painters, what is their relation to religion, to poetry, to thought. Our art critics have perhaps too much neglected this all-important field. They have been too apt to repeat the technical jargon of the studios, and to omit the primary question, What can the painter paint? Mr. Ruskin, who in so many wonderful ways has rekindled the torch of art for our whole Victorian age, in architecture, in painting, even in dress, nay, almost in literature, has done much to weaken the control of good sense over the *subjects* of art. Intent on his central idea of good work, he lavishes extravagant praise on mere *enfantillage*, goes into raptures over a baby and white kitten, systematically dwells on the painted surface, and not the painted mind. Indeed, almost the one thing about which he rarely utters a word is the human form — in reality, nine-tenths of the highest art. Following him, the art-mentors of our time will discourse largely about schemes of colour, truth in a brocade, and successful *impasto*, but they have little to say about that which precedes all these and governs the whole — how should the painter choose his subject? If the prevailing vices of the foreign schools are lewdness and bombast, the prevailing vices of the English schools are triviality and vulgarity. Our English painters, with some splendid exceptions, do not seem to live sufficiently with the higher intelligence of the time, seem to be inadequately cultivated as men, and have little access to the best religious and poetic standards of our age.

It is the object of these pages to invite some competent authority to clear the ground of this question. In the meantime, if a simple member of the shilling public may offer a suggestion at all, the following points are submitted as a rough and tentative sketch. Exhibitions of paintings in crowded galleries are a real *incubus* on art; they swamp the merits of the good and stimulate the faults of the worse. The twelve rooms at Burlington House, which have more than 2000 works, cannot properly show more than 200; indeed, 100 would be a far wiser limit. And even 100 would be strangely and cruelly out of place in any mere gallery, if they were works of real imagination and power. All pictures should be exhibited under a simple title: every word of poetry, extract, Diodorus Siculus, Macaulay's History, puns, sentiments, and ejaculations, should be strictly forbidden, as at Paris. Picture galleries are not comic annuals, nor are they Methodist pulpits, and fun of all sorts, literary dribble, and sermonising are horribly out of place in a picture. Next, Art Academies are not International Exhibitions; and we do not want Japanneries, Colinderies, and laborious costumeries from foreign lands thrust upon us simply to prove how well the painter has got up his lesson. Still less are Art Academies schools for impressing on the public mind Layard's *Nineveh*, Smith's *Dictionary of Antiquities*, Rawlinson's *Herodotus*, and all the learning of the Egyptians, the Ninevites and Phenicians. The business of painting is to vivify and beautify what we do know, and not to cram into us a knowledge of facts which we do not know. The business of the painter is not to compose small romances, but to clothe with life and grace the sights and conceptions which are familiar to us. It is not the function of art to produce a photographic resemblance of the common, simply that men may say, "It is almost as good as a photograph." It is not the duty of the painter to put into elaborate form what is uncommon, droll, and unintelligible; he has to put into permanent shape the beautiful, the noble, the suggestive.

The nineteenth-century mania for Exhibitions seems to

blind the painter, the critic, the public to some of the simplest truisms in the philosophy of art. A picture, by the nature of the case, is always *en évidence* in the place where it is, acquires or creates a certain *genius loci*, and becomes therefore part of the instinctive life of those who dwell in its presence. We cannot shut up a picture and put it away in our shelves as we do a book ; we cannot play it over again as the mood takes us, just as we can with a piece of music. There it stands for ever opposite to us like a Palace or Cathedral, continually reiterating the same impression. For this reason, drollery, riddles, anecdotes, novelettes, sentimentalities on canvas, are so horribly irritating. Does the painter of "Two of a Pair," "Her Favourite Flower," "How happy I could be with either," "Sterne and the dead Jackass," "Bugs in a Rug," "Satan addressing the Fallen Spirits in Pandemonium," "The Drunkard's Home," "Pharaoh's Daughter at Five o'clock Tea" — do the authors of these very quaint, moral, tearful, or learned compositions ever ask themselves this question — "When the Exhibition is over, will the buyer like to sit down day by day and listen to the same jest, the same story, the same bit of sapient morality, or curious bit of learning?" A slight tale, a good anecdote, an odd incident, are all very well once in a way; in a book, over the dinner-table, in an idle hour. But to have them eternally dinned into us is maddening. "Evil communications corrupt good manners" is a grand and true saying. But who could bear to have it always staring at one over the fireplace, or shouted into our ears by the public bellman? Falstaff himself would drive one crazy, if we had to listen to *Henry IV.* every time we took a seat at the dinner-table. If a comic picture is good art, why not a comic building, a droll town-hall, a laughable palace, with " surprise " windows and doors, and a labyrinth or " maze " in the basement ? And, if the queer and the sentimental be the weakness of our English friends, what shall we say to the French painter who eternises on canvas some rhodomontade fit for an anarchist orator, or a *double entendre* that would cause a blush at a *café chantant* ? A silly, tedious, vicious picture is infinitely worse than a silly, tedious, vicious song. The song, if it chance to pollute or weary our ears, is gone in an hour, and never need offend us again. The picture, like the poor, we have always with us — for ever jesting, weeping, moralising, it may be screaming or blaspheming, on the one monotonous note.

Perpetual picture exhibitions, picture competitions, and the gabble about "art for art," are making us forget these simple, eternal truths. In all great ages of art the painter was guided by the poet, the thinker, the spiritual and temporal chiefs of the society he lived in. In all great ages of art, the painter was guided by serious canons in his choice of subject; and his work was an affair of religious and public concern. In no great age of art were there ever art competitions or May picture-hunts. The painter felt that he had to dignify, beautify, purify human life, to give form and colour to the deepest ideals of his time. His subjects were made for him by an organised public opinion, expressed and enforced by the best minds of the age. And his subjects were always *simple, familiar, noble, traditional, and beautiful.*

NUDE STUDIES

1885

THIS question raises some of the most subtle problems in manners and in art, the difficulties of which have hardly yet been grasped by public controversy. Much is due to the prejudices of well-meaning but uncultured people, in whose name the "British Matron" is privileged to talk nonsense. But she will hardly be convinced by such crude pleas for "the natural" as those of a "British Girl"; and the petulant retorts of the art world do not quite satisfy the thoughtful mind. I venture to think that the outcries of worthy ignorant women deserve respectful attention and some sincere attempt to put this matter on a sounder footing. And I perceive a tendency in modern art to assert its liberty in a violent way and to claim what, by canons of true art, is illegitimate ground.

It is certain that in this matter of clothes there may be found in art, on the stage, and in society cases of license which are bad by deliberate intention. It is the duty of high art to clear itself of any such miserable association, and it is the task of morality to place the canons of purity on a rational and sure foundation. Because, in the matter of the draped and the undraped there is a very real abuse, it does not follow that all modes of the undraped are bad; neither does it follow that all modes are good. Let me try, if it be possible, to make the matter clear in language fitting *pueris virginibusque*.

What is it that constitutes decency in dress? Clearly

nothing but habit; the custom of the particular society or subject-matter concerned — in ordinary language, convention. This seems strange to some people; but it is most certainly true that there is no absolute rule as to what drapery is or is not decent. Even in the same society the conditions vary enormously. Use and custom alone determine the becoming. A Turkish lady is shocked if a strange man sees her without a yashmak and a monstrous bundle of wraps. So conventional is this covering of the face that a Mussulman peasant woman surprised in the field will often veil it with her only petticoat. Travellers tell us that a well-bred African woman blushes to be seen for the first time in clothes. The unusual use of clothing appears to her scarcely decent. Custom, habit, and convention decide the matter among ourselves. A pure cottage girl in Connemara, who sleeps in a room with men and never owned stockings, would feel uneasy in the ball dress of a princess. The princess would almost suffer death rather than share her cottage for a week. If the daughters of Leonidas went to a Drawing Room at Buckingham Palace in their Spartan tunics they would probably cause as great a flutter as they would feel themselves. No one would expect a hospital nurse to do what hundreds of innocent girls do in a pantomime; but the danseuse, again, would hardly submit to the unsparing revelations of a surgical ward. *Honi soit* is the sole and paramount rule; but then this depends on certain conventional practices being respected.

Now, is it a custom of civilised society to admit in art an absence of drapery which would now be intolerable in life? Most certainly it is; the practice of the best men, of the purest genius, agreeing with the good sense of the cultivated world, has sanctioned it for centuries in ancient and in modern times. But, just as certainly, it is sanctioned under definite conventional terms. The true question is, Have these conventional terms been uniformly respected by modern art? I venture to think they have not been perfectly observed; and it is on this ground that I wish to speak. The terms upon which the undraped is a noble subject of art are these — (1) a manifest appeal to the love of beauty, and not to appetite; (2) an ideal presentation, and not a literal transcript of individual fact; a generalisation in the imagination, and not a photographic record of the particular; (3) the observance of certain special artistic conventions as old as Praxiteles.

The representation of the bare limbs and skin of man is not only a worthy subject of art, but is immeasurably above any other form of art whatever. Not only is the human form and complexion the most exquisitely lovely thing in nature, but the subtle difficulties of painting it are so great, and the delight which it gives us when successful is so intense, that every other kind of art is distinctly humbler in aim. Much of the irritation which a "study" produces in the ignorant is due to the fact that the noble painting of the form is an almost extinct art. If we compare a gallery of ancient masters with Burlington House we shall see in the ancients infinitely more careful painting of the flesh. I do not mean that we see so many Venuses, Eves, and nymphs, but we see figures partly undraped, an arm or a foot absolutely true and living, the blood coursing beneath the quivering skin, the glow of health and purity with inimitable life before our eyes. The difference is this: — In a modern gallery, with half-a-dozen adventurous "studies," the like of which are not to be found in the National Gallery or the Louvre from end to end, we have a waxy, conventional painting of the skin wherever an arm, a bust, or a foot protrudes from those masses of "Liberty" costumes whereon the serious attention of the painter is bestowed. There seem hardly ten men in England who can draw the figure, and not one who can paint flesh, with entire mastery. Now, it needs a veritable master to paint a Venus or a Phryne emerging from the bath. Even the President himself dipped his magnificent creature in walnut juice; and Mr. Poynter's bather is a fine, firm, true, but not a magnificent creature. A Venus, an Eve, or a bather of life size is like an epic poem — it is either a sublime success, or nothing. Would that we saw in our galleries more of that marvellous texture and modelling of limb which, if it reach its highest point in Titian's Venus of the Tribune and his Flora, is perpetually present in a St. Sebastian or a Bacchus, in the portrait of a Venetian lady, or it may be in the feet of a Madonna in glory.

Perhaps our painters would educate the public better if they devoted themselves to the more constant painting of the form, and presented it in somewhat less ambitious modes. When a man can paint feet and hands like Raphael, or the bust like Titian, or the limbs of a Sebastian like Francia, he may adventure on a *tour de force* of bathers and dancers; but he had better wait till then. And always let him remember his limits of "ideal beauty" and "conventional practice." It is laughable enough to see a poor, dear old "goody" supposing that painters present the form as they see it. It is nearly as laughable to see a young girl supposing there is no harm in anything "natural." Why, my dear "goody" and my dear young lady, if painters were photographers and not painters, neither you nor any decent man or woman could stay in Burlington House ten minutes. But I am far from clear that our painters are quite as careful as they might be to observe the conditions of "ideal beauty" and "conventional practice." Abroad it is perfectly certain that neither condition is respected. The Haidées, Nanas, "le modèle qui se gratte" of a French Salon deliberately violate every one of the three canons of true art. And much work of the Van

Beers and their school belongs to the class of art against which a late Lord Chancellor directed a useful Act. In the face of such tendencies in modern art it is the duty of all honourable men who love art truly to reject the smallest concession to the accursed thing.

Convention, and convention alone, is the measure of the decent where motive and intention are perfectly pure. Neither painters nor critics recognise this quite as patiently as they should. An artist, burning often with pure love of his art, defies the conventions, and he outrages worthy people. It is quite true that conventions may need to be altered; but they must be altered slowly and by imperceptible degrees, or morality itself will suffer. It is also true that the ignorant and the inexperienced are often shocked by habits which to the experienced are mere conventions. A modest person who had been brought up by a Quaker aunt, and had never been in a ballroom, a theatre, or a picture gallery, would be pained by what to persons quite as modest, who were familiar with them, would seem innocent and proper conventions. Hence when an artist introduces a new practice he does it at his own peril. Consummate art will probably justify him; but, as the conventions of artistic morality are not his to make, but are the product of society itself and public opinion, his novelty may justly offend; and not the ignorant alone, for wantonly to offend the ignorant is justly to offend the wise.

It was the practice of the great masters to paint the male form quite as much as the female, to resort to the wholly undraped very sparingly, and rarely to paint a picture at all without the most exquisite modelling of some uncovered limbs. Under the baneful influence of the French Salon our painters are forsaking these time-honoured habits. The male torso is wholly out of fashion, though there are some who hold that Adam was hardly inferior to Eve in beauty.

The hands, neck, and uncovered limbs in subject-pieces are daily becoming more and more accessories. The undraped pieces are always "studies," and usually simple *baigneuses*. Did he of "the silver-pointed pencil" paint "studies" on canvas? Did the greatest master of flesh-painting that ever lived occupy his time with a succession of *baigneuses*? I trow the Ariadne in Trafalgar Square is worth a wilderness of "studies"; it belongs to a wholly different domain of art.

There is one specific convention on which I must be precise, however reserved be the words I shall use. From Giotto down to Ingres I venture to assert that the mysteries of the form were never displayed in painting as definitely as they were in Greek sculpture. I know nearly every gallery in Europe, and I cannot recall a single work of a grand scale and of the best time in which this is done. The art of the painter was lavished in bathing the undraped form with a subtle reserve of shadow, girdle, or tress. Even when such mighty masters of flesh tones as Titian, Correggio, or Rubens revelled in the full luxuriance of their imagination, in the Venus of the Tribune, of the National Gallery, or in the Judgment of Paris, they respected this condition. Within a generation the French school have rejected it. They treated the form in painting as the Greeks treated it in sculpture, and a nymph stood forth on canvas in the statuesque simplicity of a marble Venus. I believe that the first picture of European repute in which this was done was the exquisite "Source" of Ingres. The virginal purity of that ethereal creation created a new type in art, which in the hands of weaker men violated the old conventions while it attempted to introduce a new one. The reserve which Titian had obtained by purely pictorial resources the new school of Ingres sought by exaggerating the convention of the Greek sculptors. I take the Diadumene, a masterly, a pure "study," but in its flesh tints

2 A

not a very beautiful work, and I compare it with the Venus of the Tribune. Now the Venus, besides being beautiful beyond the dreams of poetry, is as absolutely true as it is mysterious in its grace. The Diadumene is not mysterious at all, and yet is not real. Realism carried to that point, and yet blurred by a convention violent in itself and comparatively new in the art of painting, has a weak spot somewhere. When painters attempt violently to alter recognised conventions they will cause irritation in the public. Convention is the prosody of art. And while the ignorant must be taught to accept convention, the artists must learn to respect it.

A MORNING IN THE GALLERIES

1905

Now that I have retired to a quiet life in a beautiful country I am occupied with Nature more than with Art; and it is only with a wrench that I can leave the roses and lilies for the smoke of town. But, as I do not wish to fall quite out of the modern movement, I take a look in now and then at the May shows, and had asked my friend Van Dyke, one of the young lions of the New Gallery, to point out what was best to be seen. He took me straight up to the *Lycidas*, the great sensation of the year. "There," said he, eagerly, "there is true Art. What a noble form! What a grand pose! What subtle grace in those curves of the leg! What dignity in those uplifted arms! It might be the young athlete who sat to Pheidias for the Parthenon metopes. And those old Philistines at Burlington House made a 'record' in stupidity when they rejected — actually rejected — one of the purest masterpieces of our time!"

"But is it beautiful?" I asked in my innocence.

"Beautiful?" he said quite warmly, "we don't go in for beauty nowadays. We want truth, not beauty. Art has nothing to do with beauty. The aim of Art is to be real. If you want to see a real spinal column, an honest iliac muscle, a genuine biceps, and all ten tendons of the extensor frankly displayed, there you have them."

"Well!" I said, humbly, "I am no anatomist, and I dare-

355

say this is all as it looks on the dissecting table. But what puzzles me are those ten fingers all held up in a row. What does it mean? Is *Lycidas* a Neapolitan lazzarone playing at *mora*? What is the story?"

"Oh!" said he, "a great piece of truth in Art does not need any story. It is its own meaning. Perhaps *Lycidas* is what the Boers call a *Hands-upper*; he seems to be saying 'Don't shoot, I give in.' He looks rather down on his luck, as if he has had enough. But see how truly Greek is the vitality of those limbs! How daring is the realism of those tendons! How defiant of conventions is the frankness of the pose!"

"Thank you," I said, "for your lesson in Art. If I had come here alone I should have taken it for a scraggy youth in an ungainly attitude — a sort of naked 'man Friday,' startled by the footprints of cannibals on the shore."

As I spoke we were joined by an old friend of my own, a certain Sir Visto, rather a testy amateur of the old school, who had seen all the galleries in Europe and often dined with the R.A.'s.

"You call that scare-crow Art?" he said. "Why, it is a mere cast from a very ill-shapen pugilist. And the attitude is only fit for a Fiji Islander's wooden idol."

"My young friend here," I said, "has been telling me of the magnificent modelling of the back, the ribs, and the thighs. Isn't there great merit in the way these muscles stand out clean and taut?"

"Well?" said Visto, "I grant him there is good modelling in the trunk. The pectoral muscles are well marked, and the scapula shows power, crude as it looks. But just look at those saucers above the collar-bones. The arms are those of an Egyptian mummy, and can anything be more spidery than those skinny thighs and calves?"

"Truth, fact, realism," cried Van Dyke with warmth. "*Lycidas* is not intended to be pretty. He is not one of your androgynous hermaphrodites, but a man in fighting condition, trained to the last ounce, and no girls' fancy man."

"Oh! I grant you he is a man, plain enough and no mistake; he would serve on a stand for a lesson in anatomy at a hospital."

"Is not that the highest praise?" asked Van Dyke. "He is meant to teach, to display, to exhibit fact, not to be a type of prettiness."

"Oh! dear no! he is a type of ugliness. He is a mere cast, or facsimile, of an emaciated bruiser, with his four limbs stuck apart like a child's doll undressed. Look at his flat splay feet, the corns on his long toes, and the bunion of the right foot joint. Look at him from behind, and you will see a big letter W stuck upon a pair of tongs."

"Well!" said Van Dyke rather peevishly, "we have happily got rid of the conventional Pyramid in a work of sculpture, and all the stale nonsense about symmetry in composition, a right arm to balance a left leg, and the centre of gravity to fall in the middle of the base."

"I grant you," said Visto, "there is neither symmetry, nor balance, nor centre of gravity about *Lycidas*. I was always taught that the first condition of a statue is, that it has to be viewed all round in every position. It should have at least eight characteristic points of view — and all eight ought to be at once impressive and graceful. But in *Lycidas* all points of view are equally ugly, ungainly, and unmeaning."

"Ugly, ungainly, as you please," cried Van Dyke, "but true to fact. Art needs no meaning. It does not mean anything, except '*So it is — I see it so!*'"

"Ho! ho!" laughed Visto, — "truth, fact, realism! How does *Lycidas* stand? You know, dear boy, that it is only a doll, a wax model, with wooden supports inside. *Lycidas* could not be executed in marble, or even in bronze, or any permanent material. It is only that it is a patchwork of wood and wax, that he can stand steady on his big feet. I suppose that is why they are made so long and ugly. Show me a work of Pheidias, Polyclitus, Lysippus, Praxiteles, or Agasias — marble or bronze — where a whole figure stands unsupported on its feet alone. Look at any Apollo, Aphrodite, Hermes, the Diadumenos, Doryphoros, Apoxyomenos, Niobid, Artemis, Satyr, Antinous, Heracles — they all have leg supports, or they would not stand. Why, even the 'Borghese warrior' of the Louvre, with its outstretched legs apart, has to rest upon a tree stump. Your *Lycidas* may look more natural, just because it is a doll — a toy. Talk about truth. It is a fraud; a thing stuck together to look like bronze, when we all know it could not be really made in bronze at all."

But here I thought the discussion was getting rather warm, for this sally had knocked Van Dyke out of time. So I proposed that we should all walk round to Piccadilly and see what the R.A.'s had to show us.

"We have got rid of all these antiquated conventions about Greek types," muttered Van Dyke doggedly; "what matters what Lysippus and Praxiteles did? Art is free, and makes its own laws as it grows with new ideas and younger men."

"Stay for five minutes," cried Visto, "and have a look at a bit of real Art, in that group named *Venus at her Toilette with Cupid*. Now there is beauty, grace, symmetry, truth all together. It has the subtle secret of the Renascence, the joy of life, ideal charm!"

"Ah!" I said, "by the Grand Old Man of Italian art, who has done more to keep alive the flame of Tuscan glory than any living amateur. It is a wonderful *tour de force*;

but Michael Angelo and Titian continued to work to an even greater age. Art is the most vivifying force in Nature, and makes the healthy and the happy old ever young!"

"Yes!" said Visto, "my old friend, Wemyss, I remember, was the contemporary of John Ruskin at Christ Church, and he is still carrying on some of the best traditions of art judgment, which Ruskin has long ceased to inspire. But let me tell you that the *Venus* here is not only an astonishing *tour de force*, but is in itself a fine, pure, and original composition, harmoniously conceived; lovely in all its parts, and as a whole."   .

"Oh! I grant you it is pretty, refined; well, say, beautiful, if you like," grumbled Van Dyke, "for those who care for beauty in Art. I daresay it reminds people of the old artists' idea about grace and that sort of thing."

"Can anything be more useful to-day than such a reminder?" asked Visto.

"Come to Burlington House," said I, "and as we walk along, Van Dyke shall tell us why these young fellows make such a dead set at Beauty, and why they will have it that the business of Art is to hold up the mirror to ugliness, to portray nothing that is not common, queer, or even grotesque."

"Why!" broke out Van Dyke, "we are all sick of these tea-tray prettinesses of 'The Thames at Dawn,' 'Pine Woods at Sunset,' 'Meadows in May,' 'June Blossoms,' and all the namby-pamby goddesses, nymphs, 'blue eyes' and 'golden locks,' which are very well on a bonbon box for a girl, but disgust grown men in a picture gallery. Art should be real, not conventional; and of all things the most fatal to Art is that which pleases the eye. The painter has to show people what they never saw and never could see — what he sees, and as he sees it. It does not matter what it is — a brick wall, a blind beggar, a hog, a dunghill — all are equally the subject of Art, when the artist has looked at them till his soul has grown into them, and they have grown into his soul. The new rule is — Paint just what you see, but take care that it is what nobody sees but yourself, and what nobody could like if he did see it. The business of Art is to shake up your Philistines, your Bottles, and Mrs. Grundys out of their hum-drum lives, to teach them how queer and how nasty the world can be, and often is."

"You want us all to go 'slumming' in a picture gallery?" said Visto. "You can't all be Bernard Shaws, my dear boy, and paint paradoxes and dirt all day long. Is there no alternative between weak prettiness and coarse realism? Because some painters are finikin, some babyish, and some academic, is High Art to be limited to ditchwater and rags? If we are sick of strawberry cream and truffles, we don't want to be stuffed with garlic and tripe."

"It does not matter *what* you paint," said Van Dyke, "the only thing that matters is, *how* you paint. A picture is not intended to *please* — ought not to *please* the person looking at it. It is intended to show what clever things the painter could do with his brush. Brush-work is the beginning, middle, and end of a picture. If a picture interests the public by its subject, or is beautiful as an object to view, so far it draws off attention from the cleverness of the painter, and thereby ceases to be sincere Art."

"One would think a painter was an acrobat," said Visto, "and his only aim was to show you what astonishing tricks he could play with his fingers. For my part, I don't care, as the old Duke used to say, 'a twopenny d—n' for a painter's tricks. What I want is a beautiful work and fine imagina-tion."

"Imagination!" said Van Dyke. "We don't want to

imagine things. We want to *reproduce* them — show them just as we see them. Imagination is the ruin of Art! We painters have to make things look just as they are."

"Why, that is what photographers have to do! And they beat you realists hollow at it! Is a Kodak snap-shot of a kitchenmaid taken in my backyard, Art? It certainly reproduces faithfully the look of a very commonplace object."

"It would be Art if the painter could make the backyard as absolutely true to fact as the photograph, adding colour, chiaroscuro, and tone. Let him get his 'values' right — and all is right!"

"Surely," I murmured, "it would be a dull piece to hang over one's dinner-table."

"This cursed photography," Sir Visto broke in, "has been the death of Art. It has shown artists how infinitely subtle and various are the facts in the simplest and commonest object. A bootmaker puts his own ugly mug on his trade card. Soaps, cigars, whiskies, and corsets drench us with photographs till life has become a sort of revolving panorama of commonplace, crudely realised in all its naked vulgarity and dulness. We live in a photographic *inferno*; and now Art thinks it *chic* to be equally literal and tedious."

By this time we had reached Burlington House, and I hoped to have a less lively debate. Sir Visto took us straight into the large room and stood before *The Finding of Moses*, by Sir L. Alma-Tadema. "There," said he, "is a fine subject finely treated. We want no catalogue to tell us what it represents. Any one who has ever read or heard of the delightful idyll in 2nd of Exodus sees at once that it is Pharaoh's daughter returning from the bath, and bringing the baby in his ark. The composition, the local colouring, the archaic 'properties' and costumes are all those of a master. How ridiculous it was of Ruskin to tell us Alma-Tadema always painted twilight! Is not this sunlight, and sunlight in Egypt? A fine picture! a fine conception!"

"It has too much beauty, elegance, and harmony for me," growled Van Dyke. "Why are all the girls so pretty, and so fair of skin? There is nothing prehistoric, barbaric, cruel, ghastly about the scene — nothing to remind you of the ferocious edict of Pharaoh and the leader who was one day to drown him in the Red Sea. I admit it is beautiful, if that is what you want. It is too smooth, too refined, too idyllic for me."

"Well!" I said, "the story is an Idyll, you know. Pharaoh's daughter was a gracious Princess, not a bloodthirsty tyrant, and Moses at four months had not grown to be the Prophet of Israel. The Plagues of Egypt had not yet begun. And we may imagine an Idyll if we please by way of contrast."

"Imagination is the foe of truth," said he.

Sir Visto then led us up to the President's *Cup of Tantalus*, which he called on us to admire. "Poynter," he said, "is always graceful, learned, correct, classical —— "

"Conventional —— " interrupted Van Dyke.

"See how thoughtfully every detail is studied," said Visto, not noticing his young friend, "the drawing firm, true, natural; the composition subtle; the whole atmosphere one of harmony and charm."

"Why does the child in the transparent shift stretch up on her toes when it is plain she can't reach the other's hand by twelve inches at least? And why doesn't the long girl, in the dark robe with a palm-branch fan, step down to the fountain herself?" grumbled Van Dyke.

"My dear boy," said I, "you might as well ask why did Keats see charm in a 'Grecian urn'; you don't forget how it ends, do you? —

> "'Beauty is truth, truth beauty, that is all
> Ye know on earth, and all ye need to know.'"

"I can see neither beauty nor truth," said the painter, "in these Hebes, Ariadnes, Nymphs, Sapphos, Pindars, and other machine-made Hellenisms which the Academy seems to encourage. They are crude 'academies,' as the French say, and the local colour and staging are cheap enough."

"Good work too often leads to poor imitation," I suggested, "as we saw with Raphael himself; but weak copies do not spoil the value of a true master's work."

"Come, now, let us look at the portraits," said I; "we shall not be troubled about ideals there."

"I don't know that," said Van Dyke. "Some of these smart women look as if their portraits had been commissioned, not by their husbands, but by their dressmakers as trade advertisements to puff their 'creations.'"

"There is a portrait, indeed," cried Sir Visto with enthusiasm, taking us to Sargent's *Signior Garcia*, "power, truth, character, in every line. That is a portrait which Velasquez might have owned."

"Agreed, agreed, we shan't quarrel over that," said Van Dyke; "Sargent is the one man to-day who dominates both Academy and New Gallery at once, the man who unites mastery of his brush to originality of conception — for sheer skill of hand he is matchless and unerring."

"A really great painter," said Visto, "when he chooses, and does not play tricks, or is not poking fun at his sitters."

"When does he not choose?" asked the painter.

"When he dashes off a satin gown in an hour, and flings in a lace furbelow with three dabs of his brush."

"And if he does," retorted the painter, "who could do it as well in a week's work? Besides, the gown and the furbelow have to be looked at at least fifty feet away."

"That is scene-painting, not portraiture," said Visto; "I quite agree that he has a marvellous gift of *technique*, but why does he dab his shadows in with vermilion, and why are his women rouged on the lips? Hung on a gallery wall twenty yards off, the effect is brilliant, but I call it a trick, when you look close into the handling."

"You don't mean to say that he makes game of his own sitter?" I asked quite simply.

"Well!" said Visto, "you remember the old dealer with the thick red lips and the dog putting out his tongue to mimic his master. And see how he bedizens his other multi-million-aire sitters as if he said with his tongue in his cheek — What figures of fun they are! But just come across to the grand Blenheim group."

"Surely," I said, "that is a superb piece for a great historic palace. It reminds me of the Vandykes at Genoa. What a grandiose group! The mighty Marlbrook, with the conquered banners of lilies and his descendants to the tenth generation. What life in the two boys, in the spaniels, what *bravura* in the whole composition!"

"Oh! *bravura* indeed," said Vandyke, "perhaps a trifle overdone, rather too pompously majestic."

"Why do you say making game of his sitters?" I asked simply.

"Well," said Sir Visto, "you see that, by the artifice of placing the Duchess on the step and the Duke below it, the impression is produced that she is about ten inches taller than her husband. I have not the honour of their acquaintance, but I doubt if the difference is as much as that. The Duke seems rather embarrassed by the weight of his robes, and the beautiful head of her Grace is stuck upon an elongated neck which reminds one of the new saurian, *Diplodocus Carnegii*."

"Yes!" said Van Dyke, "he has the defects of his qualities. He can't resist a sensation; and the millionaires with
their big prices are leading him to scamp it. But when he
tries his best, as in his 'Mrs. Raphael,' he is as serious as Rem-
brandt himself."

"It's a fatal snare to a painter to become the rage in the
smart world," said I, "especially when the smart world is
vulgar and tasteless. Even Vandyke and Reynolds had too
many sitters, though their sitters had beauty, manners, and
refinement."

"The worst of it is," said Visto, "that Sargent, like every
man of original genius and splendid success, is teaching two or
three other good men to imitate his *bravura* and his scene-
painting legerdemain. Sargent can make a satin gown dazzling bright with fifteen sweeps of a thick brush. But when
other men try to do it, they seem to be using a mop or a broom."

' He is the greatest master of portrait we have had since
Millais stormed the town," said Van Dyke, "and has an even
subtler eye for character."

"Yes?" said Visto; " but the genius he has for characteristic points is so keen that it betrays him now and then to
make an actual caricature — I daresay quite unconsciously.
He sees a trait in a sitter's face or figure, and in his eagerness
to catch it he makes it almost ridiculous."

"Come and look at the *Burghers of Landsberg*," said I;
"there is a solid piece of work indeed. Look at it across the
Central Hall, and you might fancy at a first glance the R.A.'s
were sitting in council. One feels that there are the very
Bavarian citizens, simple, serious, thoughtful men of business — full of character, and composed with skill and truth.
It is no bad revival of the old Dutch Corporation groups to be
seen at Haarlem, the Hague, and Amsterdam. It is a real
success in a difficult subject."

"Not much of the ideal, not quite high art," said the Connoisseur.

"The ideal be d—d," laughed the painter; "the Von has scored this time. All his portraits are first-rate. A good many of the old gang seem to have been waked up. Why, old Leader has broken out in a new place; and, after fifty years of Surrey pine-woods and commons, silvery Thames, and such serenities, he has found his way to the coast and the crags of the Cornish bays."

"A very good way it is," I added, "I know the cove well; and it has never been painted with greater truth and force. I rejoice to see a veteran, who has been too often undervalued, turn in his old age to a grand subject like the cliffs of Cornwall in a breezy sea."

And so we wandered through the galleries, each of us throwing in a word from time to time.

"How tedious it must be for those poor royalties," I said, "to have to stand year after year for official portraits whilst the artist is piling on velvet robes, gold lace, ribbons, garters, crosses, sword-tassels, and jack-boots! It's just making tailors' dummies and modistes' blocks of the poor things. How they must hate it! — but *royauté oblige*."

"There's a fine thing, indeed," said Visto, "what life, manliness, vigour, and breezy air," taking us up to Furse's cub-hunting group; "what a loss to art!

> "'Heu, miserande puer, si qua fata aspera rumpas,
>   Tu Marcellus eris!'"

"Yes! indeed, a cruel loss," we all said.

"There are some good portraits, too, as well as Sargent's!" said Visto, "Ouless, Shannon, Cope, Solomon, Fildes, Dicksee, and other less-known men. But the only man who can hold it with the great Frenchmen of to-day is plainly Sargent, and let us trust he will not spoil the rest."

"He won't spoil Ouless," said I; "he is as steady, and solid, and thorough as ever."

Nor did we neglect the ladies. Lady Butler, true and vigorous as always; Lucy Kemp-Welch, with her inimitable feeling for a horse, and the rest.

"One of the most striking facts in modern art," I said, "is the immense addition of women as painters. I can remember in the 'forties, or even in the 'fifties, no woman exhibited an oil picture. You will now see every third name is that of a woman, and in the water-colours they have it all to themselves. Why is Lady Butler not R.A., I wonder!"

"Perhaps she declines the honour," said the young rebel.

Some of us lingered beside the Peter Grahams, the David Murrays, the H. W. B. Davis, MacWhirters, Arnesly Browns, Alfred Easts, and the quiet English rural bits which are not behind their usual form. But Van Dyke was all for Stanhope Forbes, La Thangue, and Clausen.

"All good men, and sound, pure, manly work," said Visto; "but you need not suppose that this is the last word in modern art, dear boy. A picture has not only to be painted well, it must be a thing that is worth painting — interesting, original, beautiful, imaginative. As Tennyson said, you might write a very correct Wordsworthian line — A Mister Wilkinson, a clergyman — but this is not poetry. An old man with sticks, a sailor boy in a boat, a girl feeding a bird, are honest facts, which you may honestly paint — but they don't make a picture. Millet's *Angelus* has gone round the world, because it is more than an old peasant and his wife. It is a solemn and pathetic poem. To make a work of art something more than 'values' is wanted."

"It seems to me that the essential point to insist upon nowadays is the subject of a work of art," said I. "Many of these subjects that one can see on a road or a farm any day may be worth painting in small, on a canvas 16 × 10 inches. When it comes to life size, on a canvas 60 × 48 inches, as a great gallery work, it is taking it all too seriously. Everything you see, painted as you see it, true to nature in lights, values, and surfaces, may be an honest piece of handiwork, but it is not art. Your 'Mister Wilkinsons,' in or out of the pulpit, bore us. Your beggar-boys, and sheep-cots, and sandhills may be perfectly true, but utterly tedious. Unless you can show us some memorable thing, some impressive trait in your beggar, your sheep, or your sand, we do not want you to labour the matter further. And then, how sadly the habit of exhibitions reacts upon the painter. He thinks what will amuse the summer visitor, not what will rejoice the heart to be upon our walls. One of the cleverest pictures of the year, which attracts a crowd all day by its admirable life, its ingenious telling a complex story, by its intense 'modernity,' as the slang goes, would hardly be a pleasant work to hang over one's dinner-table, on so large a scale, to be looked at day after day, day and night. One's guests would ask, as they sat down to dinner — 'Well! who is she?' And there would be whispers all round. The curse of exhibitions is that they encourage painters to labour out silly japes of their own, incidents picked out of *Tit-bits*, to attract mammas by some baby nonsense, and to attract girls by mawkish sentiment. There will always be a lot of poor stuff whilst painters think only of their palettes, and not of their minds; whilst they get their ideas out of trashy novels, comic plays, and watery poems. Painters want cultivated brains as well as nimble fingers. Come, let us walk round the National Gallery before we go to luncheon."

AT BURLINGTON HOUSE

As I stroll round the pictures shown winter after winter by the Royal Academy, many questions hard to solve are wont to rise in my mind. Why is a visit to these galleries in January "a thing of beauty" — a joy for the hour, if not "for ever" — whilst the visit in May, however exciting, amusing, tantalising, is always a bit of a scramble, leaving one at dinner-time with a slight sense of fatigue, of rattle, of discord — too often of disappointment? In January I go home soothed and fresh, as if I had been listening to a symphony of Mozart. In May I struggle into Piccadilly with a feeling as if I had been stunned by a new piece of Brahms which I could not half follow, or had been to an overcrowded room where every one talked in a loud voice together, and I had missed those I wished to hear. If any one could answer these questions, he would throw some light on the mystery of modern Art — its aims, its defects, its future.

It cannot be simply that in the winter we find Old Masters and in the spring we have the Living, who are not all Masters. This year, with nearly a hundred painters, I do not see more than five or six real Old Masters. No! This year we have the English school! for, except Frank Hals, even those foreign born almost belong to us. The show includes scores of good men of our own generation — some, indeed, whom we have quite lately buried and mourned. And there are very few pictures more than 150 years old. Yet, withal, there is an air of mellowness, of sobriety, of tone, about the collection which will be sadly to seek in May next.

Of course, the painters admitted are all men eminent in their time, and many of the pictures here are first-rate examples of their powers. But, allowing for all that in their favour, the charm of the gallery lies in the sense of its recalling the great traditions of art, in a tone of harmony and quiet mastery, in a sense of the ideal. There is less of the machine, of advertising sensationalism, of those grotesque novelties, which will set our teeth on edge in May. As I am no expert, and as I go to the galleries to enjoy myself, not to detect spurious names in the catalogue, I am not going to criticise this or that picture, but simply note down a few thoughts. No one can look at the Reynoldses and the Gainsboroughs without feeling how powerful and how inspiring was still the tradition of Titian, Rubens, and Vandyke in all that century. The love of colour, of nature, of harmonious tone, was their passion — not the mania for astonishing us with something new and *bizarre*. These were the men who said when dying they were "going to Heaven, and Vandyke was of the company!" They were not afraid to be numbered in the great family of ancient masters. Nor can one see Reynolds' "Venus and Piping Boy," Gainsborough's landscapes, and Turner's incredible "Venus and Adonis," without feeling that at least down to the Victorian era the art of painting, like dress and manners, rested on a basis of tradition and "form." No doubt both Reynolds and Turner had better have left Venus and Cupids alone. It was not their line, and they could do much better things. But the hold over their souls of Titian, and what Mat Arnold would call the Grand Style, enabled them to put ideal beauty into their best work. Nowadays, of course, the aim is to be commonplace, realistic, photographic, if you are to be "convincing" to the man in the street and the woman at the "Private View." You can't play it too low down in the democratic Go-as-you-please. I think I prefer even an echo of Titian and Rubens.

No doubt the Old Boys had the great advantage of noble sitters for their portraits. The dress, at any rate of men, gave them opportunities denied to Watts and Millais. Vandyke and Lely, Reynolds and Gainsborough, printed *grands seigneurs* and *grandes dames*, who did not come to their studios dressed as gamekeepers or as actresses in a Paris fashion plate. Hands, it is said, "went out with ruffles," and perhaps the quiet dignity of heads went out with Court dress and hair powder. When Reynolds and Raeburn painted a soldier they made us look at his eyes and mouth, not at his shiny boots, epaulettes, and stars and garters. Whether gallant generals can have grown less manly to look at than they were in the eighteenth century, whether fine ladies now veil the fire of their eyes and the witchery of their smiles so as not to distract our attention from the creations of Worth and Paquin which they bid us admire, I will not pretend to decide. But some- how the formal clothes of old Queen Charlotte's Court seem to give a noble air to beautiful women better than the iri- descent satins and the multi-millionaire jewellery with which our professional beauties and our American peeresses amaze the groundlings as they stare at the walls of Burlington House in the flowery month of May.

I called Turner's "Adonis" incredible; and so it is. Here is a large picture, five feet by four, with an adipose Venus, a boyish Adonis, Cupids, dogs, and a leafy landscape, in flagrant imitation of Titian, but signed by "J. M. W. Turner." As you walk across the room from a distance you might think it a Titian. Ruskin always said that Turner could paint figures if he wished. And though this is certainly not a Titian, I think the nudities are as good as Etty's, and as a picture I much prefer it to the "Homeric Dance." We knew that Turner in his early days imitated Claude, Poussin, Vandervelde, Cuyp, and some others. Here he is trying his hand at a Titian. And so did Reynolds in his "Venus and Boy," as perhaps did Vandyke in his "St. Sebastian." Alas! that is the sad thing with our English school. They are always imitating some one. And even when the so-called Pre-Raphaelites, whose troubled story has been told us by Mr. Holman Hunt, just promoted to dear old Watts' O.M., they started with ideas about "the Primitives," whom they did not half understand, and certainly did not really follow.

Half the delight of these ancient masters lies in the memories they stir in us. One versed in the family histories of the eighteenth and nineteenth centuries sees on every side in this gallery the grandsires and grandmothers of countless persons whom he may meet to-day. How quaint are the two lovely Stanhope children, whom many living can remember as old men. What a crowd of reminiscences rise up before the Reynoldses, Gainsboroughs, Hogarths, Romneys, Raeburns, Hoppners! Who can forget the cruel tragedy of Gainsborough's bright young girl, Martha Ray? How strange to be reminded of a man who was officer in King George's army, a clergyman, a rake, and a murderer! How singular to see a picture by one who was a beneficed parson and also a Royal Academician! How many men have been "The Reverend ——, R.A."? What lessons of labour and learning in the eighty drawings by Watts! What classical refinement, what scholarship, what grace, in Leighton's "Cleoboulos and Cleobouliné" — "too waxy and mawkish," you say? Ah! well! but how lovely in line, how pure in ideal. "Caviare to the general," perhaps. Can the "general" pronounce the girl's name aright, I wonder? But a grand subject for a picture, as Leighton's subjects always were. And then to see the Rossetti and Burne-Jones imaginings all in a line, like lovely phantoms of unearthly, bloodless, supernatural beings, found more often in poetry than in canvas. Go again and again, and try to think it out!

TOBACCO

1905

WHEN the other day *The Young Man* begged me to say
how I had managed to retain my health and powers of work
to what he called my advanced age, my reason was *imprimis*,
by avoiding tobacco in all its forms. I was quite serious, for
I am a determined Misonicotinist; one of the few men of the
world who have never touched the filthy weed in their lives;
one who looks on smoking as a disease, to be shunned on
grounds moral, social, æsthetic, medical, and sexual. The
weed was first introduced into Europe at the Court of one of
the most infamous women in an age of poisoners. In an old
book of the time of Charles I., I find tobacco described as "the
spirits' *incubus*, that begets many ugly and deformed phan-
tasies in the brain." Nicotine is described by chemists as
"highly poisonous, forming acrid and pungent salts." I
would not have it supposed that my aversion to tobacco is
solely due, or even mainly due, to its deleterious effect upon
health. A sour friend of mine grumbles that it does not kill
its votaries fast enough. Nor do I protest against excess in
smoking merely. I protest against tobacco altogether as a
nasty appetite, hardly worthy of a gentleman.

I sometimes tell my young friends that smoking is the only
vice that inevitably annoys and injures the innocent neighbour.
A man may be as vicious, as coarse, as gluttonous, as drunken
as he likes to be, but he does no harm to others who do not
choose to share his orgies. But your smoker infects every

one near him with the reek of his personal indulgence, and pollutes every place he enters with his stale fumes. The habitual smoker habitually stinks. His clothes, his hair, his breath, are tainted; to some nostrils, quite sickening. The newspaper, the book, the letter he has touched, have the malodorous taint. Woollen clothes, curtains, carpets, retain the stench for days; and stale tobacco fume is disgusting even to your habitual smoker. That it nauseates women and children, and not a few men, does not at all trouble your smoker. He finds it a source of pride and distinction. It is the only occasion on which men, otherwise well bred, care to obtrude themselves on general society when in a state that makes them personally offensive. A gentleman, who from violent exertion was bathed in sweat, would not calmly seat himself in a lady's drawing-room till he had taken a bath and changed his shirt; nor, if in the hunting field he had been pitched into a fetid ditch, would he sit down in his filthy state. But when the men "join the ladies" after a dinner-party, when at the theatre the bell rings up the third act, the drawing-room and the stalls reek with stale fumes. It is merely an insolent convention to pretend that people who do not smoke themselves do not dislike the stale fumes. To many women, and to some men, they are the most repulsive of all stinks.

The stock excuse for this license to be offensive to others is the cowardly reply that it is "commonly done." In the eighteenth century, it was "common enough" to be drunk in public. In the seventeenth century, it was *bon ton* to be debauched. Tournaments, bear-baiting, cock-fighting, prize-fights, masquerades, street-brawls, and other brutalities, once common and affected by gentlemen, have been condemned by our improved sense of decency, and have ceased to be fashionable. "Fashion" has been answerable for almost every vice and for many abominations. The test is not what smart people do, but what is due to others, and what is fitting for a gentleman. The question to be asked is, by what title do you gratify a corporeal appetite in a way that makes you offensive to people you come near? A cross old man in a non-smoking railway carriage was rudely addressed by some young sparks, as they lit their cigars: "You don't object to our smoking, sir?" "Oh!" said he, "you won't object to my vomiting?" Spitting in public, snuff, and sundry brutalities of the kind, are slowly dying out under improved standards of social decorum. But one appetite, it seems, has leave to be indulged in mixed society, whatever the personal nausea produced by it in others.

The stock excuses that "everybody does it," that it is a "settled habit," are not true. Mr. Gladstone never smoked, and no one ever smoked in his presence. The same thing is true, I believe, of the late Lord Salisbury, and many very eminent men. At one of the most beautiful castles in these islands smoking is allowed to a "house party" only in a remote smoking-room. In my young days, gentlemen never smoked tobacco at a dinner-table, in a theatre, at a ball, in any drawing-room, or, indeed, in public at all. Any such thing would have been treated as an outrage which ladies would resent. Nowadays, the dinner is hardly swallowed before the rooms are heavy with smoke; the party is broken up; after a few minutes of formality the sexes are kept separate. At a house party in the country, at the theatre, even at a ball, the craving for nicotine poison divides the men from the women, the moment that freedom can be obtained with decency. Tobacco has destroyed the society of the sexes, more than ever alcohol did in the days of our great-grandfathers. It has corrupted and undermined even life in the family as well. Brothers and sisters, cousins and relatives of both sexes, may dwell under the same roof. They meet at meals, but before the repast is over, the sons and their male companions are itching to be off. They slink into their own quarters. The sisters and girls gossip, knit, play waltzes or bridge, talk chiffons or small scandal — and pretend that they like it so.

I am not going to say anything about the injury to health caused by tobacco. More men, to my knowledge, have died of nicotine than have died of drink. Over and over again I have seen young fellows troubled with heart and throat ailments from indulging in cigarettes. I knew a very eminent man who could not eat his dinner without smoking a cigarette between each course, and who fell asleep in bed with a lighted cigarette between his teeth. Naturally he died of it young. One of the most famous throat specialists told me that quite half the cancerous cases he treated were caused, or aggravated, by tobacco. He was himself an inveterate smoker, and spoke with a big Havannah in his mouth. He, too, died soon afterwards of the same complaint.

You will say — these are cases of *excessive* smoking, and prove nothing as to *moderate* use of tobacco. Quite true: but my complaint is about the anti-social, anti-feminine, anti-human habit of smoking. It disgusts nearly all women, and hurts not a few men. When I have been forced to sit in a cloud of rancid tobacco for hours, I have had a headache for twenty-four hours, and my clothes offend me for forty-eight hours more. If men crave for the stimulus, let them take care to have it in private, and so as not to infect others. If fellows must smoke, let them retire into a remote smoking-den; wash, be shampooed, and change all their clothes before they dare to mix in general society.

Of course, the smoking tribe will call me a milksop, an old "crank," with abnormal olfactories, and so forth. Well! I remember when I was a bowler to our eleven of "Non-smokers," we won in an innings; and no wonder. That is fifty-five years ago, but I can bowl a good ball still. I have been a member of the Alpine Club and two famous smoking clubs: and I founded one of them — not to smoke, but to talk. I have been about in London society and in London clubs any time these fifty years. So far from being abnormal in my sense of smell, I will not deny that the scent of a very fine Havannah in the open air on a frosty night, smoked by a pleasant friend a few yards off me, is not so offensive. It is the nasty cigarette, the stinking pipe, the rotten garbage of cheap stuff, the stale, clammy reek where smoke has been every night, which is intolerable. If I am a "crank," I can only say that fifty years ago, gentlemen, as a rule, must have been "cranks," for they used to regard a man who habitually smoked everywhere and anywhere, in mixed society, and in association with ladies, as a dirty brute. As to women smoking, I cannot bring myself to speak. I cannot get over the feeling that they do not as they should do. I will just end with the words of two illustrious men. William Morris wrote: "Tobacco seems to me a more dangerous intoxicant than liquors." John Ruskin scorns the men "who would put the filth of tobacco into the first breeze of a May morning." Yes! and into the golden curls of a child.

CARD-PLAYING

1905

THOUGH I detest the sight of cards, I am well aware that the habit of card-playing does not offend and injure the innocent bystander as the habit of smoking tobacco does. I do not call it a vice, unless it ends in reckless gambling, which it often does. But it is an anti-social, debilitating form of folly, which encourages mean kinds of excitement. "Jeune homme," said that decrepit scoundrel, Talleyrand, to a young man who declined to play with him, "quelle triste vieillesse vous vous préparez!" The old age of Talleyrand and of all such hoary sinners could not be anything but *triste*. Cards may have enabled him to forget his evil ways, but opium would have done better. "Life would be tolerable," said a great and good man, "if it were not for its amusements." He was no doubt thinking mainly of cards, which bored him. Cards bore me, the sight of them, the sight of men and women playing cards bores me. The long gasping silences bore me. The clatter when they count the points, the quarrels, the snarls, the sneers, the chuckles, the "Why did you lead that spade?" — "I knew you had the ace!" Can any jabber be more wearisome, more inane? Men and women, who are too dull to take pleasure in talk, too ignorant to read, too lazy to dance, deaf to music, blind to art, unable to keep awake, betake them to cards, as peasants in Italy make night hideous with incessant *mora*.

The noodles who brag that smoking is manly, like shop-

379

boys over their first penny smoke, tell us that cards are sociable and promote friendly intercourse. It is just the contrary. Cards strangle society, and are the death of any graceful amusement, be it talk, music, play-acting, dancing, or charades. They will say I am an old curmudgeon, and so on. Not at all! I am a particularly sociable fellow, who can always make myself at home in any company, be it a London crush, or a Pall Mall club, a big country house, or a village inn, a garden party, or a farmer's "ordinary." *Homo sum*, etc., etc. At college I played whist, "Boston," as we named *bridge*, and Van John, like anybody else, though I always found it poor fun. My father and his brothers and sisters were first-rate whist-players. I knew an old couple who sat half the night playing "double-dummy" together, and quarrelling over it like butcher's dogs. They were both very clever, very rich, with society at their call. But they were so soaked in cards that they could not read — even a newspaper; they had nothing to say to one another or to any one else; they had no interest in anything on earth, except the "odd trick" and "my last trump." When they shall hear the Last Trump, what sort of figure will they cut? The old Puritans and Quakers firmly believed that Satan had invented cards. I firmly believe there are people, who if they were offered their choice of going to heaven to sing hymns, or going to hell where cards are allowed, would follow the game, even if they had to play dummy with little devils.

Of course, my tirade against cards is called out by the modern mania for Bridge. A family game of whist or *Vingt-et-Un* is silly, but I cannot call it vice, hardly a nuisance, if it is not incessant and too irritating. But "Bridge" has become a public nuisance. It is poisoning society, desolating homes, and corrupting women. Drawing-rooms, where a graceful woman gave you five o'clock tea, have become gloomy gambling hells. House parties have become intolerable to those who are not bitten with the fashionable *tarantula*. Women of cultivation, who have lived in the best society, will not accept invitations to dinner until they know they are not to be asked to sit down to Bridge. Many a man and woman leaves a country house with the sense that they have been bored and plundered. Horrid tales reach us of the straits to which girls have been put when some old harridan has got them to sit down to a game. What happened to Elizabeth at the country places she visited is by no means fiction, but revolting fact. I have heard a real *grande dame* of the old school say to a mother — "My dear, let me warn you, never you let your daughter go to a smart country house." "Bridge" has become a vice as rampant as ever was loo in the days of Lord Hervey and Bubb Doddington.

A great many men and women hate Bridge, as many do not like tobacco. They are dragged into both, against their tastes, because it is "the thing," what "they all do now." Some women pretend to like a cigarette, because they fondly trust it will recommend them to men. In the old days such women affected a love of drink, as in our days they haunt the paddock and the betting ring. They little know what their male companions think of them. Both tobacco and cards are new habits, the "fashion of the day" — quite recent, a craze grown up in living memory. I can remember the day when smoking was the exception — not the rule, and never indulged in public, and in the society of ladies. I have said all this, because it seems to me a typical instance of the curse of our age — conventional habits. The modern craze to do "what fellows do," to wear the latest pattern of shirt collar, to vote the ticket of the "best people" — which means the richest or the most showy people — "to do the right thing," — all this has become the sole religion of the shallow, commonplace man "in our street," or "in the next villa," the whole duty of man to the average man and woman of the comfortable class. When men and women will have the spirit to live their own lives, and not to copy the lives, or rather the ways, of their neighbours, they will not think it manly to pester their neighbours with the foul odours of their own appetites, or to ruin society by forcing their friends to take a hand in their own sordid games.

GAME PRESERVING AND BATTUES

1905

I AM all for active exercise in the air, in the open country as far as possible, the wilder the better. I have been a rider nearly all my life, and was once caught in the hunting field by Anthony Trollope, who seemed to think it very funny to meet me there. I have been a mountaineer and have done the principal peaks and passes of the Alps. I know the Pyrenees, the Apennines, and the mountains of Tyrol and of Greece. I have often climbed Ben Nevis, Ben Lomond, Helvellyn, Snowdon, and have tramped any time these sixty years over the finest moors in England, Wales, and Scotland; nor did I ever feel a more glorious sense of life than when this last autumn I was taking my solitary rambles over the deer forests of Ross-shire and Skye. And withal, knowing more of mountains, moors, and forests han most professed sportsmen, I make bold to say that "game-preserving," as now practised in England, is a social nuisance and a public curse, and that "battue-shooting," as now developed, is a stupid, idle, snobbish form of sport. The man who delivers himself over to shooting as the end of life becomes a tiresome boor, intellectually below the head gamekeeper, a lump of brutal selfishness and vulgar swagger. He knows nothing really of Nature: the glories of the country are lost to him: he is blind to them; he is unworthy of enjoying them, even if he had senses to perceive them.

Now, I am neither vegetarian nor humanitarian. I can enjoy the leg of a pheasant or half a grouse. I am sometimes called a Jacobin, which is a shame; for I am a stout Conservative in many things. I see that life is being taken all round us, and indeed has to be taken in self-defence. I see a painful necessity for a lethal chamber for the superfluous or unnecessary quadruped, and I sometimes feel sorry there is no lethal chamber for the unnecessary biped. ―I am no mawkish sentimentalist. If my horse had broken his leg and there was no one to save him or to kill him, I could put the pistol to his brain myself. Or I could cut a lamb's throat, if meat must be had and no butcher could be got. A man has to do such things, just as in battle he has to use his weapon. But as to amusing myself by wantonly killing an exquisite bird such as a pheasant, or a noble beast such as an antlered stag — I should prefer to lose my own little finger. It won't do to tell me I don't know what "sport" is. I have been out on the glaciers with chamois-hunters and have seen more chamois on rock and snow than half the sportsmen of Norfolk. I have been with the hunt of wild deer in Fontainebleau Forest. I have lived for many years in Surrey, Sussex, and Kent surrounded by big preserves: — the pheasants troop across my lawn here all day long (I prefer them to peacocks) and all my life my holidays have been passed in the moors, woods, and hills. And I say your modern battue is a vulgar and ignoble butchery — and as for a "big drive" being the type of country enjoyment, I say it is the ruin of the country, and the occupation of those who know nothing of the country.

No one ever hears a confirmed battue-man show the smallest interest in the country as Nature. He is blind to its loveliness; deaf to the endless chirp, call, and notes of the songsters, the "moan of doves in immemorial elms," the sough of the pine wood; he has no scent for the fragrance of earth, and bank,

and heath. He drowns the wild thyme with tobacco smoke
— the only songster he cares for is the croak and screech of the
pheasant. All he wants are plenty of stolen eggs and a crack
place in the firing line. For this he pays in bank-notes, and
swaggers about it at his club for a week. When you meet him
at a country house or even at a town dinner-party, he can talk
of nothing but his last "bag" — "Sir George can show you
better sport than Lord S." — and when he dies, the only truthful epitaph that could be graven on his tomb is that of Graf
von Zähdarm's in *Sartor Resartus*, "quinquies mille perdrices
plumbo confecit." An evening spent with Sir George's
gamekeeper would be more amusing and far more instructive.
He does know something about the secrets of nature and the
ways of animals. He rears hundreds for every one he kills,
and whatever he kills is in the way of trade and not for amusement. To a man who really loves Nature, sucks in its infinite
forms at every pore of his body, and watches it hour by hour
and night and day, what is called "sport" is a vulgar disturbance, as if fellows handed round bottled stout whilst we were
trying to listen to a symphony of Beethoven. Few sportsmen
have seen as many moors as I have, for I have been on the
tramp for sixty years. But nothing would induce me to carry
a gun, or anything but a good stick, possibly a map and a field-
glass; nor would I lie half the morning concealed behind a
peat bank as if I were a gypsy tinker.

There is no room in this little crowded island for extensive
"preserves," which are the ruin of agriculture and the source
of endless social mischiefs. Woods swarming with birds
close to a great town breed poachers. The country lad who
takes to poaching, would not dream of stealing ducks off a
pond, or hens from a farmyard. He is the fine "young blood"
of the place, who has a taste for a gentlemanly amusement.
The rotten system of county magistracies rests much on the

2 C

game interest. Farming law, and the practice of leasing land, is built up on game questions. English rural society with all its old feudal restrictions and divisions has been evolved out of the innocent bird. He has avenged the massacre of his race by ruining British agriculture. Partridge shooting over dogs in the old way was a simple thing, and when the population of our island was one-fourth what it is to-day harmless enough, however vapid. But nowadays, with hundreds of thousands of rich men ready to spend any money to be "in the fashion," it is found more profitable in many counties to leave large tracts of lands more or less in a state of nature than to cultivate them in a regular way. Forestry is an unknown art. The woods are best left in their native tangle. Pheasants grow constantly in price, and timber falls. High-class farmers with capital will not take your game conditions. So farms go to the thriftless and more squeezable tenants; and if these are defaulters and have to quit, the birds stay on, all the more, if the land lies waste.

The idea that landlords shoot on their own lands is an old-world convention. The great proportion of "preserves" are let to outsiders, like furnished houses in Brighton or Belgravia during the season. The outsiders are men with money, usually from a big trading centre. The demand for "shootings" grows like that for motor-cars, as the luxury of the rich and a passport to "society." The Kaffir millionaire, the Colonial boss, who wants to offer to royalty a bag of 5000 per week, will give sums that run into six figures for a first-class shooting property. From him downwards, to the syndicates of sporting butchers and smart bill-brokers, there is an unlimited market for sporting rents. Distressed owners have discovered — not gold mines on their estates — but game, which, one way with another, will bring in better returns than low-class farms. So that in large tracts of English land, and still more in Scotch land, agriculture goes out of fashion and game takes its place. In the home counties, one may see miles of land quickly sinking into prairie condition, where the profits of wild things exceed those of laborious cultivation. The woods drop into swampy thickets; forestry costs money and disturbs the game: hedge-rows and fences are left to decay in gaps and fragments; gates, barns, and byres are suffered to rot. The syndicate of tradesmen from town pays regularly, and does not ask for new drainage works, repairs, and reductions, as troublesome farmers are fond of doing.

I have seen an estate where two or three small houses with suitable gardens are let to respectable tenants — retired soldiers and professional men, who keep their own places trimly cared for. But thousands of acres round them have been allowed to go waste for years, being leased for "sport" to a syndicate from the City. The woods are pathless jungles overgrown with brushwood and worthless. The pastures are masses of thistles, brambles, gorse and dock-weed, wherein thickets of young saplings have sown themselves and are forming little copses of their own. Ant-heaps weighing many cwts. stud the soil and afford ample food for the birds. Miles of fencing, hedge-rows, and hurdling are going to wrack and ruin, and no longer would enclose a cow or a sheep, even if the pasture allowed them to feed. The casuals who are called the beaters break in wherever it suits them: so big gaps and broken gates invite the tramp or the gypsy to come along night and day for anything he can pick up. The unlucky tenants who have taken farms and residences on the property find their holding covered with thistle-down, overrun with rabbits, birds, vermin of every kind with which the lands round them swarm. No care can keep their gardens and meadows in good order in the neighbourhood of such a plague. No wonder the "landed interest is distressed."

We need not fear that the means of healthy exercise are cut off, if this small island ever ceases to be a collection of shooting-boxes. The world is still wide enough for big game for those who crave for it. There is good sport and dangerous too — in the Rockies — and Africa is a big continent and far from exhausted. Let us encourage these gentry who cannot live without killing to take a turn at tigers. I don't mean in a howdah on an elephant — which is not a very noble sport — but real tiger-hunting on foot, or killing leopard from a tree. That they tell me is exciting and far from easy. But there is a form of sport which might really be practised with great benefit to the community, and would call out great qualities in the hunter. India and many other parts of the East, as of South America, suffer continually from venomous snakes and other reptiles. A man who could bring home 1000 skins of rattle-snakes would really have something to boast of. Good sport may still be had with the larger saurians — though it is a beggarly game to lie on a bank and shoot a crocodile asleep with an explosive bullet. All that need be said is this. There are still upon this planet masses of powerful and very noxious creatures — whose numbers it would be a service to mankind to reduce. And the reducing them, without taking the unfair advantage of modern fire-arms, would be a real test of skill and pluck.

The world is wide enough for fifty forms of active exertion, with or without special risks, if that is all that is wanted. Even our island has room for plenty of healthy sport, which can be indulged in without ruining the country and without outrageous expense. The fashionable craze for drives and battues is vulgar swagger to air one's purse and one's fine friends. There is neither active exercise nor enjoyment of nature in waiting on a seat about a damp cover for hours till the beaters have done their task. The "true sportsman" is the last man in the world to notice the loveliness of the land or to care for it if he did. If he says "he cares for a day's shooting because it takes him on to the moors," he might as well say he loves going to Church because it lets him see some new pretty faces! When I tramp over a Westmorland moor, or a Ross-shire deer-forest, I go alone with a stout stick and a field-glass; my course is directed by the heights whence I get the most glorious views; what I hunt is a mountain burn to its rock fall or its head spring; I can watch the grouse, or the peewit, or the heron, hour after hour without any wish to kill: the black-nosed ram, the Highland cattle, or the antlered stag, are alike a sight of joy and freshness. I would as soon kill any one of the three. Or if I had to spare one, it should be the buck.

"THE GLORIOUS TWELFTH"

August 1890

I AM amused (as I often am at this season) by the ebullitions of the enthusiastic sportsman over the return of "The Glorious Twelfth" — the Feast of Saint Grouse — who has superseded all the saints in the British calendar. Hear the other side of the matter from one who loves the moors much too well to carry a gun when he walks over them. I have known the moors and the mountains for more than fifty years; and I think few people have ever drawn from them more health, happiness, and abiding memories of beauty and peace. Ever since I was a boy I have loved the heather and the wild fowl, and the deer, and all feathered and furred things. Scores and scores of times I have spent days in watching the antlered bucks, and have traced the chamois in the Alps as they troop down to drink; I have heard the grouse swirl up from almost every moor in Scotland, from the Cheviots to Skye and from Arran to Dunrobin. I have seen, perhaps, as much of the hills as most sportsmen; but I never thought it would add to my enjoyment of them to kill anything. To us who really love the moors for their loveliness and pathetic rest, and their solitary simplicity, all this noisy swagger about killing birds is mere cant. As "the Twelfth" comes round we know that our peaceful and lovely hills are being stormed by a crowd of people who care nothing for Nature, and whose talk is of bags, and gillies, and luncheons. The effect is as if, when we are taking a quiet walk in some beloved nook in a well-known forest, we stumble suddenly on a holiday party making picnic, and our choice haunt is become like a corner of "the hill" on a Derby Day. Some years ago I took my wife and boys to visit a beautiful historic ruin which poetry, art, and a long chain of glorious reminiscences have made a place of pilgrimage to all who speak the English language. As ill-luck would have it, that very day and spot had been chosen for their annual picnic by 2000 "trippers" on pleasure bent. They seemed to be enjoying themselves; and, as far as nigger minstrelsy, steam roundabouts, and donkey-races could give enjoyment, I trust they had it. But we had little. For a short space we tried to admire the magnificent ashlar masonry of the Donjon, the exquisite tracery of the chapel windows, and to recall the passages of our great writers which lingered in our memory. But it was not to be. And I recommend all who visit those venerable ruins of the piety of our forefathers to avoid anniversaries dedicated to the outing of the tripper.

I will not enter on the big question of game and "sport," in other words, the slaughtering of harmless animals for amusement. So long as I am not expected to join I shall not interfere with the amusements of others. Personally, if I were compelled to kill something, I would rather shoot a broken-down cab-horse than a buck or a pheasant. I should at least feel that I had put a poor thing out of its misery, and that I had not wantonly destroyed a beautiful creature. But on that wide topic I will not enlarge. If persons assure us that they are never really happy unless when they are killing something, we must take their word for it. What I complain of is, that they should pretend their killing to be mere love of Nature, or that "sport" adds a fresh charm to the glory of the hills. On the contrary, many of us look on it as a stupid, noisy, vulgar desecration of hill and moor, of loch and fell. Those who really enjoy them love them for themselves, and not for the "bag" and the "drive" and the champagne luncheons and the company of gillies in kilt and tartan. All that apparatus of the deer-forest and the paraphernalia of sport can be hired by any cockney with money in Pall Mall and Bond Street; these things are no more a proof of taste or of spirit than are powdered footmen or a coach and fine team. People who find all these costly appendages necessary to enable them to enjoy a walk over a moor, do not really enjoy the moor either with them or without them. They might just as well tell us that they only enjoy pictures when they are waltzing or dancing a cotillon in the gallery, or that to enjoy music you must be free to promenade in the concert-room and chat with your friends.

The last time I went down to Perthshire I took care to go in June. What will you do when you get there? my friends said; there is nothing to kill. No, I told them, that is why I am going now; I am going to see the moors. And they thought that sheer midsummer madness. Would that sportsmen could have seen the late snow on the caps of Ben More and Schehallion, as they rose in the distance over the moors of Breadalbane, and heard the call of the curlews, and watched the white gulls fishing in the reaches of the Tay, or seen the blaze of gold from gorse and broom on Murthly moor, or listened to the roar of the Tummel and the Bran in spate. The Highlands in June are full of glory and of peace. The glens are resplendent with blossom and leaf; the burns are bursting with their springtide floods; the moors are one broad home of calm and abounding life. And it is all one's own; it is all Nature's, and theirs who love Nature, beauty, and natural life. Those sportsmen who pant for the freedom of the hillside are talking scandal in Hyde Park or sweltering in stuffy ball-rooms. Bond Street tradesmen are puffing their patent guns, boots, luncheon luxuries, and wonderful inventions to enable ladies and gentlemen to turn Sutherlandshire into Mayfair. The year draws on; half the summer is gone; the Minister, for the seventeenth time, really does hope that the House will rise next week. The sacred day arrives, and all peace and beauty are gone. Gangs of smart people pour over the country of Rob Roy, with Hyde Park barouches and Belgravian footmen. Lord's, Hurlingham, Henley, and Ascot are played over again amid the heather and the tarns. A compound essence of Monte Carlo, Wiesbaden, and Royat is dished up on the desolate solitudes of the Grampians. It's all "awfully jolly," very smart indeed, and everything is really the last thing out. The Glorious Twelfth has come back.

We who love the mountains for themselves, and the grouse, the deer, and the salmon, as the natural inmates of the mountains and the lochs, look with mixed feelings on all this hullabaloo about killing animals as Society's Bank Holiday trip. One is pleased that any fellow-mortal should be pleased; and we are not disturbed if they who live to kill regard all who enjoy the moor without killing as milksops. But to any mountaineer accustomed to the peaks and passes of the Oberland or the Bernina, these feats of the grouse-killer do not seem quite so heroic. To a traveller who has sought for beauty, and drunk in health on a thousand hillsides throughout Europe, it seems a bit of cockney swagger to turn the Highlands into one big Hurlingham — where the killing of birds is the excuse for gowns, luncheon baskets, and pony phaetons. When a short Act is passed making it penal to kill a vertebrate animal except in the way of trade, it will be possible to enjoy the hills, the moors, forests, and copses of this beautiful island all the year round. Till that day arrives, let those who love the Highlands go there before the "Glorious Twelfth of August" comes round.

THE JOLLY GIRL

1882

I was not a little confused the other day by the question of a brilliant French lady, who knows English homes to the core, "What has come to your girls of late?" said she. "The *ravissante Miss*, who used to be our idol, has taken to cigarettes and Newmarket coats." I begged her not to take so seriously the passing whims of fashion. I urged that our girls are as beautiful as ever, and in this callisthenic age both healthier in body and freer in mind. "I say nothing against their looks and their spirits," said she; "the hunting and boating and tennis for which you all seem to live, will, I daresay, improve their figures, if it does not ruin their health. What I cannot endure in a girl is a taste for the ways of men, and not of the best men — what your Charivari calls the awfully jolly girl." My national pride was wounded by this, for I had always believed that if there was anything of which England possessed the secret, it was how to produce the English girl. Long had I dreamed of "the not impossible she "; and years and years ago I had wooed and won her at last. Can it be true, methought, that we are breeding a kind of girl of whom such things can be said? This new and engaging freedom of theirs, is it all as it should be? I fell a-thinking about our new manners and resolved to use my eyes. The philosophy of clothes is complete; and no philosophic mind overlooks the subtle correlations of clothes and soul. Nor am

I hard to please in the fashions of the day. I often think I see some of the creations of Reynolds and Romney step down from the frame and move amongst us all glowing with life. Nay, I have only a good-natured smile for those passionate figures in faded green who give *couleur locale* to the "private view." The beauty of dress, I protest, is no longer an extinct art. But what are we to say to the clothes of the jolly girl? An epicene slip of a thing does she love to make of herself! At fifty yards off you would think she was still in the school-room; the slim Kate Greenaway *costume-bébé* suggests the playground and a game of romps. No! she has seen twenty, and has had her offers. Were I a marrying man I should wait, I think, till she grew to be more like a woman.

A style of the day, which I find even harder to bear than that of the grown-up baby, is the lady's version of the horsey youth. She has borrowed his billycock hat, his dog's-ear collar, his knowing breast-pocket, his gloves, his buttons, and his boots. Her hair is cut short, like a curly boy's; her jacket is made by a London tailor; Newmarket has given its fiat to her horseman's overcoat; and the flower in the button-hole is the last word of Piccadilly. Nor let us forget the whip, for no family that respects itself can live without collies all over the place. And a girl of this persuasion could as little be seen without her dog-whip as a Guardsman without a button-hole. She has contrived, too, to spoil what I take to be as pleasant a sight as the animated world affords — a fine woman sitting well on a fine horse. The poetry of motion is dismally turned into prose by the habit cut square at the ankle, the visible trousers and jockey boots. The theory is, as we all know, that the fair rider in Rotten Row is fresh from a run across country. The melancholy fact is that she has somewhat the look of a stable-boy who has thrown on a skirt. My French friend is so far right; it is difficult, indeed, to think of this female Tally-ho as entirely a thing of beauty. The women who copy the ways ôf men at best succeed in resembling boys. The special habits and interests of men, their athletic and sporting tastes, their melancholy experience of what is called "life," can no more be appropriated by a girl than our topboots and riding-breeches. She only approaches that unnatural monster, the boy who is aping a man. I am not so old or such a misanthrope but that I find myself at times amongst young people at a dance or a garden party. I see a handsome young fellow from Aldershot talking to a fine girl, the picture of youth and grace. "They are flirting, I hope, as they should," says a match-making old thing. Flirting! my dear lady; he has been telling her about that awfully jolly run with the Quorn, don't you know. And now she is asking him with an anxious look if it is really true that No. 7 is not fit. For an hour, as I sat within hearing on the bench, she has patiently committed to memory the merits of barrack after barrack and station after station — a form of feminine curiosity which he has but languidly satisfied, though he has no other topic with which to entertain her. "Aldershot," says he, "is such an awfully jolly place, don't you know." "Is it really?" says she, with feeling. "I mean," says he, "such a jolly place to get away from." And she knows who is bound to win the mile race unless Jigger Mowbray can stand the training, which is not to be thought of, don't you know. And so they go on, from mere habit, talking the talk of the smoking-room, or so much of it as can be dribbled into the ears of a pure young girl. By all that is sacred, I glow with shame when I see a beautiful woman thus put off her sex, when she certainly can never put on ours.

What are they to gain, these favourites of the regiment and the hunt, that they thus humble themselves, that they so disfigure and weary themselves in laboriously ceasing to be

women? It is not husbands, assuredly, they are seeking.
Our young friend from Aldershot does not trouble himself
to flirt with girls; he has not the remotest idea of marriage;
nor, indeed, has his fair partner, at least with the like of him.
She is not thinking of fascinating him at all; would, indeed,
that she were! Marriage is an affair of carriages and horses;
for these she must look to older men, and she does not like
older men. No! she is only filling her appointed part, the
awfully jolly girl, which her society expects her to be. Dolly
and Darling, Judy and Jo, have to do it, and so must she.
And so the poor child waits wearily in cold or rain, through the
interminable "sports," whilst hairy men with bare legs pant
round and round the ring; and she sits in a cloud of tobacco
through the endless cricket-match; nor does she blench if she
chance to be spattered with blood and feathers at Hurlingham.
And all these long hours she has to listen to the wonderful
story, how the bay mare threw a splint, how Tubby Talbot
won the cup, and what came of the row at the Rag and Fam-
ish. She is indeed weary of it all; but she will never be a
jolly girl if she cannot bear it. I wonder if she knows how
little men really care for this strange receptivity of hers. To
the young fellow this girl with her manly acquirements just
so far ceases to be woman without advancing a step towards
man. She listens to him as the fag at school listens to the big
fellow in the boat or the eleven. It is pleasant to him that the
young 'un wears skirts and has lips even ruddier than a fag.
It is pleasant to him; but not wholly to us elders and fathers.
And then the young one is not really a boy, in the way to be a
man. The soft hands will never hold bat or oar in earnest.
Thus the talk goes lounging on in that hollow way, much as
we catch it across a railway bar. The tones are perhaps
more polite; but can any one say that the sense is better?

I do not set up for a moralist; it is no business of mine to preach about frivolity and vice. My only philosophy is to think nothing human as alien to me. When I was a young fellow, if youths and maidens met, silly as might be the talk, there was always a lurking idea that we were still in the presence of women. Girls in my time expected us to treat them on the assumption that they were women, or that they very soon would be. If you could not entertain them, as women all the world over love to be entertained, they turned to one another and amused themselves. When we sat with a sweet young thing in the verandah as the band played the last notes of "Kathleen Mavourneen" we had something, I vow, to talk about besides cricket averages, the club cigars, and the right cut of a bulldog's ears. And as we never saw cigarettes in the lips of our partners, it never occurred to us to smoke between the dances.

I have no turn for satire; but I love to watch our social moods and to trace them to their causes and effects. And perhaps we may note three things at least which have led to the changes we see. I suppose the work began with that wave of athleticism which of late has swept over the land, turning the heads of not a few lads and importing some laughable customs; but, if its effect upon men was more or less manly and wholesome, its effect indirectly on women was perhaps a more doubtful gain. When the gymnastic idol was set up, and the muscular type of virtue became the whole duty of man, there were found English girls to suppose it the whole duty of woman. Physically, it may be, it strengthened those whom it did not slaughter outright. But as the girl could after all only join in the new worship as a proselyte of the gate, she fell into the social position of the "lower school" at a cricket match. The jolly girl, in fact, became a fag. When athletics are the business of life, the tone of society is naturally set by men. Was not a second cause at work in the triumphs of the famous American beauty? This fascinating being, I doubt not, on her own side of the Atlantic has planted the germs of new feminine epochs. There was nothing of the play-ground or hunt about her; her important discovery was the freedom of her sex. It may be doubted if our ancient system on this side of the ocean is duly prepared for such dash, such originality, such angelic self-possession. The type, however brilliant, is a perilous one to adopt. For the American girl, who so startles us at home, has her own traditions and habits. When she shook from her airy skirts the conventions of the Old World, she founded the conventions of the New. At home she reigns still, and imposes her law on men, concerning herself but little about mess-rooms and gun-clubs. Young ladies, you who think of adopting her adorable freedom of manner, be sure that you also adopt her shrewd and original spirit.

A word, too, as to another thing. It has been thought the happiness of this kingdom that its throne is girt about by a princely family, of high spirit and singular popularity. Wher-ever our golden youth most loves to congregate, there do we find our princes in their midst. And the ideal of life which these Royal soldiers and sailors have impressed on our mod-ern society, is an ideal perhaps more easily attained by men than it ever can be by women. So tremendous, indeed, is the pace in the new Imperial sweepstakes that only the most jolly of their sex can expect to attain a place. But be the causes three or three hundred the result is a curious social inversion. The relative place of men and women is reversed in this rapid and dazzling world. Of old, the idea was that in things social the woman was mistress, queen, and leader. Men, in her presence, were to study her tastes and submit to her law. If they could not exist without tobacco they might go elsewhere; if they wanted to be killing something, to a shooting party; and the matches discussed in a drawing-room had nothing to do with Lord's.

One is curious to know how these young bloods and sub-alterns regard the women who have got by heart their mess gossip, who have betting-books on the garrison sports, and will sit half the day to see pigeons mangled. Is such an one a girl we care to think of as wife, as the mother of the children to be, as all that woman should be and is in the world? I can imagine nothing more ruinous to womanly nature than the ways and the talk of a rather precocious lad. Is there not a bloom upon an English girl of the best old type that the camp and cricket-ground will hardly improve? Purity, simplicity, health, courage, grace, and goodness attended, like the good fairy, to bless her birth. Do mothers or fathers imagine that the winners of cups and sweepstakes have better gifts to impart? I can remember what a keen old lady said once to a mother who was mourning her lot in having no daughter — "Be thankful, my dear, you have none. In these days, who knows? she might have turned out a jolly girl!"

MAN AND THE BRUTES

1900

[Address to the Humanitarian League]

IT was with all the more pleasure that I accepted your invitation to speak on the relations of Man to the Lower Animals, because I feel that sound views about them go to the very root of a right understanding of Humanity itself, and are of vital importance to the future of our own race. We cannot understand, or respect, or rightly educate Mankind, until we come to understand, to respect, and to do our duty by the Animal kind. And our whole ethical system, I will add, must be undermined, perverted, poisoned, if we cannot learn to put the relations of Man to the Lower Animals on a healthy, scientific, social, and religious basis. To me, human nature is unintelligible apart from a right conception of animal nature in the sum; human duty involves and includes duty towards the animal kingdom, of which we are only a part; and religion, as I understand it, implies religious reverence and a sense of religious sympathy with the vast animal world, of which we are the head.

I do not admit any contrast between Man and Animals. Man is an Animal, and only the first amongst the Animals, and that in no absolute sense. I do not know what the Rights of Man are — much less shall I talk about the Rights of Animals. The only moral Right of Man that I recognise is the

Right to do his Duty. And the only Rights of Animals that I know are the Mutual Duties of Man and the Lower Animals.

I had better come to the point at once, even at the risk of paining some who hear me, by saying that I regard man's morality towards the Lower Animals to be a vital, and indeed fundamental part of his morality towards his fellow-men. I refuse to treat it as an extra, an appendix, or finishing touch superadded to our ethical creed. I do so, because I do not know what Ethics can mean, if it be not the due ordering of our own complex nature (a large and indispensable part of which is *animal*) towards the vast organic world in which we find ourselves. Of that organic world, the Animal Kingdom is the predominant part, as Man is only the predominant member of the Animal Kingdom. That is, Man does not differ from Animals, in the same way that Animals differ from Vegetables, or Vegetables differ from Minerals or Rocks. Zoologically speaking, he is classed amongst *Primates*, as one of the highest order of mammals. His physical, moral, intellectual, and therefore his spiritual, nature does not organically differ in kind from those of the highest mammals. It differs only in degree, and by a vast hereditary and secular evolution. And it does not differ in degree — absolutely and invariably.

Scientific Ethics are founded upon analysis of man's composite qualities — affective, practical, intellectual — and that harmony between all these and the organic and inorganic world that environs us, which is best fitted to secure the full development of our whole nature. I know no other basis for Ethics but this. Well! I say the higher mammals share with us, in some perceptible degree, the various qualities — qualities of feeling, of action, of intelligence. They share all of these qualities in some degree, and some of them in a very high degree. And not only do the higher mammals show them, but even some of the lower mammals, even all vertebrates, show germs of these qualities — nay, some of them are occasionally traceable here and there in the invertebrate world.

Consider what are the essential instincts or propensities of man. They are the instincts of (1) Nutrition, (2) Sex, (3) Parenthood, (4) Destruction, (5) Construction, (6) Love of Power, (7) Love of Praise, (8) Attachment, (9) Reverence, (10) Kindness or Love. No one denies that all these instincts are found in a marked degree in some or other of the lower animals. Obviously all brutes have the instincts of nutrition, sex, maternity, destruction. Many, of course, have these qualities in far more energetic forms than man. No one denies that some animals show constructive instincts, love of power, and of praise—beavers, birds, ants, bees have the first; elephants, dogs, and monkeys certainly have the other two. As to attachment, dogs often show it in a degree even rare in man. Of reverence we can say the same. Most domestic animals show the last — kindness, goodness, love. Most of the nobler mammals show germs of all our moral characteristics.

As to man's qualities of character: (1) Courage, (2) Cautiousness, (3) Resolution, brutes have them all. Many animals are as brave as man, so that the natural man calls himself as brave as a lion, or a leopard, or a game-cock, or an eagle. Dogs, horses, foxes, elephants, rats, swallows, and trout are excessively wary in danger, and most of the same animals, especially dogs, cats, foxes, pigs, and elephants, exhibit wonderful resolution, perseverance, and the will not to be beaten. It is only in the intellectual qualities that doubt can exist. No one denies the powers of observation of such brutes as dogs, cats, foxes, monkeys, and elephants. Powers of abstraction, reflection, generalisation, are often denied to brutes. But all of these can be found distinctly marked in some dogs, monkeys, and elephants. They have shown faint germs of the power to count, to reason, to classify. And no one denies to brutes the power of expression — by gesture, by mimicry, and by sounds.

Here, then, we have all the affective, active, and intellectual qualities of man traceable in other mammals, although of course the higher qualities are only traceable in germ, and no mammal exhibits anything like the completeness and due co-ordination of qualities found in man. Not only are all the qualities of man traceable in brutes, but all the institutions and habits consequent on these qualities are traceable in brutes — that is, in faint germ, in a few species, or in rare specimens of the species. Brutes have a marked and sometimes a beautiful family life; they are capable of tribal life; monkeys, beavers, bees, and ants are capable of organised activities and industries. Many brutes provide for a distant future; many amuse themselves in play; many are highly inquisitive; many are exceedingly sociable and communicative. I believe that some tribes of apes and some dogs can talk, at least can communicate ideas and wants. Some have instituted systems of education; and we can even trace the germs of conscience and of worship.

The result of all this is, that the lower animals are not separated from us by any absolute gulf, but are our feebler, undeveloped, younger brothers, as it were; below us in degree, in development, in education, in educable capacity, but not below us absolutely in kind. Some very rare examples of animals are superior in intellect to some very degraded human beings; some depraved men are much more brutal than some brutes. Neither morally, nor intellectually, nor by character are men as far above dogs as dogs are above reptiles or fishes. In some of the lower stages of civilisation, to a great extent in

Southern Europe to-day, man regards himself as absolute Lord and Master of the whole world round him, and he lumps the organic and inorganic kingdoms in one, and considers himself entitled to treat all "brutes" with the same absolute authority and want of sympathy that he shows to a forest of trees or a mine of coal. He claims the right to cut, carve, burn all alike — mineral, wood, or beast. None of these, he says, have souls. *Non sono Cristiani* — says the Neapolitan driver.

No rational Ethic or general philosophy can be built upon such a huge and monstrous sophism. Truly considered, the highest mammals, certainly what we call the domestic animals, form a part of Humanity, or are an appendix to Humanity, are the willing slaves or camp-followers of Humanity, and are its auxiliaries in the colossal task of ruling, improving, and utilising the vast world external to man — man's organic and inorganic environment and kingdom. These noble brutes share man's glorious duty, and they immensely aid his triumphs over Nature, for, without them, many of his best creations would be paralysed or impossible. These noble brutes share too in his moral qualities, and not seldom they set him most beautiful examples which nothing human but the tenderest mother and the most heroic martyr can display. The best of the brutes most familiar to us, most useful to us, most dear to us, were it only a pet bird, form a part of our household, are members of our homes, are inmates of our family, and they occupy such a place as the wisest of the Greek philosophers assigned to the slave in the ancient world. There can be no State, they said, without Family, and no Family without Slaves. We may say, far more truly, there can be no Humanity, in the highest sense, without the Brutes, and no real Humanity that has not in part incorporated the noblest and most serviceable of the animal friends and helpmates of Man.

Some of the earliest and most splendid triumphs of human civilisation turned on the subjugation, civilisation, domestication, of the brutes. Until man had secured the dog, the cat, the ox and the cow, the horse and the ass, the cock and the pigeon, the sheep and the pig, the goat and the deer, the camel and the elephant — his final kingdom of this earth was not secure. Imagine man absolutely cut off from the service and help of all of these animals, that is, that they are all wild beasts — we see him at once reduced to the level of the Australian bushman.

Our relation to the animals, at least to the nobler mammals, does not form an appendix to our human morality, much less does it form a distinct branch of Ethics, or an independent morality by itself. No! it is part and parcel of our human morality, and is inwoven with it and inseparable from it. Our duties towards our lower helpmates form part of our duties towards our fellow-beings. The highest "brutes" are our fellow-beings. Man can only regard himself as the advance guard, or as the commanding officer and leader of a vast army of living, sentient, and moral beings, whose natural function is to use, improve, and make the best of this wondrous and complex earth.

Not, of course, that this indivisible human morality requires us to treat in the same way all animals, even all domestic animals, or to treat any in the same way as we treat men. Therein lies the sophism and the distorted view of some excellent people who forbid man to do anything to a cow or a sheep that he does not feel it right to do to his neighbour. In that case he may not eat an egg, nor drink a cup of milk, which involves killing or stinting the poor calf; nor could he shear a sheep to make his coat, and leave the poor wether to shiver; nor could he geld a horse or a bull, in which case the usefulness of the equine and bovine races would be reduced to a minimum, and involve much sacrifice of human life. Nor, indeed, could he drown a kitten or a mouse, in which case mankind would soon have to retreat to another planet. Human morality does not require us to treat an infant in arms as we treat our grown-up sons, or to treat a child as we treat husband or wife, father or mother, or a Red Indian as we treat a fellow-citizen, or to behave to a rude Hottentot exactly as we behave to a cultivated Frenchman or German. All that scientific and humane morality teaches and demands is to deal with the sentient, and in part the sympathetic, animal world as the living instruments, and to a great extent as the conscious allies, of Humanity, in its vast and arduous task of developing its own highest nature, and also the fair planet whereon its life is cast and its mighty destiny has to be evolved.

This view of humane Ethics in relation to the lower animals involves an immense body of derivative details and practical applications, on which it is impossible to enter on this occasion. Every one of them implies for its right treatment a great mass of special knowledge and of very cautious deduction from facts. What I regret, is to see how often violent doctrines are preached, and furious invectives are launched *without* knowledge, *without* care, and with complete indifference to any coherent philosophy or science. I do not intend to imitate such hasty decision of intricate details, or such vehement conclusions from crude and unproven hypotheses. I came here to speak on Ethical principles, and I keep to this general issue.

Humane and scientific morality involves our regarding ourselves as akin to the whole animal world, and as fellow-workers with the higher animals and the domesticated species in the common task of developing on the planet the noblest type of animal life. That noblest type is not exclusively human life in any absolute sense. Man, in his vast secular evolution, has incorporated a portion of the lower world so inextricably with himself, that it would be impossible to separate them, or even to replace the animals in their native condition. Man has transformed the physical shape, the habits, the needs, the moral and emotional nature of many animals in a manner so irrevocable and to a degree so marvellous, that they could not be put back to their natural state. To do so, would be to degrade *their* and to ruin *our* civilisation.

Does this humane and scientific morality absolutely debar us from doing anything to destroy life, to maim, or give pain to brutes, even to the higher brutes, to the domesticated animals? Certainly not! To lay down such an absolute rule would be to put an end to the domestic species, and thus to the civilisation of animals, their sympathy and alliance with Man; and furthermore to throw man back into the lowest savagery. Civilisation has been slowly built up after secular and terrific combat with the other animal races. It is even possible that Man has only just won the long battle by the skin of his teeth or the joints of his hand, and has crushed and kept down some species that were once his dangerous rivals. In any case, it is certain that Man's victory has involved enormous slaughter, incessant combat, and incalculable and indescribable agony.

The maintenance and the development of human civilisation — and in human civilisation is involved animal civilisation — inevitably requires a continuance of combat, the perpetuation of enormous slaughter, the infliction of much unavoidable pain. It is the lot of Humanity, and we have no talisman to exempt the lower animals, not even those which serve us, much less those which war against us, plague us, or destroy us. Countless animal species useless to Man, and alas! not a few useful to Man, have disappeared from the Planet in the long warfare between Man and Brute; and,

doubtless, many troublesome and noxious species will have
to disappear in the future.   Nature means one vast whirlpool
of war, death, and agony — and Man, who did not create it,
and cannot control it, is powerless to vary this law.

What we can do, what we are bound to do, is to reduce to a
minimum this inevitable pain, to stop all needless slaughter,
to avoid waste, and wanton indifference to suffering.   What
death and pain we inflict must be in strict accord with the
necessities of civilisation, and to the ultimate protection and
amelioration of the vanguard of the animal world as a whole,
of which Man is only the guardian.   Above all, if we deal out
death and suffering to the animal world around us, it behoves
us to test our souls most keenly, that there lurk therein no
trace of enjoyment in the infliction, no brutal insensibility
to our action, no wanton curiosity, no diabolical passion of
vanity or ambition.   This is to turn into a curse one of man's
noblest prerogatives and duties.

There is no space here to deal with all the practical questions that flow from these principles — questions enormously
complicated and subtle — questions of food, clothing, labour, science, and amusement.   I reserve them all; each of
them is big enough and difficult enough to occupy a separate
lecture, or rather a whole work, a night of discussion — we
may say a lifetime.   And I will only ask you, in conclusion,
to consider how greatly the best poetry and thought of the
world has been strengthened and inspired by due sense of the
claims of brutes, the sympathy and intellect of animals, and
Man's communion with the animals — from Homer's noble
picture of Ulysses and his dog Argus to Cowper's hares, and
Burns's field-mouse, and Matthew Arnold's pets: all the
legends about the Animal World from Æsop to Kipling —
all the fine lessons of our literature from Chaucer to Walter
Scott.

THE MEANING OF HISTORY

And Other Historical Essays

BY

FREDERIC HARRISON

Crown 8vo.   Cloth. $1.75

"Mr. Harrison's writings are always interesting and always intellectually stimulating.   The present volume is no exception to the rule." — *The Week.*

"The volume places at the disposal of the reader the fruits of long and thorough study, and in an intelligible and agreeable form, and not only the sequence of history but also the development of society is outlined.   The writer deals with his themes in a large, free manner, which, nevertheless, does not lack concentration and force." — *Congregationalist.*

". . . Indeed, the brilliant and forceful style of Mr. Harrison, his knowledge and grasp, his subordination of details to general principles, fit him as few are fitted to set forth the educational value of history and to arouse enthusiasm in the pursuit of historical studies." — *The Dial.*

THE MACMILLAN COMPANY

64-66 FIFTH AVENUE, NEW YORK